The College President Handbook

The College President Handbook

A SUSTAINABLE AND PRACTICAL GUIDE FOR EMERGING LEADERS

Edited by James Soto Antony, Ana Mari Cauce,
Lynn M. Gangone, *and* Tara P. Nicola

HARVARD EDUCATION PRESS
Cambridge, MA

Paperback ISBN 978-1-68253-713-8

Library of Congress Cataloging-in-Publication Data is on file.

Published by Harvard Education Press,
an imprint of the Harvard Education Publishing Group

Harvard Education Press
8 Story Street
Cambridge, MA 02138

Cover Design: Wilcox Design
Cover Image: Westend61/Getty Images

The typefaces in this book are Helvetica Neue, Minion, and Scala Sans

Contents

Foreword

While *The College President Handbook* is intended for new college and university presidents, the range of topics thoughtfully compiled and spritely written by accomplished current and past presidents offers an opportunity for a broader audience of readers. The volume is unusual as it combines specific recommendations, observations, and takeaways filled with candor, humor, and uplifting stories for one of education's most challenging roles. Governing boards, search committees, and senior leadership would find this book of great interest and utility in their work. As a former college president for eighteen years, I wish I'd had this book when I started and could have benefited from the essays throughout my tenure.

Editors James Soto Antony, Ana Mari Cauce, Lynn M. Gangone, and Tara P. Nicola have successfully curated a wise and diverse group of presidents and chancellors who write of their professional and personal experiences across various sectors of higher education. From community colleges, small liberal arts colleges, and regional institutions to flagship state universities and medical centers, the authors detail their hard-earned experiences and share them with readers in generous and compelling ways. New presidents reading this book will be struck—and hopefully comforted—by the variety of professional experiences that prepared the authors for their presidencies. While many have risen in the academic ranks from professor to dean or provost, others enter the office as student affairs professionals bringing expertise in diversity and inclusion as well as budget and strategic planning. Others join the academy with impressive nontraditional backgrounds as a cabinet member, elected official, and successful lawyer. They write about the presidency from their experience of long service to one institution, service to two institutions, or interim status to those early in their current role. Their personal and professional backgrounds mark the diverse landscape of higher education and its rich tapestry; an inspiring collection of lives led in pursuit of the common good.

While their individual stories are diverse and compelling—immigrants, activists, graduates of their institution or those who "snuck" onto campus for a tour before an interview, board chairs, scholars, and administrators—a common thread comes out loud and clear in each of the twenty-four essays: student-focused leadership as the North Star.

THE SCOPE OF THIS BOOK

Readers will have the opportunity to delve into key aspects of higher education administration with candid assessments supplemented by sourced information and research. They will have the full scope of this unique job described as "a calling" (McCartney, chapter 2); "a calling to serve" (Gunter-Smith, chapter 22); "the face of the university" (Cauce, chapter 1); "the 'first fan' of athletics" (Kustra, chapter 8); "the storyteller-in-chief" (Christ, chapter 4); "the listener-in-chief" (Crutcher, chapter 19); "a diplomat," "salesperson," and "actor" (McCartney, chapter 2); and "a manager of change" (Gunter-Smith, chapter 22).

Transition and the Early Years

Various authors touch upon the importance of the transition to the presidency and the early years. David W. Oxtoby (chapter 3) writes about his monthly visits to his new institution between his appointment and move to campus, while intentionally avoiding big events, allowing his predecessor to conclude the year. Several authors reflect upon the imperative of active listening during the transition and early years while getting to know the senior team, faculty, students, alumni, and board of trustees. Kathleen McCartney (chapter 2) organizes worthy recommendations around two five-year terms and recalls the advice of a former colleague to "keep smiling" and set the tone for a presidency while managing time, building a team, and cultivating equanimity. Cynthia Teniente-Matson (chapter 11) urges taking the time to "reflect and write your narrative, and relate it to the institution you are leading." These early signals of listening, staffing decisions, and opportunities for particular emphasis are all key ingredients for successful presidencies. Ross Gittell (chapter 13) argues for the importance of highlighting the need for financial sustainability early in a tenure to prepare and guide the community for uncertain economic futures.

Staffing

Directly or indirectly, each president references the imperative of building a senior team and, with it, a campus culture that reflects the new president's values and aspirations. It is clear in reading the collection of essays—about everything from emergencies and strategic planning to day-to-day management—that presidents will not achieve their desired goals without an able team of colleagues working in common pursuit. Once again, early listening and assessment of senior staff are critical as new presidents are advised to "assume nothing" (Teniente-Matson, chapter 11). Some authors call out specific roles essential for supporting a president's success: senior development officer (Mills, chapter 16); executive assistant and chief of staff (McCartney, chapter 2); and the athletic director who reports directly to the president (Kustra, chapter 8).

Finances and Fundraising

The complex financing of higher education and its challenged business model is a deserved focus of several chapters. New presidents will receive real-world advice and recommended resources to understand financial statements and schedules and to "know questions to ask" the chief financial officer (Stuebner, chapter 12). Useful guidance is offered on strategic financial management (Gittell, chapter 13) and the opportunities that exist for engaged trustees to pair their expertise with staff (Stuebner, chapter 12), a necessary reality for smaller institutions especially.

Financial stewardship is required of all presidents—those serving public or private institutions, large or small—and a key component is fundraising to advance the institution's strategic goals. Fortunately, Barry Mills (chapter 16) lays out a positive philosophy for those who look to a presidency and fear the least desired aspect of the job. From building an advancement team and the prioritization required in a capital campaign, to the "silent phase" (a term I always found amusing since I never felt we were ever particularly silent on the import of securing more funds!) and "the ask"—Mills notes the importance for presidents to build confidence with donors as people generally "invest in your institution and you." Patricia McGuire (chapter 17) reflects on her extraordinary thirty-year presidency noting that fundraising builds alumni engagement and loyalty; she wisely counsels "communication, testimonials, and success" in messaging.

Diversity, Equity, and Inclusion

In the critical chapter on the role of the president in supporting diversity, equity, and inclusion, Sheila Edwards Lange (chapter 14) traces the history and "paradigm shift" in higher education from these issues as optional priorities of a president to a "necessary component" for institutional excellence and student success. Lange draws on her own experience and argues effectively to establish diversity as an institutional priority with attendant strategic communications to internal and external audiences with accountability and metrics for progress.

Communications

A common thread throughout the essays is the vital importance of communications to every stakeholder of the institution. Presidents in this volume offer specific counsel: "do not engage in conflict unless absolutely necessary" (McGuire, chapter 17); communicate in controversial situations with bias response teams; and know that quick responses are important but so is centering the institution's mission and values at the core of communication strategy (Crutcher, chapter 19). Communicating with clarity enables a president to lead by values (Drake, chapter 9), and social media platforms allow even a self-described introvert to be an accessible president to a larger campus population (Ono, chapter 18).

Shared Governance

In one of the clearest and most helpful treatments of shared governance, Michael H. Schill (chapter 5) lays out its challenges and rebuts them with examples of effective outcomes. The COVID-19 pandemic is cited as an example of how higher education was able to mobilize quickly. While shared governance may "not always be pretty and it might not always be speedy," Schill effectively makes the point of its significant contributions to the sector.

Planning

Several authors attest to the responsibility of the president to oversee planning in key areas. President Michael Crow (chapter 21) argues that "to be a college president in the first decades of the twenty-first century is to be a manager of change." How to oversee early transition planning (Oxtoby, chapter 3), federal and state legislative agendas (Napolitano, chapter 7), advancement and capital fundraising (Mills, chapter 16), and emergency management (Hutchinson, chapter 20) are all covered with personal experience and solid recommendations. Daniel R. Porterfield (chapter 23) offers a particularly thoughtful essay about being "contemplatives in action" while planning for life after the presidency.

Working with Boards of Trustees

New presidents will especially value the sage advice of several authors on the topic of how to cultivate productive relationships with trustees. Eduardo J. Padrón (chapter 10) calls out the importance of trust with the board of trustees; David W. Oxtoby (chapter 3) writes of the candor required of board relationships; and Mary Sue Coleman (chapter 6) draws from her own experience on a university board and having successfully led two large state institutions to highlight the value of one-on-one communication and active listening. Similarly, Carol T. Christ (chapter 4), who led a small liberal arts college and a large research university, notes the effectiveness of personal interaction with trustees.

CONCLUDING THOUGHTS

While the individual chapters address the major elements of a president's portfolio, the collective impact of this book lies in the unmistakable spirit and dedication of the women and men who generously offer their advice. Despite the demands ("Enjoy working hard because the work is hard by any standard," writes Kathleen McCartney in chapter 2), presidents poignantly reflect on the privilege to hold these positions as they struggle with work-life balance (Gunter-Smith, chapter 22). Consider their descriptions of the presidency: "a true gift and blessing" (Cauce, chapter 1); "bringing dreams to life" (McCartney, chapter 2); "a life-changing job [. . .] some part of it becomes you. It takes root in your heart" (Christ, chapter 4); "the gift of problems" you can solve (Borrego, chapter 15).

For eighteen years, I was privileged to serve as president of Hobart and William Smith Colleges. Fortunately, I had a committed and dedicated team to work with our board of trustees, faculty, staff, students, and the local community to advance our priorities. While we had our share of challenges and crises, I share in the joyful and appreciative reflections of this role. For those embarking on this journey, I wish you the very best. You can make a real difference. Enjoy.

—MARK D. GEARAN
Director, Institute of Politics
Harvard Kennedy School
President Emeritus, Hobart and William Smith Colleges

Introduction

College and university leaders face a dizzying array of complex challenges. In 2017, two of us worked with a colleague to produce an edited book that discussed and offered advice to higher education leaders on many of these challenges.[1] As we argued in that volume, a great number of these leadership challenges were unprecedented. Yet, we also argued that several of these challenges were more nuanced and complex incarnations of the types of challenges that have vexed leaders for generations.

Recent history is replete with examples of higher education leaders who have crashed and burned, made catastrophic errors of judgment that placed their entire institutions at risk, and have been ill-prepared to understand the complexities of the issues they faced. Higher education leadership roles are unforgiving, and the contemporary perils are many. As a result, leaders often inadvertently miss important opportunities for institutional innovation and progress. Our 2017 book intended to be part of the solution to poorly executed higher education leadership. Our goal was to outline the big issues and offer concrete advice to leaders at all levels, helping them to understand these issues and to devise their own paths toward greater leadership success.

Our original book was well received. We heard from several leaders (including deans, vice presidents, and provosts) who told us that it was a welcome addition to their repertoire of resources. Most of these higher education leaders admitted to us that the training they received for their first leadership roles amounted to no more than simply being handed the keys to their new office, and that our book helped them frame what they knew and identify areas in which they needed to become more well-versed. But we also heard that they wished the book had gone further—specifically, by helping them imagine what they would need to know to eventually become a college or university president.[2] Many told us that there was no reliable resource aimed at new college or university presidents, let alone one that could help aspirants to these roles learn more about how they needed to prepare themselves. We believe this book meets that demand.

The college or university presidency has always been an important position. Yet, these days, it is an increasingly imperiled role because many terrific people shy away from it, given the constant headlines describing the pressures and failures of college and university presidents. From managing draconian state budgets, navigating dwindling support for higher education, and facing increased pressures for transparency and communication in an era of instant media exposure, to the soul-crushing impact of the COVID-19 era on the lives of faculty, students, staff, and their families (not to mention colleges' and universities' operations), long-gone are the days when a president was simply the intellectual leader of an institution. Presidents are now required to have a broad skill set that few possess inherently. Therefore, the professional development of these senior leaders is paramount to their long-term success. Presidents who have developed their leadership skills can have a positive impact on an institution. Conversely, individuals who lack the experience and have not developed the insights necessary to manage complex challenges (or, worse, who have not learned and internalized important lessons from others' failures) can not only doom their own careers but also set their institutions back significantly.

When a college or university has a dynamic, high-impact president, great things can happen for the institution. Many colleges and universities have suffered under poor leadership or, equally challenging, have found themselves subjected to a carousel of constantly changing presidents. These institutions miss the opportunity to serve their students, faculty, staff, and communities in ways that produce long-lasting impact or that help them change, for the better, the lives of all whom they serve.

DESCRIPTION OF BOOK AND CONTENTS

There is no shortage of topics that could appear in a volume such as this and, consequently, certain choices have been made. This book contains twenty-four chapters, all written by current and former presidents. The book begins with three narrative essays from Ana Mari Cauce, Kathleen McCartney, and David W. Oxtoby. The goal of the narrative essays is to offer overarching commentary on the following ideas: *Why be a president? What do you wish someone had told you before you took your first presidency? How should you work with your board of trustees? What should the first years on the job look like?* These ideas are among the most essential that all new or aspiring presidents need to think about critically, and understand strategically, before any other work can get done. These narrative essays set the stage for the next major section of the book, what we call the tactical chapters.

Every tactical chapter offers concrete advice, written in a way that ensures the issues addressed cut across institutional types—we have asked all the authors, regardless of their specific institutional background and experience, to offer advice that any potential president working at any kind of institution will find useful. Moreover, the tactical chapters—just like the opening narrative essays—are written by a diverse array of presidents: some are from major research universities, whereas others are from liberal arts colleges, comprehensive public institutions, and community colleges. In this way, we ensure that a wide range of perspectives is offered. One benefit of this approach is that the advice given across the book is representative of the institutional diversity in American higher education. Another benefit, we hope, is that a wide range of readers will find the book appealing and useful.

Each tactical chapter addresses a specific presidential leadership area. In chapter 4, Carol T. Christ discusses how to choose a presidency, providing insights from her extensive experience leading multiple institutions. In chapter 5, Michael H. Schill explains shared governance, grounding his advice in research universities but also providing lessons that cut across different institutional types. In chapter 6, Mary Sue Coleman offers advice about how to work with a board of trustees, helping future presidents think about the many nuances of this important aspect of their role. Chapter 7 delves into the challenges and opportunities of working with state and federal legislators and agencies, with Janet Napolitano offering detailed advice and recommendations. In chapter 8, Bob Kustra explores the tricky terrain of college athletics, helping frame the broad issues any future president must consider. Because many large universities also are composed of academic medical centers and health enterprises, Michael V. Drake, MD, in chapter 9 offers detailed descriptions of these entities and discusses how to manage and lead these institutions. Eduardo J. Padrón, in chapter 10, challenges us to consider the issues of access within American higher education, rooting his advice in his extensive experience leading one of the nation's most comprehensive community colleges.

Cynthia Teniente-Matson, in chapter 11, turns our attention to the president's executive team, offering her thoughts on how to select members, how to work with them, and how to benefit from a well-functioning team. Because managing financial resources is such an important aspect of the presidency, the book contains two chapters on these issues. In chapter 12, Susan D. Stuebner addresses managing financial resources and how to dovetail that process with comprehensive strategic financial management approaches. In chapter 13, Ross Gittell explores strategic financial management, drawing on his experience leading a state community college system. In chapter 14, the book pivots to Sheila Edwards Lange's discussion of the role of the president in promoting diversity, equity, and inclusion, demonstrating how to effectively advance the goals of inclusion. Susan E. Borrego, in chapter 15, then explores the issues every president faces when working with and supporting students. Barry Mills, in chapter 16, addresses the critical topic of fundraising and advancement, while Patricia McGuire explores the importance of alumni relations in chapter 17.

Turning the book's focus to communication issues, Santa J. Ono discusses the power of communication in chapter 18, while in chapter 19 Ronald A. Crutcher (with Andrew R. Tillman and Ashleigh M. Brock) highlights how to navigate and communicate during controversial situations. Gayle E. Hutchinson picks up from there in chapter 20, explaining how to lead through disaster with courage, purpose, and resilience. Michael M. Crow and Derrick M. Anderson, in chapter 21, offer advice on how to implement a design-based process for facilitating institutional transformation. Finally, in chapters 22 and 23, the book turns its attention to the personal aspects of presidents' lives and careers, with Pamela J. Gunter-Smith discussing the all-important issue of work-life balance and Daniel R. Porterfield exploring purposeful planning for life after the presidency.

After the tactical chapters, we offer a conclusion to the book. In this conclusion, we address the recent COVID-19 pandemic, making an effort to frame some ideas that every potential president should consider. The spirit of this concluding chapter is to help aspiring presidents think about what they have learned during this challenging time. It is quite likely that future presidential searches during the coming years will ask candidates to discuss how they led throughout the pandemic. What did they learn? What did they struggle with and overcome? How do the lessons of that time inform the leaders they intend to be? The conclusion challenges readers to consider the advice from the authors in this book, coupled with their own lived leadership experiences during the pandemic, as they make sense, or find personal meaning, that will guide their future leadership work.

QUESTIONS TO CONSIDER

We believe the best way to digest this book is to read it cover to cover. However, we recognize that busy readers may choose to hop around, pulling a chapter from the book at one time or another based upon perceived need or interest. That works too. We would like to offer framing questions—questions you might consider keeping in the back of your mind as you read through this book—regardless of the approach you adopt:

- Why do you want to become (or have recently become) a president? What are your primary personal and professional motivations?
- What do you see as the principal roles and responsibilities of a president, and how do you intend to fulfill them?
- From a strategic standpoint, what are your biggest strengths, and how do you intend to leverage these strengths to help make you a successful president?

- Conversely, how will you identify what you are not good at, and what specifically do you intend to do to make sure you surround yourself with people who can help fill in any leadership gaps?
- How will you go about hiring and supporting the very best people—individuals who will help you advance your strategy and overall goals? What will you do to foster their careers and aid their development?
- What overall approaches will you use to manage the inevitable challenges that arise from such matters as athletics, budget constraints, and your work with various internal and external constituents?
- What is your approach to communication, and how will you strive to become the kind of communicator who helps your institution?
- As you think about working with your board, what are your priorities? What should you keep in mind?
- What is your vision for building diversity in your institution?
- What do you imagine your long-term, post-presidency years to look like?

This book will help you develop your own answers to these questions and to many others. Ultimately, we hope this book will help you get started on the path of a presidency. If you have already recently begun a presidency, we hope this book will provide concrete advice that will make your time as a president even more effective. The authors we have asked to contribute to this book have cherished the opportunities they were given to lead their institutions. All of them agree that being a president is both an honor and a sacred duty, and that one of your most important responsibilities as steward of your institution is to make the institution better than it was when you started. We hope this book will be part of your overall strategy to do so.

—JAMES SOTO ANTONY
ANA MARI CAUCE
LYNN M. GANGONE
TARA P. NICOLA

CHAPTER 1

Becoming a University President

A Narrative Essay

ANA MARI CAUCE

Why become a college president? Although I'm beginning my second five-year term, I never really asked myself that question. It never occurred to me that a presidency was an option. I stepped into the role in an "interim" or "acting" capacity after a fairly abrupt and unexpected departure by my predecessor. There was no real time for contemplation. But there is no question it's a position I would highly recommend to anyone with a passion for higher education, for expanding your knowledge about the world, and with a belief in the importance of utilizing analysis and data to inform decision-making and public policy.

When friends or colleagues ask whether I like the "job," my response is typically to nod, adding "the lows are lower, the highs are higher, but the highs outweigh the lows." A perfectly reasonable and accurate answer that satisfies most who ask. Yet, as any new president or chancellor will quickly find out, the devil is always in the details. This is a position best entered after careful consideration and a very candid discussion with your partner or spouse and family members, not to mention those whom you will be working with most closely, including your future board of trustees or regents.

When I entered the presidency, I'd been a faculty member at my university for more than thirty years, and I'd been working in "upper administration" for over a decade. My previous experience was by the book, with all boxes checked. I had directed the clinical training program in psychology and the universitywide honors program. I had chaired the departments of American Ethnic Studies and Psychology. I had also served as executive vice provost, dean of Arts of Sciences, and most recently as provost. My new office as president was just a dozen or so feet across the hall. How different could it be?

Having worked closely with two previous presidents, I understood the basic obligations well. In fact, I had helped the past president, who was external, make his transition. Given my many years at the university and in administration, and my time as an interim, I didn't have the same first-year tasks of most new presidents. I didn't have to get to know my colleagues, find kindred spirits, allies, or advisors. I had a pretty good sense of those I could best count on, and those who might require a more careful watch. I had a good understanding of our university's financial situation and its strengths and weaknesses. The strategic directions we were undertaking had been put in place with my active involvement, and I wasn't looking to change direction. As the interim, I'd already launched my first presidential initiative focusing on race and equity, introducing it with a talk many described as unusual in its candor for a president.[1] I also knew the regents and how our relationship worked. We had been working together for quite a while, but also I had interacted with most of them for five to ten years in my other positions.

The adjustment that was hardest for me was less about operations or tactics and more psychological, adjusting to the fact that I was really the "top dog" (our mascot is a husky) at an institution that had a big footprint in the region, state, and world. I was now at the very center, and everything came up to me. The expectations from others, and from myself, were immense. In this essay I focus on the two facets of the job I was most unprepared for: just how "public" the job is and how strongly the sense of responsibility can weigh on you. I then pivot to a brief discussion about how this had played out in 2020, a year unlike any other. I end with some thoughts about how to handle the times when things don't go as planned or as how you wish they had.

A VERY PUBLIC PRESENCE

As president, you are the "face" of the university, and your picture appears in countless university publications and in local, regional, and the occasional national publications. Sometimes, it might even be on a billboard or in an in-flight magazine. In the days and weeks following your appointment, there will be a concerted effort, orchestrated by your advancement, communications, and legislative teams, to introduce you to the public through talks or interviews with a range of groups including the local media, key alumni groups, community organizations, local business and nonprofit leaders, and a range of other civic groups or chambers of commerce. You are also likely to engage in talks and addresses to faculty and student groups across your campus or campuses. The goal is to get you to know key constituent groups and to have those groups know you. And guess what—it works!

While as dean or provost, I found it was not unusual to be recognized by students, faculty, and alumni who would take a moment to say hello while I was at the supermarket, the ballet, or even out hiking; as president, I found such encounters become daily and routine, and not just locally. And it's no longer just a wave hello or greeting in passing; requests for pictures or "selfies" or for explanations about this or that policy are more likely to accompany the greeting. I suspect this is even more the case in smaller cities or college towns. As president, no matter where you are, including the gym, you must always be prepared to be "on."

This need to be "on" is not necessarily or always a burden. Far from it! In the vast majority of cases, the acknowledgments are warm and friendly. Positive feelings about your university rub off on you, and hearing heartwarming stories about how policies enacted during your tenure or how accomplishments of your faculty and staff and students are received by the community are true highlights in what can be long and hectic days. There is no doubt that, in general, I count my interactions with the university community and public at large among the higher "highs" of the job.

But being constantly "on" also affects how you prepare for even the most mundane outing—although I still wear sweatpants to the supermarket. It also affects time management and how you plan out your day. What used to be a ten-minute walk across campus will likely take fifteen or twenty, and at times in the middle of a conversation with a colleague at a downtown restaurant, I have to look around to see who is seated within earshot before I can talk about a work situation that could be misinterpreted by others when taken out of context. In recent years, these trials and tribulations that have always come with this very public job, where discretion needs to be ever present, are magnified by a 24/7 news cycle and social media.

Most people would describe me as someone who prefers to engage. This is the case even during difficult situations or when I am with those who disagree with, or are actively protesting, policies I've enacted, opinions I've expressed, or actions by others they believe I should dismiss or discipline. When a group of faculty, students, or staff activists gather on the steps outside of the administration building, where my office is located, I tend to walk downstairs to listen or engage in conversation if I'm free. My tendency to engage is not new, but now it is critical that I be aware that anything I say is magnified by my position as president. You are the voice, as well as the face, of the university. The fact that everyone has a camera and microphone in the cell phone that's in their pocket or purse makes it extra important that you choose your words carefully and wisely. I've learned to assume that every interaction is, quite literally, "on the record" and can be shared with thousands of others within minutes, edited down to the most colorful moments without a fuller context. I try always to take a moment to compose my thoughts before answering a question or engaging in a debate. Unless you are absolutely sure of yourself, simply listening, preferably without a scowl on your face, and saying you'll get back with a response—and then doing so—is generally the best alternative. But even that reaction can come across as defensive and stilted, so it's always a balancing act.

I can recall one time when my staff urged me to enter an event through the back door, as graduate student employees, in the midst of union negotiations, were gathered outside the front door. I decided to enter by the front door anyway and engaged in what I thought was a pretty positive conversation with the students. I shared some of my own financial struggles during my graduate student years, including the fact that I had eaten my share of Top Ramen. Perhaps predictably, this response turned into the meme "Let them eat ramen!"

The state of being constantly "on" is not only potentially perilous, but it also takes up a lot of energy. It's not simply the number of hours you put in. A provost or dean role already requires twelve hours a day, often inclusive of weekends. But, whereas before I'd have several evenings a week and some weekend days when I'd work at home in jeans, sitting in a recliner with my dog and computer sharing my lap, now most evenings and many weekends I'm out and about in dress clothes and lipstick with donors, those I hope will become donors, legislators, alumni, or business leaders. Evenings and weekends become a whirl of receptions, lunches, dinners, fundraisers and galas, sometimes back to back. Even when the event is fun, and they often are, they are structured work, not relaxing. I even gave up my assigned seat at football games because space in the president's box is at a premium, and I spend most of my time visiting others across the stadium. So, make sure you save some time after events to unwind; you'll need it.

Long hours at public events and in the public eye also mean you have to plan time with family and friends much more proactively, which cuts into spontaneity. If you don't schedule this time, it doesn't happen! The days when a friend can call you up with a "food emergency"—"I made too much food and would love to have you over," and you could respond, "I'm on my way"—are pretty much over. So is the ability to count on preparing for tomorrow's work events the night before. Everything must be planned as there are so many demands coming from so many places. And you're not even the one doing the planning!

Many of us rose through the ranks, in part, because we naturally take charge and are in control. But, in jobs like this, especially at larger universities, it's important to get comfortable ceding large chunks of decisions about your life to others—including what you'll eat at a dinner, what flight you'll take and hotel you'll stay at, and what social events you'll be attending. These issues all sound fairly trivial, but you will have moments when your life will seem as if it's not truly yours. Don't put your energy into fighting a battle you will never win. Remember that others take over so you can stay focused on the larger and most critical aspects of the job. Relax into it and own this new reality. From now until you step down, this *is* your life, and if you can't learn to love it, at least get used to it. (I'm even told by others you might miss it when you're done.)

WHERE THE BUCK STOPS

It's no coincidence that the phrase "the buck stops here" was popularized by a president. President Harry Truman had it engraved on a plaque on his desk. When you enter the presidency, that's the responsibility you sign up for. No matter how large or decentralized your college or university is, you bear responsibility for every aspect of its functioning—whether it be a cost overrun on a construction project, mold contamination in an operating room, or a freshman who drank too much at a frat party. Some will say, "That's why you get paid the big bucks." And they're right. If you're not comfortable with that concept, when headhunters come a-calling about an open presidency or chancellorship, just say no. You get a short period at the start when you can blame things on a predecessor, but it disappears within months. After that, it's on your watch. In the end, all decisions at the university do filter up to you.

For the most part, people are reasonable and will give you a break when things go wrong in areas that are distant from you or your expertise. They understand that your involvement is different when a construction site was not properly secured than when there is a scandal involving a senior administrator. Still, how you handle these problems and crises, no matter where or how they started, becomes a mark of your leadership. Taking responsibility; communicating effectively, honestly, and openly; and always leading with your own and the institution's values are critical. These efforts will define you every bit as much as your successes.

CHALLENGING TIMES: SURVIVING 2020

There is probably no better example of the difficult balancing act at the heart of the presidential role than how we are navigating the triple crises of 2020, beginning with the COVID-19 pandemic, the major economic dislocations it has precipitated, and the crisis of systemic racism it has revealed and exacerbated. For us at the University of Washington, it began on January 19 when a timely research project in the UW School of Medicine led to the diagnosis of the very first case of COVID-19 in this country. At first, we all thought the coronavirus would be readily contained. When I attended the World Economic Forum in Davos in late January, it was not front of mind for me or for the world leaders there. As I was giving a talk the first week of February at Universidad San Francisco de Quito, in Ecuador, I learned we had the first presumptive case on campus, only to hear to my great relief a few days later that the student tested negative. And so again, my thoughts turned to other things and I discussed the possibility of joint projects related to climate change with my colleagues in Ecuador. But while I was traveling freely with little concern about the virus, it was quietly taking hold.

By late-February we had the first COVID-19-related death in our state and an outbreak in a long-term care facility. The first days of March confirmed there was community spread with close to one hundred reported cases, including at a local high school. On March 6, after a week of intense consultation with our university's top virologists, epidemiologists, public health experts, and our broader infectious disease advisory group, we made the decision to move to online instruction starting March 9—the first university in the country to do so. The decision to end in-person classes was anything but easy and straightforward. I worried about whether I was overreacting. At the time of the decision, we had no known cases on our campus, although that changed by the day's end. I worried that I'd be sending a message out to the world that our campus and city were unsafe. I was also worried about the potential economic consequences. We were at the end of our winter quarter, and I wondered whether students would enroll with us for spring quarter, knowing we'd almost certainly be fully online. But there was never a question but that my North Star had to be what was best for our community and its safety. The work of mitigating any economic or reputational damage needed to be dealt with, with urgency and resolve, but it had to be secondary. Indeed, the biggest long-term damage to either is not doing the right thing no matter how serious the short-term consequences may be.

Every presidency has its crises, but there is little doubt that the COVID-19 crisis is truly extraordinary. Bill Gates has called it the "defining moment of our lifetimes."[2] One of the most difficult aspects to deal with has been the constant uncertainty. The virus is new and seemingly every minute, and certainly every week, brings new information. Early on health experts believed that wearing masks should be reserved for health-care workers, and later we learned mask wearing was a critical first line of defense. At one point our experts believed installing plexiglass in some locations would provide workers a false sense of security, but later it was recommended as a best practice. And at one point, the typical college-aged population appeared to be at low risk for contracting or being affected by the virus. Now we know that they are every bit as apt to contract it, and that while their death rates are low, some do die and others will get quite ill, requiring hospitalization. As I am writing this toward the close of 2020, long-term health effects for those who remain asymptomatic or have only mild symptoms are still being debated, and we are still learning more about airborne transmission. There are still questions about how well different tests perform, how early it can be diagnosed, how long those who have had it remain infectious, and how long they are immune afterward.

We do have good certainty about how to contain the spread of the virus—wear a mask, watch your distance, wash your hands, or as we like to say at UW, the three "Ws." Yet, these are not entirely under our control on our own campuses, much less in the communities that surround us. Our ability to keep our students, faculty, and staff safe on our campuses is, in part, dependent on rates of community spread and infection, especially in public universities where we cannot bar members of the public from entering our campuses, or on campuses where a substantial part of the student body lives off campus. Yet, the responsibility to do everything we can to keep our students, faculty, and staff safe is real; so is our responsibility to make sure our undergraduates can maintain their academic progress and that our faculty and graduate students can continue to carry out their important duties, including research on timely and urgent topics related to the crises at hand.

Planning for the academic year, from estimating admission yields and dorm occupancy rates, to putting together class schedules, is always challenging and requires a certain degree of flexibility. But in the era of COVID-19, it's not enough to have a plan b. You also need a plan c, d, and e. And, once you've executed on a plan, you now know there's always the possibility that you may have to suddenly change course. This way of operating does not come naturally. Academics are, by nature, long-term planners—it's required of us in our career planning and in carrying out our research. This is, in part, why universities are often accused of changing at a glacial pace. Yet, glitches and the occasional misstep aside, it's been nothing short of remarkable how colleges and universities have responded so nimbly, moving entire curriculums online in a matter of days and weeks, getting laptops and internet hotspots to students who need them, and finding creative ways to teach classes, including laboratory and performance classes, remotely.

Universities, especially research universities with medical schools and hospitals, have also been on the front lines of the battle against COVID-19, leading the way in everything from developing diagnostic tests, treatments, and vaccines, to providing policy makers with tools to track and predict infection rates by location and demographics. Health and life science researchers are also helping us understand how transmission occurs and its potential impacts. When put to the test, our colleges and universities have proven their worth.

The majority of this work is carried out below the presidential level, by hardworking and remarkable faculty, staff, and students, including the essential workers keeping our campuses clean and our infrastructure operational. But presidents and chancellors are key to making sure there is good integration and collaboration across units, in setting the right tone of realism, leavened by optimism and resolve, and making sure that our communities remain united despite the fracturing political tensions that characterize our country at the present moment. We are also key in managing complex and multitiered communications to students and their parents, faculty and staff, whether via campuswide or more targeted emails, social media and blogs, specialized publications, or through virtual town halls.

Planning for how to continue to deliver on our missions of teaching, research, and service in the midst of a pandemic has been incredibly challenging, the execution even more so. I have no illusions about the reality that lies ahead or the difficulties that will continue as we face the winter spike in infections, brought on by holiday gatherings, more time spent indoors due to cold weather, and increasing COVID-19 fatigue. We are ready to continue to pivot as new obstacles arise.

It's also clear that the accompanying financial stresses have only begun, and they will continue to reverberate in the coming years. Recovery will likely be slow and painful. Yet, it is the crises related to systemic racism and social inequities that I've found the most challenging to deal with operationally, as well as emotionally; they are the ones I most often lose sleep over and anguish about. They are also the ones that in those all-too-rare moments of calm provide me with the most hope and optimism—because change *is* needed, and this is the best opportunity for it that I've seen in my lifetime.

Issues of social inequity, especially as they relate to Black, Indigenous, and People of Color (BIPOC) communities are very personal for me as an immigrant Latina who arrived in the United States as a refugee at the age of three, remaining on a green card until I became an adult. In this country, my parents struggled to make a living as factory workers, and finances were always tight. Like most immigrant children, I learned English quickly and served as the family translator or "cultural broker," experiencing firsthand the cruel stereotyping and condescending treatment given to those who speak English poorly and with a strong accent. It was not unusual for doctors, bankers, storekeepers, and even teachers to treat me, as a six- or seven-year-old, with more respect than they did my parents. As an undergraduate, I conducted research on how psychological assessments underestimated the intelligence of non-English speakers, and I started working in programs serving low-income Latinx youth. My primary reason for attending graduate school was to conduct research and be engaged in clinical and prevention work to help break down the barriers that kept BIPOC youths and families from reaching their potential. I was in graduate school at Yale, writing up the results of my master's thesis, which focused on the role of parental, peer, and teacher support in the lives of African American early adolescents, when my life changed forever. My older brother, who became a labor organizer and activist upon his graduation from Duke, was murdered at the hands of the Ku Klux Klan as part of what came to be known as the "Greensboro massacre." Presaging what would become all too common decades later, it was captured on film where I could watch him get shot and die, a trauma one can never truly heal from. Moreover, the police were implicated, in this case, by their absence. Five years after the murders, a civil suit for "wrongful death" found two Greensboro police officers liable.

Following the death of George Floyd, at the hands of the police in Minneapolis, I attended a Zoom meeting with students from our Black Student Union, to listen to their concerns. In describing their concerns about policing, along with very real anguish and fear, there emerged a common refrain referring to the death: "It could have been me, or it could have been my father, or it could have been my brother." Their pain was palpable; my heart and soul cried out, *"I understand—it WAS my brother."* Yet, as a light-skinned white-passing Latina, as much as I could feel and empathize with their pain, I know that I do not have to live with the same fear. I know full well that if I get stopped for speeding, I can smile and chat with the officer not once thinking he'll try to arrest me or worse. I do not fear I'll be stopped if I'm strolling through a wealthy white community. So I did my imperfect best to focus on their stories, saving the majority of my own tears for later and attending to my own retraumatization in private.

I share this story because one of the most difficult aspects of being at the top of the leadership chain is that regardless of your own lived experiences, and especially in situations related to social inequities, in the eyes of others your position of power marks you squarely as a member of the "ruling class" as I was described in some campus graffiti. Your present status comes to negate every other aspect of who you are. I've joked, with the occasional undertone of bitterness, that when I write my autobiography, it will be called *Confessions of a University Administrator: How I Became a Straight White Man.* (I am none of the above.) If you can't cry, you might as well laugh. I know of no other good choice if you seek to make a difference through leadership while remaining emotionally intact.

There is still a long road ahead for all of us trying to lead through these crises. Managing COVID-19 on our campuses and in our community, reimagining campus safety and policing, and expanding mental health services for all our students are just a few of the things on the front burner. At the same time, we are downsizing administrative units and trimming budgets—all while trying to develop a sense of community while meeting virtually. And I haven't even mentioned the many meetings related to intercollegiate athletics! Anyone considering stepping up into a presidency needs to be prepared for rapid-fire crisis management, continually divided attention, and lots of navigating through unknown and uncertain terrain. Yet, times of crisis are also times of opportunity, and the end goal is not a return to "normal," but a new and better, more equitable normal. Not simple recovery, but "equicovery" as a colleague described it. I've never felt wearier, or more energized.

WHEN THINGS GO SIDEWAYS

No matter how talented you are, or how great a team you put together, assuming you are president or chancellor long enough, sometimes things will not turn out as you planned or expected. There are different schools of thought as to how much you "own" decisions and actions that go sideways on you or turn out poorly. At a talk I attended, sponsored by an academic professional organization, a university consultant advised us that we must keep the image of the leader unsullied, as it was best for the institution. The speaker told us, "So, you should be the one who shares good news with the university community—let others share the bad news." I recall thinking dismissively at the time, "I bet people just love working for that person!" Yet, there was a sliver of truth there. Because you are the face of the university, your team will want to wrap you up in the reflected glory of your student, staff, and faculty accomplishments, while keeping you more distant from any shortcomings and errors. Having a good spokesperson who can communicate the official university perspective on difficult topics is important. You don't need to personally comment on every controversy or difficult issue. Still, when it comes to major controversies, conundrums, or outright scandals, I believe it is generally best to lean into them, facing issues head on and directly. Those who work for you will appreciate it, and so will the public.

When a problem occurs or a decision turns out to have unintended consequences, own it and then set about fixing it. Sometimes that will mean further investigation and putting together a task force; other times immediate changes may be necessary or called for. Handling problems, whether you can identify the cause or not, is generally complicated, time-consuming, and delicate. This is something I knew coming in and was prepared for. The surprise was just how personal it feels. The burden of being in charge and responsible sits very squarely on your shoulders, too heavy to shrug off. And, no matter how much you try to compartmentalize, crises, mistakes, and tough decisions will be with you long after "work hours" to the degree that nonwork hours exist at all.

Almost any president or chancellor will tell you that there's nothing worse than when someone is injured or dies on your campus during your watch. I was executive vice provost when one of our staff members, an alum, was murdered on campus by an obviously disturbed ex-boyfriend who then killed himself. I was one of the first members of central administration on the scene and spoke to friends and family members as well as to shocked coworkers and students, some of whom witnessed part of what happened. It was impossible not to feel shaken; the grief was real and powerful. There is no question that I was strongly affected, as were so many others in our community. But I was not the one being contacted for commentary by students, faculty, staff, community members, and the press for answers. I was fully a participant in the communal grieving. Though ready, willing, and able to engage in the process of figuring out how we could avoid something like that happening again in the future, I felt no deep sense of responsibility. And no one was blaming me for anything.

When something goes wrong, as president, I find it harder not to dwell on all the might haves and should haves that could have led to a different outcome. And, though my focus is on problem-solving and moving forward during my "working" hours, self-doubt, if not full-blown self-blame, can engulf you as you try to find recovery time or sleep. I've found this to be the case regardless of whether I believe any blame or responsibility is warranted, or whether others are directly blaming me, which will undoubtedly happen, deserved or not.

A few years ago a student died while walking across our campus during a period of unusually heavy snow and cold, described by weather forecasters as a once-in-several-decades event. Very quickly, through social media and more formal news outlets, speculation arose, together with anger, that we did not do a good enough job clearing the snow and/or had made a bad decision to reopen campus after classes were suspended. It was not the first, nor I expect the last time, that I've been told that I have blood on my hands. And I did play a role in decisions about suspending and then reopening classes and facilities, and the division responsible for campus maintenance reports up through my office. Needless to say, I felt absolutely awful and questioned the wisdom of the decision-making I'd played a direct role in.

I'll admit to some relief when the medical examiner found that the fall was caused by an embolism and not the slippery path, both from a liability perspective and because our facilities staff who had been working overtime in difficult conditions were also so deeply affected. But having talked to the parents and learned more about this young woman and all the promise she held, I relived that fall many times over, just as I've relived countless times the day a young man was shot on our campus, luckily not fatally, outside a venue where Milo Yiannopoulus was giving a talk, a talk many wanted me to disallow despite its implications for free speech if I had.

I sometimes tease that in the course of this job I've developed alligator skin, and I do suspect I've become better at not taking things quite as personally, differentiating between "me" and "the president." Making sure to build mental health breaks into a busy routine; keeping up a regular, or semi-regular, exercise routine; and nurturing relationships with those who really care about you, aside from the job—all are critical to keeping things in perspective. At times, I've found that having a good therapist is also a must. What I find most helpful, though, is trying to turn the tragedy or crisis into a learning, and sometimes teaching, moment. In the case of the young woman who fell, we not only reexamined our protocols for class suspension and resource allocation for snow events but also how we dealt with social media. Reflection and honest critique shift the control more squarely back into your own hands and turn your sense of responsibility and ownership into a positive.

A certain degree of thick skin is essential for a leadership job that plays itself out so publicly, but it can be a problem if you begin to detach yourself from those that you are here to serve; the position is, by its very nature, people-focused. The same caring that creates vulnerability is also highly motivating, not only for you but also for those who work for and with you. If you don't care, really care, why should they? Embrace it so that it makes you stronger, not more guarded.

You enter into a presidency in order to strengthen your institution, to provide your students, faculty, and staff with the resources they need to achieve to their fullest while making your community stronger. You will surely have amazing experiences along the way, and more than a few "pinch me" moments. Yet, it is not, nor should you ever enter it as, an easy path to fame or fortune. There are much easier and more straightforward paths to either. But, as you turn your focus on others, which is where your motivation should be, self-growth will happen. It's a true gift and blessing, the biggest surprise of them all.

CHAPTER 2

Stories, Lessons, and Reflections

··

A Narrative Essay

KATHLEEN McCARTNEY

A verse from Muriel Rukeyser's poem *The Speed of Darkness* reads, "The universe is made of stories, not of atoms."* Rukeyser is speaking to the importance of stories for our humanity. When we embody our stories, we are able to speak about who we are and what we value.[1] This chapter offered me an opportunity to reflect on what I have learned in my eight years as dean of the Harvard Graduate School of Education and my eight years as president of Smith College. Over these sixteen years, I have noticed that college and university presidents enjoy telling their stories, and alas I am no exception. The stories leaders tell reveal hard-earned lessons from their work; a good story is in essence a case study.

My leadership journey in higher education began when Harvard University President Lawrence Summers asked me to serve as acting dean of the Harvard Graduate School of Education, where I was a member of the faculty and the current academic dean. Many faculty in Harvard's professional schools study leadership, and the Education School was no exception. Therefore, I was privileged to be a student of leadership with faculty peers like Richard Chait, who studied university governance;[2] Howard Gardner, who studied the connection between creativity and leadership;[3] Robert Kegan, who studied change leadership and our immunity to change;[4] Judith McLaughlin, who studied the college presidency;[5] and Jerome Murphy, who studied the inner life of leaders.[6] I was also privileged to learn from college and university presidents who mentored me, especially, Drew Gilpin Faust, who was president of Harvard University for most of my deanship; Beverly Daniel Tatum, former president

---

* I acknowledge helpful feedback on this chapter from James Antony, Eileen Dunn, William Hagen, Joanna Olin, and Elena Palladino.

of Spelman College and a trustee at Smith College; and Lawrence Bacow, who encouraged me to apply for college presidencies when I served on the board of trustees of Tufts University while he was serving as president. Just as I have been helped by others, I hope the stories, lessons, and reflections shared here will be of use to new and prospective college presidents.

WHY BECOME A COLLEGE PRESIDENT?

From time to time, people ask me how I knew I wanted to be a college president. For me, the desire evolved over time. Like other service professions, a college presidency is a calling. By this, I mean you should feel a strong connection to the work as well as a strong inner desire to serve a community. *Servant leadership* is a term Greenleaf coined to invert the traditional notion of the leader, whereby others serve the leader; instead, wise leaders know that they are the ones who serve.[7] College presidents serve numerous constituencies: students, staff, faculty, alumni, the higher education community, and members of the communities that surround the campus. It is important to listen to those you serve. In fact, the more power you have, the more you should listen—and college presidents do have power, even when shared governance is the norm.

You should also feel a strong desire to lead an institution so that it can evolve to meet the needs of changing times. College presidents need to do more than merely steward an institution; they need to lead change, which might include new academic programs, new processes, new buildings, and new collaborations. Heifetz and Linsky note, "To lead is to live dangerously because you are leading people through change," and change is almost always met with resistance.[8] I suspect college presidents need to enjoy not only living dangerously but also sharing their visions for a better future. A compelling vision will engender a willingness on the part of community members to change.

Finally, you should also enjoy working hard because the work is hard by any standard. The hours are long, the demands for your time can seem infinite, all of the institution's problems funnel down to you, and people will misbehave. So why do it? For me, the answer is simple—the mission. The education of the next generation is noble work. This last point deserves special emphasis. The main purpose of colleges and universities is to educate students. A college president needs to appreciate that this purpose, more than research and discovery and more than alumni engagement, should be the main driver of your work. According to Erik Erikson, nurturing and guiding young people accompany middle age, a phase of life Erikson referred to as generativity.[9] In my experience, educating young people, which is inherently generative work, brings meaning to one's life.

THE ARC OF A COLLEGE PRESIDENCY

Most presidents begin their role with a plan to stay for two five-year terms. Certainly, this is how I approached planning the arc of my presidency. In this section, I offer some thoughts about the developmental trajectory of a college president with special attention to how the job changes over time.

The First Year

The first year of a college presidency is critical for success because members of your community will be looking for signals about what kind of president you plan to be. The culture of every campus is different, so your preparation for day one will be important. You may want to read a book written for business leaders called *The First 90 Days*, because much of the advice translates to higher education.[10] You should also read everything you can about the college you are serving, especially with respect to its core values. If the outgoing president is willing to spend time with you during the transition, and if you believe they can be a trusted adviser and partner, then ask them probing questions about your senior staff; student sensibilities; staff and faculty governance; key alumni who can help you, particularly as philanthropic partners; and especially the board of trustees. The trustees will be your thought partners as well as your critical friends. You should set up individual calls with each trustee during your first month. As you build important relationships across stakeholders, you should consider working with a coach who can help you process the early phase of your transition into the role, which can be confusing and lonely.

There is a principle in psychology called the primacy effect, meaning that material presented first is best remembered. In other words, first impressions matter. Many presidents want to impress their constituents by sharing their plans for the institution—plans that may have emerged through the search process. Instead, I suggest that presidents do a great deal of listening during the first year; in fact, I described my first year as a "listening tour." Trust me when I tell you that you will receive some of your best ideas from members of your community. For example, during my first year, the alumnae business leaders shared their experiences of having been channeled away from careers in business toward careers in the nonprofit sector by some faculty advisers and some staff in career services. With the partnership and support of these alumnae, my team in development and alumnae relations and I raised funds for a Center on Innovation and Entrepreneurship and created an Alumnae Business Network. While on your listening tour, you may still signal some priorities that you believe will resonate on your campus; you will no doubt mention some in your inauguration speech. The point here is not to make the mistake of believing you need to have all the answers.

During the early days, you will be evaluating your senior team, and they will be evaluating you. In your first meeting with your team, explain a few concrete ideas about your leadership philosophy. For example, you might share that you value loyal dissent—that is, speaking up to share a concern because you believe this prevents groupthink. Or you might discuss the extent to which you want to be briefed. Many presidents I know have been surprised to find that not all members of a senior team embrace a new president with enthusiasm. Early in your first year, you should decide whether to make personnel changes to have the team you need—and deserve—to be successful. I suggest new presidents outline the leadership principles they would like to see in their senior team. I wrote a memo to my cabinet in which I discussed principles such as the ability to build trusting relationships, to be transparent, to listen, to forgive others, and to be optimistic. In the memo I also explained that the cabinet and I should work together to avoid triangulation from third parties; for example, sometimes faculty members write to the president when they do not get the answer they want from the provost. It is also important to invite people on your senior team to let you know how they would like you to work with them. There are vast individual differences among people, and a good leader respects these differences, within reason, of course.

Try to get some early wins in the first year so that people can learn about you and the way you are approaching your role as a leader. In my case, I suggested that Smith College produce one massive open online course, or MOOC. Given that we are a liberal arts college that values face-to-face education, this approach might seem countercultural; however, when I began, in 2013, many higher education leaders believed online learning would disrupt higher education, even though some of our competitors were testing the waters. I invited a faculty member who taught the Psychology of Women's Activism course to teach the MOOC, as a way to showcase Smith's identity to the world. During a faculty meeting, I talked about why we should pilot new ways of working that could benefit the college, given that there were market forces we could not predict. By piloting something new, I was able to signal that experimentation could keep the college nimble.

Years Two and Three

The first year, a president learns about the rhythms of daily work and how these rhythms change month to month; for example, May is different from any other month because of commencement. A president will also have learned how the best plans are disrupted by the inevitable crises that emerge, typically with little notice. But an important new task awaits you in the second year: strategic planning. Careful time management is required to balance the competing demands posed by daily operations, crisis management, and strategic planning.

Presidents will have some rudimentary ideas about their vision going forward. A key next step is an articulation of the process for a strategic plan. It is critical to involve everyone on campus in the idea-generation stage; the more inclusive your process, the better the result. Talk with key stakeholders—students, staff, and faculty—about how to engage your community in building a plan. From the beginning, heed this warning from business management author Peter Drucker: "Culture eats strategy for breakfast." In other words, the strongest plan may fail if it is not aligned with the campus culture.

You might plan a retreat for your senior team, or you might give your team an assignment to put some thoughts on paper, or both. You might form a campus committee to consider the future of the college, or there might be an existing governance structure that you should tap for this work. You might suggest a plenary session with the board of trustees if the board would like to be engaged in this work at the governance level. Because much of your planning is likely to include new academic programs, and perhaps the elimination of some programs, it will be paramount for you to work with representative members of the faculty.

Once you have a process in place, you can turn to the real work. Developing a vision and a set of principles is the first step in strategic planning. Ask yourself tough questions. What are your comparative strengths and weaknesses, relative to peer institutions? What signals can you detect about the future of higher education, and is your institution prepared for changes in the sector? Most importantly, what are the dreams of your community? It is good to collect benchmarking data in the early phases of a strategic planning process. Sometimes data can lead you to identify strategic priorities; other times, a qualitative assessment can be just as helpful. At every step of the way you should be guided by whether a new initiative fits within the core values of your institution. An iterative evaluation of the plan should be a part of your process.

Years Four Through Eight

Institution building is a fulfilling and exciting part of the job for you and your senior team, so you need to set aside time for this work while managing the college. Once the strategic plan is written, your main job as president will be fundraising—because new initiatives require new resources. Typically, a strategic plan can serve as a blueprint for a fundraising campaign, and a compelling plan will attract philanthropic partners who will want to help you create the change you want to lead. People will tell you that development is about relationships, and to some extent it is; however, I like to think about development as partnerships. Donors want to invest in programs that are a good fit between what they value and what the college hopes to do going forward. Many development moments are moving, especially when donors explain just how much a program or initiative matters to them. For example, alumni who received financial aid as students are proud to be able to set up endowed financial aid funds to help students today. For me, one development memory stands out among all others. During my first year, I visited an elderly alumna to thank her for a $5 million gift to name an academic center. After I shared words of gratitude, she said, "Oh no, I have to thank you. This is my legacy. This means everything to me."

The Transition During Years Nine and Ten

During the last two years, presidents should assess which projects can be successfully completed before the end of their terms and which will continue. For example, a president might be working hard to complete a fundraising campaign, to finish a review of governance structures, or to build a new center. No doubt there will be some projects that you will have to put on hold for your successor's consideration. A conversation with trusted members of your team and with your board chair will help you make decisions about your priorities during the final years. They and the rest of the college community will appreciate that you continue to plan for the future even as you prepare to leave.

The search for a successor will be led by the chair of the board of trustees and will begin in earnest midyear through the penultimate year of a president's term so that the board can announce the successor midway through the president's final year. Presidents should not insert themselves in any way into the search process, although sometimes they do, especially if there is an internal candidate. Instead, the job of the president involves preparations for a smooth transition, a key part of the legacy of any presidency.

Once your successor is named, every member of the community will be excited to meet them, and so they should be. You should set up several meetings for the new president to come to campus to meet with your senior team, the student government association, a staff governance group, and a faculty governance group. Near the end of your term, you should spend some one-on-one time with your successor to share your thoughts about the culture of your institution and to answer your successor's questions. You should not try to influence them in any way about their plans for the college; its future is in their hands. I have witnessed presidents handle the transition with grace, while others seem to have a difficult time letting go, which is perhaps understandable given that most presidents have given their hearts and souls to the colleges they have led. Regardless, the needs of the institution should always take precedence.

During the transition, the president can help alumni become excited about the new president. The alumni read letters from the president, see the president at alumni events and reunions, and read about the president in the alumni magazine and perhaps in the popular press. Alumni who have served on college governance groups, especially the board, and alumni who have funded the president's priorities may have developed strong relationships, perhaps even friendships, with the president. For this reason, the president needs to send a strong signal about their support for the next president. When I left my position as dean of the Harvard Graduate School of Education, I sent a letter to prominent alumni—members of the Visiting Committee, members of the Dean's Council, and members of the Alumni Council—in which I shared why I believed that the school would be in good hands with my successor.

Some presidents resist being a lame duck until their last day in office. It may be preferable for you and your community to embrace the fact that you have less influence once your successor has been named. Maybe you should spend your last semester enjoying a victory lap as you reflect on your accomplishments. It is likely that your team in advancement—development and alumni relations—will want you to do just that, because some alumni may want to help you complete your presidency with one last gift to help you accomplish one last goal. You should also consider making one or two tough decisions that are in the best interests of the college, rather than leaving immediate problems for your successor. For example, I know outgoing presidents who have made personnel changes, restructured operating agreements, or put an end to dangerous student traditions. Then, on July 1, outgoing presidents typically have earned a full-year sabbatical, during which they should disengage from the college except when called upon by the new president for information and guidance.

FIVE PIECES OF ADVICE

Several wise books can serve as useful guides for new presidents. Two former presidents have written books that resonated with me: Nannerl Keohane's *Thinking About Leadership* and Susan Resneck Pierce's *On Being Presidential*.[11] Each of these books contains sound advice, based on theory and practice. Over the years, I have curated advice from higher education leaders who have been kind enough to share their hard-earned lessons. In this section, I share the advice I value most.

1. Setting the Tone

When I was appointed acting dean of the Harvard Graduate School of Education, I met with many leaders on campus to ask for advice. David Ellwood, who was serving as the dean of the Harvard Kennedy School at the time, shared something I take with me every day. He advised me to keep smiling, regardless of the context, because leaders set the tone for their institutions. I have come to believe that setting the tone is one of the leader's most important tasks. You will face many challenges in your role. Some may arise from forces outside your institution—for example, a pandemic or a global financial crisis that leads to negative endowment returns. Some may arise from forces within your institution—for example, incendiary views expressed by a member of your community. People will look to you for answers when they feel stressed by these challenges because they want to be reassured by their leader. During these times, you will be serving as a *holding environment*, a term coined by the psychoanalyst Donald Winnicott; that is, you will help others modulate their stress by showing them the way forward. Let your community know that together you can manage any challenge presented to your college. Acknowledge that there may be pain points, and the institution may need to change. Then let them know that you will lead the way forward by working with existing governance groups on campus. During challenging times, you may find yourself reflecting on the fact that these are the moments when the institution needs you most. Take strength from the faith entrusted to you.

2. Trusting Yourself

College presidents have responsibility for all areas of the college. It's a large portfolio consisting of alumni relations, communications, development, enrollment, equity and inclusion, faculty affairs, finance, information technology services, operations, strategy, and student affairs. You will need and will want to rely on your team for guidance, especially in the beginning when you are learning about the culture and practices of your institution. That said, sometimes you may disagree with the advice from someone on your senior leadership team. Most presidents, especially new presidents, will tell you that they made some of their biggest mistakes when they did not trust their instincts.

Alas, a mistake can sometimes lead to a national story about you and your college. After one such occasion, I was meeting with Gloria Steinem, an alumna, and she asked me what had happened. I explained that I took someone's advice against my better judgment. Without skipping a beat, she said, "If it looks like a duck, and it walks like a duck, and it quacks like a duck, but you think it's a pig—it's a pig." I laughed out loud, of course. And I learned an important lesson that day—namely, that I would rather make my own mistakes than someone else's mistakes. In other words, when I have a strong point of view, I would rather trust my judgment and live with the consequences. This does not mean that you should not trust members of your team. After all, they have domain-specific knowledge, which you may lack. That said, you must exercise your judgment after weighing all of the factors involved in a given decision. As one president said to me, our job is quality control.

It is critical for a leader to encourage healthy debate about any issue under consideration. If your team privileges consensus, remind them about the importance of loyal dissent. Sometimes, after a healthy group discussion, I am still not sure what the best way forward is, and I say so. Often, there is no harm in letting a discussion settle. Someone on my team likes to say, "Let's sit and hold," which is good advice. It can be tempting to let the demands on your time force you to make a quick decision, which can lead to a costly mistake. You will make mistakes because you are human; you will make more mistakes if you rush to judgment.

3. Managing Your Time

Time is our most precious resource. When college presidents get together at meetings, we inevitably complain about our schedules using words like *punishing* and *unrelenting*. For me, the most stressful part of the job is the schedule, which is why I discuss time management at length here.

There will be myriad demands for your time. Throughout the year, you will want to meet with your senior team as a group and in one-on-one meetings, to discuss pressing issues as well as plan for the future. A second set of meetings will involve governance groups, chief among them the board of trustees; their role is first and foremost governance of the college, while yours is management, so this partnership will be critical for your success. As important are the on-campus governance groups, especially the Student Government Association, Staff Council, and Faculty Council. Shared governance is the hallmark of the best colleges and universities because everyone has a stake in the institution. Next come the committees on which the president is expected to serve, and on some campuses, including mine, there are many. Presidents must also attend numerous academic and social events, which bring joy to the work: student research exhibitions, performances, and sporting events; colloquia, concerts, poetry readings, museum exhibitions; college traditions like convocation and commencement; and so much more. And you will also be traveling quite a lot for development and alumni events as well as for professional meetings. Trust me that when you return, a great deal of work will be waiting for you.

Managing your calendar will be a full-time job for at least one person. Make sure you have a strong executive assistant and chief of staff to work closely with the person who manages your calendar. Help everyone on your team learn that their job is not to grant every request; rather, it is to prioritize requests so that you can meet all of your responsibilities, which include time to think. Every spring, start working on an annual calendar for the next academic year. Add all the required events first, such as trustee and faculty meetings. Then think about travel obligations. Next, schedule many catch-up days when your team cannot schedule anything without your permission; I am writing this very section of my chapter during one of my catch-up days.

Tasks also need to be scheduled. Help your team understand that they need to put time on the calendar for you to read tenure and promotion files, to prepare for the board meeting, to write remarks for the faculty meeting, to sign letters, and to answer emails. Otherwise, you will be doing unscheduled, albeit important work, long into the evening. The best schedule will be undone by a crisis on your campus, which should be expected, and can even be planned for, at least to some extent; my team puts emergency time on my schedule each week. Still, the schedule will get out of control, and when it does, ask your team to cancel or postpone some meetings.

When I was the dean of the Graduate School of Education at Harvard, I would invite the president to some of our events. More often than not, someone on the president's team would decline and say, "We have to protect the asset." I came to understand that it was my job as dean to invite the president to important events, and it was the job of the president's team to ensure that the president had a sustainable schedule. Now that I am a president, I appreciate when my team protects me. There is nothing I like more than when my chief of staff offers to take a meeting for me.

A president I know once shared a story with me that still makes me smile. During his first year, he said, he was invited to five events every night, and he knew he had to disappoint four groups. One day it occurred to him that maybe he should disappoint all five. By this he meant, of course, that he had to save some time for himself and for his family. Assess what kind of time you will need to make life worth living. Early in my presidency, I decided that I would not start the work day until 9:00 a.m. Each day, I get up early so that I have time to exercise and to eat a leisurely breakfast before walking to my office. This time grounds me before the grind begins.

4. Building Your Team

As president, you will lead a team of senior people who will have the responsibility of leading day-to-day operations as well as implementing change in their respective areas. A colleague at the Harvard Graduate School of Education, Monica Higgins, once shared with me that the job of a leader is to create the conditions that enable people to do their best work; this view resonates deeply with me. So what are those conditions?

You should let your team know that you value collaboration. The best ideas typically emerge from teamwork for two reasons: teams develop more ideas than individuals, and diversity of thought leads to better outcomes. Also, for most people, collaboration is rewarding work. You should also let your team know that you want them to have agency to lead in their respective areas. Anita Roddick has written about the importance of guiding people to the "source of their own power," which is a good way to discuss agency.[12] Relatedly, let your team know that none of us has all the answers. One of my teammates has told me that she appreciates when I say, "I'm not sure how to think about this," because it models for everyone the importance of not reaching a conclusion too soon. Finally, share credit with your team. Often, you may be presenting the work of your team to others—for example, the board of trustees—and it is appropriate to acknowledge the support you have received.

Teams can be consumed by the day-to-day operations of their work. One of your jobs as president is to provide time for strategic thinking—for example, you might schedule retreat sessions several times during the year. I have found that a summer off-site retreat is a good way to provide members of my team with the mind space to think about the future of the college. Sometimes, I use a facilitator for part or all of the meeting so that I can step back from my leadership role and be a full participant. Being off-site also gives people an opportunity to have informal social time together over walks and dinners, which can strengthen relationships within a team.

Responsibility for project management typically resides with the president. Your team will outline short- and long-term projects. Begin by assigning responsibility for each and every task. My team and I use the RACI (responsible, accountable, consulted, and informed) assignment matrix.[13] The person who is accountable is the one with primary oversight for project management. During one of my team meetings, you will often hear someone say, "I am happy to take the A on that." Ask the person with the A to produce a timeline for the project. Often timelines are changed; however, it is important to have one. Otherwise, progress on some projects can come to a stop, replaced by ongoing demands. You and your team should use some of your retreat time to discuss project management; Bernie Roseke provides a useful guide to get you and your team started.[14] Projects do not just happen without careful planning.

5. Cultivating Equanimity

Recently, a new president confided in me that she found it difficult that not all members of her community liked her. I remembered feeling similarly during my first few years as a dean. Leaders new to their roles learn that very few actions will be universally admired by members of your community; for example, some will feel that a letter to the community went too far, while others will feel it did not go far enough.

A friend of mine who is a clinical psychologist once commented that a college president is a public transference figure, meaning people will transfer unresolved, unconscious conflicts in their lives to you—something that happens in all relationships to some extent. For example, some people have difficulty with authority figures, so they will question many of the statements and decisions you make. Further, no matter how hard you try to be transparent and to communicate the rationale for your decisions, there will be an information gap from time to time. And as Aristotle famously noted, nature abhors a vacuum. For this reason, people will make inferences about what you are doing and why. Some people have a predisposition to think the best, while others tend toward negative attributions.

There truly is not much you can do about this. Jerome Murphy, who served as dean of the Harvard Graduate School of Education before me, gave me this advice when I took on the role: "Ten percent of the people will love you because you are the dean, and 10 percent will hate you because you are the dean. Worry about the other 80 percent." I interpret this to mean that leaders cannot worry too much about not being liked. That said, we need to care about the naysayers and the critics because leaders serve all members of a community. When I am my best self, I can recognize that criticism is caring about the college. Try to view criticism in this light.

Sometimes you will feel mistreated or misunderstood by members of your community—a trusted colleague may betray you, students may say you do not care about them, or an alumna may post something ugly on social media. Rise above personal attacks. Sharon Salzberg writes about the eight pillars of happiness in the workplace: balance, concentration, resilience, communication, integrity, meaning, open awareness, and compassion.[15] Try to have compassion for others when they misbehave. Offer an olive branch and try to get to a better place with everyone in your community. This does not mean that you cannot let people know when they have crossed a boundary about how you will allow others to treat you. Even then, do your best to keep the lines of communication open. When I am able to act with equanimity—calm and even-tempered—I have found opportunities for personal growth. For me, this has been one of the gifts of higher education leadership.

ONE FINAL STORY

A college president plays many roles. Sometimes you may feel like a diplomat as you work to build consensus among stakeholders with varying views. Other times you may feel like a salesperson as you fundraise for key priorities. And still other times you may feel like an actor in an improvisational theater as you realize you are working without a script. On the best days, however, you grant wishes. This point became clear to me one summer when I received a letter from a young girl in elementary school who asked me to invite social justice activist Ruby Bridges, the first Black child to desegregate her elementary school in Louisiana, to speak at Smith. The child explained in her letter that her school lacked the funding to pay for Bridges's travel and honorarium, but she thought I might be able to help—and she was right. It was a memorable day when our largest lecture hall was filled not only with our own students but also with local grade school students to hear Bridges. When days are hard and I am tired, I remind myself of the privilege of bringing dreams to life, both mine and those of others.

CHAPTER 3

Assuming the Presidency

A Narrative Essay

DAVID W. OXTOBY

I certainly did not plan to become a college president early in my career; almost no one does. For the first sixty-seven years of my life, though, I lived on campus, studied at, or worked for colleges and universities—an "academic life," to use the title of the autobiography of one of my mentors, Hanna Gray. I was educated as a chemist, enjoyed an active career in research, and was able to combine that with a passion for teaching. I was fortunate to teach at the University of Chicago, an institution that both valued and supported research at the highest level and had talented students (graduate and undergraduate) whom it was a pleasure to teach. I imagined that I would spend my career there, like the great majority of my colleagues.

DEVELOPING SKILLS TO PREPARE FOR A PRESIDENCY

My interest in teaching led me to volunteer early in my career to teach first-year chemistry, which I found I enjoyed; a senior colleague invited me to join him in writing a new general chemistry textbook soon after I had received tenure, and I became the primary author by the second edition (the book is now heading into its ninth edition, passed on to other authors). That interest in teaching also led to my first administrative position in 1984 at a relatively early stage in my career (two years after tenure) as associate dean of the Physical Sciences Division, with responsibility for the undergraduate education program across seven departments in the physical and mathematical sciences. I found that I enjoyed the interdisciplinary work, developing new curricula across departmental lines, and most of all working with groups of faculty to help students learn in new ways. We developed an interdisciplinary year-long course in the mathematical sciences aimed at humanists, and a two-year course jointly with the biological sciences using evolution as an organizing principle. I enjoyed new relationships with my fellow associate deans from across the college, particularly those in the humanities and social sciences.

Having found that I enjoyed the work as a (part-time) administrator, I subsequently accepted in 1991 the directorship of an interdisciplinary research institute connecting physics and chemistry, the equivalent of a department chair position, and was invited in 1995 to become dean of the Physical Sciences Division, with overall responsibility for research and teaching across seven departments. That role gave me experience with faculty recruitment, promotions, tenure, budgets, staff management in support of teaching and research, and how to work with architects to design a new building connecting the physical and biological sciences. At the time I became dean, the university changed its basic business model to give more budget control at the divisional level, creating incentives for fundraising since gifts raised would stay within the division. I found that I enjoyed meeting alumni around the country, raising money, working with the president and provost on major initiatives, and collaborating with deans from across the university on joint projects. At Chicago, divisional dean positions are more manageable in scope than the position more typical at most universities of dean of the Faculty of Arts and Sciences. When I was not traveling for the university, I could still spend almost half my time on research and teaching, and in fact that eight-year period was the most productive time in my career for my own research.

In thinking about future administrative roles (including presidencies), it is valuable not only to have a range of experiences as an administrator at your institution but also to reflect regularly on what you enjoy doing and find rewarding. I found that setting priorities through an annual budget process was an intellectual challenge parallel to the problem-solving I was doing in my research. Most important, I found that I enjoyed working with faculty, students, and staff, both in groups and one-on-one. That is probably the most important test in exploring further steps in an administrative career.

Department chairs or deans always learn more than they want to about faculty, staff, and students in their area. My predecessor told me that the most important background I had to prepare for working with faculty was as a parent of young children, used to dealing with squabbles over minor matters. There are arguments, upset feelings, and unhappiness that you have to deal with, but also special moments to celebrate together. A lesson that I learned soon was that while you have to be sensitive to people and their concerns, you also have to be tough-skinned enough that, after turning down a request from a group, you can reengage with them right away and not "hide" in your office to avoid difficult conversations. I discovered also that although I am not an extrovert (nor is that necessary to be an effective administrator or leader), I valued being pushed to connect with people outside my comfort zone.

In exploring a future administrative or presidential role, I found it valuable also to build connections outside the University of Chicago. I was invited to join the Board of Trustees at Bryn Mawr College in 1988 and served there for twenty years. I had grown up on that campus, where my father taught mathematics and my mother was an alumna, and the college wanted a scientist to help advise on some important upcoming decisions in that area. Eventually, I became a vice chair of the board and chair of the Academic Affairs Committee. Most important, I was able to see firsthand two fine presidents, Pat McPherson and Nancy Vickers, doing their jobs and working with a highly functional board. A further opportunity to connect with other colleges arose from Chicago's participation in a network of midwestern colleges (Chicago and Washington University, together with a group of four-year colleges such as Carleton and Grinnell). We formed a coalition (ChemLinks) that received funding from the National Science Foundation to develop new materials for teaching chemistry. I enjoyed working with fellow chemists as well as meeting presidents and provosts from a group of excellent small colleges in the region. These experiences with Bryn Mawr and with the ChemLinks coalition shaped my career and led to my next steps.

EXPLORING A PRESIDENCY: FINDING A MATCH

After completing my sixth year as dean (and, incidentally, turning fifty), I began to think about what I might do next. The possibility of returning to teaching and research at the end of my second five-year term was attractive, as I had maintained my scholarly career and still very much enjoyed teaching. A number of search firms had approached me about my interest in potential positions at other research universities: dean of arts and sciences, vice president for research, or provost. While I was open to such discussions, none of those opportunities seemed just right for me. I reflected on what I most enjoyed about the various administrative roles I had had and realized that what I valued was the direct contact with faculty, close relations with students, and a hands-on approach to working collaboratively with staff. I cared more about pedagogy and innovative teaching than most faculty at research (R1) universities. These interests suggested that I should consider leaving the R1 world where I had spent the previous thirty-three years and explore a different direction.

My experience as a dean with fundraising, hiring, constructing new buildings, and working with students prepared me to consider moving directly to the presidency of a small college. The 150 faculty in my division were not that much fewer than the full faculty of many colleges, but they were all in the physical and mathematical sciences. To me, the prospect of working closely with social scientists, humanists, and artists was a very attractive way to broaden my scope of work. Just as I had moved from chemistry to broader scientific leadership roles, so moving to a college would stretch me in important new directions. I knew enough about small colleges through my Bryn Mawr experience to realize what the challenges would be, however.

If you are considering such a move, it is crucial to consider in advance what type of institution you want to work at. Does geography matter, either part of the country or city/small town? Are you ready to take on an institution that faces real challenges, or are you more comfortable with one that has had steady and strong leadership for an extended period of time? Are you prepared to work with a strong faculty and bring about incremental change over time through a very consultative process, or do you hope to bring in a transformational vision and start implementing it right away?

I took the leap and started exploring college presidencies, in part because our children were close to high school graduation, so this was a good time if I was going to make a move. (On college visits with them, I had also had the chance to see, at least briefly, quite a few colleges.) While each year many searches take place, it was important to focus on those that I was particularly interested in rather than apply all over. In the first year I explored an opportunity at a Midwestern college that did not go forward, though I learned a lot through the process. The second year, I was nominated for two opportunities: a New England college, and Pomona College, in Claremont, California.

While I had lived and studied in the Northeast, southern California was new to me and, initially, the Los Angeles area did not seem appealing. I had never visited the campus, so early in the search process (at the so-called airport interview stage), I visited anonymously and walked around the campus and the town. It is very important to do this to find out if you can see yourself in a certain setting, even if the chance of it actually happening may still be small. If you are advanced to the finalist stage (often involving the first official campus visit), it is important to know whether you are prepared to accept an offer if one is made. I found that Pomona was accurately described as "a college of the New England type" and Claremont a lovely college town, part of the thriving Los Angeles metropolitan region. I could imagine myself there.

During any search, the candidate must strike a delicate balance between bringing a preformed "vision" for what the institution might become, and hearing from the community and respecting its current realities; I approached this in the search by asking many questions, listening carefully, and responding, giving people a sense of what it would be like to work with me as president. The Pomona search was an open one at the finalist stage, so I had the chance to spend two full days interviewing on campus and meeting literally hundreds of members of the community, as well as having ample time to speak in depth with members of the search committee. I was able to meet the senior staff, who would be my direct reports—something that does not usually happen in confidential searches. By the time I had been offered the job and accepted, I felt I had a pretty good understanding of the institution and the opportunities and challenges I would have in the years ahead. I had imagined that my wife might stay in Chicago with our youngest daughter as she finished her senior year in high school, but in the end our daughter visited a fine school in Claremont and decided to transfer there for her last year.

TRANSITION PERIOD AND FIRST YEARS OF A PRESIDENCY

Between my appointment at the end of January and my starting date of July 1, I visited the campus roughly once a month. That was helpful for several reasons: first, to have plenty of time to spend with the outgoing president, who was most helpful in orienting me to what I might expect; second, to begin to get to know my senior staff, so I could hit the ground running when I started; and third, to be seen on campus and meet faculty and student leaders and gain firsthand information about their activities. At the same time, it was important during the transition months not to offer opinions about choices the college would be facing; there is only one president at a time. I also declined to come for board meetings, Family Weekend, Alumni Weekend, or graduation; while there was curiosity about me, it was much more important for the outgoing president to be fully in the lead on all those occasions. My presence would have been a distraction.

Starting any new job comes with a rush of excitement, tinged with anxiety, about what to do first and how to jump into decisions without full information. In my first two weeks, I was faced with an important decision for the college: whether to build a single new building for several departments and make some other accommodations in the meantime, or build a pair of connected buildings in one step, saving money in the long run and reducing disruption, but requiring a significantly larger fundraising effort right away. In my state of naïve optimism, I chose the latter course, which in the end turned out to be the right one.

I soon got to know my senior staff and found I was able to work well with all of them. It is important to make decisions soon about senior staff changes, avoiding an extended period of uncertainty that can be damaging to morale throughout an organization. In other jobs, I have had to move quickly to make one or more staff changes, but that was not the case at Pomona, since my predecessor had built a strong staff with only one departure in the interim (vice president of advancement, a search that I finished right after my appointment). One search consultant I spoke with recommended that I identify one member of the senior staff and replace that person "just to show everyone who is in charge." Needless to say, I did not follow that advice, nor did I hire that search firm again.

One further note for a new president: the structure and effectiveness of the "Office of the President" are critical for success. When I arrived, I did not realize how important it would be to have a special assistant (sometimes titled "chief of staff") who could be a thought partner for me and who could take certain strategic issues off my plate to free time for all my other responsibilities. When I hired a stellar individual in my sixth year, it literally changed my life. I was looking for someone with a strong mix of academic and administrative experience and was fortunate to find someone with just those qualities at a sister college without an extensive search.

The first few months of a presidency set a tone for what will come and create expectations for the community about the future. Years later, people referred to the fact that during my campus interview I asked to visit the art museum; that showed (correctly) my interest in the arts, which became a theme of my presidency. During the transition months, several faculty members took me on a tour of the neighboring city of Pomona, a different world from the wealth of the town of Claremont; they continued to speak about that visit for many years. One challenge is to know what people expect, based on what happened in the past under your predecessor. It does not mean you have to do the same things, but at least you won't be surprised. My senior staff (and the assistants in the President's Office) got used to my asking how particular things used to be done, even if I then decided to do something different. One of my first actions was to drop hard alcohol and mixed drinks from faculty receptions in favor of good California wines and beer; some faculty still have not forgiven me for that change!

One question that every new president is asked throughout at least the first year, and often beyond, is "What has surprised you about coming to [insert name] College?" It is important to develop a consistent and thought-out answer to that question, and also to recognize that the person asking the question is not really interested in the honesty of your reply! Sure, you had no idea that two or three of the departments were so dysfunctional, but don't say so. Develop a "narrative" that connects to your own idea of what the aspirations of the college should be, and certainly don't identify some peculiar feature of the college that might offend the person you are speaking with. My standard answer was along the lines of, "What surprises me is that at a college with all the recognition and accomplishments of Pomona, there is still a desire not to rest on our laurels but rather to change in significant ways in the future." I would also speak about California as a place encouraging creativity and new ideas and representing the future of the country. Now there was a lot of truth to those statements: I had been impressed through the search process at how college leadership really wanted my thoughts on what Pomona should do differently. But there was also an element of wishful thinking in my reply.

There are two parallel questions to prepare narratives for as well. One was "How does [insert name] compare to your former institution?" Now in my case that was not a very useful question, frankly, since how do you compare Pomona College, a small college located in the suburbs, with the University of Chicago, an urban research university? California versus the Midwest? Being president versus a faculty member and dean? But, needing to come up with an answer, I usually referred to the (candidly dangerous and not really accurate) myths that Pomona has the "happiest students" in the country, whereas Chicago was "where fun goes to die." (Chicago students were unusual enough to actually display that statement proudly on t-shirts!) Another popular question to be prepared for is "What do you like most about [insert name] College?" You can count on that question following you throughout your presidency. My answer (and an honest but also a safe one) was "the students." That gets a good response not only from the students themselves and their parents, but also from the faculty (who would often give the same answer) and the alumni (who remember their student days fondly). In times of student protest and occasional irrationality, loving—and appreciating—the students is not only a good answer to give but also a critical requirement for doing the job. If you can no longer say that, it is time to step down and look for another job.

UNEXPECTED CHALLENGES

Now let me return to the question "What surprised you most about Pomona College?" or rephrasing it, "What were you least prepared for when you started your presidency?" and give an honest answer. There are two things that I felt less prepared for, one of which is specific to Pomona College, and the other a more general issue for every new president.

1. The Claremont Colleges Group

Pomona College was founded in 1887 as one of the last Congregational Church foundings across the country. In 1925 a visionary president, James Blaisdell, decided that rather than letting the college grow further and become a small university, he would instead use the surrounding land from a donor (Ellen Browning Scripps) to found a number of other small colleges, so each would remain small but they would have the advantage of scale and shared facilities. He spoke of Claremont evolving into an institution like Oxford or Cambridge with a central academic core connected to separate small colleges, but this was more a marketing device to raise awareness than a close analogy. The Blaisdell plan led to the founding of Scripps College and Claremont Graduate University in the 1920s, Claremont McKenna in the 1940s, Harvey Mudd in the 1950s, Pitzer in the 1960s, and Keck Graduate Institute in the 1990s. The Claremont Colleges are unique in American higher education in having been founded intentionally as a group, not the result of later cooperation between existing institutions (as was the case with the Bryn Mawr–Haverford–Swarthmore group that I already knew).

During the search process, I had asked to meet one or more presidents from the other campuses to understand better how the group worked together, but I was told that that would be too complicated and they did not want to have to arrange such a meeting for all four finalists. So that became an important part of my education once I started. The Claremont Colleges share a common library and services such as campus health and campus safety. The academic calendars are identical, and students can freely take courses on any campus; distances are short enough that a student can take a 9:00 a.m. course on one campus and a 10:00 a.m. course on another one. Student organizations and activities are almost all open to students from every campus.

I learned about the challenges of being a president in Claremont. A typical decision that a president might make in a stand-alone college after consulting with the student dean and the academic dean becomes a consultation between the presidents' council with the two committees of student and academic deans. But the other side of this is that each president can have an impact on the future and success of more than one college, and there are presidents right next door to consult with. We used to joke that "there are more college presidents than plumbers in Claremont." Because I came from a larger university, that complexity was actually an appealing feature to me.

When I arrived in Claremont, Pomona College had the reputation of separating itself from the other colleges. We were the oldest and the richest, and we liked to do things our own way, rather than working together to agree on a common course of action. In admissions, we thought of ourselves as more connected to other elite colleges such as Amherst and Swarthmore than to our peers in Claremont. So when the other four colleges would do some admissions recruiting together, they always had to explain why Pomona was not in the room. I changed (mostly successfully) Pomona's posture with respect to the group so we were much more fully part of the joint endeavor. I was proud when, within a few years, my dean of students was saying to me "if this had been our decision, we would have done it differently, but we wanted to be consistent with the policies of the other colleges." Search processes changed so that searches involved the participation of peers from the other campuses, although that was less true of faculty searches than of senior staff appointments. The Claremont Colleges became a distinguishing feature that gave us advantages over other liberal arts colleges in recruiting students, faculty, and staff. We were able to point to real ways in which we offered the "best of both worlds": a small college with access to many more resources, comparable to what is available in a research university.

2. Working with a Board of Trustees

A second area where I felt underprepared in starting my presidency is one that applies in different ways to every new president: working with a board of trustees. As dean at the University of Chicago, I had worked effectively with a Dean's Advisory Council, which met several times a year to hear about our activities, meet faculty and students in the division, provide advice to me, help build relationships with outside groups, and donate to our efforts. I imagined that working with my own board at Pomona would be similar, but an advisory board is quite different from a fiduciary board. Likewise, at Bryn Mawr I had the experience of serving on a board of trustees, but it is completely different being a president hired by and reporting to a board than just being a member.

It took me awhile to realize how much time and considered effort was needed to develop a good working relationship not only with the board chair but also with all the members of the board (between thirty-five and forty in the case of Pomona). After a while, I started sending monthly candid updates to the board, keeping them informed of my activities, though later I changed that since I wanted instead to focus more on strategic issues rather than just list travel and events on campus. It was important to meet and communicate one-on-one with board members, which took both time and planning. My senior staff also helped to focus on what the board needed from each of them to contribute to my success.

The relationship with the board chair is particularly important. My first chair (who served in that role for six years after I started) had been very actively involved throughout the search process, so we had a close relationship even before I arrived. Since he lived nearby, we made the habit of having an extended meeting and lunch every month, as well as phone calls whenever needed. He understood the difference between management (the president's job) and governance (the board's), and we were able to be very candid with one another. I brought up problematic issues early on and turned to him right away for help and advice in crisis situations.

In retrospect, however, I do wish I had spent more time during my first years connecting with other board members. One reason is that when the board chair changes over, it can lead to surprisingly large changes for the president. With my second board chair, my relationship was quite different. Since he lived across the country, we interacted much more by phone than in person. We did try to spend a good part of one day together each year planning the year ahead, but that was a poor substitute for regular in-person meetings. While we were candid with one another, I did not feel the same connection as with my first board chair.

There are three further aspects of working with a board that are important to mention, and where I felt underprepared when I started my presidency:

- *Board dynamics during meetings.* Does the board chair actually run the meeting, or does the chair hand it over to the president after some brief words of welcome? There are real advantages to having a board chair run the meeting, with the president stepping in to make presentations, propose recommendations, and offer observations. Are all board members encouraged to speak up appropriately, or do a few do most of the talking? Is there a gender dynamic on the board where women get interrupted or do not feel comfortable expressing their opinion? Is the board spending the appropriate amount of time on strategic issues, or just focusing on small details? Does the board chair stop the meeting when an important issue is under discussion and ask for further comments before moving on? Not every board chair is equally experienced or skilled at running meetings. Training through such organizations as the Association of Governing Boards should be considered by every new board chair.

- *The role of the president in working with a Trusteeship or Nominations Committee.* Do names of new board members emerge mostly from board members or from the president? How much should the president try to "shape" a board through new members who are close to the president's strategic vision? How candid should the president be about the performance of current board members when they come up for renewal? How well is the board functioning, and is the Trusteeship Committee just letting things go or really trying to improve board processes? A number of years into my presidency, our board brought in an outside consultant to work with us on how we might change board processes to be more effective. That was a very helpful step to take.

- *How does a board evaluate the performance of the president?* In my case, during my first few years, we followed a standard process where I set out goals at the beginning of the year, which I first ran by the board chair, and they were discussed at the first meeting with the full board. Near the end of the year, I followed up with a memo describing my accomplishments in meeting those goals. That information was shared with the Executive Committee (acting as the Compensation Committee) and later with the full board, and then when my salary was set, the board chair finished with a conversation with me about my performance and things I might want to change. Several years into my presidency, though, a different process was followed one year (and only one), and it was problematic. A decision was made (with my support) to do a "360" review and to ask others in the community about my performance. Rather than phrase this as "What advice do you have for the president?" it was instead posed along the lines of "What do you think about the performance of the president?" Pomona College being an open and democratic institution, every student, faculty member, and staff member was invited to comment on my performance. And to avoid "retaliation" for any criticism, this was either done fully anonymously or with only the trustee members of the evaluation committee knowing who made what comments. Of course, the vast majority of those asked did not actually respond, and most of those who did had positive things to say. But the relatively small number of comments from disgruntled faculty and others then seemed to have a disproportionate impact and raise questions about "problems" in my presidency that affected future relations with the board for several years. While some of the critical advice was good and I took it to heart and tried to respond, some of it resulted from a dangerous step of giving people (especially faculty) a "back-channel" to the board that bypassed the president.

CONCLUDING THOUGHTS

College presidents, when they get together, invariably complain about how hard their jobs are, how unappreciative everyone is of all that they are doing, and how they do not have a single moment free to do anything personal. That is not the whole story. Those same presidents (myself included) will also say how much they enjoyed the job and the opportunity to make a positive change for a college and its future. There is no other job quite like it.

CHAPTER 4

Choosing a Presidency

CAROL T. CHRIST

I have had the privilege of leading two institutions—Smith College in Northampton, Massachusetts, and the University of California at Berkeley. The two could not be more different. Smith is private; Berkeley is public. Smith is on the East Coast, Berkeley on the West Coast. Smith has fewer than three thousand students; Berkeley has more than forty thousand. Smith is a liberal arts college; Berkeley is a research university. Smith is a women's college; Berkeley is coeducational. It would be easy to assume that leading these two very different institutions requires very different skill sets and that lessons learned at one institution would have doubtful relevance to the other. I found neither to be the case; my experiences consequently may be helpful in choosing a presidency. People often pursue their careers within a single institutional type. I believe there are real advantages in moving between different kinds of institutions; I will attempt to explain why.

BERKELEY BEFORE SMITH

When I was working for my doctorate (in English, at Yale), I imagined myself teaching at a New England college. When I received the offer of an assistant professorship at Berkeley, however, it was too good to turn down. I began my appointment in September of 1970 and spent the next thirty-two years at Berkeley. In the 1980s I took a few of the administrative positions that faculty are often invited to assume; I served as vice chair of my department, as an assistant to the chancellor for the status of women, and as chair of my department. I discovered that I liked administration and that I was talented at it. In my discipline, English, research is fairly solitary. I found I liked working with teams of people to achieve institutional goals and that I liked helping create change. I took a set of positions of progressively larger scope and responsibility—dean of humanities, provost, dean of the College of Letters and Science, and provost and executive vice chancellor. I worked for three successive chancellors and discovered how significantly the vision and style of a leader can change the shape and nature of the work of those reporting to them. The three chancellors for whom I worked had very distinct leadership styles, and I learned a great deal from each of them.

At that point in my career, I had begun getting inquiries about my interest in various presidencies. Because my husband was a tenured faculty member at Berkeley and because I still had school-age children, I routinely said no to these inquiries, but I began to wonder what kind of institution might suit me best. I allowed myself to be considered as a candidate in a very small number of searches—putting my toe in the water, so to speak—and discovered that you needed to think your way into the position—assume it in your mind—to be a convincing candidate. I found myself growing increasingly skeptical of whether I would be a good fit for the outward-facing, highly political job of a public university president or chancellor. I loved the position of provost; what I valued about it was its closeness to the faculty, its responsibility for the internal operations of the campus, and its continuing contact with students. I feared losing those aspects of the job and worried about responsibilities in areas where I had much less experience—government relations, fundraising, and intercollegiate athletics. I then allowed myself to be considered as a candidate for the presidency of a liberal arts college (not Smith); somewhat to my surprise, the fit felt right. I realized that the position involved close relationships with faculty and students as well as immediate responsibility for the operation of the campus.

In 2000, I decided to step down as provost; I had been doing the job in one form or another for eleven years (Berkeley had moved from a two-provost to a one-provost system during this period), and I felt it was time. While still harboring administrative ambitions, I decided to return to the faculty. I deeply loved Berkeley, and it was where my family was settled. However, I discovered that I had changed and that the work of leadership was more compelling to me than the work of a faculty member. At about that time, Smith College approached me about my interest in its presidency. As I went through the series of conversations and interviews in the selection process, the job felt more and more right. It was the New England college of my graduate school dreams. I had gone to a women's college myself and understood the power of single-sex education. In personal terms, it was a good time to move. My husband had just retired from the faculty and my daughter had begun college. I accepted the job.

MY YEARS AT SMITH

Going to Smith was a much bigger adjustment than I initially anticipated. The city of Northampton where Smith is located has a population of less than thirty thousand, in the midst of a fairly rural area. In that context, the president of Smith is a public personage. I discovered I had neither privacy nor anonymity outside of my residence.

The culture was profoundly different from Berkeley's in ways I hadn't anticipated. Everyone knew one another, knew each other's families, each other's children. A web of strong personal connections wove the community together, often leading to individual and personal resolutions of problems rather than policy-driven solutions. I was used to the large public spaces of Berkeley and its theatrical politics—the noon rallies on Sproul Plaza; by contrast, private spaces defined the culture at Smith. Something thoughtless, rude, or biased that one student said to another in a dining hall could roil the campus; at Berkeley it was hard to imagine how anyone would even know about such an incident. The racial dynamic was strikingly different, defined by Black/White relationships, not the more complex fabric of multiple ethnic groups in California. I early came to see both the virtues and the challenges of this very different culture.

Despite the very different characters of Smith and Berkeley, I found myself frequently using my Berkeley experience (although trying not to refer to it very often). Upon arriving at Smith, I discovered the college was facing a significant budget shortfall. My experience in dealing with the budget crises of the 1990s at the University of California prepared me with templates and strategies. Because Berkeley was so much more a policy-driven culture, I could shape policies that created consistency in decision-making. At the time I became president, Smith was in the very early stages of developing an engineering program; despite the large difference in scale from Berkeley's College of Engineering, my Berkeley experience served me well in helping the program develop. As we confronted issues of free speech, and of hateful speech, I understood how to frame the college's engagement with these issues. My deep understanding of the values of a public university led me to recognize the public aspects of Smith's mission; I began speaking of Smith as a private college with a public conscience.

When I first came to Smith, I faced the temptation of assuming that a smaller and less complex institution than Berkeley would be easier to lead. I quickly learned the error of this view. Universities and colleges all have their own ecosystems, their own cultures, and their own histories. Leading a college or university successfully requires not only understanding but also internalizing these elements of its being. Although many aspects of colleges and universities are generic, they are not experienced as such by their stakeholders. Colleges try to convince the students whom they recruit that they are offering them a unique experience, one that can't be duplicated at any other institution, and alumnae believe this to have been the case. Faculty and staff often spend their entire careers at a single institution, so imagine its character as distinctive. Admittedly, this is somewhat a Lake Wobegon effect, but the prospective president must embrace it and work with it.

I also had to resist the temptation of imagining the presidency as a glorified provostship. The position of provost is the most common route to a presidency or chancellorship, but the two positions are very different. The president is the storyteller-in-chief;

you are the face of the institution to its multiple constituencies; you set strategy. You are not the chief operating officer or the chief academic officer. It is tempting to do a new job like your old job, but it is critical to understand the differences in the respective positions. If you don't, you will not only drive your provost crazy but also will fail to realize all the opportunities for leadership that the presidency provides.

I learned an enormous amount from being president of Smith and grew a great deal as a leader. No matter how broad the span of authority may have been in your previous position, it is fundamentally different to be in charge, to have the ultimate responsibility for decision-making. You learn decisiveness, you learn to set and communicate clarity of direction, and you learn the habit of authority. Of course you work with a team, of course you inspire and empower others to shape and execute initiatives, and of course you consult widely and listen carefully. But an important element of success in these positions is comfort with decision-making and understanding its responsibility.

In making major decisions, I worked in partnership with the board of trustees, which has ultimate authority for the direction and value of an institution; one of the most important things I learned at Smith was how to work with a board. Coming from a public university system, I only knew the board of regents; I suspected the Smith board was different. In my first dinner with the chair of the board, right after the trustees had voted on my appointment, I asked her what the function was of the board; she replied, "To help the president succeed." In my experience, you need to regard the trustees as thought partners, extraordinary pro bono consultants of wide and deep experience, motivated by love of the institution. Because board meetings are intense occasions for the leadership team of a college, there is always a temptation to control the meetings as tightly as possible, perhaps through a parade of presentations, dog and pony shows. Running meetings in this way will frustrate the trustees, leading to disengagement or unpredictable outbursts. I came to think of the best model for a board meeting as the seminar. I learned to bring the board what I was thinking, and the questions that engaged and challenged me, and I was rewarded by a valuable partnership.

I also learned a great deal about fundraising at Smith. I came to understand the partnership in a good donor relationship, the ways in which philanthropic gifts express donors' values and vision for their own legacy. When I arrived at Smith, the college had a generous and deeply committed group of older donors who had graduated from Smith when the leading Ivies still admitted only men. Smith had been less successful with donors from more recent generations, so I realized I had not just a challenge of fundraising but one of alumnae engagement. There's an old saw in the development business: if you want someone's advice, ask for their money; if you want their money, ask for their advice. I held a series of salons in alumnae homes, asking guests to talk about their Smith experience and their sense of the college today. I created president's advisory councils in the major cities in which Smith had alumnae communities. We met twice a year, on a topic of immediate concern for the college—our international profile, for example, or financial aid strategy. I provided readings and questions for each meeting. Smithies, being Smithies, prepared carefully; the discussions were lively, and they resulted both in greater engagement and greater generosity.

I also learned about working with alumnae. Smith had a separate and independent alumnae association, more connected to an older model of affiliation with the college than how it might serve more recent graduates. We began building alumnae programs within the college itself focused on professional interests and career networking. Ultimately, we found a way for the alumnae association to come into the college, with excellent results for alumnae engagement and programming.

Having come from a large public research university, I was unfamiliar with many of the tools essential to the operation of a private college. I was initially surprised by how much time and energy we devoted to enrollment management—increasing the applicant pool and determining what kinds of students we wanted to attract and how best to reach and appeal to them. Financial aid was a much more complex calculus, as we tried to control the discount rate (the percent of tuition returned in the form of financial aid). We controlled many more financial tools than public universities typically do. We set tuition; we set the endowment payout; we set investment policy; we controlled employee benefits. Because the budget was so much smaller than Berkeley's, the margins were slimmer, even though Smith was a relatively wealthy college. However, financial management was easier because the college controlled so many more financial parameters than a public university does.

Smith also taught me about undergraduate education and the multiple ways in which a liberal arts college cares for its students. Shortly after I arrived at Smith, I gave a series of dinners for the faculty. Over the course of several months, I invited the entire faculty to dinner, in groups of twenty. I told my guests that they had the ear of the new president and I was interested in what they thought I should know. At every single dinner, the main topic of conversation was teaching. There was a seriousness of pedagogical intent, of earnest inquiry about how to teach even better. Although much excellent teaching takes place at Berkeley, I don't think a similar set of dinners would have produced the same conversations. I was also struck by how carefully the college created safety nets for its students, seeking to identify students in trouble as early as possible and intervene. The college felt that any student's failure was its failure.

I learned about strategic planning at Smith. I completed two strategic plans during the time that I was president. The first was the kind of plan typically developed by colleges and universities: a call for ideas was sent to the community; a large and representative committee sifted through them and chose those they felt were the best. I've since come to understand this kind of planning is not strategic. We undertook our second strategic plan shortly after the financial crisis of 2008-2009. A group of trustees were concerned about the landscape of higher education and the college's place in it; I knew I had to make this conversation central to the community. We structured a process that began with a SWOT (strengths, weaknesses, opportunities, threats) analysis and made extensive use of scenario planning; we brought all constituencies of the college together in conversation. I've since used this planning structure in a number of different contexts because it so effectively focuses attention on questions that are genuinely strategic. In my work on strategic planning, I made particular use of the ideas of Vijay Govindarajan, the Coxe Distinguished Professor of Management in Dartmouth's Tuck School of Business. Professor Govindarajan argues that the tasks of all organizations fall into three boxes. The first box contains all the things an institution does to perform its core mission as well as possible; most successful organizations are good at this. The second box is the box of deliberate forgetting, the abandonment of practices or assumptions that no longer serve the organization well; many institutions neglect the activity of deliberate forgetting. The third box is the box of innovation—and innovation with a tolerance for failure. This too is more challenging than successful execution of an organization's primary mission.

In focusing attention on an institution's future—the objective of any strategic plan—it can be particularly powerful to create a narrative connecting that future to iconic moments of its past. I learned this kind of historical storytelling at Smith; it's an important tool for any president. It builds community identity and a shared sense of past and future. This is partly what I mean when I say that the position of president or chancellor is that of storyteller-in-chief; part of your job is representing the community to itself.

Smith's history as a women's college is the most fundamental aspect of its identity. Living and breathing that identity and culture gave me a different connection to the history of women. Up to the point that I went to Smith, I had spent most of my career in male-dominated environments. I found it liberating to work in an institution focused on opportunities for women. My executive team was almost entirely female (the head of IT was the single man). We had a close and effective working relationship that taught me a lot about team building and effective execution.

RETURNING TO BERKELEY

When I left Smith in 2013 and moved back to the city of Berkeley, I expected to retire. I did some consulting—first for the Collaborative Brain Trust and then for the

Association of Governing Boards. In 2015, Berkeley asked me to run its Center for Studies in Higher Education—a half-time job that I found stimulating and fulfilling in the way it engaged me with issues in higher education. Then in 2016 the provost resigned suddenly, and I was asked to serve as interim provost. Doing the job post-retirement, on an interim basis, was curiously freeing. The institution was facing many challenges—a $150 million structural budget deficit, a somewhat demoralized executive team, and a difficult negotiation with the alumni association about closer institutional connection to the university. With issue after issue, I felt free to choose the course that seemed best for the university, even when it was not popular with some constituencies. During that year the chancellor resigned, and a search for a new chancellor began. Although a number of colleagues urged me to be a candidate, I resisted, thinking it wasn't really the right time in my life to undertake such a job. However, I finally agreed to speak to the search committee. Much to my surprise, I was offered the position.

I accepted the chancellorship because of my deep love for Berkeley; it has made me who I am. I also came to the judgment that my particular attributes and skills were a good fit for the campus's current challenges. I knew Berkeley very well and had credibility with the faculty—a critical resource at a time of crisis and change. Because I am at the end of my career, I have an independence that gives me courage to make difficult decisions when they seem in the best long-term interests of the university. The immediate challenges in front of the campus—its budget deficit, its lack of a strategic plan, its need to make more progress on diversity, and its need to rebuild community—were all good fits for the capacities I had developed at Smith and in my previous work at Berkeley. I believed that I could move the campus forward in the areas that mattered most urgently.

The chancellorship of a public university campus that is part of a large university system is profoundly different from the presidency of a liberal arts college. Major elements of my job as chancellor hardly figured in my work at Smith—for example, state government relations, relationships with the system of the University of California, and responsibility for a huge research enterprise and for an extensive range and variety of graduate programs. I had far fewer financial levers that I controlled at Berkeley in contrast to Smith. A chancellor's relationship with the board of regents is very different from the partnership between a college president and the board.

Nonetheless, many of the things I learned at Smith were transferable to my job at Berkeley. Simply having been president of another institution gave me a comfort with decision-making, with being in charge. Much of what I learned about strategic planning I put to immediate use at Berkeley. I relied upon what I had learned about fundraising and alumni relations, and even about working with an independent alumni association. I used what I had learned about storytelling.

Even in areas where the institutions were very different, I used my Smith experience and knowledge at Berkeley. I could see the undergraduate experience at Berkeley in a new light because of what I learned about undergraduate education and support at Smith; I had more sense of changes that might make a difference. My work with the Smith Board of Trustees gave me a profound appreciation for the benefits and counsel that such a partnership could bring an institution. I began to evolve Berkeley's Board of Visitors—an advisory board to the campus—into a body as close to a board of trustees as I could manage without infringing on the role of the regents. They did indeed become trusted advisors, with valuable advice about the challenges facing the campus. My understanding of the range of tools that private colleges use in regard both to budget and enrollment management gave me a broader context for Berkeley's financial modeling and enrollment strategy.

PRINCIPLES FOR CHOOSING A PRESIDENCY

My experience at Smith and at Berkeley has given me a deep appreciation for the benefits of diverse institutional experiences in a president's career. In higher education administration and leadership, people often stick to a single institutional type, but there are real benefits and insights to be gained from moving between different kinds of institutions, and search committees have more openness to different institutional backgrounds than one might assume. When I first came to Smith, I sometimes joked about the Smith bubble; however, when I returned to Berkeley, I realized that there was a Berkeley bubble. Going to Smith enabled me to see it.

As you think about your career, and about deciding which presidencies you would like to consider, I believe you should rely on several principles. First—and most important—is a deep commitment to the school's mission. As president or chancellor, you are the spokesperson for the institution, in many contexts, and to many audiences; you need to be able to speak about its mission with passion and conviction. You also need to believe yourself that you have committed this portion of your life to deeply meaningful work. Presidencies are grueling—and often lonely—jobs. Without a deep identity with your school's mission, and a conviction of the importance of its work, you will lack a sense of sustained purpose. The first test of fitness between an individual and an institution is profoundly felt belief in its mission.

But beyond mission, you need to have sympathy for, and compatibility with, the institution's culture. If the school has a strong sense of faculty governance, for example, you need to be comfortable collaborating with faculty, seeking advice, listening carefully, and altering your course when appropriate. If athletics plays a major role in a school's culture, you need to embrace being a fan. Every institution has a complex and idiosyncratic culture and history. To be an effective president, you need to learn and live the culture. Thus, you need to ask yourself, could I feel at home here? Will this college fit me like a favorite piece of clothing? In presidencies that go wrong, small behaviors and habits often become symbolic to the community of a lack of fit. You need to feel at home in the ecosystem of a place.

This fit is also important for your partner and your family. The role of president or chancellor is so public and all-encompassing that it shapes family life in ways that even powerful vice presidencies do not. The decision to take a presidency must be a good one not just for you but also for your partner. Is it a good time in their life for such a move? What will its impact be upon their career? The president's partner inevitably has a public role. How willingly will they embrace it? If you have children living at home, how will the transition work for them? Perhaps more than other career decisions, the choice to take a presidency is a family decision.

The harder question to answer in choosing a particular presidency is whether your talents and experiences are a good fit for the institution's challenges and opportunities. The answer depends on a full and careful assessment of the situation of the institution—a SWOT analysis, if you will—and an equally full and candid assessment of your own strengths and capabilities. What does the institution need? What are you good at? I sometimes compare leading a college or university to stepping in a river; the river has had a course before you enter it, and it will continue flowing after you leave. You need to respect where the river has come from and realize it will flow on when you leave. Leaders sometimes underestimate the value of historical humility; as a president or a chancellor, you are a chapter in a novel, not the entire plot. Thus, you need to figure out the trajectory of the institution and the valuable projects underway that you should continue to develop as well as the new things you wish to do.

Finally, it is critical to assess the governance of the institution. Are there deeply rooted antagonisms or tensions between major constituencies—the faculty and the administration, for example? Does the institution have a highly functioning board? Are there tensions within it? Does the board have a strategic focus? Does it concentrate on governance, not management? Does it devote attention to its own efficacy and improvement, through annual self-evaluation of its performance? Does it have a careful process for identifying and vetting new board members? Does the leadership of key committees and does the chairmanship of the board itself rotate at appropriate intervals? Is there a high level of engagement among trustees? Is there a culture of trust, candor, and inclusion? Does it have the highest standards of fiduciary integrity and ethics? Does it have a healthy relationship with the outgoing president?

Admittedly, answers to some of these questions are hard to determine in a search process, but a highly functioning board is a significant determinant of a president's success. Public boards present different challenges from private ones; they do not select their own members, and criteria for appointment (or election) are often political.

Meetings are frequently public, sometimes inhibiting the candid exchange of views. The fiduciary role of the board can be more complex, with responsibility not just to the institution but to the state. In speaking with other presidents, I often hear about their initial surprise at how much time they spend working with their boards. Because it is so key a relationship, assessment of it should play an important role in choosing a presidency.

A presidency or a chancellorship is a life-changing job. You identify yourself so fully with the institution—not only in public but in private ways—that some part of it becomes you. It takes root in your heart. This kind of connection, in which your life takes on amplitude and focus by an institutional identity, is a rare privilege. Because you are choosing what becomes a part of yourself, the choice is a weighty one—in some ways like a marriage. Choose carefully and well, and enjoy the ways it leads you to learn and grow.

CHAPTER 5

Shared Governance in American Research Universities

MICHAEL H. SCHILL

S hortly after I was appointed president of the University of Oregon in 2015, I did what many new presidents do—I visited or called several senior presidents to ask their advice. These conversations were generally uplifting and optimistic until the subject of shared governance came up. Upon posing a variant of the question—how effective is your academic senate, or what is your relationship with the academic senate?—I got a pained look or a sigh and then a litany of concerns.

Importantly, none of my soon-to-be colleagues questioned the "idea" of shared governance. The notion that faculty (and perhaps students and staff) should be consulted in connection with at least some university decisions is alive and well in American academia and supported by most institutional leaders. Nevertheless, as the recent tensions surrounding COVID-19 and decisions to "reopen" campuses have demonstrated, how that consultation takes place and whether shared governance extends to shared decision-making remain very live issues on campuses throughout the nation.[1]

In this chapter, I briefly describe the concept of shared governance, its origins, and some of the current ambiguities surrounding its meaning. A wide variation in shared governance practices exists among American research universities, some of which I describe. I conclude by examining a set of problems facing shared governance ranging from insufficient participation by all segments of the faculty, time-consuming decision-making processes, the role of unions, and the particularly difficult decisions accompanying financial contractions.

At the outset, I would like to put my cards on the table. I believe that one of the reasons why American universities have been so successful over such a long time is their adherence to principles of shared governance. I can't say I have always felt that way. My formative years as a faculty member at two private research institutions left me blissfully unaware of the academic senate or any universitywide consultative bodies. Indeed, I cannot even remember ever opening a ballot to vote for a law school representative to the senate. I served regularly and happily on my law school's appointments committees and attended faculty meetings religiously, but I never felt nor desired to have a say in university decisions.

Then I became dean of the University of California, Los Angeles (UCLA) School of Law and presided over the first meeting of my elected advisory committee. These folks expected me to discuss every important decision I would make and get their advice, even on subjects like faculty salaries! I must have looked like I had eaten spoiled food at our meeting because a couple days later the senior faculty member on the committee, a former chair of the UCLA Senate, and a widely published and admired scholar, came to my office with a set of PowerPoint slides entitled, "Why You Should Love the Advisory Committee." And you know what? I did indeed fall in love. From then on, every major decision—even those not traditionally discussed with advisory committees—was painstakingly discussed in our biweekly meetings. And while I did not accept the advice of the committee on all matters, I find it hard to remember one major decision I made that was not made better by those meetings. While my subsequent experiences in shared governance as dean of the University of Chicago Law School and president of the University of Oregon have been shaped by idiosyncratic aspects of their cultures, my belief in the value of consultation with and, in some cases, actual approval of university decisions by elected or appointed members of the faculty remains unshaken.

SHARED GOVERNANCE: WHAT DOES IT MEAN?

Except in certain limited circumstances spelled out by charter or statute, the plenary authority over university governance resides with a body sometimes called the board of trustees, the board of overseers, the regents, or the corporation. The members of these fiduciary bodies in the case of private universities are usually self-perpetuating and in the case of public universities appointed by the governor and confirmed by the legislature.[2] The trustees typically appoint and have the power to terminate a president. While the trustees normally retain ultimate authority over the university, they generally delegate operational powers to the president, often explicitly retaining the power to approve the budget, long-term debt, and, in some universities, the appointment of deans and faculty as well as the conferral of degrees. The trustees also maintain oversight over the university and are frequently engaged—formally or informally—in decisions about strategic direction and priorities. Through governing documents or custom and practice, some of the authority of the president is typically delegated to the faculty and other constituencies participating in shared governance.

While many of us take shared governance for granted, faculty participation in the management of university affairs was not always part of the American academic experience. The earliest universities were run by self-perpetuating lay boards or boards appointed by the religious denominations that founded them. The faculty of many of these universities was small, poorly paid, and not professionalized. With the explosive growth of American universities in the second half of the nineteenth century following the Morrill Act of 1862, the linkage of research to the teaching mission of many universities, and the growth of a professional faculty, power shifted to give faculty a greater role in decisions and management.[3]

For someone who likes neat categories (like most people in my profession), the concept of shared governance can be a frustrating one. Certain functions at most universities are pretty clearly the province of the faculty. These include the creation of the curriculum, the specification of degree requirements, and the selection of faculty members. Other functions are pretty much universally reserved for the administration, such as management of operations, fundraising, and external relations with governmental bodies. But there are also a vast number of functions and decisions where faculty (and perhaps students and staff) should have a say, even if that say is limited to consultation and advice.

Any discussion of shared governance today starts with the 1966 *Statement on Government and Universities* jointly formulated by the American Association of University Professors (AAUP), the American Council on Education (ACE), and the Association of Governing Boards of Universities and Colleges (AGB). According to the statement:

> The faculty has primary responsibility for such fundamental areas as curriculum, subject matter and methods of instruction, research, faculty status, and those aspects of student life which relate to the educational process. . . . Budget, personnel limitations, the time element, and the policies of other groups, bodies, and agencies having jurisdiction over the institution may set limits to realization of faculty advice. . . . The faculty sets the requirements for the degrees offered in course, determines which requirements have been met, and authorizes the president and board to grant the degrees thus achieved. . . . Faculty status and related matters are primarily a faculty responsibility; this area includes appointments, reappointments, decisions not to reappoint, promotions, the granting of tenure, and dismissal. . . . The governing board and president should on questions of faculty status as in other matters where the faculty has primary responsibility, concur with faculty judgment except in rare instances and for compelling reasons which should be stated in detail.[4]

These elements are rarely contested. Most presidents and boards admit (sometimes grudgingly) that the faculty should control the qualifications for faculty status and the content of what they teach.

Less clear is the faculty's role in the operation of the university, its strategic direction, and the allocation of resources. Back to the 1966 statement:

> The allocation of resources among competing demands is central in the formal responsibility of the governing board, in the administrative authority of the president, and in the educational function of the faculty. Each component should therefore have a voice in the determination of short- and long-range priorities, and each should receive appropriate analyses of past budgetary experience, reports on current budgets and expenditures, and short- and long-range budgetary projections.[5]

SHARED GOVERNANCE ON THE GROUND

There are over 250 research universities in the United States, and while there are not 250 brands of shared governance, there are many. In just the three universities where I have served as dean or president, the differences are striking. At UCLA, there are elected bodies of faculty at the system level, at the campus level, and in the law school. Faculty meet frequently to vote on appointments and many other issues like new programs. Only tenure-track faculty members are allowed to serve or vote. At the University of Chicago, all tenure-track faculty members are part of the senate; an elected council of the senate does most of the work, and only tenure-track faculty members are allowed to participate and vote. In the law school, faculty meetings were much less frequent than at UCLA and typically reserved for faculty appointments and promotions. Any other serious issues were usually resolved by the dean dropping by faculty offices to have one-on-one conversations. And, at the University of Oregon, the university senate is more inclusive—members are drawn from the ranks of tenure and non–tenure-track faculty, officers of administration, classified staff, graduate, and undergraduate students. In addition, an elected faculty advisory council exists to provide confidential advice to the president.

Shared governance expands beyond democratically elected legislative bodies in most universities. Faculty members in a department sometimes select the department chair who is formally appointed by the dean. A wide variety of constituents serve on search committees for administrators; even on presidential search committees, it isn't unusual to have faculty and student representation. At any particular moment scores of ad hoc task forces and committees appointed by the senate and some by the president develop policies and new initiatives. Indeed, the level of faculty engagement is sometimes so much that faculty derisively refer to it as a "service tax."

According to most sources, at least 90 percent of American universities have elected senates or councils. Most are just composed of faculty members, often only tenure-track faculty, although some have broader constituencies.[6] Part-time faculty members are generally excluded.

Judging the outputs of shared governance is difficult because there is no one agreed-upon metric of success. In general, there is a high level of consensus in the value of shared governance. For example, one survey of two hundred faculty, senate chairs, and academic vice presidents found that 77 percent of the faculty believed that shared governance was important to the identity of their institution.[7] However, when the questions got more specific in one widely cited survey of faculty and administrators, 22 percent of respondents indicated that their senate was not an important governing body; 53 percent indicated a low level of interest in senate activities; 43 percent opined that involvement in the senate was not highly valued; and 31 percent felt the goals of the senate were not clearly defined.[8] In terms of overall level of faculty influence on university affairs, large numbers responded that they exercised a high level of influence over undergraduate curriculum, standards for promotion and tenure, and teaching evaluation. Much smaller levels of influence were reported over setting strategic priorities for the institution and budget.[9] Similar results have been found in a variety of other studies.[10]

The literature examining the relationship between faculty participation in governance and institutional performance is extremely limited. Indeed, what literature exists utilizes a database compiled fifty years ago from an AAUP survey. From their analysis of the survey data, McCormick and Meiners found that the performance of the university declined as the faculty's control over decision-making increased.[11]A similar study using the same database but adopting a more refined measure of faculty control found that a higher level of control over decisions concerning academic performance was associated with increased university performance, whereas greater control over organizational management was associated with lower performance.[12] The final study finds that strong faculty governance in areas relating to faculty personnel decisions and student affairs was associated with improved financial performance, but active participation in financial planning and administration generated the opposite result.[13] In these studies, however, it is not clear that the variables used for "institutional performance" are necessarily accurate indicators of how the university is doing.[14]

SOME ISSUES WITH SHARED GOVERNANCE

The principle that the faculty (and perhaps other constituents) should be involved in the governance of universities is widely accepted. Nevertheless, consensus evaporates with respect to the question of how well university senates are performing. In this section, I discuss several different challenges for university senates.

Representativeness

Some observers criticize university senates for not being representative of the entire institution and for not attracting some of the strongest faculty members. The dirty secret of shared governance is that faculty are generally not lining up to run for a senate position, and sometimes the folks who do volunteer are not the ones best suited to further the interests of the institution. First, many faculty members do not know much about their senates and do not take the time to either learn about the candidates or vote. Voting turn-out rates can be very low. Second, there is likely to be adverse selection in who chooses to run. In fact, as reported by former Princeton University president William Bowen, "One president . . . spoke (off the record) of what he called 'the Gresham's Law of faculty governance'—if faculty malcontents are allowed to dominate campus governance, they drive away the faculty you want to involve."[15] If you were to ask a university president (perhaps over a glass of wine) to comment on the pool of candidates that typically runs for the senate, they might say that too many come from the ranks of folks who are unhappy with some aspect of their experience, want to use the senate as a podium for pushing their own personal political agendas, or are not deeply engaged and/or successful in both teaching and research. While many great faculty members eventually do ultimately serve, they often need to be recruited very heavily.[16]

Why do university senates sometimes have trouble recruiting the best and the brightest from among our faculties? Part of the problem is that many of our most successful faculty members are very busy people. They teach a lot of students; they are sought out to be mentors; they are deeply committed to their research; and they are typically engaged in national professional organizations. Faculty governance can be hard, time-consuming work. While all faculty members are expected to participate in the holy trinity of job functions—teaching, research, and service—ask any faculty member which functions are rewarded most, and they will likely say research and teaching and then chuckle about service. Thus, running for and joining the faculty senate are equivalent to providing a public good—and we can all remember from our college introductory economics class the problem of public goods and free-riders.[17]

A second problem that repels some of our best faculty members is that they do not enjoy sitting through meetings in which some of their colleagues pursue pet peeves, personal political causes, and petty animosities. Some senates or senate leaders view their role as "fighting the man," with the man being the person who sits in the big office in the administration building. Some senators may also want to spend less time on the academic matters fully entrusted to shared governance and instead engage in efforts to second guess or disrupt the decisions entrusted to the administration. While some of these discussions might be interesting, they may just not be very appealing to those with a high discount value on their time. Thus, the adverse selection problem can be devastating to a senate.

At the University of Oregon, I have found that we often need to work hard to recruit senators to avoid the adverse selection problem. I have been pretty successful in these efforts; most faculty members will think twice before turning down a personal request from a president or a provost. However, one needs to be careful to avoid any sense that the president is trying to stack the deck. I have been very careful not to recruit folks who would be viewed as "yes men" for me. In addition, I have acted in the open, often jointly strategizing with existing senate leadership on whom to ask. The point isn't to get folks who will always agree with the president to run for the senate. Quite to the contrary, for shared governance to generate value, a variety of perspectives must be working together for the common good of the institution.

Speed and Efficiency

One of the most common criticisms of shared governance comes from observers and stakeholders who are familiar with the corporate world.[18] Many look at universities, compare them to business organizations, and decry the "glacial pace of change" and how long it takes to make decisions. Indeed, the differences between corporate and university decision-making are substantial. Corporations are typically strictly hierarchical with all authority resting in the president and the board of directors (standing in for the shareowners). Universities are messy with multiple stakeholders and decision makers. While the board of trustees has ultimate authority, as described earlier, it delegates its authority to the president, who delegates again to shared governance presumably based upon expertise. Even if a stakeholder doesn't have ultimate decision-making authority, that person's voice needs to be heard and treated with respect. In short, a university's decision-making process is much more consultative than that of the typical corporation.

In addition to the collaborative and collegial nature of universities, another reason why decision-making can be slow compared to a business corporation is that the aims of a university are more varied. Under the current shareowner primacy conception of the corporation, the chief objective of the corporation is to maximize the value of equity owned by stockholders. A university's goals are much more varied. We exist to add knowledge to the world even if that knowledge isn't immediately or apparently useful or monetizable. We transmit that knowledge to the next generation, creating informed citizens and skilled employees. We promote economic opportunity for our students; we generate economic activity for our communities. We contribute to social and political discourse; we provide opportunities for cultural enrichment. And, we hopefully bring people together in a way that reduces racism through understanding. Therefore, given the diversity of objectives of the university and the fact that any decision might further some of these objectives and detract from others, is it any wonder that the process is slower and more cumbersome?

Many observers of higher education feel that our slow pace of decision-making, our need for collaboration and discourse, and our sometimes confused and conflicting objectives could prove to be our Achilles' heel.[19] The world of higher education is indeed changing rapidly: there are skyrocketing costs, diminished trust from both internal stakeholders and external observers, demands for racial equity, changing requirements in the job market, rising debt, technological advances, and more. Can we move quickly enough to change and adapt? Or, will American universities and colleges become the next eight-track music player?

As a president of a major research university, I feel the pressure of these forces. At the same time, I appreciate the deliberative and collaborative processes of shared governance. While shared governance may make it less likely that we will adapt to changing circumstances quickly, it also minimizes the likelihood of major errors.[20] American universities are among the finest in the world. While many businesses have come and gone, the Ivy League, our great baccalaureate colleges, and our flagship state universities have lasted for centuries.

Of course, that does not mean that we have to be stuck in the mud. Indeed, I believe that the recent pandemic has demonstrated that when faced with an existential threat to its survival, higher education can mobilize quickly. In one week, faculty members shifted their entire method of teaching from in-person to remote as our students dispersed to their homes all over the nation and world. Importantly, this change occurred through our mechanisms of shared governance and not separate from them. By doing this—by utilizing familiar and agreed-upon methods of decision-making—each institution was able to mobilize thousands of its faculty to keep instruction going in a time of crisis.

Of course, COVID-19 is thankfully a unique event that definitely focused attention. With respect to more typical changes, presidents need to work effectively with their shared governance processes to move things through the system. That is certainly not impossible. From over fifteen years of experience as a dean and president, I have never been unable to achieve a desired goal because of the slow pace of shared governance. Of course, that doesn't mean that everything I wanted to achieve I was successful at getting done. Shared governance is not a rubber stamp, but rather it is a deliberative process.

Transparency and Trust

One challenge that presidents sometimes have with shared governance is the tension created by its transparency. Under most versions of shared governance, faculty and sometimes other constituents should be consulted about important institutional decisions, particularly those that involve academic matters. Some of these decisions might be politically sensitive; some might involve competitive advantage; some might be newsworthy and require special arrangements. Senate meetings, however, are usually public, at least in public universities. Plus, it is likely that if the topic is even remotely controversial, it will be leaked after the meeting. The fear of leaked information may create a tendency among college and university presidents not to share information.

A failure to provide shared governance bodies with relevant information can have very negative consequences for the success of the enterprise. One of the primary problems facing many universities today is an absence of trust between administrators and the faculty. Much of this lack of trust is fueled by ideology, but some is fueled by resource scarcity. Some faculty members feel that university presidents are out to further a "neoliberal" or "corporativist" agenda privileging student demands, donor wishes, and the need for skilled workers to take their place in a capitalist economy. They see the shrinkage of the humanities and some social sciences as part of this effort. COVID-19 and debates over whether universities should have offered in-person classes in the fall of 2020 have fanned the fires of distrust. Some faculty members, often supported by faculty unions and union organizing efforts, have argued that university presidents are seeking to endanger their workforce and their communities all in the name of money.[21]

The absence of trust on campus is a dangerous phenomenon. Universities, despite being composed of folks who argue a lot for their living, need to be collegial enterprises. Shared governance suggests that we all play a role in determining the future of the enterprise. Transparency is a prerequisite to trust. So, regardless of the reason, presidents need to find a way to engage honestly with their partners in university governance. In my experience, when I felt that some subjects were not appropriate for public discourse, I had private conversations with senate leadership as well as other confidential advisory bodies. I trusted them to keep confidences. And, I was never disappointed.

Faculty Unions

In recent years American universities have experienced an increase in the prevalence of faculty unions.[22] In most cases faculty unions are limited to representing the growing number of non-tenure-track faculty members.[23] In some universities, including the University of Oregon, the union represents both tenured, tenure-track, and non-tenure-track faculty in one bargaining unit. Interestingly, the AAUP, one of the signatories of the 1966 statement on shared governance, has become one of the major sponsors of the unionization movement.[24] In fact, today, close to three-quarters of AAUP members are members of its collective bargaining units.[25]

The existence of a faculty union can complicate shared governance.[26] A fundamental premise of many labor law authorities is the desirability of maintaining a delineation between managers and employees.[27] With respect to most universities, the union represents the interests of faculty solely with respect to the terms and conditions of their employment; the governance authority resides within the senate.[28] Thus, one of the premises of shared government is that the faculty are the managers jointly with the administration of the academic enterprise. The senate often deals with issues that relate to policy and management, such as what is taught in the university, how it should be taught, and what the qualifications are to be appointed.

The existence of a union therefore blurs the already unclear lines of shared governance. Since all faculty are presumptively in the bargaining unit, senators are at once labor and management.[29] At some universities, the union through its superior organizing capacity has gained control of or abolished the senate.[30] This threat to shared governance is something we have avoided at the University of Oregon. While union leaders have sometimes served as senate president or vice president, they have sought, for the most part, to keep the two hats separate.[31]

Financial Issues

Many universities in the United States were struggling to stay afloat before COVID-19 struck. Declining student enrollments, lagging state support, increasing labor costs, excessive discounting, and expensive regulatory mandates all threatened their economic viability. COVID-19 has greatly exacerbated many of these financial problems. During the spring of 2020, some universities sustained hundreds of millions of dollars of losses generated by empty hospital beds, increased costs of instruction, and lost income from housing and dining operations. Many institutions also experienced large enrollment drops and lost tuition and auxiliary income as they opened remotely in the fall and the students they were expecting to attend did not matriculate. And, for public universities, the recession generated by the pandemic has brought about substantial state budget reductions, just as many universities were finally getting close to recovering the losses of the Great Recession of 2009–11.

Over the past decade, budget cutting for most universities has become commonplace. But current problems brought on by the twin onslaught of COVID-19 and the recession are likely to require more than the nip-and-tuck solutions we tend to utilize in normal times. Some universities have closed or merged. And others will need to reorganize their operations and possibly stop teaching some of the things they are teaching today.

Substantial budget reductions, such as those leading to major reductions in programs or department closures, need to engage shared governance. Clearly, the board of trustees or regents should at least play an oversight role since these decisions will permanently change the structure of the institution. The precise nature of faculty engagement, however, is not clear, and this lack of clarity is reflected in the 1966 joint statement. Budget reductions could be justified by any number of considerations ranging from the quality of an academic unit to insufficient student demand. While the faculty's role in making judgments based upon academic quality is paramount under almost any definition of shared governance, its expertise on enrollments, student demand, and the cost of instruction is much less clear.[32] Indeed, many faculty members have become acculturated to *not* think about the efficiency of instruction on the ground—that these considerations are inappropriate because they introduce excessive market influences into the academy.[33]

The AAUP, ACE, and AGB statement of 1966 recognizes that the role of the faculty in budgetary decisions is not nearly as great as it is for academic and curricular matters.[34] This is also reflected in the experience of university senates. Each faculty and staff member in a university senate will have on two hats when discussing budgetary cuts: the welfare of the university as a whole and their own welfare and that of their departmental colleagues. As Bowen and Tobin note, "Faculty expertise is essential in arriving at wise decisions—on academic matters certainly—but it would be hard to defend giving faculty anything approaching final authority over matters in which their self-interest is so clearly involved."[35] Ultimately, the allocation of authority or, in Bowen and Tobin's terms, "the locus of authority," will need to be determined based upon the culture of each particular institution.[36] Some universities have successfully made use of special senate committees, commissions, or task forces that can discuss the various choices facing the university in a confidential and deliberative manner.[37] Members of these task forces can be selected jointly by the senate and the administration to ensure accountability and promote trust.

CONCLUSION

It would be hard to overstate the challenges facing higher education over the next decade. Much of the polarization of our country today is reflected within the academy as universities have become lightning rods on issues as diverse as freedom of speech, racial and socioeconomic equity, police violence, and much more. Financial challenges abound as costs increase, family incomes stagnate, student debt loads rise, and state support declines. COVID-19 has intensified these challenges and accelerated the forces demanding change and adaptation.

A common view today is that universities are poorly suited to rise to these challenges because they are slow to change and adapt. Our commitment to collaboration, deliberation, and shared governance according to this view, while tolerable in normal periods, is a luxury we cannot afford in times of extreme stress.

In my view, our traditions of shared governance and collaboration are especially important as we face the challenges of the future. Universities are academic communities dedicated to producing knowledge and transmitting that knowledge to the next generation. Part of the process of learning is developing the capacity to think critically, to ask difficult questions, and to justify one's viewpoints. Shared governance, properly understood, is not about democratic governance of the university. It is instead a commitment to rational discourse, consultation, expertise, and the search for the best solutions to problems that might be intractable. Shared governance might not always be pretty and it might not always be speedy, but it has served us well and contributed to making our universities the envy of the world.

CHAPTER 6

Working with Your Board

MARY SUE COLEMAN

The Soviet Union's launch of *Sputnik* in 1957, followed by the US entry into the space race championed by presidents Dwight D. Eisenhower and John F. Kennedy, changed my life and ultimately charted my academic career in ways that I could not possibly have imagined.

That year I was fourteen and a junior high school student living with my family in Cedar Falls, Iowa, a wonderful college town. I liked science and, coming from an academic family, was encouraged to succeed in school. Fortunately, my parents saw the value of project-based learning, and one way such learning was accomplished in that era was by competing in science fairs. I also was lucky to be attending a laboratory school operated by the University of Northern Iowa for the purpose of testing educational innovations and training future teachers. In that environment, science exploration outside the classroom was encouraged and facilitated. The school atmosphere coupled with the national space race competition with the Soviet Union greatly accelerated federal and corporate funding for and community interest in science fairs. Students participating in science projects were widely supported and fervently believed they were helping the nation!

Four years of intense state and national science fair competitions prepared me well for college and a chemistry major embedded in a strong liberal arts curriculum as well as graduate school in biochemistry. Graduate education was followed by several postdoctoral fellowships, designed to hone my research skills as an independent investigator, and finally a tenure-track faculty position and a deeply satisfying nineteen-year research and teaching career at the University of Kentucky (UK).

Quite serendipitously, I was tapped to help develop and temporarily lead a cancer center relatively late in my UK career and, in doing so, I discovered that I enjoyed immensely conceiving and building campuswide research programs. Furthermore, after being at UK for sixteen years, I was unexpectedly selected by a campuswide vote of faculty members to serve on the UK Board of Trustees, a position I held for three years.

The experience of being a trustee at a research-intensive land-grant university was invaluable. I was able to observe the university from a completely different perspective and so came to appreciate the difficult issues that often confront university governing boards. I also realized that my growing interest in university administration dictated a search for new opportunities elsewhere.

The University of North Carolina (UNC) at Chapel Hill offered such a prospect. My husband (a tenured professor of political science) and I relocated when I accepted the position of associate provost for research, which was later redefined as vice chancellor for graduate education and research. During the next three years, I maintained an active research laboratory at UNC in the biochemistry department but also immersed myself in the details of helping to administer a very large research portfolio across the entire campus. My goal during those years was to streamline the "back-office" work associated with faculty research, promote collaborations across the entire campus, and increase the prominence of UNC Chapel Hill among its peers in the Association of American Universities (AAU).

Not unexpectedly, I was next recruited to the University of New Mexico (UNM) as its provost, an experience that was invaluable to my growing understanding of effective university administration. A poorly funded flagship university, UNM is nonetheless vital to economic prosperity in the state and challenged my ability to make wise academic investment decisions since money was so scarce. Regardless, I did learn how to manage limited resources well in an environment rich in students and faculty from very diverse backgrounds.

It is from that experience in Albuquerque that I was recruited to my first presidency, the University of Iowa, a tenure that lasted almost seven years. This was followed by the University of Michigan, where I was president for twelve years.

Nineteen years as a university president have afforded me all types of interactions with regents of many different stripes. While the political makeup of governing boards has changed through the years, so have the myriad issues facing higher education and research universities. But there has been one constant in my philosophy of how best to work with my governing board, and that is the value of one-on-one communication coupled with a commitment to real-time information sharing in a 24/7 media environment. Good communication is essential to building relationships and to maintaining them through challenging episodes. There is simply no substitute—not email, phone conversations, texting, Skype, or any other form of connecting. Personal communication is invaluable and, while it may at times be uncomfortable, it offers the best chance for the outcome you desire as a president or chancellor committed to the future of your university.

APPEALING INSTITUTIONS

The Universities of Iowa and Michigan share many similarities, as both are members of the Big Ten Conference and Academic Alliance and the Association of American Universities. They are large and complex with outstanding medical centers and have the distinction of representing many "firsts" in teaching, research, and discovery. They also operate very much in the public eye as ("partially") publicly funded institutions, though the regulations about public scrutiny do differ in these two states.

Having grown up in Iowa with an undergraduate degree from Grinnell College, I knew that state and its outstanding commitment to public education at all levels well, which probably helped my candidacy for the presidency of the University of Iowa. What I did not anticipate was the challenge that came with a gubernatorially appointed nine-member governing board that oversaw not only the University of Iowa but also Iowa State University and the University of Northern Iowa, as well as a school for the blind and a separate school for deaf children. Presiding over the University of Iowa for seven years, though, was excellent preparation for my next move to the presidency of the University of Michigan (U-M), which is significantly larger, more prominent nationally, and more research intensive than Iowa.

Even though I was very happy leading the University of Iowa and certainly could have envisioned myself retiring there, the attraction of Michigan was irresistible for me. The university was engaged in a high-profile defense of affirmative action in its admission policies. As a vocal proponent of this tool for many years during my career, I was eager to be part of the defense of the two cases, which many predicted would find their way to the Supreme Court. U-M also was governed differently than Iowa, by a constitutionally independent board comprised of eight individuals selected by a statewide election.

I will share several episodes that showcase the challenges and rewards of working with two different public university boards and explore how best to advance the goals of the institution while managing board expectations and occasional conflicts.

DIFFERENT STATES, DIFFERENT BOARDS

Candidates for the Board of Regents, State of Iowa may be suggested by university presidents, but it is up to the governor to present a slate of candidates (one for each open position) to the state senate, which must confirm the nominations. The nine members on this board serve staggered six-year terms with designated political representation as a Democrat, Republican, or Independent.

In other words, one political party may not hold all the seats on the board at any time. However, the governor does have the additional power of designating the chair of the board every two years, and that individual does have outsized influence in policy discussions. Finally, one of the members must also be a student (selected by the governor from a pool of nominees) from one of the three universities, and that individual may serve until graduating but for no more than one year thereafter.

These nine individuals oversee the state's three public universities (as a collective). The Iowa governing board has an executive director and a small staff located in the state's capital, Des Moines, but it is not a "university system" in the traditional sense since the three university presidents report directly to the board and not to the executive director.

By contrast, in Michigan, each public university has its own eight-member governing board. At the University of Michigan, candidates are selected through the state Republican and Democratic political conventions, and each must stand for election statewide every eight years, though the terms overlap each two years. Candidates from minor political parties may also garner a spot on the ballot, but no one outside the major parties has ever won an election. As a consequence of this system, all regent candidates must raise money and campaign throughout the state and, in many cases, they believe and behave as though they owe more allegiance to their political party than to the university that they are responsible for governing. (This same governance structure operates at the state's two other research universities, Michigan State with its board of trustees and Wayne State with a board of governors, with similar governance consequences.)

With this system there is no built-in political balance and no mandate for student representation, and as a consequence, there has been a dramatic swing in political influence in university governance throughout history. However, it is important to note that the legislature and the governor have no governance authority over the University of Michigan outside of appropriating state funding annually. Rather, the constitution of the state clearly designates that the regents "own" the University of Michigan. Rather than having an elected chair of this board, that designation rotates annually and is based solely on length of tenure so that every member has an opportunity to be the leader. In practice, though, the board operates as a "body of the whole." The board oversees not only U-M in Ann Arbor but also U-M's smaller regional campuses in Flint and Dearborn. While the regional campuses' budgets are appropriated specifically by the legislature, their chancellors report to the president of the University of Michigan rather than independently to the governing body. The U-M board is supported by a vice president and secretary who manage a three-person staff housed within the university.

CHALLENGES, PRESSURES, AND OPPORTUNITIES

University boards and trustees play a central role in the proper governance of universities. They are stewards of the public trust and help root the institution in the communities they serve, particularly in public institutions. These governing bodies must function as a bulwark against undue interference into the key missions of the institution and at their best work to support and empower their leader to address the increasingly complex issues facing our nation's leading research universities.

I firmly believe that there is no "ideal" structure for a university governing board. In both Iowa and Michigan, the boards are relatively small but for the most part are composed of individuals who are prominent in their communities and value excellence in higher education. Both states have strict conflict of interest laws that minimize the risk of mischief by individuals. As an example, in Iowa, regents may not accept any item from the university (including food) valued at more than $3.60 in excess of the per diem they receive for attending regular board meetings. The prohibition includes "free athletics tickets," a policy that I found worked extremely well. There is no designation at Iowa for emeritus regents with no expectation of benefits beyond their term as board members.

At the University of Michigan, regents also receive a per diem for meetings attended and must publicly disclose any conflict of interest at every meeting, which would include any personal or business relationship with the university. There is no prohibition on receipt of athletics tickets, but the value of these must be declared to the IRS annually unless there is a written attestation to a legitimate business purpose in support of the university mission. Unlike those in Iowa, U-M emeritus regents do retain the benefit of access to athletics tickets, admission to university events, and attendance at commencement ceremonies if they so desire.

In short, both of these boards are relatively small. Their size can be advantageous since, as president, I was in regular contact with fewer individuals. But the small size can also be challenging, as single individuals can influence directions that may not be in the best interest of the president or the university. I discovered that the overt allegiance to political parties, coupled with the necessity to raise money for a political campaign in the Michigan structure, could be particularly problematic, as will be apparent in the case studies below.

WHICH WORKS BEST?

Public universities in the United States are governed by a variety of structures and, given the seriousness with which the selection process is managed, any of them can be effective. What many of these processes lack, however, is a mechanism to bring useful expertise to the board that would be of great benefit to the president.

An example is reflected in the makeup of one of the governing boards I experienced at Michigan wherein seven of the eight members were attorneys and one was a businessperson. This description is not meant to disparage legal expertise, but that clustering of career paths did not often bring rich and varied skill sets to board discussions. In fact, it was in stark contrast to the value and importance of diversity that was vigorously promoted by the university. Private universities are able to tap a range of talents to board positions and also may use prominent board members to advance the philanthropic goals of the university—an issue that is ever more important in the public sector with the diminished state support apparent in the past two decades.

TALES FROM THE TRENCHES

Tuition Battles

One immediate and negative consequence of a single governing board I encountered in Iowa was the long-standing policy of charging identical tuition at the three universities, regardless of the drastically different missions and cost basis (at least a 15-20 percent deficit for the University of Iowa) for instruction and research. Very quickly, I came to understand that this strategy was differentially hurting the University of Iowa, as its peer group along with faculty and staff pay scales and infrastructure required for research activities were very different from the other two universities.

In fact, staying competitive nationally in Iowa was extremely challenging since even by 2000 the annual tuition at the university was only $2,906, compared with a University of Michigan tuition of $6,926. Faced with this glaring disparity, in 1998 I began to develop an alternate proposal to increase net tuition at Iowa for academic purposes, which would allocate expenses like student activities, campus bus services, health services, and building maintenance away from tuition toward an increase in student fees. As a consequence of this shift, the university's academic resources would increase by $6 million annually, but student fees would also increase to cover these very real institutional expenses.

The first step was to solicit input through student government and, to my great relief, they supported the proposal. They understood that many services students valued at the university were not academic but conducive to a better learning environment.

Following that step, and after consultation with faculty and staff leaders, I began the process of socializing each of the board members to the value of this strategy. In Iowa, law dictates that no meeting with more than three regents may be held out of public view. Therefore, it was imperative that I meet individually with each to explain the rationale for the approach and justify why it would help keep the university competitive with its peers.

Ironically, these individual meetings were enormously helpful in explaining my overall goal of improving the collegiate experience for our students and illustrated to me that developing a robust and trusting relationship with each board member was critical to my success in working with them as a group when the proposal was finally adopted in 2000. With the additional funding, we were able to address a number of faculty concerns and strengthen Iowa's academic standing with our peers.

Affirmative Action Lawsuits

Michigan's national fight to defend affirmative action in admission was my top priority upon assuming the presidency in 2002.

In 1997, plaintiffs Jennifer Gratz and Barbara Grutter sued U-M over the institution's use of race, as one factor among many, in its admission decisions; Gratz sued over undergraduate admission policies and Grutter over U-M Law School admission. The fact that lower courts ruled either for or against the plaintiffs virtually ensured that these cases would find their way to the US Supreme Court, which they did late in 2002. Michigan's strong defense of the policies made the university presidency very attractive to me as a firm supporter of the value of affirmative action; and when the position was offered, I enthusiastically accepted the opportunity to lead the institution. In their making a unanimously supported offer of the presidency to me, I assumed that the regents were as enthusiastic as I was in defending this critically important policy.

By arriving in the middle of an intensely argued principle in court cases with multiple rulings, I quickly needed to master reams of court documents and background information. Wisely, the university had in previous years undertaken a serious research project to document the life-changing impact of affirmative action policies on students from all races who graduated from U-M and had diverse experiences in their lives. The data were very clear: all students benefitted from interacting with peers from differing backgrounds inside and outside the classroom, and those advantages grew in their civic lives at five and ten years after graduation.

These rigorous analyses, coupled with my own life experiences, convinced me that the university's stance was very strong and that I could be proud of our defense arguments. However, it is important to note that this was an intense period for me as a new (to the institution) president mastering mountains of documents while also introducing myself to the Michigan community on campus and beyond. Most importantly, I needed to quickly demonstrate to regents that I was in command of the situation and its importance to the university.

Quickly after arriving on campus, I came to realize that some regents were more committed to the cause than others. This commitment was not necessarily reflected in political party alignment. I needed to balance the concerns of all board members (and other stakeholders) while at the same time be the public face of the university in a legal case being watched by all of higher education and, in particular, other public institutions. The most important board conflict centered on selection of defense attorneys for oral arguments following the consolidation of the two cases and their acceptance by the Supreme Court. The majority on the board at that time were attorneys themselves and so had strong opinions about who should be charged with arguing these important cases before the highest court in the nation. Working closely with each board member and our internal team of attorneys, we were able to forge a compromise. John A. Payton (of Wilmer, Cutler & Pickering) was selected for the undergraduate admission case and Maureen Mahoney (of Latham & Watkins) for the law school case.

Not insignificant in managing these cases was the importance of the university team, which included the dean of the law school, several key university attorneys, the provost, the vice president for communications, and several members of their respective staffs. We had only about four months to prepare and to keep the regents informed, and it was absolutely critical that there was "no daylight" between the president and critical parties.

As is widely known, the University of Michigan in 2003 prevailed in the Grutter case on the underlying principle that affirmative action could be used as one factor among many in making admission decisions. In the Gratz case, we lost on the mechanics of a point system being used by our undergraduate admission office but also prevailed on the same underlying principle of affirmative action as one factor among many. Consequently, we quickly altered our admission processes to bring practice in line with the high court's rulings. This was an enormously satisfying outcome for all at the university and especially our regents, who in the end came together to celebrate the landmark ruling, which protected affirmative action for universities across the nation.

Sadly, though, there is a coda to this victorious outcome. Three years later, in 2006, as a consequence of a grass-roots ballot initiative, the voters of Michigan changed the state's constitution to ban any use of affirmative action in public university admission. This ban was a severe blow to the university and was especially hard for our students to accept. On the morning after the statewide votes were counted, I appeared on a rapidly constructed stage in the center of campus (on the Diag) to console our students, assert that we would uphold the law, and pledge to vigorously retain the robust diversity that made Michigan such an outstanding educational institution.

Ironically, one of the opposition arguments was that low family socioeconomic status would be an effective proxy for race. Our research, however, indicated that was not accurate, and sadly, subsequent experience has confirmed that prediction. The racial composition of both undergraduate and law school classes changed drastically in 2007 when African American and Hispanic representation dropped by about half, and it has remained far below what was attained with affirmative action in the years since the vote to change the state constitution. In the end, the University of Michigan retained the principle of affirmative action for public universities in other states, so this was an important contribution to higher education overall.

Regardless of this outcome, I remain very proud that the University of Michigan and its governing board championed the utility of racially diverse classrooms to create the best and most productive educational outcomes for all students and not simply for underrepresented minority students. This endeavor has remained the proudest and most satisfying of my long and varied academic career.

Expanding Michigan Stadium

When I first visited the University of Michigan, having been named to the position but not yet president, I was aware (thanks to an earlier secret visit by my husband) of a looming challenge that would very soon confront me: the urgent need to renovate iconic Michigan Stadium.

This stadium is no ordinary venue for university football. It is the "Big House," the largest in the country, with 110,000 seats that have been filled for every home game for the past thirty-five years. In 2002, Michigan Stadium was also crumbling, with only bench seating for fans and a miserably small and inadequate press box with completely outmoded facilities for modern media and where the president had a tiny "suite" to entertain donors and friends of the university. It was also in the firing line of the Department of Education's Office of Civil Rights for noncompliance with seating for disabled individuals.

After enduring the facility for a few years, the athletics director and I decided to approach the regents with a plan for a massive renovation and upgrade. Being responsible stewards of this iconic space, we conducted extensive surveys of football fans and nonfans both within and outside U-M. The results were clear: the overwhelming majority felt it was critical that the stadium remain the largest in the country and that we maintain the practice of no advertising inside the stadium (a tradition of which I was completely supportive). It was also clear that ticket holders wanted better and more comfortable seating, greatly expanded access to restroom facilities, and more varied food options. Some wanted suite-type spaces or larger club spaces where guests could be entertained or where they could still be at the game in inclement weather. Students wanted to make sure that they retained access to at least 25,000 tickets in a good location to the field. And everyone wanted the new stadium to look impressive, even though the old one was nestled deep in a bowl and surrounded by a chain link fence with little visual appeal.

With all this input we retained two firms for the project. The first was a stadium design firm for the principal structural elements, and the second was an architectural firm charged with developing a design to accommodate the new spaces to reflect the collegiate nature of the enterprise. We also came to the understanding that this would be a very, very expensive project, with the estimate of $226 million.

When we presented the preliminary plans to the regents, it became quickly apparent that there were deep divisions among the eight about both the design and the financial model we proposed. Some wanted to retain a model that had no suites and no entertainment spaces, with the attendant differential in pricing of seats. Other regents understood our argument that without the suites' multiyear contracts, there was no way we could finance or afford the project. We even had an aggressive agitator from New York, who was not a Michigan alumnus, gathering signatures (including one from a former U-M president) and speaking frequently to prominent national journalists opposing our plan.

The discussion became so contentious that I was deeply worried that I could not get five regents (the minimum I would need) to approve the project with three required and separate votes over several months. Knowing that the discussion would go on for months, I decided on a new and radical strategy. I offered to take each regent on an individually arranged trip to tour Kinnick Stadium, recently renovated at the University of Iowa. The individual trips were important because I wanted each board member to understand that I was listening carefully to their concerns. This would also give me a full day with each regent to answer questions and present my rationale for the cost, the financial underpinnings, and the design.

Two board members took me up on the offer, so we made two individually chartered trips to Iowa City. The comparison between what Iowa had for its fans and what Michigan offered was jarring, to say the least. I showed them suites and guest reception areas. I suggested that we should have a "regents suite" for them and a "regents guest area" at the fifty-yard line that would hold sixty to ninety people and where they could host their guests for each game. They were able to see and sit in chairback seats enjoyed by Iowa's regents and a sharp contrast to the uncomfortable, too-small bench seating they currently had at Michigan Stadium.

The individual trips and intensive personal attention did pay off. When each of the required votes was taken, including the last final and decisive one, six of the eight regents voted in the affirmative for the whole project. As I predicted, every single member of the board today enjoys the new spaces and cannot imagine how they endured cramped seating and limited amenities for so long.

Free Speech and the Palestine Solidarity Movement
Six weeks into my presidency at Michigan, tensions flared when one of our student organizations announced it was hosting a national conference on the Palestine Solidarity Movement and called for the university to divest from Israel. Participants

included a speaker who, at a similar meeting held at the University of California at Berkeley the previous year, had openly advocated for the utility of suicide bombers to facilitate the creation of an independent Palestinian state.

Michigan has large Jewish student and alumni bodies. We also enroll significant numbers of Arab American students, with Ann Arbor located thirty miles from Dearborn, which has one of the largest concentrations of Arab Americans in the country. There was enormous national interest in this issue, and external groups heavily lobbied both regents and the president to ban the conference. Leading up to the date of the conference, a nasty and inflammatory spoof email was sent to selected Jewish students and faculty about the conference, heightening tensions enormously on campus. (After an intense investigation from our IT specialists, we suspected that the email was sent by a U-M faculty member who wanted to test the "free speech" resolve of administrators to permit the conference on a topic about which we personally disagreed.) We also were cognizant of some violence that had occurred when the group met on the Berkeley campus the year before.

Several regents were ardent supporters of Israel and opposed the conference in the most emotional terms, even though they understood and strongly supported the concept of free speech. One of the most difficult meetings I had with the board occurred during this time when I listened carefully to their heartfelt and passionate concerns and fears, but clearly told them that I had no choice but to permit the students to hold the event, surrounded by all the security we could assemble.

Beyond justifying my actions to the regents, I needed to use my bully pulpit as president to convey our commitment to free speech and academic inquiry. In doing this, my colleagues and I employed many different strategies. I visited personally with both Arab American and Jewish groups to explain our commitment to free speech as a public university and to security for everyone. I answered personally each and every one of the thousands of emails and letters that came to the president's office. I called or visited the university's most generous donors, explaining in detail why we were allowing the conference on campus. In fact, this event occupied about three full weeks of my time quite early in my tenure as president.

The outcome of all this preparation and concern turned out to be anticlimactic. The conference was held on a Saturday afternoon in the fall. About two hundred people attended, including two regents and many, many public safety officers, some in uniform and others in plain clothes. And yes, this was during a home football game, which dampened media interest dramatically. Regardless, I believed our actions demonstrated for the community and for the board members our willingness to host controversial speakers, avoid a circus atmosphere, and provide a safe environment for all in our community.

Unionization of Graduate Students

My most difficult and personally trying challenge came during the latter part of my tenure at the University of Michigan. Michigan has long been a union-friendly state, and at the university, there are several staff unions, with the largest being for tradespeople and nurses. Graduate student instructors at U-M also have been unionized for many years, and bargaining across these units has been relatively peaceful and harmonious.

However, in recent years, Republicans in the Michigan legislature have chipped away at unionization efforts, which has created a push for more union formation within higher education. At Michigan, the already-unionized graduate student teaching assistants mounted efforts to hold an election to include research assistants (GSRAs) in their unit to collectively bargain as members of the same union. This move would expand dramatically their number of members and their financial resources. Realizing that there was no appetite for a faculty union at the University of Michigan, but being pressured by their party to help expand union representation in the state, the Democratic majority of the board of regents strongly supported unionization efforts by GSRAs against my and my cabinet's advice.

University leaders and I firmly believed graduate students conducting research were first and foremost students, and treating them as employees would corrupt the academic environment. This position had long been reinforced by the Michigan Employment Relations Commission (the state body responsible for unions). Virtually all academic deans and faculty supported this stance and viewed with dismay the actions of the Democratic regents, who at that time controlled the board.

The issue became so heated that when Republican legislators moved with legislation to ban GSRAs from organizing, U-M regents ordered administrators—particularly the vice president for government relations—"to take all available action" to fight the legislation. This meant that our highly respected and long-time vice president was "ordered" by the board to meet with every single legislator and make the argument that U-M strongly supported the right of graduate student research assistants to unionize. The board, during a heated private meeting with me, voted (including only the Democrats) to muzzle my voice by "preventing" me from speaking about the issue at all.

I knew I was at great peril over this issue, but I suspected that the board action would backfire; every legislator clearly understood that the argument did not in any way reflect my or my leadership team's views. In fact, before the crucial and heated meeting with the board, I had made a public statement at one of our monthly board meetings arguing vigorously against unionization, and that viewpoint was reprinted in every subsequent news article about the unionization debate. My position was never unclear.

The regent directive did backfire spectacularly. Not only did the legislature pass a new law preventing GSRAs from unionizing, but the following year the citizens of Michigan voted overwhelmingly to convert Michigan to a right-to-work state, meaning that union membership could no longer be mandatory for any worker.

This episode was the most contentious and most openly politicized debate with regents in my twelve-year tenure at Michigan. It was a very sad one for me because I believe it illustrated a central weakness of the method through which regents are selected for the University of Michigan. Regents were more committed to political party than to advice from university leaders about what was in the strong interest of the institution.

LESSONS LEARNED

From these experiences, I learned a great deal about the importance of having the president take and advocate positions that directly affect the university and perhaps all of higher education. If I were to offer a checklist for a new president, it would include this advice:

- Listen to your board and communicate with them regularly. Individual relationships and cultivation of those relationships are critical, as is a "surrogate" (in my case, a vice president for finance at Iowa and a vice president/secretary of the board at Michigan) to create a buffer between the board and the president.
- Agree to respectfully disagree but know that there will be instances when you must disagree. Frequently, board members will respect the president more for a willingness to fight for a firmly held principle than to capitulate to please them.
- Always work for the future good of the institution. Board members may (most often and routinely) think only as far ahead as the end of their terms (with reappointment or reelection most prominent in their minds). University presidents and chancellors, however, must focus twenty-five to fifty years into the future. That should always be a guiding principle for leading a research university.

CHAPTER 7

State and Federal Government Relations

JANET NAPOLITANO

In today's hyper-political environment, one of the most important fields of engagement for a college or university president to master is state and federal government relations. All higher education institutions—particularly public ones—are profoundly affected by state and federal budgets, legislation, election cycles, and other political factors. Higher education operations and government relations intersect on academic affairs, research policy and funding, student financial aid, international students and faculty, capital projects, and health care, just to name a few key areas.

College and university leaders who are not keenly aware of these dynamics when they assume their roles will become quickly and starkly aware of them on the job; I cannot overstate the importance of understanding and respecting the political and regulatory landscape in which higher education institutions operate. New presidents will also soon realize that managing federal and state government relations takes significant resources—both time and budgeted dollars—which are well spent if dedicated wisely.

As a former governor, federal agency leader, and public research university system president, I have had the opportunity to see these dynamics play out from several different vantage points, at both the state and federal levels. In this chapter, I share the lessons and insights I have gleaned along the way—the good, the bad, and the ugly. My hope is that this chapter will help individual higher education leaders and their institutions, as well as contribute to the advancement of higher education as a whole in our society.

NOT AT HOMELAND SECURITY ANYMORE

Thinking back on my first day as president of the University of California (UC), it feels like a lifetime ago. After nearly five years as US secretary of homeland security, I looked forward to a change of pace, a different and more optimistic slice of American democracy. I was taking a sharp turn away from counterterrorism and disaster response and looking toward investing my time and energy in America's youth.

I was familiar with the University of California's reputation, of course. But I admit that I was not anticipating the complexity of the system's operations and its budget, or some of the thornier issues surrounding its state and federal government relations. This was 2013, a politically charged and fiscally challenging period for higher education (and that pressure hasn't relented much since).

The minefields were everywhere, and it took time, experience, and expert advice to understand them better. State politics—particularly in California—are vastly different from federal politics. A public university is not the same as a federal agency. And the University of California in particular—with its extensive breadth and rich history—is a whole different animal.

These differences were both structural and cultural. For starters, California is more liberal than the rest of the country or Washington, DC. The state also has a generally populist streak exemplified by its initiative process, which allows voters to legislate or amend the state constitution through the ballot initiative system. Unlike several other states that allow ballot box legislating, once a measure qualifies in California, it requires only a simple majority vote to be approved. California also allows recalls of elected officials and repeals of state laws through elections. And California state legislators have term limits, while federal elected officials do not.

Meanwhile, I learned that decision-making at UC was a very consultative and democratic process. University leaders are expected to be more collaborative with stakeholders such as students, faculty, alumni, and others. At UC in particular, we operate under a "shared governance" structure, which gives faculty a stronger voice in the decision-making process.

As I got to know my new institution, I grew to hold a great deal of respect for the importance of government relations, and the skill and finesse it takes to successfully carry out strategy and achieve the institution's goals. Government relations is both an art and a science. And it's an area where college presidents can set the tone and agenda in a highly impactful way—for good or for ill.

Whether as a lone president promoting your own institution or as a higher education leader advocating alongside your counterparts, four key principles should inform your approach to government relations: humility, service, adaptability, and availability.

These principles break down into four broad attitudes or approaches that we explore in this chapter:

- *Humility*: I am here to listen. I am open to suggestions.
- *Service*: How can I help? Here is what my university is doing that could be relevant to your local community, the state, and the nation.

- *Adaptability*: My institution and I are nimble, and we are willing and able to evolve.
- *Availability*: I am prepared to jump into the fray when necessary—not just to direct others, but to do the hands-on work.

With these principles in mind, this chapter addresses the broad strokes and some of the gritty details of leading a strategic, dynamic government relations operation that will set up your institution, and you as its leader, for long-term success. We cover the importance of cultivating relationships and building an advocacy infrastructure, as well as branding your institution as a resource and effectively managing legislation. Let's dive in.

CULTIVATING RELATIONSHIPS

In my twenty-five-year career in public service, I've seen firsthand how relationships can make or break a leader's—or an institution's—plans and aspirations. To advocate effectively on behalf of organizational priorities, university presidents must support and empower their government relations staff to build strong connections with law-makers at the state and federal level. By nurturing and sustaining these relationships, universities can position themselves to communicate about their priorities and needs in real time, share major achievements and milestones, alert state and federal leaders to bad news (preferably before they hear it elsewhere), and build general support among lawmakers and stakeholders.

It's true that relationship-building can command a significant investment of senior university leaders' energy, time, and resources—so much, in fact, that some presidents may be tempted to put this work on the back burner or delegate it entirely to their staff. Don't.

These connections are essential, and they often benefit from the direct engagement of the institution's leader. Managed thoughtfully, they form the foundation of a comprehensive government relations engagement strategy that can advance critical legislative and policy objectives.

To cultivate and tend to these connections, the University of California maintains dedicated government relations teams in both Sacramento (California's state capital) and Washington, DC. From advocating for state and federal investments in specific programs to interfacing with key governmental agencies and assessing and influencing hundreds of pieces of legislation every year, these offices serve as central hubs through which all of UC's legislative analysis and outreach flows.

Government relations staff also play a critical role in guiding the university's strategy on issues that impact the entire higher education sector and helping to coordinate those efforts with industry groups and fellow universities. In California, for example, UC is one of three segments of public higher education, and we work closely with our colleagues in the California State University system and the California Community College system, along with the Association of Independent California Colleges and Universities. In addition, we collaborate regularly with national groups such as the Association of American Universities (AAU), the Association of Public and Land-grant Universities (APLU), and the American Council on Education (ACE), as well as California-based organizations such as the Campaign for College Opportunity, the College Futures Foundation, and the California Coalition for Public Higher Education.

It's important to remember that the vital work of government relations does not begin and end with the legislative session. Nurturing relationships of all kinds by maintaining robust channels of communication and information-sharing is a year-round, 24/7 endeavor that requires investment and focus from a range of senior leaders and policy experts, in addition to on-the-ground staff.

To make the most of these efforts, here are some best practices I've learned in my time as an elected official *and* a university president.

Make a Concrete Plan

Make sure you have the right people leading your government relations offices. Then empower them to design and follow a thoughtful and strategic roadmap to build and nurture relationships with elected officials and legislative staff. Effective government relations staff are often well connected and experienced in policy making. It helps if they are nimble, skilled in relationship management, and able to play the long game. They must be compelling communicators, have credibility with legislative and government administration leadership, and possess the confidence to speak truth to power when necessary.

Once you have your team in place, let these experts guide you as to how *you* can be most effective as part of that strategy and make the time to support their efforts by carrying out your part of that plan. For example, this could involve participating in events and briefings, writing personal correspondence, and taking part in other engagement opportunities as they arise.

Listen and Offer Solutions

One of the worst missteps you can make as a university leader is to approach lawmakers with the assumption that your relationship is a one-way street, that your institution is entitled to their support, and that your requests and needs should always be their top priority. College leaders must be fierce but humble advocates. The most authentic and often effective way to finesse this is to ensure that your university is serving as a resource, a think tank, and an innovation generator, offering ideas and connections to lawmakers to address the problems they and their constituents face.

At UC, we host regular legislative roundtables, affording the opportunity for frequent, casual conversations between university leaders and elected officials on the issues of the day. We also provide regular briefings to key government leaders and their staff on their topics of interest to showcase our faculty and academic endeavors. It's important in these settings that you don't just make asks—you also must offer solutions. We dive into more detail later in this chapter about how to position yourself and your institution as a resource.

Keep Channels of Communication Open, No Matter What

Make sure you pick up the phone and share both good *and* bad news—preferably before a legislator hears it elsewhere. Delivering good news is the easy part. It's much harder to be the one bearing news of a failure or disaster. But it is essential that legislators hear from the institution directly before learning of a problem in the media or from an angry constituent. This builds institutional and leadership credibility, and the trust engendered pays big dividends over the long term.

When you're lucky enough to have positive news to share, consider incorporating legislators or other government leaders into your announcements and events. Include a quote from them in your press release, offer them a few minutes to speak at your campus event, or find another way to give them credit for their support in a public way.

In addition, don't discount the opportunity to engage with legislative staff. Your preference and instinct may be to work directly with elected officials, but this isn't always possible—and that's okay. Legislative staff members are valuable, behind-the-scenes partners. They have significant institutional knowledge, and they keep legislation and other issues moving forward. Learn who they are, respect their roles and expertise, and keep in close contact with them.

Finally, keep in mind that some policy makers may not be aware of, or have an appreciation for, the full benefits that a higher education institution provides the public. This is especially the case when policy makers haven't had much exposure to universities, or when a higher education institution does more than educate students. (For example, in addition to its teaching and learning functions, the University of California manages a robust research portfolio, has three affiliated national laboratories, and operates five academic medical centers as well as a statewide division of agricultural and natural resources.) In these cases, government leaders may feel that their support entitles them to a certain level of engagement and flow of information, similar to how a donor might view their relationship with a university. Be patient and gracious. Continue to demonstrate your institution's value, and make sure your elected officials aren't surprised by any news coming out of your university.

BUILDING AN ADVOCACY INFRASTRUCTURE

For universities of all sizes, winning the attention—and support—of local, state, and federal leaders on funding and other priorities can often feel like a battle to the death. As a former two-term governor, I can attest that the most successful advocates manage to cut through the noise and get the outcomes they desire by communicating their priorities clearly and strategically, in tandem with a broad coalition of partners and stakeholders who share their goals.

That's why it's critical for new university presidents to develop a smart advocacy plan with broad buy-in and participation by senior administrators, governance board leaders, students, faculty, alumni, staff, and external validators. College leaders should work with their government relations and communications staff to design a robust, multichannel advocacy program that can foster or cement positive relationships with elected leaders, promote the institution's core mission, influence legislation and funding decisions, and communicate vital information about the university to stakeholders and the general public. Be prepared to invest in this work, particularly the digital infrastructure needed to execute your advocacy strategy.

With this type of investment in mind, the University of California in recent years has refined its advocacy enterprise to incorporate new technological tools, tailor advocacy opportunities to individual needs and circumstances, and target both "grassroots" and "grasstops" supporters. We employ a two-pronged approach: first, staying on top of and in the mix on budget and legislative negotiations; and second, using creative communication and engagement strategies to grab attention and generate support that move the needle on advocacy.

I encourage new higher education leaders to implement similar strategies as soon as they are able. Below, I share how the University of California has successfully put these tools into practice.

Enlist Your Best Storytellers

As a university president, I've been alarmed by recent data showing that Americans are questioning the value of a college degree and have increasingly negative views of higher education. A 2019 Pew Research Center survey found that "only half of American adults think colleges and universities are having a positive effect on the way things are going in the country these days."[1] Nearly 40 percent said colleges and universities are having a *negative* impact on the nation, up significantly from 2012.

I posit that this view is not because a college education is any less effective or transformative in the lives and opportunities of Americans, but because of other factors affecting the reputation of higher education institutions. This topic alone could fill an entire book. But in the context of state and federal government relations, it's instructive in understanding that universities cannot be the only voices telling their own stories. We need other, more trusted voices to speak on our behalf with a unified voice. To do so, we must take the time—years, decades even—to build and empower broad coalitions of advocates.

At UC, we pay special attention to student voices. Students are some of our most authentic advocates, and they are heard loud and clear by lawmakers. In my time at the university, I have focused on building trust and engaging with student leaders over the long haul. For example, I host a regular lunch with the UC Student Association president where I get to hear directly from a student leader about their constituents' needs and concerns. When students have this kind of regular access to university leaders, they are much more likely to answer the call for joint advocacy. Students have been instrumental in helping UC secure state and federal funding, particularly around basic needs such as food and housing, as well as in advocating for financial aid reform.

We have also put great care into forging strong alliances with external organizations and associations, such as local business groups and specialized industry organizations, who share some of UC's goals and can assist in specific areas. These groups will vary by geographical area and the priorities of your institution. Get to know them early so you can work together when needed.

Keep in mind that this kind of engagement won't always go your way. Students and other allies will still have their own agendas, constituencies, and voices. But when you create clear and accessible lines of communication, you provide a path to partnership on issues that matter to both entities.

Customize Opportunities for Engagement

Colleges and universities have more than one audience, and they must speak to and mobilize them all. Though challenging, this *is* possible if you take care to execute your messages thoughtfully and with authenticity. One way to do so is by tailoring your outreach based on advocates' interests and affinities.

In recent years, the University of California has devoted resources to building and expanding the UC Advocacy Network (UCAN), made up of students, faculty, staff, alumni, and other friends of the university, who are regularly called upon to take action on issues of importance to the institution.

When a new advocate joins the network, they are asked a series of questions, such as which issues they're most interested in; which UC campus they're associated with; and whether they are a student, faculty or staff member, alumnus, parent, employee, or another ally. Someone who graduated from UC Berkeley may be especially interested in supporting undergraduate education. On the other hand, a UC San Diego faculty member may be more focused on research, while a UC parent may only want to get involved if financial aid is at risk. In every case, we can use the information shared with us to reach out to advocates with tailored calls-to-action.

When it comes to "grasstops" and one-on-one advocacy efforts, the tailored experience becomes even more important. "Grasstops" advocacy refers to efforts that utilize thought leaders and influencers who may already be well connected with government leaders and policy makers. This is where university leaders and their staff must do more legwork: Is there an alumna who's especially close to an elected leader and can make a call at a key moment? A former public official willing to publish a compelling op-ed on the institution's behalf? A philanthropist able to introduce university leadership to other well-connected supporters? Once you determine the most effective way to activate a particular ally, university leaders and government relations staff must employ every tool in their relationship management toolbox to carefully cultivate these advocates and provide whatever customized support they need to take the next step.

Go Organic

The digital age provides us an opportunity to build affinity and share important content in more organic ways. At UC, we increasingly aim to create shareable, interactive, visually appealing content that can catch fire in its own right. One highly effective example of this was a video series we produced in partnership with Vox Media called "Climate Lab," an exploration of how to change the way we think and act on climate change. The series showcased UC's commitment to sustainability and highlighted some of our most exciting research discoveries. It was a prime example of universities providing real-life solutions to people's problems. But the series also became incredibly popular online—one of the videos got more than 4.8 million views on YouTube—generating excitement and good will among viewers.

BRANDING YOUR INSTITUTION AS A RESOURCE

As I wrote earlier, Americans don't hold the same common view we once did about the value of college and the importance of investing in the higher education dreams of young people. The reality and the common perception of reality are growing increasingly divergent, and that is partly on us as higher education leaders. Whether it's the Varsity Blues scandal, free speech skirmishes, or the cases of sexual harassment at colleges and universities, these missteps at best—and failures of the system at worst—have dealt some damaging blows to the credibility of higher education institutions. The resulting lack of trust is poisonous when it comes to gaining allies and advocating for support.

Thankfully, colleges and universities get frequent opportunities to (slowly) rebuild that trust with the public and lawmakers by providing public service through education, economic activity, and other endeavors. But the element I focus on here is research.

In times of both calm and crisis, state and federal leaders need access to reliable, evidence-based information that can help them make timely decisions, and that is where higher education institutions shine. There is a powerful symbiosis in the role that colleges and universities can play in informing and supporting their communities—from the local to the national—about issues of the day. The better we perform in this role, the more valuable we become to the public and to decision makers.

Your institution can most effectively establish its reputation as a service and information provider by getting personal and practical: give the public and its elected officials the information and concrete solutions they need to solve their most immediate problems. In UC's case, we tackle everything from cancer and wildfires to agricultural pests and cybersecurity. Our faculty's research has led to the discoveries of vitamins E and K; CRISPR-Cas9; vaccines for the flu, hepatitis B, and polio; the nicotine patch; and treatments for AIDS and Alzheimer's disease.

More recently, however, we turned the power of UC's research on the COVID-19 pandemic. And we made sure our state knew it.

In the spring of 2020, shortly after California Governor Gavin Newsom issued a stay-at-home order for all Californians to slow the spread of COVID-19, UC's state government relations representatives held a briefing to provide up-to-date information on the pandemic in a format that allowed legislators and their staff to ask questions specific to their constituents. I attended this briefing, along with Dr. Carrie Byington, the leader of UC's health enterprise and an infectious diseases specialist. The facts we shared, combined with the service-oriented and personal nature of the briefing, provided a measure of calm and stability in the midst of a daunting crisis. I believe that briefing directly benefitted the public and boosted UC's standing as a vital resource in the eyes of some of California's most influential leaders.

As higher education leaders, we are keenly attuned to the needs and challenges of our own institutions. But we must not forget the needs and challenges within our larger communities—cities, counties, regions, states, the nation, and the world. Universities have the privilege of educating the next generation, creating new knowledge, and fueling innovation. No other institution has the ability and the firepower to do all of those things under one roof. But we must work harder to channel those efforts toward our communities' most urgent needs and then ensure they are aware of these contributions. This way, we position our institutions as partners and resources for state and federal governments and for the public at large.

You can begin by focusing on these strategies:

- *Find out what issues your state and federal leaders care about and what problems their constituents are facing, and then connect them with relevant research and experts on your campuses.* Legislators aren't shy about their priorities—the easiest way to find out what they care about most is to ask them or their staff. (In fact, they will appreciate if you do this.) You can also identify their priorities by looking at which pieces of legislation they've introduced or supported and which groups they speak to the most. If your institution includes multiple campuses or is spread out over a large area, map out those priorities and the corresponding campus resources by district so you can keep track of them more easily and follow up with legislators as needed.

- *Ensure your campus community understands the value of tailoring some of its research and innovation to the needs of the state and nation.* Provide and solicit the support and tools researchers need to get this done and cultivate collaboration with communities on the campus level. A good example at UC was AB 2664, a state bill that led to the investment of $22 million to accelerate innovation and entrepreneurship across the university system. Thus far, that funding has allowed us to support more than five hundred new start-ups and existing companies and helped launch at least forty-seven new products.

- *Be bold about taking on society's largest problems.* Internalize the idea that addressing these problems is, indeed, the role of universities, particularly research institutions and public universities. Climate change, immigration reform, a global pandemic—nothing is too big or insurmountable for American higher education. We have the rare combination of thirst for knowledge, innovative spirit, and passionate students, faculty, and researchers to get it done.

MANAGING LEGISLATION

Managing legislation is a central function of a university's state and federal government relations function. It involves close monitoring as well as active lobbying to pass, defeat, or amend legislation of importance to the institution. This effort requires a solid policy analysis apparatus and effective relationship-building and management.

The work here is relentless, unforgiving, and absolutely essential. At UC, state and federal government relations staff are responsible for evaluating the impact of, and crafting the university's public positions on, numerous pieces of state and federal legislation. In some cases, government relations teams work directly with elected officials and their staff to draft legislation. In addition, they testify on a regular basis in front of state legislature and congressional committees, as well as prepare UC subject matter experts to do the same, in hopes of informing and swaying policy makers.

For public universities in particular, budget bills may be the most important pieces of legislation—and most critical advocacy focus—of the year. But it's also important to keep a close eye on the long list of proposed changes to state and federal statutes.

Next are a few tips for managing legislation effectively.

Get to Know Your Budget

Before you step foot on your new university's campus, study your institution's budget inside and out—not just the numbers themselves, but how they can work for or against you. For example, how much of your budget comes from state and federal funding, as opposed to other sources? Are those amounts restricted to a particular use? How has the institution dealt with past state or federal budget cuts, and what have those reductions meant for the university? What are your college's unfunded liabilities? Which areas of state or federal code are legislators most likely to leverage in order to achieve behavioral change at your institution? Where can you match the priorities of policy makers with university programs and research priorities?

Be Prepared and Realistic

You win some, you lose a lot. That's just the reality of politics. Take a moment to appreciate those infrequent wins, even if they feel like small potatoes (they never are). I recall one example in which UC's state government relations office sponsored four bills over the course of seven years to modernize the university's competitive bidding procedures to allow the consideration of factors beyond "lowest price." Not the sexiest of policy making! But it was a delicate and collaborative effort, and the data has borne out that UC is getting a better product at a lower cost today as a result of this legislation—an important accomplishment for an institution partly dependent on taxpayers' dollars. That's a win in my book.

Don't Be a Bystander

Universities can, and should, take an active role in the legislative process by supporting bills that have already been introduced by other parties. These can be bills with direct positive impact on the institution or higher education as a whole, or they can be bills the university generally supports (or tolerates) that are introduced by legislators the institution is trying to cultivate. Sponsoring or publicly supporting legislation this way is an effective strategy for building relationships with key policy makers, advancing your institution's goals, or both. During my time at the University of California, we actively sought to support bills that expanded federal financial aid and California's basic needs programs for students—bills that weren't only beneficial to UC but also focused on areas of importance to key leaders. In this way, UC cultivated the relationships and credibility necessary to earn a seat at the table for future legislative efforts that could affect us negatively and require direct intervention to manage.

Occasionally, managing legislation requires your institution to demonstrate its commitment to a particular principle or course of action *before* a bill is introduced. This is exactly what UC did in 2015, as Congress was crafting legislation to address sexual harassment and sexual assault on college campuses. A number of senators wanted to introduce legislation that would require universities to provide an independent advocate for survivors of sexual assault on every campus. We thought this was an excellent idea and decided to move forward immediately to offer this resource, even though the bill had yet to be introduced. By the time the legislation passed in Congress, UC already had a compliant program up and running. We were able to go back to our senators, endorse their bill, and cement ourselves as a national model for other higher education institutions as they established their own programs.

Even if recent attempts to roll back federal protections for survivors of sexual harassment, sexual assault, and sexual violence move ahead, UC will continue to have a strong process in place for providing resources and holding people accountable, while still adhering to the federal guidelines. The policy pendulum often swings back and forth, and having a solid process in place that was informed by stakeholder input can and will withstand those pendulum swings.

Take Calculated Risks

Lastly, managing legislation occasionally means taking a much bigger risk: if and when the legislative process fails, higher education institutions must consider taking legal action to further their goals and uphold their values.

The most ambitious example from my time as UC president was the lawsuit the university filed to halt the Trump administration's rescission of the DACA (Deferred Action for Childhood Arrivals) program—a program I helped launch back in my days as secretary of homeland security in the Obama administration.

We filed the lawsuit in 2017 in response to an unlawful executive order, after years of advocacy in support of comprehensive immigration reform, which never resulted in Congressional action. It was a carefully considered and crafted legal action to protect members of our university community, as well as others across the country, who would be unfairly and capriciously harmed by the rescission of this program. We paired this action with meaningful services and external campaigns to both garner and show support for our undocumented community members.

The victory in that case came almost three years later in June of 2020, when the Supreme Court agreed with us that the administration's attempted rescission of DACA was unlawful. It was a win not only for UC and our DACA community members but also for the 650,000 DACA recipients living in the United States at that time.

The lawsuit was a bold and somewhat unusual move—how often does a university president sue the federal agency she once led to protect a program she once created? But regardless of the personal meaning this case had for me, it was a necessary action and a strong stand for what is right and what is fair. UC didn't shy away from a legal challenge that reflected its institutional ethos. And the risk we took paid off.

As I write this in the summer of 2020, it's unknown what the future holds for DACA or comprehensive immigration reform in our nation. But this much is clear: Through this lawsuit, we demonstrated that universities can—and should—take calculated risks and tackle large societal problems on behalf of our campus communities.

THE LONG VIEW

Beyond the specific tactics I've set out in this chapter, perhaps the most important advice I can share with new university and college presidents is not to get bogged down in the losses or victories of a single day, academic year, or legislative session.

The surest fact any leader faces is that you will make mistakes. They will often be public and will likely have consequences that are difficult to stomach. We all know that, of course. But we often expend too much energy avoiding those mistakes, downplaying missteps, or shying away from risk. Resist the temptation to dwell on the losses and injustices, large or small, that are an inevitable part of the job. Take the long view, and that is this: no matter what our reference point is, what battle we are fighting or win we are trying to secure, we need to ground ourselves in what really matters—not just the outcomes of our own tenures, but also the lasting impact of our institutions; not just the accomplishments of our individual universities but also the strength of higher education as a whole and the world-changing impacts it makes possible.

CHAPTER 8

The President and Athletics

BOB KUSTRA

In the early days of one of my presidencies, I often joked in speeches that it wasn't clear to me if I had joined a university that happened to have a football team or a football team that happened to have a university attached to it. Too often, it seemed like the latter rather than the former, as the most feedback I received about the university usually came on Monday after the weekend football game, and those people weren't commenting on the quality of our engineering program. The role athletics plays in the life of the university will differ from school to school, conference to conference, and division to division in the National Collegiate Athletic Association (NCAA) or the National Association of Intercollegiate Athletics (NAIA). But at any level, the emphasis on athletics is significant, and as president, you should be prepared to spend a considerable amount of time supporting your athletic program and those directly responsible for its effective operation.

In this chapter, I address how the athletic department can help brand the university and serve as an important ally in fundraising and building community and state support for the university. I cover your relationship as president with your athletic director, compliance officer, and faculty athletics representative and offer some advice on how your chief financial officer and university counsel can assist you and your athletic department. You will read my thoughts on how to position yourself as "first fan" of athletics and yet retain the presidential credibility all of your constituencies expect. I also touch on your responsibilities with your athletic conference and the NCAA and NAIA. Finally, I address how the issues of social justice and racial equity so prominent in our society today may present themselves in athletics.

Much of this chapter is rooted in my experiences overseeing a university with a prominent Division I athletic department and my roles on the NCAA and athletic conference governing boards. The particulars of my examples may be rooted in Division I, but the lessons are universal. I realize that not all of you will be presidents at institutions with highly visible athletic departments. But regardless, athletics plays an outsized role in the life of a college or university, no matter the size of the department or the institution. Large or small, prominent or not, the athletic department will require your undivided attention among your various responsibilities. If you do this well, then athletics will be an asset to your institution.

THE ROLE ATHLETICS PLAYS IN THE LIFE OF THE UNIVERSITY

Branding the University with a Successful Athletic Brand

As president, you may inherit an athletics program with years of proud tradition, sustained by the campus community of students, faculty and staff, alumni, and the community and state at-large. In some states where the university is the flagship, you will find yourself owing an explanation to fans across the state on why the team lost last weekend. For every sport, there will be a specific fan constituency devoted to that sport and helping you and your athletic director understand the importance of the sport to its student-athletes and to the university overall. You may not keep track of wins and losses on all of your sports, but you will hear from fans who do.

Your university's brand as evaluated and scored by the larger community your university serves will be impacted to some extent by the success of the athletic program, and you will be held responsible for the overall success of that program. Early in your presidency, you should make it clear to the media and all the constituencies you serve as president that you are, indeed, the number one fan of the athletic program. Over time, you will learn just how engaged you must be to reassure fans and donors that you value the athletic program. That may require an occasional visit to a soccer or wrestling match, but it will likely mean attendance at all football games and as many basketball games as fit your schedule. That should put you in good stead with the fans, alumni, and the community in general as you progress through the early stages of your presidency.

The athletic brand can enhance the overall reputation of the university and attract faculty, staff, and student talent that a university without a successful athletic brand can find more difficult to achieve. For example, the Oregon athletic program managed to take its famous "O" up and down the West Coast to promote its athletic program while the university went along for the ride, and today its "O" brand is also the university's brand that promotes academic as well as athletic success.

Whenever the media asked me to justify the size of a coach's salary or the overall budget of the athletic department, especially that portion coming from student fees or the university's budget, I was quick to point out how much funding we would have to generate for our marketing efforts if we did not have the benefit of the advertising that accompanied every athletic contest. And, needless to say, the value of that advertising quadruples in the case of high-profile victories such as conference championships, bowl games, and the NCAA finals. Just ask Butler University in Indianapolis, whose men's basketball team made it to the Final Four a few years ago.

On the flip side, when the athletic department fails its mission to deliver a quality athletic experience for its students and to graduate student-athletes in a timely fashion, it can set back a university for years. Penn State's coverup of sexual predation and Michigan State's similar experience come to mind as two universities that suffered beyond athletics, showing how the athletic brand can impact the university. The University of Montana also learned the hard way how the handling of sexual predators on the football team can hurt enrollment and send a university into a financial and enrollment tailspin. In that case, noted outdoor author Jon Krakauer's book *Missoula: Rape and the Justice System in a College Town* spread the word of the mishandling of sexual violence cases that dramatically impacted the university's enrollment. These cautionary tales should serve as reminders of the drastic consequences if you do not act with the student-athlete's welfare as your first and last consideration—and what happens when you do not act with the highest degree of transparency in dealing with such issues.

Athletics Can Provide the Building Blocks for a Diverse University Campus

Building a diverse campus community of faculty, students, and staff still remains a challenge for many universities. For those campuses in states and locales with few minority populations, it can be especially difficult to attract a diverse talent pool of candidates for university positions or students from diverse backgrounds.

I know something about this issue, having spent my fifteen-year presidency at Boise State University in a very "white" Idaho. On more than one occasion, we lost faculty candidates and prospective students we recruited to Boise State because they did not see many people of color around town or on our campus during their official visit.

On our campus, the athletic department, by virtue of its aggressive recruiting of minorities, is one of the university's most important tools in diversifying the campus. By highlighting the success of student-athletes of color, the university can assist enrollment management efforts to recruit more minority students. Marketing and communication strategies that highlight the success of African American student-athletes can send a signal to high school students of color to consider a university even though they may have no interest in competing as a student-athlete.

Athletics as an Ally in University Fundraising

Athletics often introduces the university to donors who may contribute initially to the athletic program. Then, the donor learns more about the university's overall priorities for faculty support, student scholarships, and the other compelling needs of the university; that piques the interest of the donor to give to university priorities other than athletics. Most importantly, from the standpoint of the athletics department, which might jealously guard its donor base for fear of losing financial support, it was not in my experience that athletics lost donors to academic priorities. Donors expanded their giving to programs across the university, including athletics.

Athletics Builds Community and State Support for the University

The role of athletics in building state and community support for the university will differ greatly depending on the competition university athletics has in the community and state. Some universities and their athletic departments compete for attention with professional teams across town or other athletic programs across towns or states, making it more challenging to leverage the athletic program for community and state support. Whether it's branding your university, filling seats at athletic events, or fundraising, the challenges of sustaining fan interest can be substantial if you are competing for attention against a professional team that captures too many of the headlines and sports reports.

In a Division I school, with football and basketball in particular, building support is about getting fans in seats and bringing in the revenue for the department to support Olympic sports such as swimming or soccer that usually cannot raise the revenue to sustain themselves.

A university in close proximity to a state's flagship university will find it difficult to gain public attention for its programming—athletic or academic—when the flagship is sucking all the university oxygen out of the region. I served as president of a university just down the road from the state's flagship, and it was very difficult to compete against the steady stream of media acclaim heaped on the flagship. Conversely, when I moved to Boise State, a city without a professional team and with the land-grant university seven hours away, I learned how a university can benefit from occupying a predominant position in the community.

An institution that is the only university in a town or state with a successful athletic program has a significant advantage in using the program's success to imprint the university's brand on the community and state as a result of its successes in athletics. Whether it's a board member, a prospective donor, or the fan in the stands, athletics builds state and community support for the university in areas that have little or nothing to do with athletics. For example, often branding the university with its athletic brand works to the advantage of the university's enrollment management plan. I've met many students who explain that their parents had been taking them to football and basketball games for years, and it was a foregone conclusion that their favorite team's university would be their choice when the time came for college!

Indeed, the president's strategic thinking can help university colleagues across the university build those connections between university athletics and the larger community it serves. For example, without question, many of the media opportunities

I had over my years as president came from sports reporters and TV commentators covering games. Although the ostensible purpose of the interview was athletics, I always used the opportunity to update the media with the latest developments across campus. As you prepare for interviews with the media about athletics, consider how you can also give a shout out to academic and research accomplishments of the university. I always credited the athletic program as serving as the window to the university that allowed us to showcase academic and research successes, thereby increasing the stature of the university.

Similarly, how might your college of education use the football or basketball program to build stronger relationships with school superintendents across the state or region? The dean can invite the superintendents to a pregame dinner and the game, where at some point between plays, the superintendents can be introduced to the fans, thereby honoring the work of K–12 educators but also impressing the superintendents, who will go back to their districts with favorable impressions of your college of education and the university in general. I leave it to your imagination to replicate this effort across colleges with the various constituencies served by your academic departments.

THE ATHLETIC DEPARTMENT

The Athletic Director

The athletic director (AD) will be one of your most important direct reports. And if you find yourself at a university that has the athletic director reporting to some other administrator, you have a problem. The NCAA holds the president ultimately responsible for the performance of the athletic department, and handing the athletic director off to another administrator is a formula for "loss of institutional control," the NCAA's terminology for an athletic department out of control. Do make sure the athletic director reports directly to you.

If the NCAA ever informs you that your university committed a major violation of NCAA rules and regulations and there is "loss of institutional control," your coaches responsible for the infractions and the athletic director will be called before the NCAA for a hearing, and you will not be staying home to observe from afar. Instead, the president will be prominently seated at the table, creating the distinct impression that you were ultimately responsible for the "loss of institutional control." Those are not my words, but the words the NCAA attaches to the most egregious violations of its rules.

Most presidents move to their offices from positions in academic affairs, financial affairs, student affairs, and other administrative backgrounds. As well versed as you may be with your former areas of responsibility, few presidents come to the office with experience in intercollegiate athletics. Whether it's the hiring of coaches and their supervision, the recruitment and support of student-athletes, the byzantine rules of the NCAA or the NAIA, or any number of AD responsibilities, most presidents new to the job have a steep learning curve compared to their command of other administrative responsibilities.

For that reason, it is imperative that you have the utmost confidence in the AD's integrity and command of the athletic enterprise. As important as expertise is in all things athletic, it's the integrity component that must come first. Presidents have failed thanks to athletic directors who did not level with their presidents in the face of crisis and promoted instability in the athletic department. Honesty is the best policy as far as your athletic director sharing all challenges of their department with you and seeking your advice on how to handle a difficult coach or student-athlete. If the president/athletic director relationship is solid and built on trust on both sides, you can sleep at night knowing the department is in good hands.

As a new president or chancellor, you cannot spend too much time with the AD as you learn the ropes of the department and its teams. One of your first requests of the AD should be to take you around the department to meet the coaches and learn about the sports your university offers. This meet-and-greet will give you firsthand knowledge of the department and will show you are interested in the athletic program and that you support their efforts. It will also convey a message, directly or indirectly, that you will be paying attention and taking NCAA and departmental rules seriously as the ultimate decision maker at the university.

One of the most important messages you can deliver to the coaches is the simple fact that you trust your AD and you will follow their advice and counsel on those few, but most important, decisions that require presidential sign-off.

One area you can reinforce with your AD and the coaches is the university's priority of graduating student-athletes in a timely fashion. Coaches' contracts are usually loaded with incentives based on won/loss records, conference championships, and post-season play. I believe those contracts should also include incentives for the academic success of student-athletes. If you report to a board that requires board approval of coaching contracts, board members may require such incentives; but whether it's your governing board or your own commitment to the academic success of your student-athletes, academic incentives for the coaches send a message to the athletic department that the university and its president are committed to the academic welfare of student-athletes and their long-term success.

Most athletic programs have at least one sport that qualifies as the university's or college's "power" sport, raising much of the revenue for the athletic budget and branding the university with its success. That sport will, in some cases, have a coach who may find it difficult to "suffer" under an AD and will expect more independence from the AD. To paraphrase George Orwell's famous line from *Animal Farm*, all sports may be equal, but some are more equal than the others; but you cannot allow one coach to skirt your athletic director's oversight.

No matter how you ultimately decide to treat the power sport, at the outset of your presidency, it is wise for you to demonstrate the confidence you have in your AD and not allow any coach to drive a wedge between you and the AD. That is a formula for disaster down the road when the coach takes advantage of your relationship and cuts corners that damage your relationship with your AD. Worse yet, you just might find yourself at the NCAA headquarters in Indianapolis before a committee explaining a major violation or, worse yet, loss of institutional control.

Once the coaches know and understand the complete confidence you have in your athletic director, there is no reason why you cannot develop collegial relationships with them. In fact, such relationships that morph into friendships might come in handy when a coach is recruited by another school and your AD asks for your help in persuading the coach to stay put rather than take off for greener pastures.

Building strong relationships with coaches also can assist in their recruitment efforts. I offered coaches the opportunity to bring their recruits and their parents to my office so I could help them understand our academic mission and what academic opportunities were available to our student-athletes. Not all coaches took me up on the offer, but those who did greatly appreciated my building an even stronger case for a prospective student-athlete joining our team. On many occasions over the years, a parent of a student-athlete would tell me how much they appreciated the opportunity to meet with me and learn more about the university beyond the athletic department.

At the beginning of the academic year, I would always host (and I recommend you do the same) a meeting of all coaches and student-athletes where the president signs off on an NCAA-required document that acknowledges the president's oversight of and responsibility of athletics. You cannot miss that meeting. For one thing, it's an opportunity for you to kick off the new year with a passionate and energetic show of personal support for the athletic program. It will go a long way in helping the athletic staff know that you are behind them and the number one fan of the athletic program. I also found a way to insert into that speech of support a warning of the consequences of cutting corners off NCAA rules and regulations and the importance of supporting the student-athletes in their studies as well as supporting them on the field, court, or wherever they compete.

It is also important for the community of donors, the media, and the university community to hear of the confidence you have in the athletic director. In my speeches to fans, athletic donors, or in conversations with sports reporters, I always included the confidence I had in my athletic director's leadership. There can be no better way to assure their success with coaches than for them to hear that you have the AD's back, so it will do little good to go around them to get to you.

The Unique Role of the Compliance Officer

Historically, the compliance officer has been hired by the athletic director and reports directly to the AD. The reason I head this section the "unique" role of the compliance officer is that it will probably be the only position in the athletic department that deserves dual reporting lines—one to the AD and the other directly to the president. At the end of the day, it's the latter that will underscore the fact that the president is ultimately responsible for the athletic department in the eyes of the NCAA and your governing board.

In 2005, I was invited to join other presidents in a meeting with late NCAA President Myles Brand. Brand called the meeting to discuss the importance of the president taking ultimate responsibility for athletics and helping the assembled presidents understand they were the ultimate deciders on all things athletic. He underscored the importance of the compliance officer in helping the athletic department understand the rules of the NCAA and assuring that coaches and staff stayed within the boundaries of those rules.

At one point, Brand asked for a show of hands as to how many presidents had the compliance officer reporting directly to the president. Not many hands went up, and mine was not among them. But the message was clear: do not allow your athletic director to confine responsibility for compliance to their office and prevent the president from meeting with the compliance officer regularly. There must be accountability running directly from the compliance officer to the president.

After hearing Brand's directive, I returned to campus and immediately called in the compliance officer to inform him that even though he was hired by the AD, he would now have a direct reporting line to me. I would meet with him regularly, and he understood that he was protected by my office from any retaliation he may experience for enforcing a rule or calling out a coach for a violation. Such meetings were also opportunities for me to learn of new NCAA rules or court decisions that impacted intercollegiate athletics.

One area that must be of particular concern to you is the enforcement of Title IX of the Education Amendments of 1972. According to the law,

- When a school knows or reasonably should know about possible sexual harassment or sexual violence, it must promptly investigate to determine what occurred and then take appropriate steps to resolve the situation.
- A school must take proactive steps to address individual and systems factors contributing to sexual harassment and violence.

- A clear written policy against sexual harassment and violence, as well as clear grievance procedures, must be in place.
- Schools must have a designated point person to receive and investigate Title IX complaints.
- Parties involved in a sexual harassment or violence complaint must be treated fairly and must have ongoing access to a transparent resolution process.
- Access to an internal/institutional investigation and resources regardless of whether outside legal or police involvement is pursued must also be available.

You cannot overlook or deal lightly with a student-athlete infraction or conduct issue. Sexual violence or sexual impropriety of any kind merits careful review by university officials beyond the athletic department. I relied on our university counsel to review such cases and assure me that the toughest and most appropriate sanctions were applied. If you have a relationship of trust and confidentiality with your university counsel and your compliance officer, it will serve as yet another check on your AD or a coach who might gloss over a serious incident that brings great harm to the people involved and to the university as well.

Faculty Athletics Representative

You have another direct report who can enhance your ability to monitor the athletic department and, at the same time, build a liaison between your faculty and the athletic department that might improve what can be a difficult relationship between these two stakeholders. From time to time, you may hear from faculty who complain about the "bloated" athletic budget or a coach's salary or just the misguided priorities of the university when it comes to athletics versus academics.

Here's where you might receive some assistance from the faculty athletics representative (FAR). The FAR is appointed by the president and serves at the pleasure of the president. The FAR is the intermediary between the athletics department and the faculty, and also represents the university, along with you and your athletic director, at the NCAA. FARs serve on committees of their counterparts both at the conference and NCAA level. On some campuses, the FAR is not necessarily viewed as a neutral arbiter between athletics and the faculty. Faculty may view the FAR suspiciously as a tool of the athletic department, too quick to defend the athletic department even when things go wrong.

Because, as president, you are the appointing authority in this case, your job will be to make certain that the FAR reports directly to you and you expect to hear of any concerns your FAR hears or sees in athletics or about athletics, especially from the faculty. There have been cases in which student-athletes are not treated fairly in the college classroom by a faculty member who might not understand the rigorous game schedule during the playing season or who simply resents the privileges of student-athletes. The FAR can help faculty understand the need to deal with student assignments and even attendance differently than other students. The FAR can go a long way in improving the image of the department in the eyes of the faculty but can also be that extra set of eyes you might find valuable in watching for any irregularities in the athletic department that escape the attention of your athletic staff.

The Athletic Budget

Controlling the costs of the athletic budget ranks as one of the president's greatest challenges, even at institutions that do not sponsor "big-time" athletic programs. Every president wants winning seasons, and that comes with the cost of escalating coaches' salaries, increased scholarship and student-athlete support, and other pressures on the budget, especially in the revenue-producing sports. Needless to say, football and basketball coaches alone can gobble up most of the personnel budget in an athletic department budget. Of course, they can also deliver the revenue the department needs to support Olympic sports that cannot begin to cover their costs.

Given the pressure on athletic directors to balance budgets that can career out of control, very sophisticated and complex relationships have been built in recent years with firms that specialize in overseeing and managing the marketing opportunities for athletic programs. A marketing campaign offered to the athletic department by an athletics marketing firm may look like a revenue bonanza to the athletic director, but it may not register so well with faculty or the larger community if it conflicts with the shared values of the campus or community. For example, efforts to partner with alcohol companies can meet with opposition from campus partners or governing boards as the university struggles to define the values it upholds for its students against those dollar signs waved before athletic departments in contracts with marketing firms. It's always best for your athletic director to inform you of any plans for a new relationship with a marketing company or a new marketing campaign.

The most effective guarantee to assuring the athletic budget turns a profit is the oversight and support of the university's chief financial officer. The CFO plays a critical role supporting the AD and the budget officer for the athletic department. A close and trusted relationship between the university's CFO and the athletic department's budget officer will assure there is effective financial oversight of the athletic budget. There will be times when your athletic department will require the university's budgetary support for an athletic venture. Or it may be the use of the legal or financial tools of the university in introducing a new initiative in athletics. Your CFO is your guarantee that the request for university support is reasonable and does not sink the university in debt or involve questionable financial practices that come back to haunt you and the university.

Booster clubs also provide athletic departments with substantial revenue to cover expenses that cannot be covered by the university's contribution to athletics or other revenue sources such as ticket revenue. Booster clubs like to hear from the president regularly, both to gauge the direction and success of the university, in general, and to hear of the president's support of the athletic program. Lunches or dinners with donors to the program are also important ways to show your support for athletics. These events provide a great opportunity to call out the success of your student-athletes, your coaches, and your athletic director.

Although your staff in athletics will work directly with the booster organization to raise funds for the athletic budget, there is no substitute for the AD rolling up their sleeves to cultivate donors to athletics and score significant gifts for the athletic program. There can be a competition between the athletic department and the university advancement office overseeing all university fundraising; the president's job should be to encourage a strong and collegial relationship between the two offices. As president, you are the lead fundraiser at the university, so it will be incumbent on you to demand a strong working relationship between the AD and the vice president for advancement and development. In larger universities, the foundation will be independent of the university administration, and if you find yourself at such a university, you will be responsible for fostering a close working relationship with the executive director of the foundation.

Cost-Saving Measures

The constraints of tight athletic budgets mean that you, as president, will have to make some tough decisions. One of the most difficult choices you and your athletic director will ever make is the decision to drop a sport. Although it doesn't happen very often, sometimes the budget can no longer sustain a sport, or Title IX and its requirement to keep men's and women's sports on an even keel may require the dropping of a men's sport. In recent years, many universities have added women's sports for Title IX reasons, and sometimes athletic departments are required to pare men's sports for these reasons. Alternatively, the passage of time and changing fan interests no longer make a sport as attractive and sustainable as it once was. Another sport may make more sense in building the university brand and keeping aligned with fan interest in a community.

I learned something about this challenge when I decided to bring men's baseball back to the university by eliminating men's wrestling so we would remain in good stead with Title IX requirements. Wrestling attracted few fans and did not generate enough revenue to support itself, like many of the Olympic sports. No matter the sport, pockets of die-hard fans will fight tooth and nail to keep it. Wrestling is certainly no exception, and the aficionados will come out of the woodwork as they did with my decision. In the end, wrestling went by the boards and baseball was back, but it was not an easy time dealing with fans whose hearts were in the right place in support of their favorite sport. If you find yourself in that position of dropping a sport and perhaps adding another, do your due diligence carefully before making the announcement and have substantial support in the community and fan base for your decision. Of course, you will want to make sure that any major decision such as dropping a sport has the support of your board; otherwise, you may find yourself leaving with the team you dropped.

The student-athletes of the dropped sport will have at least two important concerns when they learn their sport is dropped. First, since they will likely be on some form of aid, full or partial tuition, how will they now pay for their education? Given the fact that they came to the university with a good faith commitment that the sport would be around for the length of their undergraduate experience, the best and fairest policy is to allow the student-athletes to use their scholarship for the rest of their undergraduate studies. This policy will go a long way in satisfying, to some extent, parents of the students who will be quite upset with the news the athletic department is dropping the sport.

Some student-athletes and their parents will prefer to move on and compete at another institution. The AD can probably figure this out on their own, but the athletic department should make every effort to pave the way for such students who choose to transfer to another program where they can compete.

Eliminating a sport is one of the most difficult decisions a president and athletic director will make, and it should not be taken lightly. Review with your AD just how the news will be rolled out, and how staff will assist coaches and student-athletes to accommodate any transfers to other schools. Make sure you are in a great place with key stakeholders—especially your board—should the day ever come that you have to go down this road.

THE IMPACT OF COVID-19. The impact of COVID-19 on revenue sports such as basketball and football has significantly challenged the athletic budget. With games postponed or canceled, ticket revenue has taken a dive and, so often, that is the revenue that supports the Olympic sports of the athletic department. As a result, athletic departments must find new and innovative approaches to balancing the budget.

The most obvious is dropping certain sports that have such a small fan base that they cannot be justified in our post-COVID world. The other option is to reexamine coaches' contracts when they are due for renewal. Over recent years, excessive coaches' contracts have caused consternation on and off campus, especially as student-athletes discover they may have some bargaining power given the size of a coach's contract. Many athletic directors must be considering how to use this new moment in time to deal with the salary issue. That will be no easy task and, short of that, you can explore with your athletic director the possibility of reducing the size of coaching staffs and even consolidating some of the Olympic sports so that one coach oversees more than one sport.

COVID-19 presents new challenges, but it also presents new opportunities to re-examine the role and standing of athletic competition at our universities and colleges. Most schools have "club sports," many of which have developed into very successful enterprises that compete with other club sports in the region. They are usually over-seen by the student affairs division of the university and depend on private giving for their support. The student-athletes often organize their own fundraising to support their sport. Coaches volunteer for the love of the sport, certainly not for the remu-neration they receive. To the extent that athletic competition is modeled after the true Olympic model, it may well be that the club sport model is more akin to the role athletics should play in the life of the university as opposed to a "pay to play" model that looks more "professional" than "amateur."

INTEGRATING ATHLETICS INTO THE LIFE OF THE UNIVERSITY

The president is the "first fan" of athletics, although some may not agree the presi-dent dare be called that title for fear it would compromise the role they must play in holding athletics accountable. No doubt, the president is ultimately responsible for the success or failure of the athletic program, and some would argue they cannot be a cheerleader for the program and possibly miss important clues to managerial or ethical issues that require the president have a completely objective perspective.

Critics of presidents who become so enmeshed in the life of the athletic program call them "jock-sniffers," which is not a term you want to identify with your presi-dency. Drawing that line between appropriate presidential behavior and jock-sniffer behavior is not the easiest of tasks, and I do not know of any guidelines that spell it out. Clearly, you will have to decide between behavior that can make you look like a fan buffoon, surrendering to the fan hysteria of the moment or the adulation of a win-ning coach, or behavior befitting a president who is ultimately responsible for apply-ing the highest standards of integrity and sportsmanship to the athletic department.

Common sense and good judgment are the best aides in seeing you through what looks presidential and what crosses the line into jock-sniffing territory. For example, one president led the football team out onto the field at the outset of every game. Applying the common sense and good judgment metric, it just doesn't seem like the place to find the university's president. On the other hand, when our women's bas-ketball team captured the conference title, the team members and the coaching staff climbed the ladder after the game to cut the net from the basketball hoop, a tradition for the victorious team. The coach and the team asked me to climb the ladder also and cut one of the net strings. That seemed to me to be a way to honor the players for a great season and still keep me out of jock-sniffing territory.

There is a fine line between behavior that is becoming of a president and that which borders on clown antics, such as leading the team onto the stadium field. You did not successfully navigate the search process without the search committee and the board having determined your ability to make decisions in the best interest of the university and your presidency. I am confident you will know what works and what doesn't when it comes to your image on campus and in the community as the university's number one fan. That said, keep this in mind: as a president, you should be the number one fan of everything the institution does. So, if you will be the "first fan" of the football team, make sure you also publicly represent yourself as the top fan of any academic department when it receives accolades, or the student debate team when it wins an award, or of faculty members who are recognized with national or other prestigious honors. In other words, your fanaticism should be spread around the institution so that no one can accuse you of being a fan solely of athletics.

There will be days when you will have to make an unpopular decision regarding athletics, and fans will disagree with you. But make sure fans know from your past allegiance to the program that you have the best interests of the athletic program in mind even when you have to make a tough decision about a popular coach or athletic director that tests their loyalty to the university.

As I filed away those moments when fans applauded my devotion to the athletic department, I knew the day might come when I would have to call in those chits to convince fans that a particular decision I had to make regarding athletics was done with the utmost concern for the long-term viability of the athletic program. In my case, that day came when I fired the athletic director for NCAA violations, including "loss of institutional control." He had served in that capacity at the university for thirty years and had many booster friends who were not pleased and attempted to reverse my decision. In the end, my decision stood because I had demonstrated by example over the years that I had the best interests of the athletic program in mind, even when it meant the termination of a popular athletic director.

Developing Faculty Support for Athletics

The athletic department, with some coaches paid outsized salaries when compared to faculty compensation, may not be viewed as equals in the same educational endeavor on campus. In keeping with my previous thoughts on the value of the athletic program in marketing the university, the president's challenge is how to help faculty and staff look beyond a few salaries that appear exorbitant and see those salaries as part of the larger marketing and communication strategy for the university. Therefore, your job will be to bring your faculty colleagues along by building bridges between academics and athletics. I can think of two ways to make that happen that neither cost much nor require great effort.

Assuming your athletic booster club has a weekly review of games during the season, ask them to invite a faculty member to the luncheon each week to be introduced as the "faculty coach" of the week. Also, when prospective student-athletes and their parents visit campus to consider enrolling and joining a team, individual sports will hold meetings for the prospects and parents to hear about one or more of your sports. If your AD or coaches don't think of it, offer to have them meet faculty who can describe the majors that are of interest to the prospects. Such an effort not only showcases the academic opportunities the prospects have but also gives faculty a stake in the game, so to speak.

Many faculty members at your institution are engaged in research or scholarship that either directly applies to athletics or is of interest to athletic staff and/or boosters. You might also consider inviting some of them to speak about their work, thereby fostering deeper connections between the faculty and the athletic department. Similarly, many faculty members are engaged in terrific work with students (enterprising teaching practices, inspiring fieldwork experiences for students, collaborating with students on research, etc.), many of whom might be student- athletes. Getting these faculty to talk about what they are doing with students in and out of the classroom and using those discussions to stimulate interest among coaches in the teaching work within which the faculty are engaged can help to break down the perceived barriers between coaches and faculty members. After all, both coaches and faculty members are teachers; getting them to see the commonalities that exist in their roles can go a long way toward building helpful collaborations and alliances rooted in shared interests.

The faculty athletics representative can be very helpful in this regard. The FAR can build the connections between faculty colleagues and coaches that will lead to new relationships and friendships for coaches and faculty that underscore the value of their teaching roles.

THE PRESIDENT'S ROLE IN REPRESENTING THE UNIVERSITY IN ATHLETIC ORGANIZATIONS

Unless you find yourself at a university or college that is independent of an athletic conference affiliation, you will be called upon as president to participate in conference meetings with your fellow conference presidents. Your athletic director will also attend these meetings, and each conference will approach the issue of attendance differently. Some may have the presidents meeting separately from the ADs, while others will have joint meetings or a combination of both.

I found the conference meeting to be very valuable in gaining a better under-standing of the issues facing intercollegiate athletics and interacting with presidents dealing with the same challenges I faced as president. It's a great learning experience for you to bounce ideas off veteran presidents who have experienced so many of the challenges you are about to face.

When conferences negotiate media rights contracts, there is much at stake for ath-letic departments and their universities or colleges. At this moment you need to take stock of your staff's expertise in the byzantine world of sports media. Do make sure you have expertise at the conference table when the conference commissioner or their staff explains how each member of the conference will fare financially from a new contract with a media company. Such expertise will lie either with your AD, CFO, or university counsel. If you are not confident with the level of expertise in any of these, then it's time to seek outside counsel. There are lawyers and consultants for hire who can assist in understanding the implications of a particular relationship with a media company on your athletic budget.

Fan viewing preferences are changing significantly as a younger demographic takes to mobile devices, tablets, and personal computers to view athletic contests. The power conferences still enjoy the financial windfalls that come with signing up with ESPN and other networks, but smaller conferences are finding their traditional relationships with TV media to be less attractive than in the past.

Stepping in to provide new viewing opportunities are digital sports media com-panies that offer what has become known as Over the Top platforms, essentially deliv-ering content over the internet directly to the consumer on the device of their choice. In this new world of digital media, the ideal is a contract for digital consumption but also with the right to contract with regional partners for linear TV coverage where you can get it. Some conferences do require its members to sign over their rights for the length of the TV contract, which locks the school in for years. That is to be avoided if possible, but there is no guarantee you can pull that off in these days of digital dis-ruption of sporting events.

Your athletic director will probably understand these new options available to conferences, but you should also be comfortable with the new approaches to media rights, and always stay focused first and foremost on maximizing your school's reve-nues from new media rights contracts.

How the NCAA Will Impact Athletics on Your Campus

The recent announcement by the NCAA that it will permit student-athletes to benefit financially from the use of their name, image, and likeness is a game changer that will definitely pop up on your radar screen as you oversee athletics on your campus. It's too early to know just how the NCAA will implement what is known as "pay to play," but rest assured it will upend long-standing assumptions about the student-athlete's role as an amateur.

You may find yourself answering questions about the NCAA's decision even though it's certainly not something for which you can be held responsible. Your job will be to figure out how to live with it and still call intercollegiate athletics amateur sports. You may want to point out to fans and boosters that it's difficult to justify the size of coaches' salaries while players who are responsible for so much of the athletic success are not somehow compensated for their services.

Recent focus on racial and social justice prompted by the police killings of people of color on our streets will challenge athletic departments and coaches as they attempt to address this issue of compensating student-athletes. We have already seen how professional athletes have united in support of Black Lives Matter and called for reforms to deal with systemic racism in our society. Although higher education in America has led reform efforts addressing diversity and inclusion on campus, this issue of racial equity will raise the bar on how universities and colleges are to treat student-athletes of color whose athletic success contributes to the financial and athletic success of the university.

We have applauded our athletic departments for increasing the number of underrepresented students on campus by recruiting large numbers of African American players over the years. As commendable as that may be, their role and standing on your teams may be viewed differently today than it was in the past. If the white coaches are pulling down those excessive salaries thanks to the athletic abilities of Black players, it won't take much in today's world to raise some very serious questions about just what a university owes a Black student-athlete whose athletic accomplishments kept the stands full and financial coffers of the athletic department in good shape. And that athletic budget pays for those Olympic sports where you will find very few student-athletes of color. So here's a couple of thoughts on how your athletic department can achieve racial equity in this regard.

Too often, coaches steer athletes to that easy major, and four years later the student-athlete moves on with an academic background not marketable in the workplace of the future. Some parents and their students have very specific career objectives, and they will have no interest in a major recommended only because it's the path of least resistance to eligibility. Some, however, may not be ready to connect a particular major with a particular career trajectory that interests them, so they take the advice of the coaching staff and choose a major that will guarantee four years of eligibility.

I've seen some student-athletes leave the university without a degree to pursue a professional sport, only to return later to finish up, this time not to satisfy eligibility but to prepare for a job and career. If nothing else, athletic departments should make career plans and objectives—beyond professional opportunities—for each of their student-athletes early in their student experience. Some players may not be ready to connect a particular interest with a career goal, but a good faith effort on the university's part will work for many, especially for those who do not intend to play a professional sport.

For those student-athletes who do return to pursue a second degree, the university owes them the cost of that program given how it skirted the issue of career preparation the first time around, in favor of eligibility. This policy may not affect many players, and it may be difficult to administer, but it's a sign of good faith that the university did not just use "Black labor," in the case of student-athletes of color, without giving them equal opportunity to pursue their career goals when they return for a second degree.

My thoughts on this subject come from two directions: first from my experience as a university president and second from my teaching experience at one of the most selective universities in America, just in case you think steering a student-athlete to an easy major is limited to open enrollment universities. During my teaching days, I was taken aback to meet so many football players in my class, only to learn later that they were steered there by coaches who considered it to be an easy major. (To this day, I wonder if that made me the "easy" professor!) You might ask the athletic director how their coaches deal with recommendations for a major and engage them in a discussion of how to accommodate student-athletes who return to complete their degree or to seek a second degree. I believe this is a cost to be borne by the athletic department or the university, not the student-athlete.

CONCLUDING THOUGHTS

You are responsible for the overall success of your athletic program, and it will require far more time and effort than face time at athletic contests. Your athletic program can be one of the pride points of the university, but it can also bring you and the university considerable embarrassment and shame if you and your staff are not forever vigilant in holding your AD and coaches responsible for a program of integrity and success in all respects.

Meet with your athletic director regularly and hold them responsible for a culture of compliance that respects and upholds NCAA rules and regulations. Gain their complete confidence in your commitment to make the athletic program the very best in your conference and make sure you have complete confidence in your AD's leadership of the department. Do not skimp on the time you allot for you and your staff to follow the work of the athletic department, from its budget, the conduct of its staff, and success of student-athletes, to the larger issues before your athletic conference that impact the branding of the university. And, remember, do this work no matter what the size or scope of your athletic department might be—any athletic department can be an asset or liability to an institution. Don't assume the problems, or the opportunities, are confined only to those institutions that host big-time athletic programs. Following those guidelines will bring you the personal satisfaction of having successfully led an athletic department in a time of great change, and it will bring distinction to your university or college.

CHAPTER 9

Academic Medical Centers and Health Enterprises

MICHAEL V. DRAKE, MD

A cademic medical enterprises are some of the most complex and managerially demanding components of the modern American university. As health-care providers, they interface with the public in ways both widespread and deeply personal. Because they are endeavors devoted to education and research, their mission to produce professionals and knowledge to ameliorate suffering is one of the clearest illustrations yet of higher education's value to our society broadly. And as academia's nexus with the $3.6 trillion US health-care industry, they are economically vital to the institutions and communities of which they are a part.[1]

These factors combine to make medical enterprises important and beneficial parts of our universities. To effectively lead them, university presidents must first understand them—their mission, structure, and culture; the ways they complement the broader educational enterprise; and how they can challenge even the most seasoned leaders.

This chapter will be most beneficial to new presidents of institutions with academic health centers or their components. Yet I believe its contents can be useful to leaders of all colleges and universities. At a general level, studying organizations of varying sizes and composition yields valuable lessons that can be applied to one's own situation. More specifically, knowledge of the complicated nature of academic medicine and how it interacts with other parts of campus can help guide leaders as they chart a course for their own institutions. Whether they are contemplating launching a school of medicine, a new allied-health degree program, or an affiliation in the health education or health services arenas, the costs and benefits of such decisions can be made clearer—creating better outcomes for institutions and people alike.

ACADEMIC MEDICAL CENTERS AND MEDICAL SCHOOLS

Throughout this chapter, the terms *academic medical center*, *academic health center*, and *academic* or *university medical enterprise* are used interchangeably as they apply to all health enterprises in a higher education setting. Traditionally, however, an academic medical center refers to a medical school and its affiliated teaching hospital.[2] The broader academic health center comprises these two entities in addition to training for other health sciences vocations, such as dentistry, nursing, public health, or veterinary science.[3] The distinction is one of educational scope, not focus. Each is dedicated to providing patient care, training health professionals, and advancing quality of life through research—the tripartite mission that has long guided academic medicine.

This three-part charge gives academic medical enterprises a significant role in the modern health-care system. It also places them at the center of the many communities they serve. Collectively, these institutions supported 6.3 million jobs and accounted for $562 billion in economic impact annually—or about 3.1 percent of the United States' gross domestic product in 2018.[4] Regional economies depend on them to create and attract talent and to generate innovation and entrepreneurship with far-reaching effects. Additionally, university health enterprises often provide care to the sickest and neediest of patients. Their wealth of clinical expertise, ability to deploy leading-edge therapies, and, frequently, their historical status as safety-net providers create a unique set of responsibilities. One analysis found that these institutions, despite being only 5 percent of all hospitals nationally, provided 37 percent of all charity care, accepted 26 percent of all Medicaid hospitalizations, and received 38 percent of patient transfers from other hospitals not equipped to treat those with complex needs.[5]

Today, academic medical centers stand at the pinnacle of science and technology. Yet they were not always such intellectually rigorous or essential institutions. Except at the most prestigious university programs, entrance requirements for an American medical school in the latter part of the nineteenth century typically consisted of a high school education or simply the ability to pay the necessary fees.[6] Courses were generally superficial and short—some measured in weeks—and graduation was assured to all.[7] Few programs included instruction in the basic sciences or even hands-on clinical experience.[8] Most of our hospitals, too, were a far cry from the venerable institutions of education, research, and patient care we know today.[9]

Despite this chaotic state of affairs, a movement for reform was already building. It began with American physicians traveling to Europe for advanced training and bringing home with them a vision of modern academic medicine and the academic physicians who practiced it. They found fertile soil on the campuses of Harvard and the universities of Pennsylvania and Michigan. This momentum was further catalyzed by the opening of the Johns Hopkins Hospital in 1889 followed by the Johns Hopkins Medical School four years later.[10] The closely affiliated institutions quickly became the model for medical schools and teaching hospitals nationwide.[11]

The Johns Hopkins model also helped inspire another watershed in the history of university medical enterprises. Abraham Flexner, author of the landmark 1912 report on the state of medical education in the United States and Canada, visited Johns Hopkins first before embarking on site visits to all of the countries' 155 medical schools.[12] The report, which codified ongoing reforms in the field, outlined four broad imperatives. They included requiring students to earn a bachelor's degree prior to entering medical school; employing a more standardized curriculum rooted firmly in the sciences and emphasizing practical experience; providing education by physician-scientists who engaged in teaching, research, and patient care; and instilling a spirit of inquiry in each student. Flexner believed this final goal could be best achieved by locating medical schools within institutions already dedicated to uplifting society through the creation and dissemination of knowledge: universities.[13]

Although the marriage of medical education and universities was hardly inevitable, both enterprises benefited from this new arrangement. Including medical education in a university's portfolio further proved its value to society and authority in the advancement of knowledge. Affiliation with a university enabled medical schools to distinguish themselves from lower-quality peers, which made fundraising significantly easier. It also legitimized academic medicine as a career separate from clinical practice.[14]

The affiliation of hospitals with medical schools and universities was also mutually beneficial.[15] Previously, American hospitals had seen little reason to grant inferior-quality medical schools access to their patients.[16] In the late nineteenth and early twentieth centuries, however, they began to adopt a more expansive interpretation of their traditional service mission. This meant advancing patient care not only in their own wards, but broadly through research and the pioneering of leading-edge clinical techniques. In the increasingly scientifically rigorous, university-affiliated medical schools, they found ideal partners. Hospitals gained access to university facilities for basic research, added prestige as scientific institutions, and gained an expanded workforce of medical students and distinguished academic physicians who would deliver an ever-greater quality of clinical care. Medical schools, of course, at long last secured access to the facilities necessary to advance their students' experiential learning.

Through these close institutional relationships—the effect of which is amplified among medical schools and universities that own their own hospitals—educators have a direct influence on the training of interns, residents, and postdoctoral fellows by having protocols built into the patient-care algorithm that take full advantage of these trainees. So, rather than being a purely patient-care-first enterprise in which students have to find a way to fit, leaders of the medical school and hospital can work together to deliver world-class patient care while maximizing educational and research opportunities within the medical center and across the broader university.

BENEFITS AND RISKS OF THE UNIVERSITY-MEDICAL ENTERPRISE PARTNERSHIP

The partnership between medical schools, hospitals, and universities helped solidify a reckoning in medical education; professionalized the field of medicine; and sparked tremendous advances in medical science. In the century since they first affiliated, the advantages of these relationships—to themselves and to society broadly—have only grown.

If universities are concerned with creating broad public benefit through education, research, and service, few of their many offerings provide more clear and immediate benefit than a university hospital that is raising the level of health and medical care in that community. It is tangible, immediate, and measurable. Academic medical centers also routinely provide the highest quality of care available. Several studies have illustrated that patients treated at academic medical centers experience better outcomes than those treated in nonteaching facilities—regardless of the size of the institution or the severity of a patient's condition.[17]

This benefit extends to members of an academic medical center's campus community, who themselves need health care. In addition to having access to the significant resources and expertise of a university medical enterprise, student clinics on campuses with academic medical centers are far more likely to be accredited by a national certifying body.[18] Faculty and staff can, likewise, take comfort knowing they have outstanding health care near at hand.

The health benefit of having an academic medical center in a community or on a university campus is made acutely clear by the COVID-19 pandemic. The centers provide care to those in their immediate communities and beyond through referrals; drive research to understand and treat the disease; and are the source of myriad innovations to care for patients, protect health-care providers, and aid the public during this extraordinary time. Schools of medicine and the other health professions are also making significant contributions. They are graduating students early to help alleviate staff shortages, coordinating medical reserve corps, and supporting those on the front lines in ways large and small.

A university that provides care for its students and employees to a great degree can tailor that care to provide higher quality at a lower price by using the campus as a place to model healthy behavior. The benefits in terms of improved health and well-being are obvious. Modeling this behavior can also create meaningful savings financially. The Ohio State University, for instance, leveraged the expertise of its medical center and health sciences colleges to advocate for and incentivize employee wellness, yielding negative trends in health-care costs several years in a row.[19] This approach to cutting costs comes during a time when increasing health-care costs are common for employers and employees alike.[20]

The research function of academic medical centers is also extraordinarily significant. According to the National Science Foundation, universities with medical schools spent $56 billion on research and development in 2018 when funding from federal, state, institutional, and other sources is combined. Approximately half of this was associated with medical schools.[21] This magnitude advances a university's research mission considerably. It also provides compelling opportunities for collaboration across disciplines. From health-care financing to biomedical engineering to social determinants of health, there are countless investigations for which faculty in the medical enterprise would be effective and excited partners to their colleagues in the humanities or the social and natural sciences.

Close institutional affiliation also creates opportunities for leadership at the medical enterprise to interact with academic leadership across campus to open avenues for better collaboration, improved care, and the provision of synergistic services. The latter includes wellness programs—physical, mental, and more—that go beyond disease prevention to increase quality of life. Finally, if managed correctly, the marginal revenue from clinical services can feed the academic mission by supporting teaching and research.

Academic medical enterprises create tremendous benefit to the broader university, but they can also pose significant challenges. Although clinical operations can generate substantial revenue to advance complementary strategic objectives, providing patient care is also an extraordinarily expensive endeavor. Medical centers generally, and hospitals and clinics specifically, must be managed very professionally to minimize the risks and maximize the advantages to the university as a whole.

Providing patient care also allows a university to interface with the public in ways it otherwise may not. The university thus has many opportunities to do miraculous things—pioneer innovative therapies, save lives, and more—which build public support. There is, however, always a chance for the opposite to happen. Incidents of malpractice, ethical lapses, and other issues can quickly erode public trust and support. Some of these issues can be tragic in human terms, and others can result in tremendous financial liability.

STRUCTURE OF ACADEMIC MEDICAL CENTERS

When the term *medical center* was first used to describe closely affiliated medical schools and teaching hospitals in the 1920s, and the term *academic medical center* was employed for the first time in the years following World War II, the terms already encompassed a variety of organizational structures.[22] Now, as then, each university medical enterprise is unique. In broad terms, however, they fall into two categories: those that are part of the larger university governance structure and those that report to a separate fiduciary but coordinate their operations.[23] Most institutions fall somewhere between the two ends of this continuum.

Among those models with a single fiduciary, leaders of the medical campus may report to the university's president or chancellor, who in turn reports to the university's board of trustees. This degree of structural integration has the opportunity to enable the most alignment across the institution since campus leadership is directly involved in the management of the medical enterprise. A notable drawback to such an arrangement is that a medical center, for instance, oftentimes has policies and procedures that must be extraordinarily responsive to patient care and financial pressures. Yet the deliberative structure at most universities is not designed to move as quickly as a medical enterprise sometimes requires. This model also requires a high level of sophistication among campus leadership to manage the complexities of a medical center.

In a second model of single-fiduciary integration, the medical enterprise reports to a committee of the board of trustees and, through the chair of that committee, to the full board. Institutions in this arrangement benefit by having a focused set of people in campus leadership who are dedicated to the medical center—a benefit that can be multiplied by including subject-matter experts in this board committee. However, the policies and procedures of the traditional side of campus still may not be nimble enough for many within the medical enterprise.

A third potential structure is the medical campus having a separately incorporated board, which handles the affairs of the enterprise in a fiduciary or an advisory fashion and reports to the university's board of trustees. This body tends to be more significantly supported by subject-matter experts. It has the burden, however, of making more decisions and ensuring those choices are aligned with the general campus. In this case, additional autonomy for the medical enterprise creates a more streamlined decision-making process that is generally beneficial to itself and to the broader campus enterprise.

The final structure is a separate medical enterprise with its own executive leadership and board. This structure tends to be the most efficient from the standpoint of the medical campus, but it has a smaller degree of built-in connection and alignment with the rest of the university. In these circumstances, the benefits of having an academic medical center on a university campus are often minimized. There can also be a degree of friction between the interests of the university and the medical enterprise that may or may not be resolved effectively for the greater good.

These are only four of the most prominent models. Other structures certainly exist at points between them or on other positions on the spectrum from full integration to complete separation. One configuration is also not more closely associated with success than another—outstanding examples can be found of each. Additionally, the issue of operational alignment is distinct from that of how integrated structurally the medical and traditional academic campuses of a university may be. While one structure or another may lend itself to a greater degree of alignment operationally, it does not guarantee that alignment.

CHALLENGES OF MANAGING ACADEMIC MEDICINE

Regardless of how the academic and patient-care operations of a medical enterprise are organized, the challenges university presidents face in their management are extraordinarily similar. They can be internal to the medical center, the university more broadly, or between these components. They can also be external. College campuses are truly unique environments, but they and the medical enterprises they host are hardly immune from issues of public perception and the broader forces shaping health care and higher education in the United States and beyond.

Academic medical enterprises demand a tremendous amount of time on the part of a university president. This is a function of the size of medical centers—in terms of budget share, staffing, and capital assets—and the deep investment people and their families have in the medical care they receive and its outcomes. Any controversy in this space, then, can easily become a first-tier issue and overwhelm other strategic goals. Active management to minimize such risk is critical.

As previously described, the culture at a medical center is quite different from that on the more traditional, academic side of a university campus. Consider that the physicians who frequently run teaching hospitals and medical schools, as medical students, each completed a stint in the emergency room or has experience with patients who became emergently ill under their care. In these situations, a provider must gather, organize, and process a huge amount of information very quickly. Contrast this to the shared governance structures found within many universities today, which rightly provide the opportunity for a wide variety of stakeholders to craft and contemplate policies and decisions. Neither structure is more appropriate than the other; they are simply different processes designed for different environments. Yet it is often a university president's responsibility to manage the inevitable friction that arises and to serve as a bridge between these two worlds.

Medical centers also present unique talent-management issues within higher education. Whereas a professor of history, for example, often has to move to another city or state to find a comparable program and position, medical faculty can often join another hospital or practice in town. This ease of moving from one position to another presents retention issues at a medical center that can be very challenging. These challenges are in addition to the ongoing work of managing any enterprise with a significant concentration of highly trained and often self-directed individuals.

University presidents also share with executives of other anchor institutions the challenge of managing staff who may have relationships with prominent community leaders and those to whom the executive reports. This challenge can be an issue among higher education institutions broadly—as any faculty member could have a social relationship with leading community members. Yet these relationships can be particularly challenging in the context of a medical center. A member of the medical faculty who is the long-time physician of a board member, prominent donor, or political leader can bring that relationship to bear if there is a conflict or difference of opinion with a university president. This situation can be uniquely challenging to those university presidents who are not, themselves, physicians or health-care providers, as their perceived judgment in matters relating to managing a medical enterprise will oftentimes be seen as less worthy than that of the well-connected family doctor.

Regardless of whether an enterprise is public or private, for-profit or not-for-profit, its leaders must attend to the business side of the endeavor. This is also the case for academic medical centers and higher education more broadly. Costs must be contained, revenues maintained or expanded, and pressures of competition must be managed in an age of more concentrated nonacademic health systems.[24] They must remain at the leading edge of medical and educational innovation. Added to this issue is the ever-increasing regulatory burden placed on colleges for training, screening, credentialing, and more.

In addition to pressures on academic medical enterprises' bottom lines, a more expansive interpretation of the traditional tripartite mission is taking hold. Clinical teams are broadening their focus from treating disease to preventing it by promoting wellness across a variety of dimensions. Research, while becoming specialized to an ever-greater degree, is also expanding in scope to encompass the many social, economic, and historical factors affecting health.

Medical education is also continually evolving to keep pace with biomedical innovation and the increasing complexity of clinical care and the organizations that facilitate it. Additionally, there has been an almost incalculable increase in the amount of information being processed at academic medical centers compared to a generation ago. Electronic medical records have enabled an unprecedented degree of connectivity among care providers—a connectivity that simply did not exist in the age of handwritten records—but it can also be an incredible burden.

Related to this connectivity is the sheer volume of information available and the increasing sophistication and accessibility of tools to help make sense of it. At the end of the twentieth century, the medical student who could memorize research articles and what they concluded was the star. Now it is the student who can rapidly look up those articles, make sense of their findings, and deploy that knowledge in a meaningful way. This is a huge change for higher education broadly, and medical and clinical education in particular.

This explosion of knowledge, and the novel therapies and procedures it enables, has also driven a greater degree of specialization in medicine and among medical faculties. The triple-threat, tenure-track faculty member who saw patients, taught students, and conducted research was once the standard. More recently, however, the ability of these individuals to effectively compete at a high level in these areas has been challenged by specialists in each category. A surgeon who is dedicated to operating regularly and perfecting their technique will generally be more proficient than a colleague who is in the operating room just once or twice a week. The same goes for those who primarily pursue research—who regularly write and submit grants—versus those who do so only part time.

While the decline of triple-threat faculty may give pause, differentiation into those who predominantly provide clinical care and those who are predominantly research scientists is an entirely natural progression. The next evolutionary stage is to have the same level of focus on pedagogy, with dedicated faculty spending a significant fraction of their time educating medical students and other health science professionals as effectively as possible.

Hospital stays are also far briefer than they once were. Previously, patients scheduled for surgery would be admitted the night before and stay until they were fully capable of going home. For medical students, this meant the opportunity to spend a great deal of time with patients and learn throughout the arc of their care. Now, patients come in the morning of their surgery, quickly head back to the operating room, and move on to postoperative care. Then, as soon as they are stable enough to be discharged, they are sent home.

Medical faculties have grown as well, creating greater opportunities for faculty to focus solely on providing patient care. This was a rarity several decades ago, but these individuals now comprise the majority of medical faculties. Additionally, revenues at academic medical centers—and costs—have continued to rise. Medical enterprises have gone from making up a significant share of university budgets to routinely half or more.

Also of tremendous importance in higher education and health care is the appropriate balancing of the benefits and costs of providing additional or higher-quality services. Both college degrees and medical treatment are frequently expensive. Yet when are they too expensive? In the classroom, for example, if a $10 allocation can educate a student well, then imagine what $100 or $1,000 could do. At some point, however, additional gains in learning may not be worth the substantial additional investment required to achieve them.

This challenge is exacerbated significantly in the world of medical care by innovation and its attendant ethical questions. Thanks to the vision and creativity of research scientists and health sciences leaders, diseases that once ravaged humanity can now be managed or treated entirely. Yet these treatments are extraordinarily expensive. In some cases, an individual course of therapy for a single drug to treat one patient can easily cost hundreds of thousands of dollars. For that one patient, access to that drug is a miracle. But this cost multiplied by the millions of people suffering from the same condition becomes an untenable financial burden on any health-care system or society at large.

Simply no one has enough money to afford treatments like these at a scale large enough to meet the needs of every patient who requires them. The way forward, then, is a question of ethics—to which there is no easy answer.

STRATEGIES FOR SUCCESSFULLY MANAGING ACADEMIC MEDICAL ENTERPRISES

The broad tenets of managing an academic medical center effectively are very similar to those of any large and complex enterprise. Understand its structure and culture, and the environment in which it operates. Get to know people and their work. Communicate with clarity and candor. Lead by values—using principles centrally held by the institution and its leadership as a guide through times both unremarkable and unprecedented.

A new president or chancellor would first want to spend time learning the organizational structure of their institution's academic medical enterprise. Developing a thorough understanding of the medical center's culture would be the next logical step. As stated previously, the culture of a medical endeavor will be different than the traditional academic side of a university. Most of the individuals running or working in a medical center will have trained to provide clinical care—as a physician, nurse, or other profession—in an environment in which significant constraints often are placed on the time and information with which one has to make decisions. These constraints carry over into their management style, and this style can be off-putting for those unfamiliar with it. An appropriate reading of texts describing academic medicine, and resources such as this, can be helpful in this regard. In-person tutorials to appreciate the work of those throughout the enterprise—from the corner office to the community clinic—would also be important.

The incredible importance of communication cannot be overstated. The job of running a university is hard enough that if there is anything less than complete clarity in communication, the challenge can easily become overwhelming. Additionally, many of the most difficult issues a university or medical center faces arise from the failure of someone, somewhere, to actively communicate in a timely fashion. The other side of this is that what was not communicated well to begin with is never as troubling as what results.

Leading by values is also essential. Values act as guides during new and uncertain times, and they ensure we remain on course throughout the day-to-day. Over time, they also keep us consistent and accountable as individuals and ensure our institutions continue to advance their founding ideals while evolving to meet the challenges of an ever-changing society.

Leading by values can be described many ways. But one example, related by a gentleman who worked in the office of former US Attorney General Janet Reno, is instructive. During morning meetings to determine the course of action on a particular policy or issue, she would first ask, "What is the right thing to do?" Then, after settling what was right, she would ask, "Is it legal?" She would go on to weigh the political costs and benefits. Finally, after considering these three factors, she would ask whether it was viable financially. This is the concept of leading by values in action—determine first what is right; then weigh matters of the law, public perception, and money.

The values anyone chooses to live by are the result of deeply personal decisions. Yet they can have a very public effect. When we are leaders of universities and academic medical enterprises, our ability to adhere to these values during extraordinary times can shape people and communities in profound and varied ways.

In many ways, academic medical centers are the heart of the American health-care system—elevating well-being, driving innovation, and preparing future clinicians to provide effective, compassionate care. They are also vital partners to the sciences and humanities across our campuses. These many roles make them a unique and, on occasion, extraordinarily difficult management challenge. Yet it is one we can and must meet.

In little more than a century, academic medicine has propelled medical education and patient care in the United States to previously unfathomable heights. Sickness will always be with us, but the pioneering innovation that takes place every day in academic medical enterprises across the country and around the world has made a meaningful and measurable difference in people's lives. This promise makes the challenges worthwhile and provides all the incentive we need to understand academic medical enterprises, manage them effectively, and maximize the good they can do for society today and for years to come.

CHAPTER 10

Turning Point

....

American Higher Education and the Challenge of Access

EDUARDO J. PADRÓN

On a small patch of green in downtown Miami stands a seven-foot sculpture of a young boy. The boy walks, bent by the burden of a large box strapped to his back. He is alone, as he was almost sixty years ago, a refugee in the hallways of Miami's Freedom Tower. Adjacent to the tiny sculpture park, the Freedom Tower echoed the uncertain footsteps into American life for wave upon wave of Cuban exiles. Many were youngsters, sent forward by their parents to escape the new regime. They walked those hallways with their homes on their backs.

In 1961, at the age of fifteen, younger brother in tow, I entered my new American life in the Freedom Tower's hallways. Operation Pedro Pan, a clandestine US-led effort, brought fourteen thousand Cuban youngsters to American shores, our parents fearing indoctrination and government-mandated separation.

My mother was unambiguous in her parting instructions: no matter what—sick, hungry, or tired—I was to gain a good education, a college education. That meant applying to the famous colleges I'd heard about in Cuba: Harvard, Princeton, MIT, and Yale. Fortunately, I had a local backup; my only acceptance letter came from Dade County Junior College, opened just months before I arrived in Miami.

This fledgling experiment, originating in renovated chicken coops, relieved a critical measure of uncertainty. These brightly lit classrooms became a home away from home for homesick immigrants. The faculty and staff responded to us with enormous care; it was clear that an institution of great purpose and commitment was forged in those early years. In me, a foundation was established that guided my life and work for many years to come.

I reveled in the chance to learn. I remember, to this day, the feeling of self-discovery that burst into my awareness. It propelled my education through a doctoral degree in economics from the University of Florida and led me to the doorstep of a career with a major American corporation in Delaware. Before heading off to start my new job, however, I returned to my roots in Miami. "Chicken Coop College" had become one of the largest higher education institutions in the state of Florida. Upon hearing of my career choice and intention to move to Delaware, one of my former professors looked stricken. "Why would you do that? Your place is here. You're a teacher."

I thought about it. I wanted to give back to the place that gave me a chance. I told myself I'd teach for a year and then move on. But a lot can happen in a year. I taught for several years and went on to become academic dean and then campus president. In 1995, I was appointed college president and served for twenty-four years until my retirement. It was the job of a lifetime.

We tell our lives in stories, often the ones that shape the course of our lives. While my story unfolds against the backdrop of a large community college, what I've learned will, hopefully, prove valuable to anyone entrusted to lead an institution of higher education. I begin with events that shaped my understanding of leadership and the fundamental purpose of our institutions. Purpose leads directly to the heart of the institution—students, each bearing unique vulnerabilities and strengths. Communication, team building, and engagement follow as the crucial elements in support of students and the institution. I then address what is clearly a turning point for both higher education and American society, and how presidents and their institutions are called upon to author a new story for a pivotal time in our history.

THE IMPORTANCE OF MISSION

Several years into my tenure at what is known today as Miami Dade College (MDC), a brilliant member of the English faculty told me his story. "I call it the 'quickening,'" he said. "It's that moment when a student is captured by learning itself. The thrill is in their eyes. It never goes away."

I knew this experience firsthand. I had come to see MDC as the great equalizer, a dream factory attuned to a basic thirst to grow in each student. For all the glamor and gloss that Miami has grown to represent, it remains one of the poorest communities in the country. For the overwhelming majority of the county's high school graduates, as well as its service-dominated workforce, MDC remains the only possibility of a college education and true economic mobility.

Miami Dade College's inaugural class of 1960 numbered 1,328 students. Sixty years hence, still true to its open-door roots, MDC hosts more than 160,000 students at eight campuses and additional outreach centers. It is the nation's largest degree-granting institution. The student profile is among the most diverse and exceptional for the socioeconomic challenges inherent to South Florida. But one data point remains the most remarkable to me: nearly 55 percent are the first in their family to attend college. Crossing this threshold, creating a generational precedent, strikes at the core of poverty and its tangle of implications.

I experienced this as a student and observed it in classrooms and from every vantage point I occupied in fifty years at MDC. The college's mission statement begins with the declaration that "Miami Dade College is Democracy's College." This was well-considered wording. We felt our work was about the most elemental of society's responsibilities: to honor the potential of each person and provide the chance to realize it.

More importantly, our goals and accomplishments had to confirm these principles. We set overarching goals, to be demonstrated via measurable outcomes and data:

1. Access *and* excellence would mark MDC's essential character. We needed to prove the open door to higher education was not a revolving door.
2. Make MDC the school of choice.
3. Eliminate the achievement gap between white students and students of color.
4. Ensure that the distribution of faculty and staff matched the diversity of the Miami community.

Democracy is not asked to guarantee prosperity, but the opportunity to learn and prosper is the backbone of an authentic democracy. I think it is a principle often assumed but not yet realized in our higher education community. We prize talent but not always the opportunity that unlocks it. Such is our ongoing national conversation, never more urgent, about the quality of our institutions and the freedom to learn.

TAKEAWAYS

- Prize opportunity as we do talent.
- Access to higher education will break the cycle of poverty.
- Create ownership of the institution's mission and goals; engage faculty and staff in articulating the foundations of the institution.

STORYTELLING

My years as a student at MDC spurred an evolution in me. The day I spoke up in the Pan American Club meeting and realized people were paying attention, listening to me, remains vivid in memory. Each new chapter in my story has asked me to uncover another expression of myself. And events like the days I spent at the Orange Bowl—where President John F. Kennedy addressed Cuban exiles following the Bay of Pigs debacle, and where years later I roamed the football field, offering entry to the community's college to newly arrived Marielitos—further engraved the college mission in my understanding.

When I became president of MDC's downtown Wolfson campus in 1980, the surrounding streets—indeed, the entire downtown—remained a forgotten wasteland. Establishment of the campus years earlier had been a gamble, and the downtown backdrop clearly compromised the campus's appeal.

Town-gown relations have not always been uppermost for college presidents, but I assure you the investment will reap serious rewards. For a college in downtown Miami, new connections were essential. I began to understand that leadership is often about telling a new story. Along with a merry band of colleagues, I determined that we would begin a new story of Miami, with its very own community college at the center of the narrative.

The new story, at first, appears outlandish, staged in the surroundings of the old. And it begins with a parade. Eight o'clock, Saturday morning, Northeast Second Avenue in downtown Miami, circa 1980, is the old and muted wasteland. But now it's a parade route, flag bearers draping colors from around the world. It is Commencement Day. Hundreds of capped and gowned graduates flow into the street, through the flagway, new touching old, the few bemused, sleepy-eyed denizens of Second Avenue.

Inside the Olympia Theater, the former silent movie palace, the flags take center stage. One by one, sixty-five flags announce the homelands of the class of '85. *"Afghanistan . . . Antigua . . . Argentina . . ."* and the feeling grows until *"Cooba"* shakes the walls and *"Haiti"* signals get up and shake. And finally, the last flag, the *United States of America*, the roaring embrace, the sound of a new story.

In the years that followed, the Wolfson campus served as the center of a downtown renaissance. Small but consequential forays like *Lunchtime Lively Arts*, a weekly outdoor arts potpourri, drew scores of downtowners from their desks, armed with bag lunches. And we lit up the night with events like *Paella Fest*, where Spain's foremost chefs danced around giant woks, serving hundreds of Miamians in formal evening attire. MDC's little campus in downtown Miami was becoming the hottest ticket in town.

I joined with business leaders to found the Miami Bayside Foundation, a nonprofit that created loan programs, small business training, and technical assistance for minority-owned businesses in the downtown district. It has also provided nearly eight hundred scholarships to minority students to attend MDC and local universities.

Sometimes you need others to tell your story. MDC's launch of the Miami Leadership Roundtable brought together US presidents, foreign heads of state, congressional leaders, media voices, and renowned artists. With each fascinating story from the likes of Bill Clinton, Mikhail Gorbachev, Mitt Romney, Oliver Stone, and many more, MDC's role as a civic entrepreneur grew.

But it was storytelling itself that placed MDC at the center of the community's ongoing rejuvenation. In 1984, the college hosted *Books by the Bay*, a modest two-day author soiree. Like the downtown campus, a literary event was a longshot in a city branded more for "Miami vice" than cultural acumen. But twenty-five thousand people attended the event that showcased just twenty-five authors. Miami Book Fair, now approaching four decades, has become South Florida's beloved arts and culture event, bringing renowned authors from the US, Europe, and South America. "All America looks at the Miami Book Fair as a paragon of what a city that loves books ought to be like," wrote the *LA Times*. And colleges across the country began to look to MDC for what a college could mean to its surrounding community.

Not every college president will deal with wave upon wave of immigrants and the literal makeover of a major city. But it will be something in your surroundings that compels your attention and response. The stream of immigrants from 1960 onward gave rise to the need for bilingual education. In the heart of Miami's Little Havana neighborhood, MDC's InterAmerican Center (IAC) soon became higher education's largest bilingual learning endeavor. Similarly, MDC's fourth campus was born from urgent care. The dire shortage of nurses spurred the fast-moving story of the college's medical campus. It now produces 60 percent of the county's nurses. The baccalaureate in nursing was MDC's initial four-year degree, followed by the physician assistant bachelor's degree.

The story continues. . . .

TAKEAWAYS

- Sometimes, leadership is about telling a new story.
- Sometimes, boldness is required to bring about change. Never be afraid to fail; never accept failure. Everything will be alright in the end. If it's not alright, it's not the end.
- Sometimes, start small and build on your success.
- Sometimes, let others tell the story of your institution.
- We tell our lives in stories; craft memorable experiences that generate pride for students, faculty, and staff.
- Always be aware of emerging needs in the larger community and beyond; determine if and how you can respond.

HEART. BRAINS. COURAGE.

You will often hear people describe works of art, particularly films and books, as well crafted. You hear them say, "It was very well done." I ask, "Did you like it?" And the response oftentimes is, "Yeah, it was okay." Art, like life, needs the fullness of romance. It gives us the exquisite, with the now and again ragged edges. We revel and relish and root for the extraordinary—and the ordinary—people who enter our stories with the full range of their humanity in view.

Our students, at MDC and around the world, arrive in every imaginable condition. Whether timid, exuberant, whip smart, or undernourished, they will be the central players. We will have charismatic presidents and brilliant and venerable faculty, but those who pass through, who quicken and flourish in our midst, are the once-in-a-lifetime personages honing their own stories. As a wise observer once told me, "If you want to tell the college's story, line up three MDC faces on a billboard. Underline with 'Heart, Brains, Courage.' There's your story."

At MDC and institutions across America, heart, brains, and courage are often obscured by poverty. Two-thirds of MDC students are low income, and 46 percent live in poverty, according to federal guidelines. And economic life insinuates itself deep into educational and personal life. Sixty percent of students arrive at MDC underprepared for college-level classes, and the same percentage work while enrolled, many full time.

Poverty offers considerable challenges, but whether low income or not, high achiever or not, nearly everything at the college threshold is new for students. It should be a critical point of focus for every college president, one fraught with academic and personal challenges. The greatest number of students are lost within the first six months, and far more are overwhelmed in the earliest days.

The work of Stanford professor Carol Dweck speaks to the mindset that accompanies each student to campus.[1] She distinguished between *fixed* and *growth* mindsets. In simple terms, using a prime culprit, one says, "Math is not my strength." Period, end of story, fixed limit. The other says, "Math is not my strength *yet.*" As Dr. Dweck wrote in an article for *EducationWeek,* "Feeling that math is hard is the feeling of your brain growing."[2]

Dr. Dweck's work underscores students' need to uncover a deeper layer of themselves, essential resources that are foundational to learning. Brains are only one aspect. Heart and courage need to be nurtured as well.

Despite many MDC enrollees' lack of college-level skills, our experience demonstrated that very few actually lacked the necessary intellect to be successful. Far too many, however, believed their own stories: "I'm not smart enough; other students are better than me; I don't belong here." Researchers labeled this experience *imposter syndrome.*[3] From elite universities to community colleges, students arrive vulnerable to the edicts of their own self-judgment.

But simple approaches can help students find a more authentic view of themselves, one that allows them to push back in the face of the inevitable disappointments. For example, the peer mentoring program at The University of Texas at Austin pairs older students with new arrivals.[4] A few words from a veteran student to an overwhelmed freshman—"I went through the same feelings that you're feeling now"—can change an individual's trajectory. "Really? I thought I was the only one."

Many years ago, with the help of the Bill & Melinda Gates Foundation, MDC faculty and staff engineered a model of student progression and support. Preorientation correspondence led to in-person orientation sessions, personal advisor meetings, and development of personal learning plans. These steps proved a critical launching pad for student engagement. With early focus on a major of study area, students moved on to faculty mentors in their second semester.

For MDC, with its very large incoming class, much of this format was new and very challenging. Our advising professionals and faculty underwent a sea change, asked to break with old ways of thinking and take on new responsibilities. In your role as president, your new perspective will reveal obvious need, and the inevitable pushback against change. Traditions are guarded, bound up with how we view ourselves. But institutions live and breathe through each one of us. Change runs through us.

TAKEAWAYS

- Romance of learning—fall in love a thousand times.
- Heart. Brains. Courage.
- At the college threshold, everything is new for students. Be aware of their vulnerability and help them engage and own their learning.
- Change begets resistance; dialogue breaks down barriers.

OUT OF THE BOX

As president, you will surely have days when the buck stops at your door and it won't move. The job can feel isolating. You're in the box, alone, at the top of the organizational chart. Hierarchy in full bloom, encoded in the deepest recesses of your brain, including all the people living in the little boxes below you.

Believe it or not, a simple remedy does exist. My three most important steps to breaking hierarchy's bonds and most other organizational conundrums are (1) communicate, (2) communicate, and (3) communicate. Identify your many constituencies and utilize the full range of communication vehicles, from the old-fashioned face-to-face and the even more old-fashioned print (newspapers and magazines will welcome your opinion pieces), to the already old-fashioned email, and the soon-to-be old-fashioned SMS, blogs, video conferencing, websites, and online media that suit your messaging needs.

Building a healthy, robust organization is difficult; it takes patience and time. Listen and listen well. Not just in the beginning, though you will need to do the obvious reconnaissance. Even if you've already spent years at the institution, I promise you, your eyesight and your hearing will change; much will be different than before you moved into the box at the top. Ask questions. Feel for the atmosphere that exists. Is it free and open? Is there laughter? Fear? Most organizations have a little of everything, and a lot of some things.

The most important communication, however, will be with your team, the group of people you depend upon to help you steer the direction and progress of the institution. You'll want the best of the best around you, and that translates to heart, brains, and courage. It will fall to you to dispel the constraints of hierarchy and break open the boxes. You'll need real dialogue with these people—honesty, passion, knowledge, creativity, boldness, and courage. If you can achieve this, you will have an invaluable asset. A small army, at the ready, to tackle any challenge. And each will take this experience outward to their teams. This is how organizations are transformed.

Of course, a much larger army does exist. But you must leave your office. The workload can be daunting, but don't get stuck inside. Take a walk. Smell the grass. Surprise the registration folks. Drop in on a dean. Most important, talk to the students. They will make your day.

TAKEAWAYS

- Communicate. Communicate. Communicate.
- Listen.
- Build your team.
- Break the hierarchy.
- *Heart, brains, and courage* also applies to the adults.
- Get out of your office! *Now!*

TRUST

As Mr. Murphy has made clear, if something can go wrong, it will. The life of a college president will have its inevitable missteps, but the one place I understood I could ill afford to slip up was with my board of trustees—my bosses.

Trust is the cornerstone I sought to maintain with each board member. Rule number one in keeping faith is "no surprises." Whatever the news, board members must hear it from the source, never second hand, and never ever from the media. Rule number two is to treat board members as the unique individuals they are; find the approach and attention required to ensure each is aware of important developments. Moreover, invite their expertise and ownership. Board champions for the college's efforts are invaluable.

Board relations can be complex and subject to all manner of pressures, but trust and regular communication afforded me the freedom to do my job. Meet regularly and provide each with the monthly meeting agenda in advance. And make those board meetings as uneventful as humanly possible.

TAKEAWAYS

- Communicate. Communicate. Communicate.
- Trust.
- No surprises.
- Handle with care.
- Invite expertise.
- Don't screw up.

TWO AMERICAS

When you're president, understanding that campus challenges exist in a larger universe is a critical reality check. Our institutions reflect, for better or worse, that larger universe. Presidents across the full spectrum of American higher education have an opportunity to change the way our institutions serve the country.

The challenges are well known by now. The *New Yorker*, addressing economic inequities, quoted Irving Fisher, perhaps the most respected economist of his day, in a 1918 address to the American Economic Association. He warned that we face "a great peril," one that will "pervert the democracy for which we have just been fighting." Dr. Fisher concluded, "We may be sure there will be a bitter struggle over the distribution of wealth."[5]

More than a century later, before the very same American Economic Association, Anne Case, Princeton economist, said simply, "American capitalism and democracy are not working for people without a college degree." She is coauthor, with husband and fellow Princeton economist Angus Deaton, of *Deaths of Despair and the Future of Capitalism*.

"The people who are really getting hammered are the people with less education. It's almost as if there are two Americas, one for people who went to college, and one for people who didn't," said Dr. Case at a Brookings Institution conference. *Deaths of Despair* explores the collapse of the American middle class and the epic consequences that accompany the loss of meaningful work. Data show the cruel effects in suicide and life expectancy; opioids, illness, and access to health care; broken families and loss of community engagement, right down to the simple act of voting. Right down to personal dignity.

Balancing capitalism and democracy has always been a delicate affair. No silver bullet exists for a social order so tilted and hobbled. But the authors of *Deaths of Despair* demonstrate that access to higher education is central to restoring balance and the economic mobility inherent to a healthy democracy.

Buried far deeper in our national story are racial disparities, which are also embedded in practices that remain apparent in higher education. The Education Trust's recent report *Segregation Forever?* challenges the nation's top 101 public colleges to finally reflect the nation's racial diversity.[6] The report assigns grades of "F" to 50 to 75 percent of the most selective public colleges for admission of Hispanic and Black students. The report shows that in the past twenty years, little progress has been made.

I believe higher education, like the nation, is at a crossroads. Colleges and universities have scratched at the margins of this challenge for too many years. Without significant change, higher education's graduates will perpetuate the age-old imbalance that has fractured American society. The achievement gap will continue to waste the vast potential of so many students in waiting.

Business and industry are waiting too. A survey by the ManpowerGroup identified 46 percent of American employers who can't find the workers they need. The US Chamber of Commerce says this is keeping 40 percent of businesses from taking on more work.[7] It should be no surprise that undergraduate enrollment overall was down 8 percent between 2010 and 2018, amounting to 1.5 million fewer students, who were disproportionately Black and Hispanic.[8] The United States fell to thirteenth in the world for the number of twenty-five- to thirty-four-year-olds with at least an associate's degree.[9]

Some years back I met a young man leading the development of a new college. He told me neither SATs nor grade point averages would be significant in selecting students. "We're looking for a particular quality," he said. "We're looking for students with grit."

I have witnessed endless examples of this quality of grit. But here we sit, in thrall to rankings from *U.S. News & World Report* and other sources. Measuring institutional excellence by the number of students excluded is insidious and morally corrupt.

Presidents new and old are positioned to address these inequities. Higher education should be taking the lead in making access and success a national priority. Rest assured, this effort will confront the deepest traditions of venerable institutions and the current rush to exclusivity. But the distinction could not be more apparent:

striving to win on the pages of *U.S. News* versus addressing the national priority of erasing the achievement gap and fueling a healthy economy. I'm not saying the road will be easy, but the choice should be clear.

TAKEAWAYS

- Two Americas: those who went to college and those who did not.
- Human beings thrive with meaningful work and suffer without it.
- Change our institutions, change the country.
- Higher education and the nation at a crossroads: can we close the achievement gap?
- Let go the rankings; let in the talent.

INVESTMENT

What is also clear is that higher education cannot do this work alone. Just forty years ago, not a single country in the world graduated even half the students completing college in the US. But the ensuing years have seen zealous efforts to reduce tax revenues, resulting in steadily diminished education spending. The 2017 package of tax cuts, which sponsors promised would "pay for itself," reduced corporate tax collections by one-third.[10] But this is not new. States collectively cut spending to colleges and universities by 16 percent, $9 billion in real terms, between 2008 and 2017. Per-student funding fell by more than 30 percent in eight states, while only five states spent more in 2017 than in 2008.[11]

College presidents can take the lead in delivering a message to state legislators and can call on partners in every realm of the economy to support the priority of funding for higher education.

The loss of revenue has pushed the burden onto students, particularly those from low-income families. In those same years, average university tuition has climbed skyward by 36 percent. Ten years ago, student fees paid about one-third of university operating costs; now they pay nearly half.[12]

In community colleges, the trend is even more severe. In my tenure at MDC, state funding has plummeted from a statute-mandated 80 percent of operational costs to under 45 percent. In Florida, state funding to community colleges is half the allocation per student to universities and two-thirds of the K–12 allocation. Students' yearly full-time costs at MDC, still among the lowest in the nation, have risen by 350 percent over the past twenty years. The burden on low-income families too often puts college out of reach, reinforcing a ruinous cycle of poverty for individuals and communities.

If *Deaths of Despair* highlighted the loss of meaningful work, what shall we say of a society that fails to value learning? That society is sure to not only lose its way economically but also erode its civic and social bearings.

Somehow, though, a false narrative clouds this reality. According to American Public Media (APM), 71 percent of Americans believe higher education funding is on the rise or holding perfectly steady.[13] Once again, time to tell our story.

TAKEAWAYS

- Reduced tax revenues = diminished funding for higher education.
- Diminished funding for higher education = financial burden on students.
- Devalue learning = society in crisis.

STORYLINES

If students are the central characters, then how and what they learn are the main storylines. How you tell the story of your institution will be unique, told in language that appeals to diverse constituencies. The community college story is one of quick response to pressing workforce needs, and deep, durable learning for professional careers. At MDC, we understood that our essential storylines, our academic and workforce programs, needed to attract students more attuned than ever to the shifting economic environment. That goes for the eighteen-year-olds as well as the thirty-eight-year-olds in search of a new foothold in a fast-rushing economy. That same story, from perhaps a different vantage point, needed to impact state legislators and foundations, and especially our potential partner employers.

New Economy, New Workforce

Several years ago, I received a phone call from the CEO of a Florida-based biotechnology firm. The firm specialized in devices used in heart surgery. He told me the traditional bachelor's degree in biology from local universities wasn't meeting the demands of his industry. Biotech was flourishing in South Florida. Could we help?

One year later, with partner support from local and national biotech firms, we developed a state-approved bachelor's degree in biological science with specialties in biopharmaceuticals, bioinformatics, biotechnology, and biology education. An associate's degree and advanced certifications were soon to follow. Several hundred graduates now work for our partner firms.

Partnerships beyond the campus cannot be stressed enough. The economy is much too fluid, with new knowledge being applied that affects curriculum, students' job readiness, and ultimately, the strength of the emerging industries in the region.

Many years ago, MDC partnered with the Beacon Council, Miami-Dade County's economic development agency, to help ensure a viable workforce for relocating companies. Today, MDC's eight academic schools work with partner industries to address curriculum development and access to current equipment and technology. Faculty-industry dialogue ensures teaching and learning are up to date and supports job readiness. Each school offers stackable learning options, including short-term technical and professional certifications through associate and baccalaureate degrees.

MDC was among the first community colleges in the nation to develop bachelor's degree programs, a break with an old tradition of two-year degrees. Pushback came from universities, but workforce data demonstrated that Florida was importing thousands of workers to meet industry needs. These were the storylines that drew strong industry support and legislative approval, not to mention interest from the best students emerging from the county's high schools.

Of significant note, MDC's bachelor's degree graduates average thirty-one years of age, a key segment of the community assuming roles as teachers, nurses, scientists, and other much-needed workforce support. MDC bachelor's degrees are much less expensive than other institutions for both taxpayers and students. To date, MDC offers thirty bachelor's degrees and targeted concentrations across all of the college's academic schools. Ninety-four percent of graduates secure jobs in their field, at average annual wages of more than $58,000.

Once again, partnerships are central to building new and timely programs, efforts that pay off for these companies at the point of the workforce spear. For example, Google, Amazon, AWS, Facebook, NextEra Energy, and others helped us develop the Cybersecurity Center of the Americas, Data Analytics, Cloud Computing, and Robotics. The Tesla Start program led to MDC's Electric Vehicle Service Center, Tesla's only educational partner in Florida.

Partnerships have driven other key workforce projects including MDC's Idea Center, supporting ideas to market entrepreneurship for students and the larger community; Miami Animation and Gaming International Complex (MAGIC), offering degree and specialized courses; Miami Culinary Institute (MCI), fulfilling South Florida's growing need for chefs and restaurant management; and MDC Works, in collaboration with the US Department of Labor and Florida Department of Education, offering career exploration via interactive, virtual, and augmented reality.

TAKEAWAYS

- Partnerships with employers are essential.
- Data is important to make the case.
- Faculty-industry dialogue ensures job-readiness curriculum.

The Enduring Strength of Liberal Learning

With all the effort to respond to a fluid workforce, it would be a mistake to devalue the need for a strong liberal learning foundation. Employers were also telling us that liberal learning mattered more than ever, beginning with communication, critical thinking, and cultural awareness. We asked ourselves the question, "What does it mean to acquire an MDC education in the twenty-first century?"

Several years ago, MDC developed its Learning Outcomes program, rethinking outcomes and how we measure them. After extensive research and debate, faculty established ten liberal learning outcomes. These outcomes were embedded across the curriculum, along with specifically designed assessment instruments. Emphasis was on traditional subject matter, now including technological acumen, but equal importance was placed on critical thinking, knowledge of diverse cultures, ethics, aesthetic appreciation, and, perhaps most importantly, civic and social awareness. Beyond awarding tickets to various careers, our aim was to deliver graduates who could become change makers and discerning citizens.

The last word in liberal learning goes to the arts. For presidents needing to engage the surrounding community, the arts are the natural connection. They link to the diversity of the community and draw partner support both locally and nationally. In addition to the Miami Book Fair, MDC presents a year-round calendar of arts programming that includes the Miami International Film Festival, MDC Live Arts, and MDC's Gallery System, with exhibits open to the public at each campus.

TAKEAWAYS

- Liberal learning for the twenty-first century is still the foundation of higher education.
- Learning outcomes and advanced assessments can deepen learning.
- College graduates: change makers and discerning citizens.

Success Stories

At the height of the Miami Heat's championship years, a friend posed a question: "Who, by chance, would you like to bump into and offer to buy lunch, the unfortunate homeless person or Shaquille O'Neal?" His point was clear: don't cry foul over the state legislature's diminished support. Don't lament the unmet need. Stand as tall as Shaq and tell your success story. And tell it in language your audience understands.

Money talks. Numbers add up. In the midst of a decades-long stall in economic mobility, MDC's students have jump-started their economic standing. In a study by Harvard economists, MDC ranks first among Florida colleges and in the top four nationally among nonselective, four-year public colleges in promoting economic mobility.[14] Thirty-six percent of students move up two or more income quintiles, while 5 percent leap from the bottom to the top income quintile. From college-of-last-resort to college of first choice, MDC opens its doors to all: 90 percent of students choose MDC because of quality, cost, and specific programs.

And be sure your local community knows the value of hosting your college. Every single dollar that society invests in MDC yields $12.10 in added taxes and public sector savings (e.g., reduced crime, lower unemployment, better health). MDC contributes more than $3.4 billion to Miami-Dade County's economy annually, accounting for approximately 2.5 percent of its gross regional product.[15]

If students are the heart and soul, faculty are the backbone of the institution. Faculty relations can be difficult. Faculty are constituency, colleague, collaborator, and sometimes adversary. Turmoil marked my early years as college president, but both sides worked hard to establish an honest dialogue. Confronted by many students who struggle with the rigor of college-level work, the faculty is dedicated to teaching and their creative pedagogy is impressive. Each year, MDC awards peer-reviewed Endowed Teaching Chairs, with grants of $7,500 per year for three years, to outstanding MDC faculty. Teaching and teachers matter.

It should also be noted that the *Chronicle of Higher Education*'s "Great Colleges to Work For" program has awarded its highest honors to MDC for the past fifteen years. This is a "hats off" to the staff and faculty who breathe life into the workday. Engagement matters.

Telling your story via anecdote is important and can be dramatic. But numbers have their own rhythm and resonance. The importance of internal institutional research cannot be overestimated, for both storytelling and decision-making. Numbers matter.

And once again, partnerships matter. Currently, sixty-five institutions welcome MDC graduates, including Smith College, MIT, Georgia Tech, Kettering University, and all of Florida's state universities.

For community colleges, an Honors College is an attractive option for outstanding high school students. MDC provides a full scholarship in an intensive associate's degree program. Graduates who transfer to the nation's most respected universities are genuine success stories.

A final note on confronting the ever-present challenge of funding a dynamic, ever-evolving institution: a robust, strategic effort to attract additional grant and corporate funding is essential. In the past ten years, MDC has earned between $40 and $50 million annually in grants from private foundations, including Gates, Lumina, Kresge, Ford, and others, as well as federal sources. The MDC Foundation also contributed substantially, focusing primarily on building a devoted base of alumni support.

TAKEAWAYS

- Money talks; find the variables and data that distinguish your success.
- Economic mobility is the balm.
- Connect with faculty; they have success stories galore to tell.
- It all matters: teachers, engagement, numbers, and partnerships.
- Be strategic and find additional support.

ALUMNI POWER

History has bestowed a special relationship on MDC and its surrounding community. Generations of immigrants and low-income graduates have established new economic precedents and family traditions. And their loyalty has helped MDC to build an unprecedented community college alumni tradition. The Miami Dade College Foundation has nurtured relationships with thousands of MDC alumni and has established the Miami Dade College Hall of Fame. Each year, the foundation hosts a gala induction ceremony that has yielded more than a million dollars annually in student scholarship support. Inductees range from professional athletes and Pulitzer Prize awardees to local leaders across the workforce.

Those who excel helped jump-start the alumni community more than thirty years ago. MDC's *Everywhere You Turn . . . Successful Alumni* campaign saw billboards across the city with lawyers, doctors, chiefs of police and fire safety, government heads, and more. Many called us, asking to be part of the campaign and support the college. The same goes for the current campaign, *I Am MDC*, stretching from bumper stickers to Facebook and Twitter and back to the *Miami Herald*. We called it a Rolodex long ago; today it's an electronic database, but we never missed a chance to build our base of support.

It was that base of support that allowed the college to establish the American Dream Scholarship, fulfilling the promise that anyone in the greater Miami community would have the resources needed to complete an associate's degree at MDC.

TAKEAWAYS

- Give alumni every chance to give back.
- For community colleges, remind those doctors and lawyers and police chiefs where they got their start.

BE STILL . . .

As one story appears to end, another certainly begins to unfold. I am certain that higher education has never held a more central role in the story of this country, but for both, it will surely be a new story.

So much has changed, even before a pandemic laid bare age-old reckoning with race and inequality, and found our democracy stalled before the moment's challenges. The founding ideals of this country read with the same great promise as they did hundreds of years ago. But what we seem to have forgotten is that institutions were never charged to fulfill those ideals. It was always people. Each of us, understanding the depth of our own promise, working in concert, in community, would bring greatness to bear.

For this once-upon-a-time anxious immigrant, transformed time and again, now steps removed from the complexity of the president's office, I understand one simple tenet more strongly than ever: learning is transformative. Our charge in higher education should be deep and profound: to shepherd this transformation in each student. Take special care of each one. Hold them accountable and help them grow into the next phase of their lives.

Can you remember all of this in the midst of the job's complexity? Not all the time, that's for sure. But come back to it because all the layers of complexity sit atop this purpose. Be still. Ensure that you have space and time to reflect, alone, and in collaboration. Pay close attention to what is unfolding in front of you, but also listen to the quiet voice within you. Be witness to learning as building a house dedicated to learning is the job of a lifetime.

CHAPTER 11

Building Your Executive Team

CYNTHIA TENIENTE-MATSON

As the board announces your appointment, your presidential spirit is ignited with a whirlwind of elation and futuristic ambition. You are likely juggling competing priorities and a myriad of important voices seeking attention. As you move forward, either independently or guided by a transition team, anchor your vision around the existing team. In the early days of the presidential journey, the executive team members are critical co-collaborators. Your aspirations and vision will navigate the assembly of the future leadership cast that can enact your vision.

This chapter provides a self-directed anticipatory lens with various probing questions and exemplars intended to guide your thinking about the executive team. The framing begins with building blocks such as affirming your docu-story, understanding the institutional "truth," and preparing for the unexpected. The spirit underlying the narrative should prompt aha moments that range from self-validation to "okay, think different" and offer an early alert warning for missteps. Some ideas or suggestions include anecdotes braided by personal experience and professional advice acquired from interviews, leadership roundtables, and good old-fashioned hard-knocks from higher education professionals. I hope the ideas and concepts help you seize this moment to embrace who you are, what your presidential leadership will embody, and guide your "how-to" ideation for a high performing team.

SET THE STAGE

There are several approaches to building an executive team, but the bottom line is always about leadership fit, work style, and the organizational culture you intend to create. As Jim Collins describes in *Good to Great*, "Get the right people on the bus, in the right seats"—in other words, identify the who before the what and the how. In higher education, organizational context matters; as you determine team needs, the who matters. Academe values the shared governance consultative approach. As presidential searches evolve, there are increasingly more "closed" selections, and there should be sensitivity with the senior team if the process precluded an open campus visit. As other chapters indicate, a savvy president will assess and identify essential relationships, community connections to the existing executive team, and the regional politics impacting the campus and its key players. These findings may influence the speed at which you assess or rebuild your executive team.

Start with the end in mind. Imagine the last day of your presidency. What do you see? To frame the development of an executive team, as eager and enthused as you are in the transition and onboarding, be sure to direct your energy toward goals and outcomes. Imagine a team that can achieve that foreseeable future.

What does the board expect you to accomplish? If you are part of a system, what does the system head (i.e., chancellor or president) expect you to achieve? Forecasting results provides clarity for the types of individuals, expectations, and the sense of urgency you desire from your executive team. As you set the stage and tone for your presidency, you signal to others what to expect and should launch the support needed to lead the campus. In the early days, resist temptations to say yes to every request; it is impractical and may diffuse the perception of who you need on the team. Remember, you can't do everything first.

KNOW THYSELF; BE AUTHENTIC

Knowing thyself is a simple concept. The actualization is a process of deliberate discovery guided by self-awareness and authenticity. To this point, you have held many leadership positions, but this role, at this moment—this presidency—is different. Building an executive team starts with an in-depth understanding of who you are, how you work, and performance expectations. If this is your first presidency, self-probing may be more in depth. Contextual questions about who you are, typically, can only be answered by you. A personal story is important because it creates connectedness and relatability to those around you, particularly on the executive team. Take the time to reflect and write your narrative, and relate it to the institution you are leading; this transcends into your documentary or docu-story. The following are starter questions to help guide a deeper dive into oneself:

PERSONAL INFLUENCES
- Who am I? Think about your familial upbringing.
- What are my values or moral perspectives? Think about what defines you and how you lead.
- What experiences have led to this point? Think about crucible moments.
- How does my family influence who I am and what I do? Think about the effects of others on your whole self.

INSTITUTIONAL INFLUENCES

- Why were you chosen to lead the institution? What's your fit to the institution?
- What's your narrative? Ensure it is relative to the mission or vision of the institution.
- What is the timing of your presidency? Orient your team-building with the institutional tempo: the beginning of the academic year, mid-year, or following a tragedy or scandal.
- How will influences from your predecessor impact the leadership team?

Understanding who you are comes from an earnest place, and it bears repeating that authenticity matters; your narrative should square up who you are, how you got there, and what's ahead. The president must ably articulate and embody the vibe, integrity, and personas of the institution. The president is not a soloist but guides a multidimensional approach to getting work done—the role of setting strategy, organizational execution, and culture. Simply put, how does the president think, act, and do? A few probing questions may help:

- Will I benefit from a 360-feedback before I start?
- Do I recognize my biases?
- How do I think and make decisions? Think about values or input that guide your decision-making.
- Do I have a specific strength that is a differentiator for the campus?
- Am I aware of my weaknesses and how they may impact my leadership?

Focus on guiding your self-direction, capitalizing on prior self-assessments, scanning results to reinforce natural tendencies, and articulating how you will lead to inform building the executive team. Also, identify areas for self-improvement, and, if needed, call on critical colleagues for direct and candid input. Greater specificity about your behavioral tendencies ensures self-understanding and self-managing and can improve your capability to manage others. A word of caution: do not assume your strong suit and prior accomplishments will be the predictor of future successes. When the president has a deep understanding of their whole self—expertise, knowledge gaps, and blind spots—it tends to inform who is needed to ensure the development of a strong executive team.

KNOW THY CAMPUS

Some boards seek a comprehensive management audit to understand the current state of affairs and to inform the strategy or traits needed by the president. Management audits or reviews are most useful when they provide anonymous insight into organizational perceptions and culture. Although an external review will provide insights, I have found it best to assume nothing. Instead, thoughtfully inquire and intake information from many sources, including colleagues who have previously worked at the institution. As practical, document your findings to determine insights and areas of caution.

MEET THE TEAM

Is there a best way for the president to meet the senior leadership team? The selection process itself impacts the orientation, and the executive team may be present when the board announces its selection. An open search process provides an inkling of the senior leadership team's style and connectedness, in contrast to a closed search, where there is no interaction. Irrespective of the circumstances, never speak ill of your predecessor; whether a planned or abrupt exit, graciously focus on their legacy, particularly with the executive team.

Without a doubt, a team assessment begins before your official arrival. Some presidents prefer a ten-minute chat for self-introductions and transition logistics before an in-depth discussion. Consistently, do what is practical, with the entire team or individually. Ask about customary greeting protocols; assume nothing. Do you prefer handshakes, fist bumps, hugs, or another standard greeting unique to the campus? When it comes to physical touching (i.e., hugs, back slaps, arms around the waist), avoid creating discomfort for yourself and the executive team. Again, assume nothing.

BRIEFINGS

Request specifically curated briefings tailored to unique campus circumstances and include open-ended inquiry, with bios or resumes from the executive team. Before your arrival, this initial communication will signal to the leadership team how you expect to receive information, and you'll gain a glimpse of how the executive leaders present themselves. A few interrogating questions include:

- What are the greatest assets? What are the challenges? What are the highest priorities?
- Where are areas of promise?
- What's working? What's not working?
- What are personnel issues, grievances, or detractors?
- What financial pressures or structural deficits are concerns?
- Are there pending acquisitions, audit findings, legal actions, or regulatory matters that require your attention?
- How does your executive area reflect equity and inclusion?

These lines of inquiry and analyses should inform sense making and prepare everyone for in-depth individual or group meetings. Ideally, there will be a commonality in perceptions about opportunities and agreement on the challenges. Briefings accelerate your understanding of the culture, history, and current state of affairs from those entrusted to lead the campus and help to scaffold an executive team retreat.

LEAD BY LISTENING TO THE TEAM

Briefings provide a nonthreatening opportunity to listen and gain a glimpse into the work style of the cabinet. A fellow CEO said to me that, at this stage, senior leaders should act like "Every day and every interaction is a job interview." You are building a relationship, and listening is vital; I suggest you listen *so intently* that you're burning calories.

As the listening tours progress, triangulate perceptions, including the effectiveness of the senior leadership team. Now you have a tangible product from each team member, a rich understanding of the role they play, and early indicators about fit on the team.

You may desire an external engagement for a leadership audit of an area in question or a strategic review of the executive team. For example, how does the campus leadership advance equity, diversity, and inclusion? An independent assessment documents the caliber of the team and highlights misalignments or dynamics that require attention. You gain speed, openness, and a thematic map provided by the review team, although these engagements may be expensive. There is credibility in a third-party examination of the leadership team, and it may foreground expectations.

THE PRESIDENT'S STAFF AND THE PRESIDENT'S OFFICE TEAM

The presidential staff are vital to your team; they are the lifeline to daily communications, operations, and interactions with board members or other essential constituents. Again, assume nothing. Invest time, ask probing questions to understand their philosophical approach and administrative expertise in managing presidential operations. The president's office staff are your front-line representatives; their actions, personalities, and tone should reflect your style:

- How does someone get an appointment with the president? Who screens invitations and how?
- Are there standing meetings with faculty leaders, students, staff, and the executive team? Will these continue?
- What activities are within the day-to-day operations of the president's office?
- If there is a president's spouse, is there support for their activity?
- Are there board priorities nestled within the office of the president?

ACCESS VERSUS GATEKEEPING

Based on what you learn, do you want open access or gatekeeping? In today's connected workplace, there are endless ways to communicate directly with the president, like text messaging and social media direct messages (DMs), WhatsApp, and video calls or dances (i.e., TikTok). One president shared with me, "I don't do email. If I need to know it, someone will message me, tell me, or text me." I appreciate the pitfall of endless emails. If you intend to avoid email, assign the formalities and expectations associated with the president's office to staff. At the onset, be clear what your immediate needs may be, for example:

- Is there a shortlist of callers who may disrupt your daily routine?
- Do you have any family or personal needs that require immediate attention?
- Do you have external board obligations or speaking engagements that require support?

Also, recognize that a long-standing presidential team may have trusted relationships with board members, donors, or other community leaders. There will be an onslaught of calls and gatherings to introduce you throughout the community. Pay extra attention to the staff team.

In some circumstances, the president may opt to bring along a confidant, such as a presidential aid or chief of staff. If you are fortunate enough to do so, that person is a built-in trusted advisor and understands the idiosyncrasies of your presidency. Such a decision may be vital to a smooth transition; however, it can also cause uneasiness within the existing organizational structure. Be cautious and conscientious in communicating the role and relationship with the executive leadership team.

If your spouse will play a role in the president's office, be clear about expectations and boundaries. One cabinet member shared, "The president's wife joined cabinet meetings. It impacted the openness of dialogue and team effectiveness." The president's spouse can be a vital asset to facilitate communications and personal needs. However, the staff need clarity on spousal duties. Be up front if they are a presidential delegee for specific areas such as invitations, appointments, event management, or initiatives.

THE ORGANIZATIONAL STRUCTURE: TRUTH UP

One college president shared, "Not all who came before you were stupid. People make the best decisions, with the best information before them at the time." Although your fresh eyes may see situations differently, where practical, recognize the executive team's as-lived experiences. As you crowdsource intel, resist the temptation to jump to conclusions or harden your opinions too soon. Compartmentalize the extracted narrative from the stakeholders. Their voices paint a portrait of the *current* truth of the organization. A few ideas to shape your thinking about organizational structure:

- What do you know now that you did not know in the interview?
- Is the existing strategy clear to executive leadership?
- Are the processes or systems for decision-making obvious?
- Are there critical campus relationships or union agreements you should understand?

Take sufficient time to understand the preexisting strategy, organizational structure, decision-making framework, relationships, and shared governance mechanisms already in place:

- Will you continue the existing leadership team meeting structure, or will you replace it?
- Is there a pressing problem that requires immediate intervention or resolution?
- Does the external view of the campus align with the insider view? For example, think athletics.

First impressions matter; use the early momentum wisely. A new president offers a moment for change, reinvigoration, or a refocus to pause decisions by the team. As practical, skillfully balance external influences on the organizational structure and priority setting for the team.

ORGANIZATIONAL HEALTH: TRUTH UP

As one president said, "You can't fire everybody. You need people to do the work." Personnel changes disrupt the flow of information and operations, and there is usually an impact on institutional history and workflow:

- What is the state of current personnel in the executive team?
- How much change can the existing organizational structure handle while maintaining effectiveness?

It may help if you recognize the organizational health "as is," rather than what you want it to be. For example, when there are multiple interims in executive roles, anticipate hesitancy in decision-making or successive turnover. Gauge organizational capacity to act at scale when senior positions are temporary appointments. There is always an abundance of work. Recognize limitations to how many simultaneous changes can occur while sustaining an organization, particularly with interims. Be cautious about tempo, so as not to jeopardize organizational health. Remember, you cannot do everything first.

SENSE MAKING

Early on, likely within the first one hundred days, even without a campuswide strategic planning forum, the picture of the team and campus dynamics has moved from ambiguity to clarity. By now, you have heard or seen various iterations of the organization from many voices. It may help to use a retrospective model to transfer your mental picture onto a thematic map. Sense making is ongoing; it helps identify themes or what's working, and diagnose what needs immediate attention. Organize and frame the information gathered in your transition and early assessment of the senior team.

For instance, in whichever way works best for you (i.e., paper, computer, marker board), you might create four columns labeled "Working exceptionally well," "Satisfactory. Needs refinement," "Broken. Needs immediate attention," and "New Initiatives." See table 11.1 for an example of how to organize information under these headers.

TABLE 11.1 *Organizing themes to create a thematic map*

WORKING EXCEPTIONALLY WELL	SATISFACTORY: NEEDS REFINEMENT	BROKEN: NEEDS IMMEDIATE ATTENTION	NEW INITIATIVES
• Outstanding vice president for research • Diverse • National reputation • High-caliber research activity	• Student academic performance • Organized across three vice presidents • Insufficient accountability • Moderate graduation rates • One interim vice president, one announced vice president retirement, one strong vice president • No gender or racial diversity in leadership • Possible reorganization	• Multiple donors disgruntled with athletics decisions and performance • One donor dissatisfied with the performance within a named college • Inconsistent stewardship, inconsistent communication • Negative feedback about a vice president; may not be salvageable	• Create a new academic program • Transfer to a new athletic conference

Another simple method to organize your data for gathering and framing observations is a universally understood green (go), yellow (yield/slow down), red (stop) light technique. As other chapters describe, the presidency is a marathon. Still, pain points require a sprint to ensure the organizational structure will enable you to reset strategy and create a high performing team.

CREATING THE EXECUTIVE TEAM WITH #HIP (HIGHLY IMPACTFUL PEOPLE)

You know who you are, who you have on the team, and where you need to be. The complexity of the organization is before you, and the immediate initiatives are apparent. Remember, you can't do everything first, so identify three to five significant areas of focus for your first year. If you opted for an external review, the results have identified people or pockets of talent that align with the strengths and opportunities of the institution. Your information gathering has set the stage.

Identify the highly impactful people on your team.

It is beneficial to start from a position of strength, so engage the critical actors who can achieve your priorities. Do you want the senior leaders to stay on the board? If someone is vital to the future state of the institution, make sure they know it. Early on, it's impossible to overengage or overlisten. Talented people always have the most options, and you want to ensure there is no confusion that those at the highest levels of the organization are necessary to create a high performing team. Remember, as your team is getting to know you, affirm their importance, engage them as thinking partners, and solidify their role on the team. Be generous with praise, where warranted. As you examine talent, the questions are more granular:

- Who stays? Are the right people in the right seats?
- Are there rising stars who can step into leadership roles now? Engage them early.
- Are you at risk of losing high performers? Identify them. Engage them.
- Are there critical areas with unfilled vacancies that jeopardize future performance?
- Are there succession plans for key positions?
- Does the cabinet reflect the diversity of experiences, skills, and perspectives of the community it serves?

REASSIGN, REORGANIZE, OR REMOVE

If you are fortunate, all cabinet members magically fit with your work style and are the right people to cocreate and enact your vision. If not, consider the three *R*s: reassign, reorganize, or remove. Or, as Jim Collins suggests, "get the wrong people off the bus." It's worth exploring all possibilities, with strategic advice from human resources or legal counsel, before removing anyone. Ideally, before your arrival, the board will have released anyone who is genuinely incompetent. As you identify a misalignment, explore possibilities; a technically competent person with a positive attitude is prime for reassignment to a position better suited for their talents, or the "right seat on the bus."

In some cases, reorganizations align with leadership talent or elevate new opportunities. If reassignment does not fit, there is likely an incongruence in either work style, pace, or leadership practices. A few simple questions may help clarify the obvious:

- Is there a shared sense of urgency or shared work ethic?
- Is there a joint agreement on opportunities and challenges?
- Is there a level of trust? If not, can it be developed with time and clear dialogue?
- Do others on campus respect the person?
- Is there resistance to change?
- Do you have a problem spotter versus a problem solver?

One president once told me, "Hire slow, fire fast." If you need to remove someone, don't hesitate to make leadership changes within your honeymoon period. Everyone is watching, and it will become glaringly obvious if the senior leadership team is not working well together.

Whenever vacancies occur, by removal or by attrition, implement a credible selection process. There is value in using executive search firms, particularly those with depth in background checking candidates. Your initial hires are crucial, particularly if you have a prior history with them; having such a relationship not only becomes a value judgment on your credibility but also reduces the odds of a wrong hire. Never tolerate illegal or immoral behavior—new hire or not. Transparency rules. In the case of a bad hire, share what is permissible and always inform the board or system head about dismissals.

THE EXECUTIVE TEAM: DETERMINE THE CRITICAL POSITIONS

It bears reiterating that senior academic and administrative roles are complicated and face an enormity of challenges as they are continuously balancing new expectations while preserving quality in teaching and research activities along with the business of running a campus.

Holistically review the composition of the executive leadership team, and ensure critical positions create synergy by building on strengths and filling in weaknesses.

Cabinet members should be respected and held in high regard. If they have been on campus for any length of time, rest assured someone is unhappy with a decision they made along the way. Avoid confusing unhappiness with a lack of respect. Everyone will not get along all the time, but avoid dysfunctional behavior.

Generally, the cabinet includes the provost, chief financial officer, chief student affairs officer, and other members varying by institution size, Carnegie classification, and regional influences, to name a few. The span of control between the president and executive team varies to meet the unique needs of the campus but usually encompasses between four and ten. The variations include enrollment management, institutional advancement, general counsel, research, athletics, information technology, marketing and communications, diversity, and so on.

There are also variations on meeting structures:

- Weekly cabinet meetings with detailed agendas about a broad range of topics, or biweekly cabinet meetings with one or two strategic issues
- An extended monthly cabinet meeting that includes academic deans
- Periodic roundtables, leadership councils, or executive summits with deans, chairs, and other administrative managers

There are no hard-and-fast rules, except what works best for you to achieve the desired culture and strategy. Initially, an off-site extended cabinet meeting is ideal for sharing early perceptions or expectations with the executive team. Later, a retreat provides a forum to incubate ideas, engage in team building, and foster cohesion. Gauge the readiness and timing for team development within the first year. A facilitated retreat should establish short-term initiatives and long-term strategy.

LASER FOCUS EXPECTATIONS

One vice president said to me that adjusting to a new president was like "getting a new job, without going anywhere new." This statement captures the essence of new expectations and necessitated self-adjustment because the leadership style of the new president was markedly different. At the onset, as you contemplate the executive team, help them avoid assumptions about your expectations.

COMMUNICATION

It should be evident that communication is critical, and the clarity of expectations can mitigate unintended missteps. As president, you are consistently messaging early and regularly about expectations. Assume nothing. One president says, "When in doubt, shout it out," and this easy-to-remember adage supports the universal "no surprises" rule. The president's staff will create systems to monitor, prioritize, and anticipate your needs once they understand your preferences. Here are some other topics that you should not overlook sharing with the team:

- How do you prefer to receive information? Be explicit. If you prefer text messages over emails or email briefings before face-to-face meetings, now is the time to share.
- What constitutes an emergency, and when do you want to know about it? Be clear.
- Do you want to know about communications between staff and board members?
- When will you talk with the media?
- Will you have an open-door policy for students or parents?

Keep in mind that the new team may be excited or nervously anxious about your arrival. Make it easy; answer the unasked questions:

- Are there times of the day or night you have declared off-limits?
- What nuances help you function best? Exercise? Sleep? Certain foods? Certain habits?

The president is in the proverbial fishbowl; if you know your triggers, share them in advance. The presidency is nonstop and demanding, so do your part to preempt conditions that create negative energy.

DELEGATION

One president shared, "I delegate everything. I expect the cabinet and staff to handle it." Delegation works best with experienced colleagues who also happen to be mind readers. They know what you need, when you need it, and deliver without fail. Absent that, you may need a feedback loop, such as a shared mobile app, Google docs, or regular updates at face-to-face meetings. Assume nothing. As you rely on the cabinet to work together and accomplish the business of the university, you may need a feedback loop on several initiatives or selective follow-up on items of critical importance. Whichever it is, make it clear. Who will follow up directly with you or your delegee, and when?

It's best to avoid micromanaging; however, if you intend to micromanage an issue of high importance to you, make it clear that you are intentionally doing so, especially when you delegate activities and request updates.

TRUTH-TELLING

One president shared with me, "These are complex jobs, but one fundamental concept to uphold—honesty is always the best policy." The most vital inner workings of the senior leadership team are grounded in truth-telling and integrity. It should be unabashedly straightforward that you will not shy away from bad news and the truth. It may be useful to share your intentions with direct and concise explanations of what you mean when you insist on frankness, honesty, and integrity. It helps to provide an expectation along with an exemplar for clarity.

> *Expectation*: Act with integrity and candor with the president and cabinet colleagues.

> *Exemplar*: Offer phrases to the cabinet that exemplify what you expect them to tell you, such as "it may be a mistake," or "have you considered an alternative," or "there are errors or factual misstatements." Gain impact by sharing in writing and repeating in a formal setting your expectations for honesty. Be openly welcome to a shared expectation to avoid situations that compromise the campus or put the president at risk.

TRUST

Truth-telling builds trust, which advances the betterment of a common purpose. Teams displaying trust tend to share feedback openly; they readily explain their thought processes and admit when they don't know something. The team members are accountable and look out for each other; they engage before a hot topic lands on the president's desk. The ultimate appearance of trust is visible when the executive team advances the institution's needs ahead of their division or departments.

Trust is a bilateral and fundamental value in building cohesion. Use the presidential voice to engender trust with the team and, in individual meetings, offer direct and constructive feedback.

DIFFERENCES OF OPINION

One president shared this: "I'm but one voice at the table. I don't expect everyone to agree with me." Set the stage and grant permission to disagree, with respect. There are varying degrees of difference; the spectrum includes reasonable, healthy disagreement to divisive undermining and everything in between. Establish an agenda that culls out competing ideas or critical feedback to ensure all perspectives are shared and, where practical, invoke the "no surprises" rule. No one wants to learn about an initiative that impacts their area at a cabinet meeting.

A difference of opinion or a bona fide dispute is tolerable, albeit uncomfortable, even when the parties agree to disagree. Create an environment of opposition for the right reasons:

- Is the activity potentially illegal or unethical? There's no scenario where this is acceptable.
- Does the decision embarrass or compromise students or appear to be discriminatory?
- Will the university be at reputational or fiscal risk or assume unnecessary liability?
- Will the actions create an adverse impact on a particular group or create unintended consequences?

Take time to discuss the difference between day-to-day issues and controversial conversations, if possible, before they arise. All viewpoints matter, and ideally, consensus prevails; otherwise, final decisions reside with the president.

A repeated pattern of disrespectful disagreement is undermining and a signal of dysfunction, and that cannot go answered. One president reflected about an adamant clash between the CFO and provost. The president invited them both to a closed meeting, listened to all sides, and made a decision; the provost vehemently and publicly disagreed and subsequently resigned. There was no trust or ability to create cohesiveness for the team.

BUILD A DIVERSE TEAM

The president must lead, and the cabinet must act purposely to create an inclusive culture. Seek ways to hear diverse and different voices, and look for signs of marginalization or deficit thinking. Recognize that fear of retribution may prompt some to withhold feedback or skirt engagement. The cabinet should look for those whose experiences or authenticity may not fit the organizational norms or culture.

Use it, don't diffuse it. Use the presidential voice to champion awareness, knowledge-building, and institutional capacity for diversity, inclusion, and equity. As you build a team, seek out candidates who have broad backgrounds that complement or share missing perspectives. Where practical, mentor diverse candidates in senior roles and recognize that this may require an additional investment of time to teach someone to be an effective administrator and cabinet member.

EXPECT THE UNEXPECTED

One president shared that on his first day, "The campus experienced a multistudent death resulting from an accident on an academic field trip." Another shared, "The system head was terminated the first month into [new president's] tenure," and another said, "I had to fire the CFO for malfeasance." No one is ready for every unknown circumstance that might arise, but you must be poised to lead and direct the team in unexpected situations. Create a circle of trusted colleagues outside the institution where you can vent, refresh, and reenvision the next steps. There is strength within the presidential circle. Use it.

The prolonged period of disruption caused by the pandemic, racial injustices, and an economic downturn have changed how we operate. COVID-19 has fundamentally rewritten how we behave and think about an open campus environment—a fundamental value in higher education. Everyone has embraced technology, including boards, for emerging and uncharted demands; the president's mindset and honest communication can catalyze confidence during unexpected and uncertain times.

Higher education moves slowly within a world that hurries along rapidly. Managing within a pandemic has uprooted all sense of normalcy and thrust all leaders into a warp-speed transition to remote instruction with varying teaching and learning modalities. As one provost shared, "The yellow notepads disappeared." We've reset, at least momentarily, that higher education can be swift and responsive, where warranted, without bypassing shared governance. And we know that remote work is doable. We can expect the business model to change to meet future needs. Funding constraints are inevitable, especially in the aftermath of the pandemic. Political winds will impact your university as local, statewide, and national politics shift. Be prepared for the unexpected and be ready to repeatedly motivate your team. These crucible moments will influence your campus, and a high-performing executive team will have a competitive advantage in the uncertainties of tomorrow and be poised for the opportunities ahead.

CHAPTER 12

Managing Financial Resources and Strategic Planning

SUSAN D. STUEBNER

In March 2016, when I was appointed president of Colby-Sawyer College, a private comprehensive college in New London, New Hampshire, of approximately one thousand students, one of the things the trustees wanted to do was renovate the kitchen in the president's house before my arrival. The previous president and his wife ate most of their meals out because the kitchen was barely functional. I was grateful for this gesture by the trustees for personal reasons and for the hopes of using the house much more actively and having a space to prepare food.

By June, the previous president had moved out, but there was no progress on renovating the kitchen. It was an awkward spot for me: I did not want to pressure this to happen when there were many other needs at the college, but, since the trustees had approved it, I wanted the renovation to proceed before my move in July. Over the previous months, I had asked for several financial documents, including a ten-year review of operating revenues and expenditures, the latest budget to actual document, and financial statements. I also asked for a number of enrollment measures, such as a ten-year history of applications, acceptances, deposits, and information on financial aid leveraging. By June, I realized that our incoming enrollment figures were much lower than expected, and we were going to have a sizable deficit to which to attend. The kitchen became less and less important to me, but our chair of the board wanted it done, so I pressed for more information.

Beyond the elements that I requested, one of the most frequently neglected schedules that is of utmost importance to review is cash flow. And from my request about the kitchen in mid-July after arriving on campus, I discovered that the college had been using restricted funds for a major building project simply to balance the budget for the past two years, masking the underlying structural deficit and exhausting funds for a kitchen rather than for the real priorities at the college.

One of the trustees felt so strongly about the kitchen that she donated a gift to get it done, so that small detail was accomplished. But as a first-time, new president, I discovered that the college had over a $3 million structural deficit for operations plus an additional cash deficit of nearly the same amount and projections for lower than usual enrollment for the upcoming fall. There was much work to do, and none of it was going to be easy.

ROLE OF THE PRESIDENT AND THE BOARD RELATIVE TO FINANCES IN HIGHER EDUCATION

While the board of trustees serve as the ultimate fiduciaries of any institution, it is absolutely critical for the president of the college to be adept with reviewing financial schedules and knowing what questions to ask of your chief financial officer (CFO) upon arrival and throughout your presidency. While the chief financial officer should be asking these questions as well, this cannot always be assumed; the president must have a broad and deep understanding of finance, especially in this era of challenging demographics, pandemics, and other stresses that have hit our institutions. If a president feels as though they do not have these skills, there are a number of conferences or books they can access. A number of seminars for new presidents include at least a module on understanding the basic financial schedules and review the types of strategic questions that should be asked. Kent Chabotar, former president of Guilford College, has also written a number of articles and authored a book on strategic finance that can help a president develop a strong financial foundation.

Having a strong board with some financial allies can be a huge help in this regard. Upon my arrival at Colby-Sawyer, the chair of the board rotated, and I was fortunate to have someone who had significant financial savvy. He had been asking the right questions of the staff prior to my arrival but not getting the appropriate answers to understand how cash was being used to mask the underlying problems at the institution. During my first year of the presidency, one of the major goals my chair of the board and I shared was to populate the various financial committees—Audit and Risk as well as Finance and Investment—with strong chairs who could be partners with us in truly uncovering all of the institution's financial challenges and, more importantly, helping vet the plan to ameliorate the situation. I again was very fortunate to inherit a number of strong trustees. The Audit and Risk Committee was chaired by a former partner of one of the top four accounting firms, and our Finance and Investment Committee chair had extensive financial expertise as well. Between the chair of the board and these two committee chairs, I was lucky to find myself with an instant team of trustees on whom I could rely for assistance in making sure no points were missed and that the turnaround plan was sound.

One of the other decisions we made around this time was that all trustees needed to have a better understanding of the college's finances. For several cycles, even though the Finance and Investment Committee met frequently, all board members received a thorough finance update at the full board meetings where the content mirrored what we discussed at finance meetings. We covered basic things like definitions of the operating budget, reviewed the operating budget, identified issues with cash flow, underscored the importance of the endowment (including how much could be spent and under what circumstances), and talked about debt.

Another financial teammate that was under a great deal of scrutiny and discussion at this point in time was our auditing firm. The trustees were unclear how the administration could have been spending restricted funds with no mention from the auditors at previous meetings. The auditor's role is to provide an independent assessment on the college's finances and practices, and so this was a concern to the trustee leadership and to me. We met with the top partner in charge of higher education at the firm and made some changes to the structure of our audit. We changed the partner in charge of our audit, who seemed to have become too comfortable with the college account. We had the top partner in charge of higher education as one of the reviewers of the audit.

A final key player in the governance of higher education finance is the chief financial officer. Having someone you can trust and who can give you accurate, timely, and effective information is critical. I ended up having to make a change at this position early in my tenure—earlier than desired as a new president—because the quality of information was simply not present. As president, I was having to get far more involved in the finances than was helpful given the number of cuts and strategic issues to which the college needed to attend. One of the trustees called me the best chief financial officer with whom he had ever worked. While I was grateful to have these skills to see us through this turbulent time, I needed to delegate more if I was going to be president, not chief financial officer. And unfortunately, this required a new chief financial officer. While most strong chief financial officers will come from a background of having some accounting experience, this is not always necessary. What is most important is that the CFO have the ability to ask questions of the financial data in a significant manner and understand the variety of schedules and components that make up a chief financial officer's responsibilities. In addition, at a smaller college such as Colby-Sawyer, it is important that the chief financial officer not only be able to delegate tasks to their direct reports but also to roll up their sleeves and do project and strategic work.

ASSESSING FINANCES ON YOUR CAMPUS

While new presidents always have a lot of questions to ask, it is important that presidents continue to stay in close communication with their chief financial officers about a number of schedules:

OPERATING BUDGET. I find the most helpful tool when looking at finances is a ten-year history of the actual revenues and actual expenditures related to an operating budget. Not only does this help you see in which years expenditures may have outpaced revenues, it also enables you to identify trends across the divisional areas of where there is significant growth in a positive or a problematic manner. Because Colby-Sawyer is a traditional institution, one of the areas of significant growth we saw that was initially a puzzle to me was in the use of adjunct faculty. This did not make initial sense to me as our full-time faculty did most of the teaching. Two elements were putting pressure on this trend: (1) the college was growing its nursing degree, which required more adjuncts than full-time faculty, and (2) we had to make a number of personnel cuts my first year, which required hiring adjunct faculty to fill the gaps in academic content. Without the ten-year review, it would have been difficult to know what questions to ask and to get the right answers.

BUDGET TO ACTUAL. It is also very important to stay current with how the institution is doing during the current fiscal year. The budget to actual schedule highlights what areas are on track to be within budget and where any problem areas may be that are running too high in terms of expenses. There may be logical explanations for the trends, but there may be a need to have a discussion with the divisional vice president to fully understand why the expenses are running ahead of projections. Many times it is a timing issue—for example, travel for admission occurs mostly in the fall and spring, and that significant line item may be running near 100 percent before the fourth quarter. But sometimes it is not a timing issue and interventions need to occur.

CASH FLOW. It is critical that presidents understand the ebbs and flows of their cash stream on campus. Typically, cash will be steady in the fall and early winter months because that is when tuition dollars are collected and cash is coming to the institution. However, the fourth quarter—March to June—can be a period when cash is very lean, and it's important to be able to see from a cash flow summary whether the college will make it through this time without any interventions. Colby-Sawyer, like many small private institutions, has an operating line of credit, and we rely most heavily on this line of credit in the fourth quarter, especially in June. In my first year at Colby-Sawyer, we had to transfer $1.8 million from quasi endowment to cash because of the deficit practices that were ongoing.

AUDITED FINANCIAL STATEMENTS. Another source of financial information are your audited financial statements, which typically are available in the fall if your fiscal year runs July 1 to June 30. The audited financial statements have three primary schedules: statement of financial position, statement of activities, and cash flow statement. It is important to remember that any audit shows these three statements as a point in time. The statement of financial position shows assets, liabilities, and changes in net assets. When you are president, understanding what drives the changes in net assets is a very important measure. The statement of activities is close to an operating budget in that it shows the functional areas of the college. This statement also breaks out the revenues and expenditures by restriction of donors. Understanding whether the college is operating within its means is the primary question to answer with this statement. The statement of cash flows provides a snapshot in time of cash on hand at the end of the fiscal year. It is important to understand what drives the differences in a year-to-year analysis that are shown on the statement. Often it is a timing issue, but it is important to ask the question why cash is greater or lower than the previous year on the larger items.

A college's financial statements are sent to the Department of Education (DOE) each year and are used to calculate the DOE's financial strength ratio. This ratio uses data from your audited financial statements to calculate a score up to a maximum of 3.0. Schools that have a score under 1.0 are deemed at risk and often have to work with the DOE to provide additional information about their finances. This process is in place for any school that receives federal financial aid. Thus, another question for you as president and your CFO to ask your auditors about major financial decisions is how it will impact your DOE financial strength score.

ENDOWMENT. A good trustee committee paired with an investment advisor is needed to adequately monitor and grow the endowment. At the same time, the president should not delegate all activities relative to the endowment to trustees. It is important to understand what proportion of the endowment is restricted (that is, must be used for specific purposes such as scholarships) and what part is unrestricted. It is important for the trustees to understand these definitions as well, including how much board-designated or quasi endowment exists. Board-designated or quasi endowment includes funds that the board authorized to place into the endowment and, as such, they have the authority to use in the future with fewer restrictions. Most institutions have a cap on annual spending at 7 percent of the endowment of the restricted and unrestricted portions (though the recommended amount is much closer to 4 percent); however, in times of emergency or when a strategic project arises, the board may determine they want to allocate a portion of the quasi endowment, and they may do so at a value higher than 7 percent. It is also helpful for the president to at least annually have a conversation with the chief financial officer about the spending formula calculation—typically a twelve-quarter or three-year trailing average of the endowment value—and to ask how many funds might be underwater (at a lower amount due to market returns than the original gift).

For a president, it is not essential that you are familiar with every fund in which your endowment is invested; however, it is critical that you are familiar with the institution's investment policy statement (IPS) and are able to ensure, along with your chief financial officer and investment firm, that the college is staying within the parameters of the IPS. The IPS outlines what types of funds an endowment will be invested in and at what ranges. It also typically speaks to an institution's philosophy about the spending formula for operations as well. Most institutions have endowment strategies that are lower risk and made with an eye toward long-term growth. There may be instances where this changes; however, since the endowment is to last in perpetuity, it is important not to make very risky choices with that money. A good trustee committee is essential to the management of the endowment, and it is important for the president to be well versed enough to ask good questions of decisions being made at the global level to ensure the IPS goals are being met and that the endowment is protected from unnecessary risk.

DEBT. It is also imperative that a president understand how much long-term debt the college carries as well as any lines of credit that are used for operations or other purposes. Many times, long-term debt requires covenants, or standards, which the college must achieve in order to remain in good standing with the lender. Understanding the terms of the debt as well as what the college needs to do operationally to remain in good standing is very important for a president.

CAPITAL NEEDS AND DEFERRED MAINTENANCE. A final area that is critical to understand is the college's current capital needs and approach to deferred maintenance. Does the institution have funds set aside for these important expenditures, or is it reliant solely on gifts to cover capital needs? All colleges and universities have capital expenditures as our infrastructure typically includes aging buildings and the need for state of the art information technology. Understanding what the sources of funding for the highest priority areas are in this category is crucial. In a perfect world, an institution would have a capital budget in addition to an operating budget that covers the most critical items. Absent this, it is important to talk with your chief financial officer and trustees about how gifts will be used and what level of gifts are needed to cover the main costs. Delaying spending in these areas often causes problems with even higher price tags, so staying on top of capital needs is very important.

WARNING SIGNS. When examining these components of an institution's finances, there are some warning signs for which to monitor.

If you have one or two senior officers who consistently have expenditures that outpace their assigned budget, this is a sign that either insufficient funds are allocated to that area, or the particular senior officer may not be as strong at budgeting as needed and additional help may be required. Reviewing the budget to actual percentages throughout the year is important in terms of seeing what areas may be outpacing the allocated budget and where insufficient funds are being spent. The percentages can be deceiving—as mentioned earlier, certain areas are very cyclical and may have their expenses front-loaded, so the percentage used may be quite high even with much of the academic year remaining. Being able to understand the context behind the percentages is important.

With cash flow, it is critical to have a cash "budget and actual" statement that helps you as president understand if you are meeting cash flow needs. There will be times when the institution is lower on cash, especially the fourth quarter, but if for some reason the actual is not meeting the budgeted amount, that would be worrisome. Another warning signal would be if the college had to access an operating line of credit right around the time tuition payments are due and cash should be more abundant. Having a good rapport with your CFO around cash is critical.

One of the most important warning signs around debt is any covenants the college has and not being able to meet them. It is important that as president you understand the covenants, if any, associated with your long-term debt and how different financial decisions might impact the covenants. Here again, it is crucial that your CFO works closely with you and relies on assistance from your auditors about how certain gifts or other large amounts of money might be credited and in what fiscal year so that you have the best chance to meet your covenants.

For the college's endowment, one of the warning signs to monitor is how well the endowment compares to benchmark performance measures. If your funds consistently underperform, you may not be invested in the right types of funds within the categories of your IPS. It is also important to keep an eye on the percentage allocation of your funds relative to your IPS. There will be instances when the Investment Committee determines it is okay to go above or below the values of the IPS, but those instances should be short term in nature.

In a perfect world, colleges and universities should budget for deferred maintenance, but this is not always the case. Absent a capital budget, it is very important that a president work with the CFO to know the primary sources of funding possible for dire capital needs. Even if there are not sufficient funding sources, understanding the primary maintenance issues for each building is one way to keep track of capital needs and work with both trustees and donors on funding. Neglecting capital needs only amplifies future costs associated with them. At Colby-Sawyer, we are fortunate to receive approximately $1 million in estate gifts each year, and until we can fully fund a capital budget, the trustees and I have determined that these unrestricted gifts are best used to help protect the institution's physical plant.

APPLYING FINANCES IN SUPPORT OF OPERATING AND STRATEGIC GOALS

Operating Goals

There are a number of methods for building an annual operating budget. Some basic tenets are to communicate the broad assumptions for the budget to the campus community so they are aware of the overall pressures on the budget. It is also important to set a schedule for approval with your board of trustees. At Colby-Sawyer, we set tuition and fees for the following year at the fall board meeting, which allows us as a tuition-driven institution to begin to estimate revenues. We spend the early months of each calendar year asking budget managers to present their estimated expenses. We present a tentative budget at the spring meeting in May, which allows us to begin the fiscal year based on our best knowledge of enrollment and revenues. Our final budget is approved at each October meeting, once enrollment and financial aid outlays are confirmed.

Beyond the basic calendar of approvals, there are also different approaches to building a budget. At Colby-Sawyer, we do a version of zero-based budgeting each year in which each budget manager is responsible for articulating why each budget line is included and why the specific amount. A purer form of zero-based budgeting is to have budget managers start from scratch each year and rebuild a budget based on the current year's needs. Many institutions also simply do an incremental budget, wherein the overall budget of each budget manager increases by a certain percentage and the budget manager can allocate the specific line items within their overall budget to meet that increase as needed by programmatic demands.

There is no "right" way to do budgeting, and it should serve the circumstances of your institution. At Colby-Sawyer, we have gone with the modified zero-based budgeting because we still are working with very little margin and have not had a situation where we can provide incremental increases across the board yet. Thus, it helps us to have each budget manager reflect on and justify each budget line to ensure that the expenses are absolutely necessary.

One of the budget items that typically is handled separately from the operating budgets is salaries and benefits. At Colby-Sawyer, any new positions requested are vetted by our Senior Leadership Team, a group of vice presidents as well as a representative from the faculty and from the staff, to determine whether the request fits with our strategic plan and is needed. In many cases, we need to reduce costs elsewhere in order to add a new position, so this kind of deliberative process is important for our institution. At other schools, it may be the president's or provost's office alone that allocates new positions, but rarely does that responsibility sit with the vice presidents, at least at small private institutions.

The president's role in setting operating budgets is to help keep the budget managers and other decision makers focused on strategic priorities and goals as they make their determinations about what costs might be needed in any given year.

Once an operating budget is built, one of the strategies that we have found particularly useful with the board of trustees and at community forums is to do scenario budgeting in terms of a best, middle, and worst case, depending on various factors. With student demographics in the Northeast forecasted to decline precipitously, one of the scenarios we often review is differing enrollments and the impact on the budget. This kind of scenario testing helps decision makers at all levels understand what factors influence the budget and assists with seeing the big picture.

Strategic Goals

One of the most important tools an institution can have is a strategic plan that helps drive decision-making, including informing the budget. In the absence of strategic priorities, anything within an operating budget can be argued to be important. However, with a strategic plan in place, planning priorities and measures help determine whether something is truly needed to help the institution achieve its goals.

Just as with budgeting, there are a number of ways to develop a strategic plan. At Colby-Sawyer, we used a very inclusive process whereby the Strategic Planning Committee, a group of faculty, staff, senior officers, and me, led multiple groups through sessions to identify our key priorities. We ended up with a strategic plan that includes three promises to students: a sense of place, engaged and personalized learning, and a transformational experience. It was very encouraging how the different constituents—faculty, staff, trustees, alumni, and local townspeople—all articulated themes that were congruent with what ended up being our promises to students. The Strategic Planning Committee then determined several strategic priorities that must be met in order for us to keep our promises as well as measures for each of those priorities. We monitor the priorities at least twice a year and share them with the various constituencies. The planning process took several months in order to be as inclusive as possible and to enlist the input of many groups. But the plan in place now helps guide us on how to make decisions around the budget, staffing, and new programs.

Once the institutional plan was in place, the college also embarked on a more streamlined planning process to take advantage of a strategic opportunity related to our nursing program, one of our largest and most successful programs in terms of outcomes. A group of trustees, the chief financial officer, and I met over the course of several weeks to imagine what Colby-Sawyer could be, and we determined that pursuing the health sciences was an opportunity that offered us a potential pathway to distinction in a highly competitive marketplace in New England. We were able to sign a $3.25 million partnership agreement with Dartmouth-Hitchcock Health that focuses on tripling the size of our nursing program over ten years, doing workforce development through a new associate's degree in health science and two new tracks in our master's of nursing program, and introducing five new undergraduate programs in health sciences. This particular planning process was much faster and occurred in my fourth year versus the more inclusive approach which began my first year.

Regardless of the type of planning approach adopted, it is important that the president play a role of facilitator and guide. As the individual with the broadest institutional lens, the president must ask questions throughout the planning process that help others maintain an institutional view as well. It is also paramount that any planning process is tied to the finances of the college. A plan without funding sources is likely to fail and frustrate many constituents. One of the ways to ensure that a plan is linked to funding is to create specific measures for the strategic plan that are financially oriented. At Colby-Sawyer, some of our financial measures include having a balanced operating budget, the endowment value, the total raised each year through our annual fund giving, our alumni participation rate in giving, and progress toward our overall goal in our comprehensive campaign.

Communication with Constituents

When it comes to financial planning or strategic goals, one can never communicate enough as president. At Colby-Sawyer, we have a culture of all-campus meetings at which faculty and staff attend at least two to three times a semester. These meetings provide me as president with an opportunity to speak about critical issues at the college, and we have used these sessions to share the same information that is shared with trustees around enrollment, finances, advancement, academic affairs, and student life, among other topics.

I also provide a monthly email to campus about key issues facing the institution so that there are as few surprises as possible between the all-campus meetings. And each vice president is charged with updating their respective areas about strategic issues as they arise as well. But one can never communicate enough, especially in times when resources are scarce and employees may be feeling anxious or on edge about the fragility of their own roles—a lesson that has been reinforced for all presidents over the course of the coronavirus pandemic.

My approach has been to be fully transparent with the campus community about the details of the college's finances. While I believe this transparency helps the community trust in my leadership, it can also be a burden on them when there are financial scarcity issues. That said, I believe full transparency helps all members understand the challenges and provides an opportunity to invite ideas and solutions from others. What savings might they see in their areas that have not yet been identified? What ideas do they have for the institution that the senior officers have not thought of themselves? We also find that budget managers are far more likely to adhere to their budget parameters when they have the full institutional picture. Transparency plus a mechanism for feedback can be powerful tools.

One of the challenges with transparency is that when funding levels do return to a point where there are funds that can be spent strategically, it may be hard for the campus community to develop those ideas. At Colby-Sawyer, the budget has been in scarcity mode for so long that when we were able to develop ideas for a major grant and/or when we had funds to spend, it was challenging for our staff to get out of scarcity mode—even when given permission to think big. I think each president has to find the right balance between being authentic in communications and how transparent to be about finances. It can be scary for an institution, and you might lose some of your good talent. That said, I have found it to be respected and desired more so than my keeping the details to myself.

CLOSING THOUGHTS

As I have attempted to outline in this chapter, it is critical for presidents to know as much as possible about their institution's finances and strategic goals. Although many presidents may not have come up through administration, and this kind of institutionwide budgeting and forecasting may be new, ultimately the president plays a crucial role as a fiduciary and must work hard to get the information that they need to make good decisions. While there are many constituents who can help, namely the board of trustees, senior officers, chief financial officer, and budget managers, ultimately it is the president's role to know and understand the college's finances.

The kitchen in the president's house turned out very well. Sometimes during college events when I pop into the kitchen to say hello to dining services, I marvel at how far the college has come. The coronavirus has certainly stalled some of our momentum, but the college has achieved balanced budgets several years in a row, we successfully completed a capital campaign, and our endowment is growing. We have a strategic direction in the health sciences that has helped us diversify our revenue streams through the creation of a master's program in nursing and an associate's degree in health sciences. And we have checks and balances in place so that we know how cash is being used and for what purpose. We still have more to accomplish by way of taking care of our people through salary adjustments and increases, but we have a much more solid foundation than we did five years ago. Like most institutions, we have strengths and we have challenges. And thanks to a donor, we have a beautiful kitchen that is well used for events where we celebrate our special college community.

CHAPTER 13

Strategic Financial Management and the College President

ROSS GITTELL

One of the most important functions of the college president is to make sure their institution has the financial resources and wherewithal to sustain its work and support its mission.* Financial sustainability is one of the key areas of focus for higher education leaders. College presidents are increasingly trying to figure out the financial sustainability piece—sustainability as in how to ensure the resources necessary to support thriving, vibrant organizations that can continuously fund and reinvest in the people, activities, technology, and physical plant that support the needs of students and other stakeholders.[1] This chapter focuses on how college presidents, particularly new college presidents, can work toward achieving financial sustainability by focusing increasingly scarce resources on strategic priorities and on what the college does most successfully.

COMMUNITY COLLEGES AS CASE STUDY

The chapter, in part, uses community colleges as an illustrative case study. It draws on my nine years of experience as chancellor of a seven-college community college system in New Hampshire. Focusing on the financial practices of community colleges can provide insights for presidents of all higher education institutions, as the financial challenges of community colleges make effective strategic financial management a constant priority. The fundamental underlying consideration is that without long-term financial sustainability, community colleges, and any higher education institution, cannot sustain their long-term mission-related work.

* I would like to thank Tammy Kolbe, associate professor of Educational Leadership and Policy Studies at the University of Vermont, for sharing her insights and perspectives on effective processes to allocate education resources when I began my work on the chapter.

While all of higher education, even before the 2020 coronavirus outbreak, operated with financial concerns, community colleges in many respects had the most significant financial challenges: community colleges tend to operate with more limited financial resources and support student populations with greater need for financial, academic, and personal support than those served by many four-year colleges and universities.

Community colleges particularly over the last decade (2011–2020)—with the end of their enrollment growth period in the aftermath of the recession of 2008–2009—have addressed significant financial challenges. One perpetual challenge is navigating how to finance the changes needed in order to improve student outcomes and generate higher student enrollment, thus providing more revenue in a period of increasingly tight budgets.[2] For community colleges in this period, there has been an increased need for a strong and consistent focus on core mission and strategy as well as an emphasis on ensuring that limited resources are allocated to institutional priorities aligned with the college's mission. This has required a shift in the framing of financial decision-making toward a strategic finance focus.

A strategic finance focus prioritizes resources needed to achieve core objectives over a long period of time. In the case of community colleges, strategic finance initiatives emphasize achieving broad access and improved student outcomes. Community colleges' access mission necessitates that they keep tuition as low and affordable as possible; yet, at the same time, the public and private funding support they receive is low relative to other institutions of higher education. With regards to private funding, community colleges also do not have the base of well-to-do alumni to draw on for fundraising that many universities and colleges with bachelor's and graduate programs have.

On the cost/expense side, community colleges tend to also operate at a disadvantage. The reason is their relatively small size (making it difficult to achieve scale efficiencies), broad range of programs and courses offered to serve the needs of a diverse student population, high percentage of part-time students enrolled, and the individualized supports their students require. Many community colleges serve rural areas with low population density; have lower average class sizes than bachelor's and graduate institutions; and have more costly developmental education, advising, and financial support needs.

Adding to the financial challenges of community colleges is that their two main sources of operating revenues—tuition and public funding—are not only low but also are highly variable relative to many four-year institutions. Community college enrollment (and tuition revenue) tends to vary with the general economy: when the economy is strong, the unemployment rate low, and the opportunity cost of college high, community college enrollment tends to go down, and the reverse is true. Public funding support is also highly uncertain, varying with state and local economies, revenue, and executive and legislative changes.

At the same time community colleges have these significant financial challenges, student outcomes need to be improved given that six out of ten students do not complete a degree within six years of starting at a community college.[3] Improving student outcomes is a high priority of community colleges but a costly one.

The need to use limited financial resources strategically toward improving student outcomes and to be positioned to make an effective case for more resources heightens the necessity for effective strategic financial management at community colleges, and thus the value of focusing on community colleges in this chapter.

THE NEED FOR STRATEGIC ALLOCATION OF RESOURCES TO ACHIEVE MISSION

"If we are to preserve access, ensure affordability and increase attainment, in a world of constrained resources and fewer students, then we must get a better return on investment from current resources through understanding levers to change the business model, which will require a strategic approach connecting financial practice with institutional change models and culture."[4]

Financial decisions should be focused on the institution's priorities that are most important for achieving its mission. The priorities of an institution should emanate from a strategic plan, developed with broad stakeholder engagement, that is aligned with an institution's mission and aspirations. The plan should include identification of organizational priorities—and the key resources (e.g., human, physical, and intellectual), activities, and functional capabilities—necessary to achieve the institution's mission. The plan and the institution's priorities should be transparent and drive budgetary and other decisions.

Making and framing decisions with a focus on longer-term priorities and continuation of mission-related work can help to engage broad stakeholders in budgetary decisions in a positive and purposeful way. This approach can create a framework for positive engagement on long-term planning and budgeting, and can also help to overcome resistance and animosity to difficult budget adjustments associated with unanticipated revenue shortfalls or expense increases—such as a sharp decline in revenue in response to the 2020 global pandemic.

A strategic finance approach has all financial decision-making focused on having the resources and capabilities needed to achieve core objectives on a sustained, long-term basis. For community colleges, this means having the resources needed to provide affordable access to higher education and to have strong student outcomes on an ongoing, sustainable basis.

Strategic financial management requires acting on main revenue and cost drivers, such as tuition and faculty and staff salaries and benefits, and making decisions so that the college invests in programs and practices that support the long-term net positive revenue position and are aligned with the mission and priorities. It requires institutional identification and focus on what matters most and at what cost and with what benefits to students and the institution. And it necessitates how the mission-critical work can be financially supported over time.

The financial decision-making under the president's leadership should be done with as much transparency as possible and with clear assignment of responsibility and accountability. Transparency and accountability should be embedded as much as possible in all financial decisions made throughout the institution and in formal and informal discussions about the budget.

TEMPORAL FRAMEWORK OF STRATEGIC FINANCIAL DECISION-MAKING

There is a temporal framework to financial management. This includes the immediate/short-term, intermediate, and long-term time frames. In all temporal frames there should be the informing and involvement of division heads and the most relevant campus stakeholders, and an embedded "feedback loop" with ongoing budgetary and financial learning and adjustments with experience. Documenting and learning from the outcomes of financial decisions should inform ongoing efforts to refine financial decision-making in order to best serve the institution and its stakeholders.

Immediate financial decisions are reactions to unanticipated occurrences that are not budgeted for and are of significant immediate financial consequence, such as expenses related to an external event like the 2020 coronavirus outbreak. Shorter-term financial decisions can happen as part of an annual budget process, or outside the formal budgeting context, and involve addressing a current situational budgetary concern. The latter can include a revenue shortfall or cost that was unexpected.

The immediate and short-term budgetary/financial management responses can in many respects be the most difficult and of the highest visibility for the college president. While needing to be done in a timely manner and to address an immediate or short-term situation or concern, the decision should be made with a strategic frame. For the immediate and short-term financial decision, this will be what budget action should be taken that not only addresses an immediate/short-term budget challenge or concern but also meets longer-term strategic objectives as much as possible. Another way to frame it: What action can help with current financial concerns while positioning the institution best for longer-term financial sustainability and success?

Shorter-term financial management can often involve identifying and addressing organizational "slack," or cost inefficiencies in services, activities, and/or programs. It can also involve comparing costs and benefits and return on investments (ROI) with different programs and activities and reducing or even eliminating programs and activities that have the highest net cost to the institution or lowest ROIs.[5] With the latter, it is important to recognize that ROI means different things for different stakeholders—the *R* is not only the dollar financial returns. For students it can include reduced or stabilized tuition cost, reduced time to degree, and a reduction in excess credits, while for institutions it can include increases in net revenue and reduced unit costs. For systems of colleges it can be a reduction in duplication of efforts, creation of shared services, and more effective support of student success.[6]

Applying an ROI lens has to touch on a college's culture and be recognized as a change management process. It is important for colleges to have a framework for ROI conversations. That framework must reflect different views of ROI for different stakeholders and be used as part of active engagement across the college in strategic financial practice.[7]

The ROI assessments, even while done in a short-term/immediate temporal frame, need to consider longer-term strategic consequences—for example, whether a program cut negatively affects the institution's core value proposition and what it means to students and for the institution's position relative to peer and competitor institutions.

Short-term financial management can be focused on reducing unneeded, low-priority, or low ROI programs or services, or removing lowest-priority staff and activities. The former, the cutting of unneeded programs or services, may be commonly referred to as reducing "organizational slack." The latter, the cutting of lowest-ROI activities, is commonly referred to as "activity-based" budgeting as compared to cutting program budgets by equal percentages.

Intermediate-term financial management is focused more on reallocation of resources toward higher ROI areas that are more closely aligned with strategic priorities and with what is working at the institution. These changes are more structurally focused, rather than situational and in response to immediate financial concerns. At community colleges this effort has involved focusing on reallocating resources and spending away from programs and services with declining enrollment and benefits to students and employers and shifting them to programs and activities with growing demand, increased benefits to stakeholders, and good long-term prospects. The focus on program and activity performance and trends can ensure that financial decisions are not only aligned with longer-term mission and institutional designated priorities but also with what has been actually high performing (i.e., working) at the institution.

Longer-term financial management should recognize and plan for longer-term variability and vulnerability in revenue and funding sources and the institutional cost structure. There should be financial modeling based on historical trends and known or expected trends and changes in all major revenues and expenses, overall and by major program and activities, and with contingencies and alternatives modeled. Contingencies on the revenue side to model should include, for example, the influence of general economic factors and cycles, demographic and student trends, and competitive factors on key revenue line items such as tuition, fees, investment returns, fundraising, and personnel costs. On the expense side, factors to consider can include how changes in the economy, demographics, and competition could affect staffing and faculty costs and how these could be influenced by changes in program delivery and technology deployment.

EXAMPLES OF APPLYING MISSION-BASED FINANCIAL DISCIPLINE TO PRACTICE

Some illustrative general examples of strategic financial practices commonly deployed by community colleges are provided below. These include examples of immediate/short-term, intermediate, and longer-term strategic financial management decision-making.

IMMEDIATE/SHORT-TERM:
- *Financial decisions made during coronavirus outbreak in March 2020.* At community colleges and other institutions across the nation, immediate, situational, mid-semester financial decisions had to be made in timely response to the global pandemic in March of 2020. For New Hampshire's community colleges, immediate financial decisions were framed in the context of "doing the right thing" for students, faculty, staff, and the communities served by the community colleges. The right thing in this case was ensuring the health and safety of students and employees while not sacrificing the priorities and mission-critical work of the colleges during a crisis period for students and the nation. This decision involved incurring significant unplanned expenses to continue the semester with students and faculty engaging remotely and required funding the purchasing of computers, supporting technology, and Wi-Fi access for students and employees.
- *Immediate financial decisions were made in the context of an unanticipated crisis and potentially highly destabilizing situation.* Addressing any barriers to

mission-critical work immediately was the top priority, with understanding that the dollars to support this effort would be funded as necessary by operating surpluses that had been built up over time and reserved for contingencies such as the situation at hand. Fortunately, for New Hampshire community colleges and other colleges across the country, some of the dollars needed to meet the added expenses in the spring semester were made available in US federal funding from the Coronavirus Aid, Relief, and Economic Security (CARES) program. The CARES Act support totaled in the multiple millions of dollars for New Hampshire's community colleges and helped to financially support the decision to address the immediate crisis at hand by continuing education and training programs for students while addressing health and safety concerns.

It is important to recognize that for New Hampshire's community colleges, and many other colleges and universities, the mid-semester decisions involved taking on some significant financial risk. In the case of New Hampshire's community colleges, sound long-term financial management practice to have annual operations end regularly with contribution to reserve funds allowed the colleges to make immediate financial decisions without putting the institutions at immediate risk of being without adequate funds for continuing operations.

- *Considerations made about opening college campuses for fall 2020 instruction on campus.*[8] Soon after the March 2020 pandemic response decisions were made, there were active discussions and information and intelligence gathering about whether to open the college campuses for the fall. It was clear that for these colleges there was high risk of significant revenue shortfalls associated with the pandemic; this would be due to declines in enrollment, tuition, room and board, and other auxiliary revenue at the same time as there would be significant increased costs associated with addressing pandemic health and safety concerns and for using technology to increase agility in instructional delivery. This meant budgetary expenses not directly related to the pandemic would have to be cut significantly.

The key, which was exceedingly challenging given the highly dynamic and complex situation, was to try to ensure that the situational response to the immediate revenue and expense challenges was also strategic so as to not negatively affect the strategic priorities and position of the institution. This would include not allowing the situational financial challenges to lead to expense reductions in non-pandemic-related areas that were mission critical. It also meant to not let concern for potential losses in revenue or high expenses related to healthy and safe campuses (e.g., expenses associated with testing and enabling social distancing) lead to decisions to open campuses or to minimize pandemic-related expenses that could result in a long-term decline in the reputation and integrity of the college.

INTERMEDIATE TERM:

- *Making structural academic program and activity investment and reallocation decisions based on which programs and activities operate with the highest (and lowest) net positive operating revenue.* Recent surveys of college chief financial officers have highlighted that future investment in new staff, faculty, and activities would increasingly need to come from reallocation of existing resources. In addition, new programs or activities will need to eventually support themselves, rather than benefit from increases in net revenue from enrollment growth or other sources. As noted by Rick Staisloff, "Once an institution has identified its economic engines (the programs and services that make the largest contribution to financial sustainability), it can direct resources toward them and to its strategic academic and financial goals. The college should be in a position eventually to harvest resources for reinvestment in new strategies, thus moving dollars, people, and time away from simply maintaining the current model, and toward an investment in the college's future."[9]

  Doing this type of return-on-investment analysis requires accounting for historical program and activity-specific operating revenues, expenses, and projections on net return on any new investments or changes in programs and activities. Investments (and reallocations) should be directed to the most cost-effective programs and activities that are aligned with strategic priorities and long-term economic and demographic trends. Removing financial and other resources from the programs and activities with negative or the lowest ROIs that are not mission or key stakeholder critical should also be a priority.

- *Using technology to enhance student support.* The individualized supports community colleges offer—which begin as soon as students enroll and commence their college courses—are important for the eventual success of many community college students. Recently, more attention has been paid to using technology to cost-effectively provide these services. The cost of in-person 24/7 support can be prohibitive and thus require alternatives, especially technology-based alternatives. Efforts are being made to identify a "sweet spot" where technology can be used effectively to support student success at lower cost than in-person support, while recognizing limitations of the use of technology for some student populations and support services. The key is to find an appropriate balance of benefits for financial sustainability and mission achievement.

Community colleges can review the documented performance of different potential advising technology vendors, and learn from assessed experience of other colleges, when making decisions to invest in technology-enabled student support platforms.

- *Partnering with school districts/K–12 education on early college education/ concurrent enrollment.* A growing area of enrollment growth for community colleges is with early college and concurrent enrollment programs with local high schools. These programs can contribute to lower cost and greater access to higher education. At many community colleges, decisions have been made to continue to operate these programs at discounted tuition and financial loss. While the immediate net revenue per student is negative, early college and concurrent enrollment programs can create a stronger pathway to eventual community college enrollment, increase visibility and a positive reputation for the institutions, and align with the access and affordability mission of community colleges. For some community colleges, including in New Hampshire, their investments (i.e., operating at net loss) in early college and concurrent enrollment programs are "paying off," at least in part, in that the strong positive benefits and reputation of the early college and concurrent enrollment program have contributed to increased public state funding over time.

- *Awarding of credit for prior learning.* In New Hampshire and at community colleges across the nation, there is consideration of providing credit for prior learning. The credit for prior learning presents some unique financial implications: on the one hand, there is loss of revenue from courses not taken, but on the other there is the potential to increase student headcount and course enrollment over time. Specifically, more students, particularly adult learners, might be attracted to enroll knowing they will get college credit for their work experience and have the potential for accelerated degree attainment at lower cost. With the financial assessment of prior learning, institutions often consider its cost and benefits in specific demographic and labor markets, including how it would affect enrollment over time, revenues, costs, and institutional outcomes like improving college access and completion.

With credit for prior learning, there is the trade-off between awarding no or low-cost credit for prior learning and future revenue generation from new enrollment of students who, without such a program, would not have enrolled in the college. The longer-term financial consideration is with regard to financial sustainability of the credit for prior learning: Can the college sustain this type of program, at what cost or with what benefit, and how does this program contribute to institutional mission and position relative to other activities and programs?

LONG-TERM:

- *Investments in developmental education that improve student retention and graduation.* In New Hampshire and in many other community colleges, a particular approach, corequisite remediation, has been deployed in math and English developmental education. Corequisite delivery requires increased expenditure in instruction because of embedding individualized tutorial-type support within traditional entry-level college courses. In addition, it can result in lost revenue as students are not required to first take developmental education courses with no college credit obtained before taking an entry-level college course. Decisions to adopt a corequisite approach have been made for both mission-related and financial considerations. On the former, a corequisite entry-level math and English approach in community colleges has been documented to have a significant positive influence on the likelihood that students who are not prepared for college-level math or English courses will complete the college-level course; a much higher likelihood than if they had completed the developmental course before enrolling in the college-level class. On the latter, corequisite instruction can have net positive financial benefits longer term through increased student retention, leading to longer periods of enrollment and tuition revenue generation. The driving factor in corequisite implementation is its proven ability to improve student outcomes. While the move to corequisite education may seem clear and straightforward, the reality is that it has involved colleges losing short-term revenue with the loss of stand-alone developmental education revenue, and increased costs of instruction in corequisite first college courses. But there is a longer-term payoff of increased student retention, improved student outcomes, and the generation of additional tuition revenue.

- *Decision not to seek support for free community college.* While adopting a free college policy funded by state government would be in support of community colleges' access and affordability mission, the uncertainty of public funding being sustained for free college and the potential for state support not to meet the financial needs for sustained delivery of a quality education had a strong influence on the decision not to pursue free community college in New Hampshire. It might thus be said that, at least in general terms, there really is no such thing as free community college that could be pursued as viable over a longer-term period. At least this was the belief in a state with a long history of limited public funding for higher education and without a broad-based sales or personal income tax base to support free college over a sustained period.

  Similarly, many colleges might want to increase scholarships for students based on their need. While well intended and aligned with most colleges' missions, if sustainable sources of funding for the scholarships are not iden-tified, the commitment to increasing need-based funding may not be realized and can, unintentionally, put the quality of education and sustainability of the college at risk. That is why there is a need for a strategic finance approach even for the most well-intended objectives.

WAYS TO OVERCOME CHALLENGES TO STRATEGIC FINANCIAL DECISION-MAKING

For a college president, effectively focusing on strategic financial management issues will require overcoming some significant barriers in many higher education insti-tutions.[10] Perhaps the most significant is the academy's traditional resistance to a so-called business approach to institutional decision-making.

There can be negativity and cynicism when presidents give priority to financial factors in decision-making. Many faculty and student support professionals resist financially based decision-making out of concern for their own programs and ac-tivities being subject to considerations apart from their academic integrity and/or direct benefit to students. They often lack the longer-term perspective that financial sustainability is critical to their work and the ongoing academic and student support work of colleges.

Also part of the problem is the background and training of many finance profes-sionals who have operated in higher education. They have tended not to be from an academic background or be strategically focused. The common background of higher education financial managers is often very different than other (nonfinance) college administrators, who tend to have little formal financial training and often enter their positions with limited experience making difficult financial decisions such as reduc-ing staffing/faculty during extended periods of enrollment and revenue decline. Many current higher education CFOs might have difficulty relating short- or longer-term financial decisions to academic and student priorities, and many administrators out-side of finance might have difficulty applying some basic financial principles. Even in some sense more limiting can be insufficient attention to, and background and training in, strategic management for higher education financial managers and other administrators in higher education.

What is proposed here would be a new role for not only presidents but also for many financial officers in higher education and for other higher education adminis-trators who do not have *finance* in their titles. The strategic financial management ap-proach outlined in this chapter requires that institutional priorities and mission drive how dollars are allocated, and not the other way around. As highlighted through-out this chapter, it is essential to have a well-conceived and strongly communicated strategy that clearly identifies core priorities toward achieving the institution's mission, and the strategy should be used to frame strategic financial practice.

Unfortunately, higher education currently suffers from a relative paucity of well-documented, strong strategic finance practice, and good evaluation of financial practices overall. There is limited knowledge about what works in terms of financial best practices in higher education and on specifics such as how to do an ROI analysis with respect to educational programs. Also lacking is the data and data availability across the institution required to support strong strategic finance practice. Financial and institutional performance data related to institutional priorities and mission should be modeled and available to managers throughout the institution to support the strategic financial analysis and practice.

On the flip side of having limited well-documented practices and institutional financial data to support strategic finance decision-making is the opportunity for presidents to develop campus-based solutions with improved strategic financial practice at their institutions—especially in the post-coronavirus context of heightened financial challenges and constrained resources. In the past, college presidents were not particularly lauded for their financial management acumen as much as they were, for example, for expanding programs, promoting research, and attracting top faculty talent. This, however, was changing before the 2020 coronavirus outbreak and has accelerated. College presidents' strategic financial management abilities and performance will be of increased interest and importance.

REQUIREMENTS FOR STRONGER STRATEGIC FINANCE CAPACITY

The requirements for new college presidents to develop stronger capacities in strategic financial management include:

- Highlighting early on in your presidency the need to address financial sustainability to sustain the important work of the institution
- Using a strategic investment argument, or that the use of limited financial resources must be aligned with institutional mission and with what the institution does best
- Leading by example with strong, sound, and consistent practice in strategic financial management
- Staying the course, even in the face of challenges to difficult decisions being made, such as eliminating programs and reducing faculty and staff positions when enrollments decline
- Operating with transparency and accountability with active sharing of financial information, analyses, and decisions

- Incorporating financial sustainability considerations into all financial management and strategic planning practice
- Gaining governing board and internal leadership support for financial sustainability and a strategic financial management focus
- Keeping the board and leadership involved in and informed about strategic financial decisions made and the process and analyses used
- Instilling a data-informed culture with a spirit of curiosity and inquiry, as well as supporting faculty and staff in their use of metrics and financial data[11]
- Establishing a financial data infrastructure to support strategic financial analysis[12]
- Ensuring faculty and department chairs receive strategic finance training and support (there is a need to train faculty and department chairs on the economics of programs and classes and to implement financial accountability structures in academic planning)
- Using commitment to financial sustainability and accountability to garner increased support for the institution

CONCLUSION

The strategic financial approach I have described here helped me, as chancellor of a resource-challenged community college system, to ensure a stronger and more sustainable future for community colleges in New Hampshire. The approach has also been of significant value to me in my new role as president of Bryant University, a private residential university in significantly better financial standing than a large majority of community colleges. As I began my presidency at Bryant in July of 2020, a strategic financial approach helped to guide budgeting in response to unanticipated revenue declines and expense increases directly resulting from the 2020 global pandemic. It enabled the institution to make difficult financial decisions addressing the immediate financial situation, while minimizing the potential negative impact on mission-critical work.

For many institutions and college presidents, there will be a need to build strategic financial management acumen and capacity. This will be a paradigm shift, particularly for college leadership that comes from the faculty or from a student support background without financial management or strategy training. When building the strategic financial capacity at a college, college presidents, particularly new college presidents, need to strive to achieve a "virtuous cycle," having each of the required items discussed in the previous section support each other and collectively help to support advancements in institutional strategic financial management practice. The ultimate goal is to use strategic financial management in support of sustaining the important work of your college.

CHAPTER 14

The Role of the President in Promoting Diversity, Equity, and Inclusion

SHEILA EDWARDS LANGE

I am an activist president. I start with that since this positionality has shaped how I lead, and it is the lens through which I see the complex landscape of higher education. I have been the student demanding racial justice; the staff advocate for students of color; the chief diversity officer managing the campus enterprise for diversity, equity, and inclusion (DEI); and now the college president responsible for it all. Over a thirty-year career in higher education management, I have seen the paradigm of DEI shift dramatically from a concept rooted in representation to one today that is essential to an institution's core mission of educating students. In this chapter, I discuss that paradigm shift, explore the expectations of presidential leadership in this new reality, and offer advice to new presidents who will be expected to elevate and pursue DEI as a strategy for institutional success.

THE PARADIGM SHIFT

In the late 1980s I was fortunate to be invited to serve as special assistant to a college president who was a national leader in the field of education. We coauthored a chapter in a book that projected what higher education could expect in the 1990s.[1] In this chapter, we discussed how Clark Kerr, president emeritus of the University of California, predicted that equal opportunity in higher education would manifest itself as a struggle for greater proportionality of racial diversity in the student body and faculty; and that we could expect a backlash to admission and hiring practices that fostered this proportionality. *One Third of a Nation*, a report of the Commission on Minority Participation in Education and American Life, had been published in 1987 calling upon higher education to strengthen its efforts to increase minority recruitment, retention, and graduation. Admission practices to increase representation, affirmative action, and race- and gender-based policies became common strategies in higher education institutions across the country.

As Kerr predicted, however, the 1990s brought about great change and conflict over issues of diversity and inclusion in higher education. While institutions were pursuing a representational strategy, students, staff, and faculty who were being recruited were not having positive experiences on campus. Issues of isolation and explicit bias in the tenure process were common complaints that drove many faculty of color to exit institutions in such large numbers that it was referred to as a "revolving door" by many scholars.[2] Student attrition and a persistent gap in graduation rates prevailed even as institutions put structures in place to better support outcomes for students of color.[3]

As the 1990s drew to a close, institutions were being called upon to do more even as their practices were being challenged legally. Diversity advocates called for institutions to move beyond representation to be more inclusive of the histories and lived experiences of people of color in their curricula, and more sensitive to the intersectionality of student and faculty identities. Legal challenges such as the landmark Supreme Court case *Grutter v. Bollinger* in Michigan challenged the use of race in college admission and focused national attention on diversity in higher education. The Michigan case forced institutions to be more explicit about why and how diversity related to the mission of higher education. Research and documentation about the value of DEI in higher education ballooned as part of the defense in *Grutter v. Bollinger*. By the time the case was settled in 2003, scholars, activists, and higher education leaders had developed a compelling case for the inclusion of people of color in the academy as a solid strategy for mission fulfillment in higher education.

This paradigm shift, from diversity as an optional priority to its role as a necessary component to institutional excellence and student success, propelled institutions to develop new language and structures for its pursuit. Colleges and universities became more self-reflective about the role of the institution in the success of its students and faculty of color. This shift changed the focus of the problem from the individual to the institutional structures that serve as barriers to student and faculty success. The chief diversity officer (CDO) role was elevated with the emergence of the National Association of Diversity Officers in Higher Education (NADOHE) in 2006. CDOs are now typically cabinet-level positions reporting directly to the president and charged with transforming institutions to be more inclusive and supportive of student and faculty success in the academy. Prior to 2006 only a handful of colleges around the country had senior leaders reporting directly to a president with this level of responsibility. NADOHE developed standards for the position and elevated its importance through scholarship in its *Journal of Diversity in Higher Education*.

EXPECTATIONS OF PRESIDENTIAL LEADERSHIP

With the emergence of executive-level leadership for DEI work on campus, expectations of the college president's role have expanded. It is now routine for campuses to list experience leading DEI as a required qualification when searching for new presidents. Following are six of the most common expectations for presidential leadership in DEI:

- *Personal understanding of and fluency about equity in higher education.* The president must be able to speak to the value of equity in the institution and why it is important to the mission, vision, and goals of the college. They must also be able to articulate how DEI aligns with their personal values as a leader.
- *Establishment of DEI as an institutional priority that is integral to mission fulfillment.* The president has to work collaboratively with campus constituencies to include DEI in strategic planning and accreditation reports. Because DEI is articulated as a required qualification for presidents, boards of trustees include it as part of presidential performance reviews. Successful presidents keep their boards engaged in the work through periodic reporting and/or planning efforts.
- *Strategic communication about equity-related issues to both internal and external audiences.* The president is expected to communicate broadly about what the campus is doing related to DEI. Silence on critical equity-related issues happening on campus and in the broader community is perceived as not caring about those issues and can lead to fierce criticism by faculty, staff, and students. Issuing statements on everything from immigration policy to police brutality and gender identity is expected and must be carefully managed.
- *Development and implementation of policies related to national politics and free speech on campus.* Even as the president is called upon to issue statements, they must ensure that the campus remains a place where differences of opinions can flourish and be expressed. As the nation has become more polarized politically, vocal conservative and liberal organizations jockey for a place on college campuses. To deny one over the other can lead to legal challenges and negative social media directed toward the campus and its leadership.
- *Proactive management of campus, community, business, donor, and alumni expectations for engagement.* The campus has many constituencies, and they all have different understandings of why DEI matters to the college. The president is often the only person in the institution who has relationships with each of the constituents and must manage conflicting expectations about campus work on DEI. Strategic engagement with constituents before an equity-related crisis presents itself on campus or in the community helps the

college be proactive in problem-solving. Developing and strengthening those relationships can also assist presidents in developing a broader perspective on the impact their DEI work is having outside the campus walls.

- *Accountability and metrics for progress (in collaboration with a CDO if one exists).* Articulating DEI as important to the institution consequently means that presidents must be able to report on progress of the work. Qualitative and quantitative metrics beyond anecdotal evidence are required, and the president must know where the institution stands on each of them. Collecting and analyzing data on student completion, faculty/staff composition, and campus experiences disaggregated by race, gender identity, sexual orientation, and other identities should be standard practices.

Like most change, this paradigm shift in DEI work and subsequent expectations for presidential leadership was initially incremental and then propelled forward by unpredicted external forces. The 2003 Michigan Supreme Court case; the 2014 Black Lives Matter (BLM) movement in response to the murder of Trayvon Martin and, more recently, the murder of George Floyd; and the racial reckoning taking place at the time of this writing are all examples of unpredicted external forces that have changed higher education considerably.

ADVICE TO NEW PRESIDENTS

With all the racial unrest in the country, many of our students, faculty, and staff are engaged in protests and activism both off and on the campus. In this era, college presidents must be responsive to the new paradigm for DEI on campus in order to be aligned with their campus and surrounding community. While I identify as an activist, that is not the usual descriptor for college presidents. No matter where they stand politically, every president must be able to provide leadership for successful DEI work on campus and know their position on equity issues. For example, in the aftermath of the murder of George Floyd, presidents were being asked to weigh in on defunding the police and the creation of antiracist organizations. My advice for new presidents is know where you stand, assess where your campus is positioned on the issues, and forge a path forward that is inclusive and responsive to the campus and surrounding community.

Knowing where you stand is a critical first step in this work. You must have a clear understanding of what your stance is on something like defunding police or dismantling institutional racism before you can lead the campus on these issues. I cannot express how important this is when you are confronted by a student, faculty, or community member and asked to explain why the campus is engaged in DEI work. Or when you are asked to express your opinion about the campus relationship with local police or your own security staffing. Or when you are asked why racial equity should be elevated above other dimensions of diversity like gender, sexual orientation, or socioeconomic status. You have to know where your personal views diverge from the campus community you are entrusted to lead. They will not always be in alignment, and you will struggle with that dissonance in this role.

Understanding where your campus is on DEI issues will help you considerably in the role of president. As a new president, you will quickly need to assess the depth and breadth of DEI activity. Who are the leaders for the work on campus? Does the campus lead with racial equity, and how is that manifested in programs and activity? How are you structured, and who is being held accountable for advancing the work? What does your governing board expect, and what is the level of engagement they have in the work? Is your campus community more liberal than the town in which you are located, and how will you address that in town-gown relationships?

As president, you are expected to walk the walk of DEI, not just talk. That means you will need an actionable plan and path for moving the campus forward that is inclusive and responsive to where your campus and surrounding community are willing to go. The process of assessing this most likely started with your application for the role. If the campus and board have declared that DEI is important in the president's job profile and interview process, then they are most likely ready for an aggressive and bold plan from the president. If the application process was silent or timid about DEI expectations, then that is a signal that the campus may still see DEI as optional or student focused rather than as a necessary component to institutional excellence. It doesn't mean the campus cannot shift to the new paradigm, but it will require more intensive work by the president to help it get there.

PERSONAL REFLECTIONS

I became a CDO just after the ruling in the Michigan case and was leaving the role just as the BLM movement was starting. As CDO at a large predominantly white research institution, I managed a portfolio of student support services, worked with deans and other senior leaders to improve the diversity of faculty, partnered with community-based organizations to address equity-related priorities, created new organizational structures to improve the university's use of women- and minority-owned businesses, and engaged with the board on their interest in DEI.

When I moved to the role of president at Seattle Central College in 2015, I had no idea that DEI work would continue to be a significant part of my portfolio. After all, community colleges are open-access institutions, the racial diversity of the student body far exceeds that in large research institutions, and the credentials needed to become faculty are more flexible. I assumed that the college would already have structures in place to support students of color and the faculty would reflect the students in our classrooms. Fortunately, nine years in the CDO role prepared me to be very successful in meeting expectations related to fluency about equity, and promoting DEI as critical to mission fulfillment and accountability. As a new president, however, I struggled with the strategic communication, free speech policies, and the conflicting priorities of constituents.

Very early in my first year as president, it became apparent that issues related to faculty diversity, curricular inclusion, and student opportunity gaps by race were prevalent on my campus. These were not issues I expected to find in my urban community college with its long history of social justice and activism. As I examined the work of DEI on my new campus, it was focused primarily on student representation and multicultural student support. The college had not reflected critically on its own role in opportunity gaps and lack of racial diversity in its faculty. We had a director of multicultural student services, but no one focused on hiring practices, inclusive curriculum, or institutional policies. By the end of that first year, I created the CDO role and provided resources to create an office that would help me as president address these issues. I had an advisory committee help craft the job description and benchmark what other community colleges in the state were doing. Using data to highlight the dissonance between who we espoused to be as a campus in service to communities of color and the experiences of our students and faculty of color was fortunately received well by faculty and staff, and we experienced no pushback for creating the CDO role.

As a campus, we have been able to make progress on faculty hiring and academic offerings that are inclusive and meaningful to communities of color. All faculty searches now include training on implicit bias in the search process, and we have seen better racial outcomes in hiring faculty as a result. We launched a social justice emphasis in our associate's transfer degree that allows students to get transcript acknowledgment for taking five or more courses focused on race, power, and privilege in the US context. Just recently we partnered with the local school district to develop a grow your own teacher diversity program that won national recognition and promises to be a new model for increasing the racial diversity of teachers in that district.

There are many things for me as a new president to be proud about. My ongoing struggles with strategic communication, free speech policies, and the conflicting priorities of constituents remind me that I still have much work to do. The constant calls for me to issue statements about the campus stance on equity-related things on the local or national stage are overwhelming at times. My communications team has had to develop criteria for us to determine when we issue statements from the president. Even with those criteria, the pressure to speak to everything within hours or days of it happening continues to come from students, faculty, and community members. When I stood up as a Black woman speaking out against anti-Black policing recently, I was bombarded with negativity from both the conservative right and liberal left for either taking the campus too far or not far enough. Even now, the campus is examining its free speech policies after a three-week takeover of part of campus by BLM activists and homeless individuals.

As an activist who has challenged institutional status quo all of my career, I am finding the role of president both rewarding and problematic. It is rewarding because I get to put DEI theory to practice at an institutional level and dismantle structures that impede progress. It is problematic because I am now considered administration and am viewed as too conservative by other activists as I seek to balance the sustainability of the institution with its radical transformation of today.

As I have negotiated the role of president, I have found it helpful to continue to examine institutional capacity for DEI work. I constantly query what resources and partnerships I can leverage to further progress on goals. Partnerships with business had increased the number of paid internships that we can offer students. I have learned that utilization of an advisory committee on equity broadens the innovation of the college's work. Our advisory committee includes faculty, staff, and students who push us to do more. I have also learned that the learning never stops. My own education—and that of my team members—is crucial to continued fluency about educational equity and our campus work. My advice to new presidents is to do the same. Diversity, equity, and inclusion in higher education have changed, and presidents must keep up with the field in order to effectively lead that change.

CHAPTER 15

Remember the Reason We Are Here

Working with and Supporting Students

SUSAN E. BORREGO

The connection between college and university presidents and students is a powerful influence on campus climate and the quality of the student experience. Equally important is the president's advocacy for student success and providing leadership to the campus and senior team to develop and implement campus practices and relationships that will enhance student success. Support will look different depending on the particular campus you serve. However, an authentic, courageous, and emotionally intelligent president who is present and asks good questions will make a positive impact on the lives of students on any campus.

After thirty years in higher education, my experience has taught me not to assume that "putting students first" or "student success" means the same thing to all campus constituencies. I've learned that "success" means different things across campus. It is essential for a new president to plant a pivot foot in the mission of the campus to facilitate and prioritize the development of *shared* strategic goals for student success. Working to establish clear outcomes—defining what student success looks like, how it will be measured, and how the campus will prioritize these commitments—must be an early step each president takes. It must be a decisive step that leads in the direction of progress and achievement.

WHO ARE YOUR STUDENTS?

Student populations have shifted dramatically over the past fifteen years, and many of us still carry an old picture of students. As improbable as it seems, our faculty and staff often do not know *who* our students are. Those of us looking at the data struggle to find ways to translate it into meaningful information, a data story, that communicates effectively. A simple fact sheet early in the academic year could be helpful to campus constituencies, but it must include the nuances and context that are crucial to knowing who students are. Student populations are complex and vary greatly across institutional types. The president is the chief student advocate and the last word on the budget necessary for strategic student support initiatives. It is critical you get a clear picture of your unique students and their challenges on your campus.

Many campuses are organized in ways that assume the bulk of our students are "traditional" eighteen- to twenty-two-year-olds. Today, slightly more than half of the 16.7 million students enrolled in postsecondary education are traditional-age students.[1] While traditional-age students make up 78 percent of the students enrolled in four-year public institutions, student demographics are shifting to include a growing number of younger (think dual-enrollment programs) or older students, particularly in part-time and two-year programs.[2]

Also, more women than men are enrolled in higher education today, with women making up 56 percent of the total undergraduate enrollment. Despite an overall decrease in enrollment numbers in higher education starting in 2010, the percentage of students who identify as Hispanic, Black, Asian, two or more races, American Indian/ Alaska Native, and Pacific Islander has been increasing. According to the National Center for Education Statistics (NCES), between 2010 and 2018 the enrollment of individuals who were two or more races increased by 120 percent, and the number of nonresident alien undergraduate students increased by 42 percent.[3]

Our students are mothers, fathers, working class, and wealthy. We have Dreamers (undocumented students), increasing numbers of students with disabilities, students who are LGBTQ and/or gender fluid. We have trans students, students who, having chosen their gender identification, expect we will know how they want to be addressed, *he/she/they*. We have veterans. The populations are ever-changing. My point is that we need to get rid of the term *traditional* and be prepared to be light on our feet. We must let go of our assumptions about who students are and actually get to know them. As president, you will ultimately know only a handful of students, but knowing them will help you learn more about all your students and how they experience your campus.

The thirty-five-year-old and younger students on our campus are far more tech savvy than many faculty and staff. When I am around them, I hear them poke fun at those of us over forty for our technical skills! They say we don't speak their language and talk about institutional messages that sound like texts from "Grandma!" They think we are far too sensitive to negative posts on Facebook, Twitter, or Instagram. The students I have worked with do not seem as impatient or angry in person as their social media presence sometimes communicates. Additionally, they have consumed far more content than most of us, in bits and pieces, so they are aware of a lot of issues but may have less experience actually dealing with those issues.

From my perspective, social media is a mixed bag. Many students have told me about being bullied on social media throughout middle and high school. Having experienced social media bullying myself in my role as chancellor at the University of Michigan-Flint, I cannot imagine the amount of pain students live with, every day, for years, that's caused by the steady stream of negative social media. This experience also shapes their own online behavior. That said, social media channels can be potent tools to communicate broadly and engage otherwise tough-to-reach audiences. Students get much of their "news" electronically, in real time, and look for answers in the digital space. Remember, anything you tweet or post is public and likely to be distributed more widely than you might imagine. Many presidents use a range of platforms, sharing posts about campus events, awards, campus highlights, and accomplishments, and students do appreciate it. During the Flint water crisis, I sent tweets inviting students to meet me for breakfast or lunch at local restaurants, and it was a great way to actually talk with, and listen to, students without all the planning of a formal event. I believe talking directly with students, even knowing they are not going to agree with you, goes a long way.

DON'T ASSUME; KNOW THE DATA

Knowing the data about who your students are and what challenges they face on your campus is essential to correctly crafting your institution's priorities. When you arrive, you will likely be handed an institutional description of your students. You will be told who they are and all about the challenges they're facing. Do not assume these descriptions are accurate or that the student stories are up to date. One campus data story I was told was that first-time freshmen students were dropping out because they were working multiple jobs. I discovered the reality was that 96 percent of first-time freshmen on that campus were, in fact, not working. Clearly, they were dropping out for different reasons, and we needed to know why. On two other campuses, with large transfer-out rates, I was told that students were transferring to other, more prestigious four-year universities. After looking at the data, on both campuses, we found out most were actually transferring to local community colleges. Discovering that students were choosing to leave us to attend community colleges led to a set of interventions entirely different than what we would have used if they had been going on to four-year, more highly respected institutions. You cannot develop and enact a purposeful retention plan if you do not know what is driving student flight from your campus.

Knowing the data helps you and your team prioritize more effectively. If signature student support programs are in place, work with your team to establish a way of regularly reviewing the outcomes of those efforts. You must disaggregate your data and pay attention to the ways students are experiencing your campus. A caveat about data: it is important to know how these data are defined. Much of our higher education data are based on "first-time, full-time" student definitions from the US Department of Education (DOE). For those of us on regional public campuses, half or more of our first-year class may be transfer students. Therefore, it is possible that you are looking at data that include only half of that class. Well, that's not very helpful! If you ask how many students receive financial aid, you could get four or five different statistics. Again, not helpful. Do you want to know how many students are Pell eligible? How many received institutional aid? What information do *you* want and need? When you peer through the lens of your experience, you have to make sure you're seeing all you need to define the path for the success of your students. This is the most important reason you got this job. *This* is your responsibility.

You do have to be able to talk with your team and have the conversation about the data and how the data stories you tell are built and told. You do not need to spend your time digging up the data yourself, but you need to have it. Remember, asking for data sometimes scares people. Make sure they know you want it in your hands so that you are able to truly see and accurately prioritize actions and that you're not looking for fault.

All of us make unexamined assumptions about others. We're informed by media, generational differences, our past experiences with students, and a host of other factors. These assumptions may have *nothing* to do with who our students *actually* are and what their lives are about. In each decade since the 1980s, students have been organized into generational groupings. While the generational approach to identifying characteristics of boomers, millennials, or gen Xers and more has been somewhat helpful, there is a downside to what can become dangerous stereotypes. They allow us to think we *know* who students are without taking the time to *learn* who they are.

No doubt, there are some commonalities as a result of cultural influences, but the caution for us is not to rely solely on those descriptions. A first-generation Latino student from Los Angeles will be shaped by vastly different cultural experiences than a legacy student from Kalispell, Montana, who will be very different from an Indian student raised by immigrant parents in Sacramento. Also, students raised by immigrants have distinctly different experiences than students raised by refugees. Think about the budget implications of using the term *Asian* to categorize students. This will lump Vietnamese refugees in the same category as Korean immigrants. The needs and budget resources and the ways they're allocated for these students may be very different. This is a place where you, as president, must lead toward inclusivity. It is only through knowing and understanding who students are that you are able to prioritize. If your data are not disaggregated, if your team is not paying attention to student service and the lack thereof, your support efforts and your students will unnecessarily suffer.

CHANGE

Students tell us they are concerned about a lot of issues. To me, three stand out, demand greater focused attention, and are particularly relevant today: issues of inclusion and diversity, mental health, and college affordability.

INCLUSION AND DIVERSITY. Don't allow campus language to undermine students. I attended a conference of higher education human resources leaders and college presidents regarding diversity issues. One of the participants was describing current students as being "naive white kids from all-white high schools." That may be true on some campuses but was not my experience, nor the experience of many others in the room. On some of our regional and/or urban campuses, students arrive with better skills in working across differences than some of our faculty and staff. I've seen Black and Muslim students form very strong bonds and support each other around issues of oppression. I've seen straight students step forward and become allies, supporting LGBTQ and trans students while many campus administrators are still struggling to figure out what to do about bathrooms for trans students. This has been true on many campuses since the late-1990s, and students can be great participants in making the campus more inclusive.

I have been involved with issues of equity and inclusion at every level in my career. One of the tricky aspects of the presidency is that it is a position of influence and leadership, but less likely to be directly responsible for implementation. This is why it is so critical to work with and through your senior team, keeping the principles of diversity and inclusion at the very center of your campus climate conversations, budget, and overall strategy. One of the first things I did at my last campus was to ask the senior team and deans to prioritize time for all of us to spend a few days focused on diversity. We engaged in training sessions in actively combatting racism, both through our language and our own perceptions, and examined our role as leaders in fostering diversity, equity, and inclusion. If this is an area in which you have little experience, take some time to increase your own understanding of cultural humility and the history of systemic racism in the academy.

MENTAL HEALTH. Right now, there is a greater understanding of student mental health issues across campus, but it's still connected to a difficult conversation when it comes to resources. It is crucial that you work with both your senior team and your board as a champion for mental health support. The student community needs to hear your advocacy and commitment to providing meaningful mental health services.

I did not grow up in an environment where we talked about mental health. I did not know anyone who had been to therapy or was a therapist! Early in my career, I had to work on my own stigma around mental health issues. This work involved learning about mental health interventions and promising practices regarding campus mental health issues. I now know how crucial it is that the president be an advocate for student resources for mental health, for building and nurturing a climate that takes mental health seriously. Students are calling for more resources for campus mental health; they are incredible advocates and will leverage support from the president to reach out to their peers and carry this critical message even further.

COLLEGE AFFORDABILITY. College affordability is a huge issue to students, and they find many supportive partners on campus and echoed throughout the college's culture. You therefore must walk a fine line between the actualities of higher education costs and communicating return on investment and relevance to students and their families. According to the Brookings Institution, college is not really getting more expensive, in spite of what people believe.[4] While the sticker price of college has increased dramatically, the net price, what students are actually paying, has stayed fairly steady. Many of the tuition increases I've been part of amount to less than the cost of an iPhone (without the data plan!). However, that does not make the discussion about tuition increases easy.

I have primarily worked at regional comprehensive universities that had large numbers of first-generation, low-income students, so financial aid was a concern for both the institutional budget and student success. We know that financial aid is complex, but it is also an area that can make a real difference for students. Being creative with financial aid is important as it specifically relates to your students. For example, on one campus, our financial aid was structured so that it was going to all need-based students at the greatest need level. We then decided to take a more focused look and identify students with less need who would actually benefit from a smaller amount of aid. We also developed a "Finish Strong" pool of resources for fiscally struggling students who were within a year of graduation and needed additional resources to graduate. This is another place as a president where you cannot "do" the work of financial aid experts, but you must be clear about your priorities and the need to track data that inform where institutional money can be leveraged for the most impact.

Our students expect us to be knowledgeable, and they *deserve* for us to be knowledgeable. We not only must be informed but also constantly refreshing our understanding in the ever-changing stream of knowledge regarding issues of diversity, mental health, and affordability. We must commit to being culturally competent and humble, and providing the necessary leadership for campus to become more equitable. Students expect transparency with little definition about what that means. There are often not right or wrong answers, or single ways of doing things. We cannot meet all student demands, but we can engage them and be honest, and we can communicate. It really serves a president well to create relationships with students and student groups before issues arise. If we are not fully present, deeply engaged, and nimble in action, we cannot possibly build the relationships that are going to help increase student success.

NO SMALL AGGRESSIONS

At every campus I have been on, I've listened to students describe the devastating microaggressions they experience in the classroom. These experiences eviscerate the idea of an inclusive campus culture. These microaggressions have a poisonous impact on student retention, which of course is an institutional issue. Some campuses have found powerful and effective ways to prepare and engage faculty in efforts to create more inclusive classrooms. The difficult reality is that many more have not yet developed, or even embarked on finding, ways to effectively work with faculty to increase their skills of managing classroom climate. In many cases, administrators think they cannot "require" any kind of equity training for faculty. In some cases, there is strong dissent that microaggressions even exist, and thus microaggressions in the classroom remain, year after year. As presidents, we cannot shrug our shoulders and ignore this issue. We have to continue to be not only visible in our support of an inclusive campus but also effective. The provost and deans can work with the faculty to make inclusivity a priority even if it cannot be required. I believe faculty can have the largest influence with their colleagues in working to develop more inclusive classrooms.

LISTEN

Throughout my career I have been surprised by how easily some people can dismiss or underestimate students and their concerns, including mine when I was a student. It has always been interesting to me that we commit to supporting students in finding their voice, yet when they do, if they disagree with ours, that voice becomes problematic.

For me, one of the greatest (not simplest) aspects of working on campus has been my ongoing learning curve regarding students and all they have to teach me. Students have influenced my policy changes, laughed and cried with me, asked me to meet their family, come out to me, and shared grief and love. Some of the most powerful lessons I have learned with students are about differences and "otherness" and their experiences on my campus.

There is so much room for learning even when a student situation is challenging. Some of my most rewarding experiences are the positive relationships that came from a difficult student encounter. Four months into my first year as chancellor, I was on my way to a campus holiday gathering when I heard there was a "die-in" for Black Lives Matter on the second floor, so I decided to show up. While there, I heard other students yelling down the hall, "White lives matter!" One of the students yelled to me, "Chancellor, why are you here?" I said, "To bear witness." As I got ready to leave, I was struck by how isolated the students were on the empty second floor. I encouraged them to bring the die-in downstairs, thinking there would be people around. And they did. After the die-in, several of the students wound their way through the holiday gathering, starting a spoken-word poetic performance, an impromptu moment of asking us to pay attention. The party attendees were caught off guard but were polite. Two students made their way to me to tell me we needed to work on diversity issues. When I said, "I agree," they looked at me, then at each other, and left. I worked respectfully with that group of students throughout the rest of their time on campus.

A core of students will be active, at times strident, and they may have a short time frame in their expectations for change. They are thinking in terms of change in four years because they want to see the results of their work. It isn't always simple to be present with students and, often, by the time they see the president, they are frustrated and angry. There is no magic here; mostly we need to take a breath and listen. Don't promise you will do anything more than listen and find out more information. I don't mean to sound harsh here. You want to be supportive of your staff as you support the students; you do not have the full picture, and you likely are going to need someone else to deal directly with whatever the issue may be. You will often need to walk a fine line with multiple constituencies, but listening and being present will go a long way toward students feeling seen and heard.

IT'S THE STUDENTS

My background in student affairs has served me well as a chancellor. There are faculty who believe, somehow, that you will not be able to support the academic mission if you have not been a full-time faculty member or academic administrator. The issues college presidents are now facing have changed over time as have the backgrounds of those filling the role. Just as the profiles of students have evolved, so have the needs for different kinds of leaders with diverse skill sets and experiences. There is no size that fits all. There is important work for you in making sure the academic community realizes the value of a nontraditional path, should you come from one. Likewise, should you come from a more traditional career path, there is value in your recognizing the expertise of others who do not come from such a path.

From my time in student affairs, I've learned senior leaders can support students through a few key avenues. One of them is through facilitating strong connections with the student government.

When it comes to shared governance with student government, make sure your student representatives are treated professionally and supportively, as they can be excellent allies and critics. Involving them in campus discussions demonstrates your commitment to mutual governance and taking them seriously. In the context of shared governance, make sure student voices are heard. Beyond student government, athletes, artists, and Greeks, do not forget to include a broad range of students in your communication plan and relationship building.

You also have a valuable sightline into your student body: your dean of students or vice president of student affairs. An early reach is to have that person manage a list of student university committee assignments and facilitate those appointments. These are too often neglected; students' lives are moving fast and they don't get the slots filled, but then the story becomes "students are not involved in decision-making." Making this commitment and fortifying this relationship early can build an important bridge. Sometimes you might be tempted to create some sort of a student advisory panel, but be careful not to undermine the existing student government organization. All of this will be very dependent on understanding the culture of your campus and student shared governance. If you ever hear one of your cabinet members dismissing students with the line, "Well, you know, it's just students," be forewarned. If someone says that in front of your students, they will swiftly know they are not taken seriously.

One commonly accepted principle is that a great deal of learning takes place outside of the classroom. Many student affairs professionals have graduated from programs that teach about student development, supporting student learning *in and out* of the classroom, and about how to create environments that enhance student learning. We have managed protests, responded to student deaths, worked with those who experienced cyberbullying, talked with parents, and helped students identify what they need to be most productive. We tend to be engaged with students in a variety of aspects of their lives. Consequently, we are current with the breadth of students' needs and understand who they are as people.

If you have not had a great deal of background working with students, do not hesitate to rely on your vice president of student affairs or dean of students. Make sure they know you want a schedule of opportunities to meet students and attend events, plays, and concerts. You should also indicate interest in attending any other critical events. If there is an athletic program, attend some athletic events. Take some time to walk around campus, or maybe have a meal in the student cafeteria or the transfer student lounge. In the last few years, an increasing number of presidents have moved (or been moved) out of their positions because of student issues that blew up on campus. Student affairs divisions can be an afterthought. But in light of today's litigious society, issues of sexual harassment and assault, campuses being held more responsible for student behavior, and the critical work of creating complex inclusive environments, it is shortsighted to allow the student experience to be lodged low on the campus priority list.

STUDENT SUPPORT

As presidents, we have to stay current on many things. Understanding students' issues, their campus experiences, and what supports they need to achieve success *must* have a place on your agenda. Over the past decade, there has been a great deal of research into student success, and at the end of the day, we know it isn't rocket science. Retention and completion are the results of students moving through our system, fiscally, academically, socially, and emotionally. The cold reality is that our systems can be less than coherent, and when combined with the myriad issues facing students, dropping out becomes easier than moving forward.

Let me say that again.

Dropping out becomes easier than moving forward.

Because my background is in student affairs and enrollment management, I had a great deal of experience with systems. Most of our systems have evolved but not as quickly as the technology around us. There are places where someone made a decision without knowing the ways in which that single decision had an impact on multiple systems. For example, I once noticed long lines coming out of the financial aid office and students going back and forth between the bursar and financial aid; everyone was frustrated. Ultimately, we discovered that software both offices relied on was broken, so in this case the solution was a simple fix.

Another system that can be a barrier is wait lists. On many campuses we still expect students who want a space in a full class to show up the first week of classes and wait for someone to drop out. These old practices can really disenfranchise students who are working or relying on bus transportation, to name just a few. Additionally, this process can be handled electronically, but too often we have not kept up with technology and are not using such a system. Multiple "back of the house" operations are central to supporting student success. Ask your senior team to process map student systems, and encourage them to work with student government to hear from students where there may be processes that simply no longer work.

THE DISRUPTION OF ORGANIZATION

Significant processes related to academic policy, practice, classroom climate, and non-curricular issues have huge impacts on student progress. Academic-related organizational issues that often have nothing to do with curriculum can cause deep disruption for students. This often amounts to a slow-moving ground battle between faculty and administrators where the lines between academic freedom and professional practice are blurred. We know how higher education creeps forward slower than nearly everything around us, and sometimes too slowly to serve many students. Consequently, it takes the president and a strong provost partner, working within and through their teams with faculty leadership, to create the urgency to move the needle toward greater support of students. It is critical to have a provost who is your partner to work on the kinds of academic changes that will increase student success and enhance student experiences.

Research shows that clear degree pathways greatly bolster student progress, and it is very difficult to develop and maintain clear, functional pathways. For all kinds of reasons, there is often a huge disconnect between what deans believe is happening and what students actually experience. Once a provost and I brought three students from different majors to a cabinet meeting to give examples of degree pathways in their programs. In every case, organizational challenges made four-year degree completion impossible. Because pathways involve curriculum and course scheduling, and they are a lot of work, developing them can be difficult. What faculty teach, as well as the curriculum, is theirs to manage. However, the organizational practice of creating degree pathways that allow students to move effectively and smoothly through their academic program should not be a point of contention. Developing such pathways requires careful attention to details, such as when courses are offered, what enrollment bottlenecks exist, and the extent to which students are making progress through academic programs.

THE GIFT OF PROBLEMS

I have been in higher education a long time. I am still stunned by how little attention is paid to campus bureaucracy that unintentionally gets in the way of student progress. Campuses have decentralized, more so as resources have gotten tighter. At times, that can mean things like eliminating the campus operator, so now the admissions office is taking those calls. No one in admissions was trained to be the campus operator, but now staff are taking and routing incoming calls. This task takes significant time away from their admissions work, which begins to suffer real consequences. Perhaps the financial aid office has gone through a technical transition. School opens and financial aid is awarded late to students because of an unexpected glitch in the system. Students begin to get eviction notices from campus housing offices because they have not paid their bill, but they cannot pay their bill because they do not have their financial aid. Yet, both financial aid and campus housing report to the *same* supervisor! Systems often seem complex for those of us who work on campus, but imagine what it is like for students. And they are *paying to be here!*

Sometimes, bureaucracy evolves in ways that just plain don't work. Remember, there are all kinds of people who do not want you to know if or when things aren't working! The reason is that they're scared—afraid of taking the blame for mistakes, worried about bringing you bad news, and terrified to be identified as the cause of problems. From my experience, this is often because previous leadership has doled out punishment more often than praise. Your job as president is to make sure you and your team are ruthless when it comes to identifying and solving these problems. When someone brings you a problem, see it as a gift. The process of finding and solving problems means opening the windows to success. When you're new, you have the ability to confront things that aren't working without the baggage that comes from them being created on your watch. You have to make sure the campus community really knows you want to root out problems to clear the way for positive momentum. Blame has no role to play because, in your eyes, everyone starts with a clean slate. Encourage community involvement and find ways to reward participation that makes campus successful.

ADVISING ADVICE

Academic advising is another critical service for student support and success, yet it is too often disjointed and, when so, poses a barrier for students. Through the course of a student's time on campus, there are lots of academic changes, typically only recorded by the registrar's office. If no coherent communication and strategy are applied to academic advising, students will suffer. Advising can work in many different ways, but the "how" is less important than the understanding that effective advising is essential to student degree progress. It is important that you, as president, call attention to your clear expectations that this critical area is working for students.

I have worked with all different types of advising systems. The specific form advising takes will vary often by campus type and size, and multiple advising formats are successful. What is essential is that there is a clear, universitywide commitment to advising as a central aspect of student success and that it is working well. This is another place to pay attention to the data about where students might get stuck. Pay attention to majors where students might be dropping out in significant numbers, which may or may not be an issue. For example, if students are switching majors, that isn't necessarily bad. I would wonder if they were getting appropriate advising as pre-frosh or in their first year. Different delivery systems may be appropriate. Instead of face-to-face advising, would Zoom be a better option? On some campuses students are required to get a faculty signature to register for fall. However, faculty are on ten-month contracts and often not on campus for summer signatures. New students want to get their courses and be assured they are ready for fall. This is another place where staff must understand issues of inclusion. From my perspective, the advising staff function a bit like concierges. They are often on the frontline and know more about students and the bureaucracy that gets in their way. However, on many campuses, advisors are not at the table when it comes to drafting and reviewing policies or operations, and they offer a significant view on the student experience. As president, you want to hold a high standard for advising on your campus and make sure you ask for reports and data that demonstrate advising is functioning smoothly for students.

PREPARE FOR PUSHBACK

Activating your priorities can be more difficult than you'd think. They may require additional resources, new accountability expectations for faculty and staff, and reorganization of student services to be more coherent and streamlined. Many campuses have been working on student success initiatives for several years; however, most often the work is slow going, too slow to actually benefit students. Much of what is needed may be disruptive to a variety of campus entities, and even if there is room for improvement, there is likely to be pushback. This is where the president's role as advocate and influencer is critical.

USE YOUR TEAM

The president's job is to inspire others on their team to "do the work," and there are multiple ways for the president to influence success mindsets and practices and to interact with students. Students are successful when the campus is successful. This is where the president-as-champion role is important. Making a case that every campus employee is an educator helps to keep the focus on student success and creates a more holistic, supportive environment for students.

Building this shared approach begins with your cabinet. I have had the good fortune of working with senior partners who are excellent in their specific duties and understand deeply the role their division plays in supporting student success. At the risk of sounding overly simplistic, leading the ongoing conversations about student success as the center of campus business practices serves as a continual reminder of the critical nature of support. The cabinet is ultimately not going to interact with students on a daily basis like campus staff will. Instead, their ability to nurture and support their staff is at the core of supporting student success. Over the last decade, there have been numerous examples of institutions finding ways to support students. Little did we know that there would be such a heavy lift regarding institutional policies, as well as academic, business, and support practices. Advocating for students, supporting your senior team, holding high expectations for student success, asking good questions, and being very clear about your expectations are important to power student success on campus.

YOU WON'T SLEEP MUCH

I know higher education is changing. What keeps me awake at night is wondering if we are going to lose our ability to work across differences to nurture and build inclusive spaces. As a society, we are so polarized—we can shut out news and voices we disagree with, and we do not have to be open if we choose not to. And as I write that, I think about the students I have worked with, their high expectations of me, and their push for inclusivity and justice.

And I am hopeful.

I am grateful for my career of working with students. At times I think I have learned even more than they have. My job has included being with students in the highs of winning a national championship and also being on the sidelines with them when they lost a national championship by an "own" goal they scored on themselves. I have seen students persevere and triumph and achieve things they weren't sure they could do. I have stood with them when they failed, when we lost a student, and when the campus was in crisis. Many times it was not easy, but it has always been meaningful work.

I used to wonder how those presidents who shook every student's hand at commencement kept smiling. Until I did it. I realized my smile came from celebrating each of their achievements.

None of us is perfect, and you will make decisions that no one is happy with. Students' needs are changing, students themselves are changing, and everyone will want your time. If you are honest, stay at the table, take students seriously, and show up, student interactions will be one of the things that sustains you and reminds you of why you do all the other things you do!

Each of us is temporary, but the content of our actions and the results of our efforts have lasting effects. You may lead the university, but you do not own the university. We are caretakers of the special places that grow the future. Our footsteps will be erased and our words will go silent, but our work remains.

CHAPTER 16

Fundraising and Advancement

BARRY MILLS

When I first took the job as president of Bowdoin College, I found myself being questioned by my family, friends, colleagues, and nearly everyone: "Why would you take this job? It is all about fundraising. Who wants to spend all their time asking people for money?" And during my tenure as a college president, I was often asked by alumni, students, and staff, "How much time do you spend fundraising? Isn't the principal job of a college or university president to raise money?" People assume fundraising is nearly 100 percent of the job. And people are convinced that the job of asking for resources and support is uncomfortable and unseemly, at best.

At the same time, when I took the job of college president, my most trusted advisor and chair of the board reminded me of this reality. He advised me with assurance that no matter how successful I may be with the students, the academic program, research, the faculty and staff, and the alumni, if I didn't raise money for the institution, I would not be a success.

My guess is that, as a new college president, you expect fundraising will be a big part of your job, and you probably have heard much the same reaction and advice. However, I am confident that you would not have become a president unless you can be involved in all aspects of your institution beyond fundraising to make a positive impact. The other chapters of this volume confirm that the job isn't all about fundraising. In fact, to be a successful president one must commit more than 100 percent effort, 24/7, and be eager and willing to dive into the entire academic, research, student life, and business aspects of your institution. But, the practical reality of university and college life (as well as any business) is that without resources, it is incredibly hard to support all of the activities of your institution and promote the aspirations you have for sustainability and improvement.

So, welcome to the world of development and advancement.

Many of you have previously been provosts, deans, department heads, and in the academic world for your entire careers, while others (very few, however) have been nontraditional presidents who come from other walks of life (I was a nontraditional president). Regardless of your prior position in the academic world, the role of president is very different in so many respects from your past leadership jobs. The president of a college or university today is viewed by many as the personal embodiment of the institution, representing what most external and many internal constituencies experience as the institution. The weight of this responsibility and the burdens of the role are heavy for all new presidents, regardless of their past experience. And, from a fundraising perspective, in large measure your position and the perception of your position ensure that your role as president is central to the success of the development enterprise.

It will come then as some comfort to understand that the road to success in development is the same as the road to success generally as a college or university president. All of the work you will do to communicate and execute on your goals and aspirations for the institution; the work you will do to build trust and respect with faculty, students, and alumni; and the work you will do to live and breathe your institution are a predicate to your success as a leader of your institution and as a leader of its fundraising efforts. As you gain the respect of your institution broadly and people understand your goals and aspirations for the institution, you will put yourself and your institution in a position for success to raise funds.

Simply put, folks want to support, financially and otherwise, leaders in whom they have confidence and respect. It matters enormously if you are well liked, but most important is that as a leader you have to work to be respected and build confidence. And for major donors—and even all donors—it is all about their confidence in the institution, which is often about their confidence in their president. Success in fundraising and more generally as a president is complicated, but it is remarkably hard to be successful unless and until you develop with your community that intangible sense of trust and respect. From my perspective, "being comfortable in your own skin" is essential to leadership and vitally important to success in getting alumni and organizations like foundations to invest in your institution and you.

A sense of trust, respect, and confidence are determinants of success at colleges and at large, multifaceted universities. The president's role in fundraising at a large university is especially vital, and all of the qualities discussed above apply. However, at a large university the role of the president in fundraising is different from that at a small college because of the important partnership with deans of the colleges and the leaders of programs and institutes at the university. One of the key jobs of the university president is choosing deans of these colleges and other program leaders who have the capacities to lead fundraising efforts as well as the academic programs of their college. The distributed nature of a large university adds another level of complexity to fundraising, but the president remains critical to the success of the fundraising efforts.

In my experience, college and university presidents take on these positions because of their enthusiasm for the institutions they lead and their passion for teaching, learning, and research. You can take comfort in that passion for your college or university because it is, in large measure, the key to your success in fundraising. Because you believe in your institution, so long as you can articulate the mission and a set of goals for your institution in a genuine manner with a sense of passion, you are on the road to success. And, because you believe in what you are doing as a mission and not just as a job, the task of communicating that mission and set of goals can, and in my experience will, be rewarding for you and the institution and, very importantly, even be fun.

THE PHILOSOPHY OF FUNDRAISING

Before we discuss the mechanics and some of the practical issues of the fundraising effort, it is important to step back and consider why and what exactly the fundraising effort is designed to achieve. Regardless of the wealth of the institution or its size, it is critical for the institution to understand the strategy and goals to be achieved.

The strategy and goals are set by institutions in a variety of ways. However, as a starting point for a college or university president, it is essential for the leader to understand where the institution is headed and to identify the primary sets of needs and opportunities for the institution from their own perspective. The president often cannot and should not set forth these needs and opportunities by fiat, but it is important for the president to have a general roadmap for themselves.

You may be asked as you assume the role of president about these priorities. While you may have some fairly concrete sense of the institutional needs as you begin in the position, you may be well advised to take some time to articulate fully these priorities as you get to know the institution from the perch of your new role as president. Learn and listen to your community broadly over the first months of your tenure.

All colleges and universities are governed by the principles of "shared governance." This elusive concept varies in practice and intensity among colleges and universities. But as a general matter, unless the institution and its constituencies have some shared sense of the priorities for fundraising efforts, there is a strong opportunity for complaint and dissension, and the fundraising efforts will unlikely succeed. The consensus-building effort is often achieved in practice by efforts of institutions to create and implement strategic planning and/or through planning for a capital campaign to raise money for the general funds of the institution and, if relevant to the institution, its endowment. The exercise of strategic planning and setting priorities for a capital campaign is essential to successful fundraising. Hopefully, the goals of the president and the president's roadmap are recognized in that planning; it is also essential that the community of the institution, broadly conceived, understands and buys into the plan for the future.

That is not to say that opportunistic fundraising isn't important—institutions and presidents must be nimble to take advantage of opportunities. But, as a general matter, institutions and presidents should seek to raise money and accept funds principally for priorities or strategic initiatives identified by the institution, rather than ad hoc in response to the financial support opportunistically showing up. The practical issue here is that gifts rarely support the long-term costs of a program or initiative, and university funds often must supplement the donated money. Unless there is a plan and the initiative fits within the strategic priorities of the institution, a gift for something that may seem "cool" or in vogue at the time always has the potential to be an unfunded mandate in the future or the "sink" for funds that are otherwise necessary for more central activities. Bottom line: get the institution to understand where it is headed and where resources are required, and then focus intently on raising money around those priorities.

In most fundraising plans, the strategy for fundraising is inextricably linked to the "life cycle" and financial condition of the college or university. Nearly all colleges and universities raise money on an annual basis for general operating expenses from alumni, parents, and friends. Beyond these annual fundraising efforts, however, there is always the question of whether the institution is seeking endowment dollars or money that is currently spendable. Although not a binary decision by any means, it is important for the president to understand the institution and whether, and how much, money raised is necessary for the short-term needs of the institution or to set a path for the future through endowment.

As an example, if there are necessary capital projects that require funds for construction, the president may focus on these needs and the necessity of raising short-term spendable money. On the other hand, if there is a need for money for financial aid (as there always is) or to fund a new program, raising money as an endowment to support these efforts over the long term may be the focus. As noted, these decisions are not binary; but it is important for the president to understand how the money will be used and how to focus the discussions around fundraising based on the needs of the institution.

Many institutions with very small endowments or no endowment set goals for their new leaders to grow or establish an endowment for the future stability of the institution. This is often a correct strategy; however, it is important to remember that endowment spend rates are usually in the range of 4 to 5 percent per year, so unless the endowment is moderately significant, the endowment will not over the medium term provide the institution with much growth potential. Another way to think about this issue might be to focus on ten- to fifteen-year spendable gifts that would allow for a more significant contribution to fund the desired initiatives over a moderately long period of time for the institution. And, when the initiative is a success, it will be possible to build long-term endowment to support the project.

The point is that there is no simple one-size-fits-all solution to college finance and fundraising, and it is important for the president to be creative and flexible in leading the fundraising effort and planning process.

Finally, an important issue that has become more evident in the past few years is from whom and for what is the fundraising effort focused. Many colleges and universities have found themselves in controversies over what money is being raised for, who is giving the money, and what types of control the donor has over the institution. These are complicated issues; there are some who advocate that a college should be willing to accept funds from whoever is willing to donate, while others object strongly to accepting gifts from donors without questioning their motives for giving. The president in today's world must be cognizant of these issues and address them directly with the board of trustees and their institution broadly conceived. It is important to remind and reinforce these values with the faculty and the administrative staff of the institution so that everyone understands the "rules of engagement" and the importance of these issues.

I would remind the new president that one of the primary responsibilities of a president is to protect and preserve the reputation and integrity of their college or university. So it is essential in considering these issues that careful and thoughtful consideration is given to each gift consistent with the principles and mission of the institution. These are complicated questions where there are often no easy answers, but it is essential for the president of the institution to face these issues in a candid and transparent manner.

THE ADVANCEMENT TEAM

The president is the leader of the advancement efforts of a college and university, but no development operation can be successful without an experienced and comprehensive team. Generally, advancement teams are created for major gifts, annual fund operations, parent giving, foundation grants, planned giving, and stewardship (including the party planners and foot soldiers who make events happen seamlessly). The number of these folks is always surprising to new presidents as these operations are rather people intensive. Often in a large university, each college may have its own team of advancement personnel or a hybrid situation of college-specific teams supplemented by central university resources and staff. This is a major people investment that, if successful, yields important resources to the institution.

Most importantly, the president has to identify a development leader—the head of development who is often the vice president for development or advancement or has an even more august title—with the skills and experience to lead and organize development efforts. This development leader must be someone with whom the president has a personal rapport and who understands the personality of the institution (and the president). Personal rapport and trust are essential because the president and the head of development will spend a lot of time together soliciting and stewarding donors on the road traveling together. The development leader will also often be the face of the institution and represent the president with trustees and other important participants in the development work; as such, this leader must be someone who can interact with, and be admired and liked by, various constituencies.

The choice of the senior development officer is one of the most important hires for a new president. In most cases, there will be an entrenched development leader, and the new president will need to make the tough judgment as to whether the existing person is still the right person. This decision can be complex and political because the senior development person will likely have deep relationships within the trustee base and alumni community. The existing development leader may be the right person to continue in the job for all those reasons, but if the chemistry is not right between the president and development person, hard choices will be required. The president doesn't have to be best friends with the development leader, but the leader must be experienced, someone the president can trust and respect, and most importantly, someone who can raise resources for the institution.

Diversity in its broadest sense is also very important in crafting a development team. One key to success in development relates to the bond created between the development folks and the alumni, parents, friends, and foundations. The constituencies are diverse in so many ways that we typically think about diversity, but they are also diverse in what people are interested in as a vocation and avocation. So having a staff of development folks who relate to the donor base on a personal and professional level is essential to creating the bonds necessary to successful fundraising.

Technology is also crucial to the success of fundraising efforts and will become more so into the future as artificial intelligence matures. Presidents must be prepared to invest in the technology of development operations. However, it is important to pay attention to the development systems to ensure that the legacy systems adopted are right for the institution because once the technology is adopted, the frictional costs of change are high. Presidents are rarely experts in the technology, but paying attention to technology issues and getting advice from people who are trustworthy and reliable are essential—the costs of doing this right are high, but the costs of getting it wrong are higher.

I have thus far emphasized the central role of the president in development, together with the development senior leader. In addition, it is always very helpful to identify and encourage important trustees and donors to the institution to become engaged in the development enterprise. Folks who have supported the organization have a unique position of credibility in talking about why they donate and are often deeply ingrained in the institution's alumni network. The volunteers' ability to ask for support is an important partnership to be nurtured by the president. Of course, it is important to make sure that these volunteers are raising funds for the institutional priorities and not their own agendas.

One area central to successful development efforts in today's world is planned giving-bequests, annuities, trusts, and structured gifts. Often the fruits of these efforts will benefit the institution long after the president is gone. It has always been important to get the institution included in the will of donors and alumni. Although people can always change their wills, it is often the case that people do not do so. But, today with folks living longer, parents to take care of, children to educate, and uncertain economic times, many donors in a position to support an institution are looking for creative and flexible ways to support. Having a team of experts on staff or retainer to work with donors on these often-complicated gifts is important.

Finally, a president will always be told by development professionals that the bigger the development office staff, the more money it will raise. It is true that the development team should be extensive enough to support the development potential, but it is most important to have talent and organization rather than scale for scale's sake. Seeking out talented and experienced development staff who can become "infinite return" players is often more effective from a dollars-raised perspective and a cost perspective than the sheer number of development employees. This issue is always a tension in organizing a development operation, and a new president must be prepared to test and question the assumptions involved in building the development enterprise, as overhead is expensive.

THE CAMPAIGN

A milestone in the career of every college or university president is the commencement of a capital campaign to raise resources for the institution in an organized and focused endeavor. Nonprofit organizations today are often said to be perpetually in a campaign with one beginning as the last just ended. In a college or university setting, a president should expect that the momentum to commence a campaign will start three to four years into the leader's term and will extend for somewhere around five years. The president of the institution is expected to lead the campaign, and one's success is often measured by the success of the campaign's fundraising efforts.

In anticipation of a capital campaign, as discussed earlier, the president should think long and hard about the priorities of the institution and how many resources are needed to achieve these priorities. Often these priorities are established by a strategic plan developed by the college or university community in advance of a campaign or by committees established to develop the priorities. It is important in any case for the president to have developed in advance a clear vision of these priorities that lead the community in the strategic and campaign planning. And it is important prior to the commencement of the campaign for the president (or deans, in a large university) to establish a process for transparency with the community at large so that there is institutional adoption broadly of the campaign goals. This process is complex, cumbersome, and can take time, but it is essential for the campaign to be a success.

Campaigns, whether at a college or at a university, consist of fundraising goals established for priorities and then classified in buckets around annual fund commitments, spendable dollar commitments, planned giving, and endowment. How these buckets are organized and their relative size all depend on the needs of the institution or the separate colleges within a university.

The fundraising goals of the campaign should be realistic given the prospects of the institution. It is difficult for a president alone to make a determination on the size of the campaign and whether it matches up to the needs of the institution. The leader of the development team as well as the board of trustees will be very influential on this issue. There are outside consultants available who can test for the institution the appetite and capacity of the community and who can provide relevant outside competitive data. Setting a stretch goal for the institution is important, but the value of a capital campaign is the emotional and competitive "juices" that engage when a campaign is announced because generally the community wants to "win." The stretch goal established, therefore, has to be linked to an informed sense of what the institution has the capacity to raise, influenced by a generous dose of optimism.

Before the campaign is publicly launched, the institution will go through a "silent phase" where fundraising from major donors and foundations will occur to generate commitments somewhere in the range of 50 percent of the intended goal. The role of the president in this process is the most intense fundraising effort a president will generally be involved with during their tenure. This phase will have the president meeting far and wide with important donors explaining the purpose of the campaign, its priorities, and "making the ask."

Some presidents become comfortable asking for money. All presidents are generally more than comfortable explaining the priorities and making the case. However, many presidents need some time and experience asking for a dollar amount directly in a face-to-face conversation with a donor. A new president should not feel self-conscious if this "ask" feels uncomfortable. It is often difficult for many to directly ask for money from a donor. A new president should have confidence, however, that the priorities are important, the institution is vital, and the need is real. With that confidence, it becomes easier to ask for funding; but many still find the "ask" to send chills through their body. Like many things in life, practice helps. The more the president asks for resources, the easier it becomes. And, it is important to remember that in asking for the money, you are asking a donor to do something that matters to the institution, and the donor will feel good when the gift is made—even if the donor at the outset doesn't make the president feel that way.

A president may still be successful in the campaign even if it's just not in them to make the ask. In that case, bringing along the advancement person connected to the donor is a good option or engaging an important trustee or volunteer also works. But, in all events someone must be engaged with the president who can make the ask for a specific number—the advancement world can feel mercenary, but, in reality, it is about the health and future of your institution. I often would tell my board that money is not what we are about, but without financial support we cannot be the institution we aspire to be.

The "silent" stage of the campaign is generally over when there are commitments for about 50 percent of the target goal. Prior to hitting the target, however, an enormous number of logistical details must get organized for the next stage of the campaign. A communications strategy in print and social media must be ready to launch. There is often a major campus or big city event where hundreds of alumni, parents, friends, and supporters come to celebrate the "campaign kick-off." Planning for this event is complicated, and it is important to get it right in tone and scale reflecting the personality of the institution. And, there must be a strategy for "soldiers" to take the field to interact with hundreds of donors to generate the funds for the remaining half of the campaign target. A president is well advised to be engaged in all of these planning efforts, but if the president follows the advice set forth above about building a broad-based and effective development team, the team will do most of the heavy lifting with the president on deck to interact with important major donors and to show up and perform at the events.

From the institutional perspective, the president is viewed as the personification of the campaign, so the pressure the president feels can be intense. And, because the success or failure of the fundraising efforts is tied to the success of the campaign, presidents feel even more pressure for success. This is true not just in a small college but also in a larger university where deans and provosts are doing much of the work of the campaign. The intensity and pressure during this capital campaign period, along with all the other presidential responsibilities, can be draining.

Given all of the intensity around the campaign from setting priorities, getting trustee and community engagement and support, traveling to countless events, and the vast number of conversations with donors and public performance required, the president would be wise to remember these initiatives are a marathon and not a sprint. Although it is easy advice to give, but hard to make happen, it is essential for the president to remain optimistic and balanced through the process and to not take anything too personally, except of course the success of the big gift. The president of a college or university has many jobs and the addition of the campaign pressure is an added burden, but part of the job. So the most important thing to remember is the president needs to take care of themselves emotionally and physically and avoid burn-out. Finding ways to have fun during the process is essential. And, from experience, there is a lot of fun to be had interacting with a vast number of interesting people during the campaign. So, enjoy the process.

Finally, it is important to remember that institutional needs and priorities arise all the time and can be urgent for the institution. Often these needs are not coincident with the strategic planning for or execution of a capital campaign. Colleges and universities often create fundraising initiatives around these "one-off" priorities. These initiatives often require similar planning to a full-blown capital campaign. Accordingly, donors and presidents in today's world often feel accurately that the institution is perpetually in a capital campaign. In many instances this is true and reinforces even further the need for the president to maintain balance and perspective in the never-ending and seemingly insatiable fundraising efforts. This balance and perspective are important not just for the president personally, but also very important for the donor base to understand and be responsive to the needs of the institution in a way that minimizes donor and volunteer exhaustion from giving and participating.

TWENTY-FIRST CENTURY COMMUNICATION

Just twenty years ago, the modes of communication between a college and university and its community were tried-and-true alumni magazines, president's letters, reunions, regional events, print communications, and the general print media. Obviously, the world has changed dramatically, and the adoption of social media by a college and university is crucial to development success. Although this social media message is firmly established and successful in the for-profit business world, colleges and universities have been late adopters and to this date are not as adept or focused on their presence, identity, and communication through social media. Getting the college or university message out there is even more complicated because the number of voices that can broadcast about the institution is infinitely dispersed.

My own view is that the chaos of social media about colleges and universities, while complex and often incorrect and misleading, is on balance quite positive and allows alumni, parents, and friends to communicate organically in ways that can benefit the institution and create bonds that will be important in development efforts into the future.

It is essential then that the president assembles a team of social media experts (including young people and students) to assist the institution in getting its message out through video, Twitter, and all other forms of social media and to employ these modes of communication on a real-time velocity. It is important because this is the manner people get information and develop opinions; it is critical to ensure that the message and narrative of the college and university are out there in the social media as the college and university seek to be portrayed. It is a complicated and new world, but the importance of bolstering an institution's social media presence is a lesson that would be well learned by college and university leadership.

Social media is also an opportunity to generate resources in small donor amounts that in the aggregate can be very important to the advancement efforts of the institution. There are obviously many models for success in the political environment and the nonprofit world. In the future, these social media efforts will be even more important for colleges and universities because competition for donors' resources will be even more intense.

At the end of the day, however, the personal relationship among the president and the advancement team with major donors still remains vital. While it may be informed by social media, the personal connection continues to be the avenue to success in raising philanthropy for the institution.

FINAL REFLECTIONS

Fundraising is a critical role for the new president through their tenure for all the reasons discussed in this chapter. It is demanding but very important work. For many years in the past, colleges and universities relied on the bonds connecting alumni to the institution as the main catalyst for financial philanthropic and stewardship service and support. These bonds continue to be important and must be nurtured.

However, in today's complex and competitive higher education and nonprofit world, alumni bonds to the institution need to be nurtured based on "ideas" and initiatives. Donors are being solicited by nonprofits every day—from their colleges, schools, hospitals, religious institutions, social justice and environmental organizations, and on and on. There is tremendous competition for philanthropic donors. The best way to get a donor's attention is with concrete proposals for programs and initiatives that will improve the college or university.

Donors today are much more focused on immediate or medium return for their philanthropy. Regardless of whether the gift is currently spendable or for endowment, donors today are eager to understand how their gift will make a "difference" to the institution and how the impact of that gift will be measured and demonstrated. These donors often are not exactly asking for a return on their investment, but more and more donors and foundations speak in these terms of establishing metrics for success. It is important to respond to this demand for accountability.

Many presidents find this desire for proven impact from philanthropy less than attractive. This ambivalence to these new trends is understandable since it is often hard to be held accountable, and impact is often difficult to measure in a university or college environment. However, the trend demanding impact of gifts puts the president squarely in the position of why they have taken on the role of president. The president takes the job because they are looking to improve the institution in positive and meaningful ways—it is all about those "ideas" that move institutions forward. And so, the role of the president in advancement and development is totally consistent with the motivations of taking on the role of president in the first place. And the goals of the donors seeking impact is, in reality, consistent with why the president assumed their role. The new president and the mature president will be well served to continually be innovating and developing new "ideas" for their institution and ways to measure success (advice, I might suggest, that transcends the president's fundraising role). And out of these new programs and initiatives, philanthropy will follow enthusiastically.

It is precisely the opportunity to develop these important programs and initiatives that makes the job of president so exciting. And I am confident that the engagement with alumni, parents, friends, and foundations in support of these programs and initiatives will be invigorating to the president, particularly when they are successful. So to the new president: it is perfectly understandable that you may be apprehensive about the development role. But, I encourage you to view this role optimistically because it can be great fun and will lead to success for the institution and for you personally.

CHAPTER 17

The Importance
of Alumni Relations

PATRICIA McGUIRE

E very college president was a student once; hence, every president is also an alumnus or alumna of a college or university. This obvious fact may obscure a dimension of a new college presidency that is critically important to understand: the impact of the alumni culture on the institution. While the faculty and student cultures are obvious areas of importance for new presidents to comprehend, the alumni culture may be even more influential over the long term on the ability of the institution to change; to engage in substantive and sustained innovation; to welcome new student populations; to develop significant sources of financial support; to open career pathways for students; and to develop the volunteer leadership essential for good governance. Where the alumni culture is open, progressive, and supportive of a growing institution, the president will likely have important allies and advocates among alumni leaders. But where the culture is retrograde, inbred, defensive of tradition, and suspicious of change, the president will face significant obstacles in moving forward with innovation.

UNDERSTANDING ALUMNI CULTURE

A healthy alumni culture is essential for most colleges and universities to thrive. We love to brag about the achievements of our most accomplished alums, even if we look away when alumni sometimes are in the news for the wrong reasons. At the same time, presidents are often ill prepared for the costs of alumni culture and some of the great weirdness that goes along with the long traditions of the most entrenched parts of the group.

Alumni culture is necessarily rooted in some nostalgia, not all of which is harmful. Most alums have in their mind's eye a fading photograph of the institution as it was on the day they graduated, and most have little or no knowledge of the institution beyond that day except for what they read episodically in the alumni magazine or experience at occasional reunions.

New presidents have to understand the touchstones and taboos of the alumni culture, knowing how to use a cherished tradition to rev up the troops (let's cheer for the Tigers; onward Purple and Gold!) while also knowing when to confront what is unsustainable (no, we no longer allow segregated clubs and organizations; Greek life must follow the rules).

Presidents also have to help alumni to understand the role they play in welcoming and supporting new generations of students while (gently but very firmly) making sure alumni understand that their loyalty and charitable gifts do not give them an "ownership" share in the place. Colleges and universities must be free to thrive, grow, and change for the needs of each new generation of students; no single group of graduates or donors can claim "ownership" in a way that blocks innovation and change as the institution strives to keep pace with contemporary expectations for higher education.

This chapter considers alumni culture through the lens of several case studies based upon my thirty years of experience as president of Trinity Washington University (historically, Trinity College, Washington, DC). While aspects of the Trinity experience may seem, at first blush, to be unique to our institutional mission and characteristics as one of the nation's historic Catholic colleges for women and now a small university with some coeducational programs, I have chosen topics that have broader significance for the range of challenges new presidents may face when learning about the alumni culture on their own campuses.

THE WATCHDOGS: THE INDEPENDENT ALUMNAE ASSOCIATION

"But the alumni won't like it!" can be the most intimidating words a new president might hear, an implied threat that represses innovation and undermines strategy. The implied threat is spreading ill will among graduates, leading to withholding donations. New presidents may find it hard to ignore the threat, but they must do so or risk failing at their top priority: to make the college or university as successful as possible.

"The alumnae won't like it!" was a rallying cry that had repressed necessary change at Trinity College in Washington for decades. In 1989, when I became president of Trinity, the college was on the brink of collapse with just about three hundred full-time students. A relatively new program for part-time adult students known as Weekend College was thriving, but traditionalists among alumnae leaders demanded that the program be closed in favor of a "restoration" of the traditional full-time undergraduate residential college, an impossible task in the modern era. As a traditional alumna myself, I well understood some of the concerns about changes that seemed to impinge on our fond memories of dear old Trinity.

I had just completed a three-year term as president of the Alumnae Association of Trinity College (AATC). So, in one sense, I knew the alumnae association and its biases intimately. However, I was ill prepared for the blowback I received from my very first day as the college president when I learned things I did not know as the association president. While I knew that our beloved alma mater had struggled with low enrollment for many years, I did not know how severe the financial situation was until I sat in the president's office for a few days and reviewed the college's finances in some detail. I learned about management and administrative issues that had festered during several interim presidencies. I also encountered a faculty in deep despair and a student body confused about why nothing ever got fixed.

I assumed that the alumnae association would want to work with me to make the changes necessary to save our alma mater. How wrong I was! The trouble began when I asked for a meeting with the leadership of the AATC to discuss a necessary change in the association's structure in order to start an urgent capital campaign for Trinity.

The AATC, like many alumni associations, is an independent corporation and has been since its establishment in 1911. I did not seek termination of the independent corporation, but I did seek management oversight of the staff person—the executive director of alumnae affairs—whose position the college subsidized but who reported to the AATC Board of Directors, not the college president. I needed the alumnae director to work in full cooperation with our institutional direction. I also sought the AATC's engagement with our new strategic plan that called for much greater alignment of association activities with the college.

Immediately, the AATC leadership declared that I was threatening the historic independence of the association. They sent inflammatory letters to all alumnae, gave interviews to local media who suddenly "discovered" Trinity after years of obscurity, and bonded with senior faculty who also felt threatened by the strategic planning process.

When I asked the AATC leaders why they were so aggressive about an issue that didn't seem to move Trinity's interests forward, they responded insistently: "WE are the 'watchdogs' on Trinity," they said. "We are the ones who make sure that what you are doing will not harm our beloved alma mater!" There it was. The main rationale for independence was to bring pressure to bear against the college administration to ensure that no changes would occur that they deemed offensive to tradition.

In their missives to the alumnae, the changes the alumnae leaders denounced included everything from having a business administration major in a liberal arts college to keeping the main chapel locked when not in use for security reasons—changes my predecessors had made years previously. But I was responsible for the most controversial change that resulted from our strategic decision to start recruiting in our own backyard in the District of Columbia: the shifting demographics of the student body. In the 1990s, Trinity experienced a paradigm shift from a predominantly White, Catholic residential women's liberal arts college to a predominantly Black, religiously pluralistic, and highly diversified university.

Fortunately, the Trinity Board of Trustees rose to the challenge, intervening in several important ways. The board chair told me to concentrate on my job, which was to reorganize and strengthen Trinity, and not get distracted by the dispute with the AATC. The board chair and other trustees also met with the AATC leadership and held firm to the board's direction to undertake significant strategic change including focusing on educating the women of DC.

What I learned from this difficult early conflict served me well across the decades: First, do not engage in conflict unless absolutely necessary; better to let the fire burn itself out. Second, there is no substitute for a great board of trustees who will carry some of the load. Learning how to step back so others can exert leadership is crucial in times of conflict and was an important early lesson for me during this unhappy era with the AATC.

As I traveled around the country talking with alumnae about the strategic plan and Trinity's future, I realized that most alumnae really wanted a healthy, thriving Trinity, and they simply did not understand what the fuss was about. But the appearance of conflict, all by itself, was disheartening and a disincentive to giving. By increasing communications about Trinity's strategies and the context for higher education and women's colleges, over time the alumnae and I were able to move past the conflict and focus on Trinity's future.

Trinity's story of overcoming conflict with its formal alumnae association suggests several key strategies for new presidents:

- Study the formal organization that represents the alumnae and alumni of the institution and understand its relationship to the college programmatically, financially, and in governance. Some universities also have significant alumni organizations beyond the formal alumni association (e.g., sports booster clubs or similar groups), and understanding the structure, finances, and relationship of these organizations to the institution is also important. Be sure that the university's board of trustees understands these organizations and their legal structures in case challenges arise.
- Cultivate the elected alumni leaders as important partners in communicating about the college and sustaining the support of its graduates. At the same time, develop a broader base of alumni and alumnae friends, supporters, and volunteers who can be effective communicators about strategic plans and the vision for the institution's future.

- Educate the larger body of alumnae and alumni about higher education today, particularly regarding issues that are likely to drive strategic change and cause resistance among alums (e.g., online learning, changing demographics, and new programs or program elimination).

DEMOGRAPHICS, AFFINITY GROUPS, AND CHANGING ALUMNI CULTURE

The "watchdog" faction of any alumni association is most often intensely focused on preserving tradition. The very idea of change is kryptonite to their cherished memories of their alma mater. When change involves the institution's demographic characteristics—the race, ethnicity, gender, sexual orientation, language, religion, socioeconomic status, culture, and abilities of students—the reaction among some alumni groups can be treacherous.

"We are concerned about *declining standards*."

"We don't mind diversity, *but are they Catholic?*"

When Trinity alumnae made these and similar statements in public meetings at the height of our controversy with the alumnae association in the mid-1990s, I found myself ill equipped to address the racism and classism that were fueling this very public problem. I had to deconstruct my own biases and fears about discussing race in the public square, and more, I had to develop the ability to confront the ugly comments without bringing further harm to Trinity. Fortunately, I had some exceptional friends among alumnae who were not afraid to call out their classmates, and working with them helped me shape a response strategy that moved beyond the immediate tensions to longer-term solutions.

One of the most effective strategies we adopted (and still use today) is inclusion of our students in alumnae events; at the annual reunion, for example, we have a large group of students working through the weekend, and the alumnae love getting to know them—by the end of reunion they are exchanging social media contacts and vowing to stay in touch! Over time, as our more active alumnae told their friends about the wonderful young women they met at Trinity, the negativity faded, and soon I received messages of praise and pride for Trinity's progress in making social justice a real part of our mission.

By the year 2000, Trinity's success had grown along with the majority Black student population. We had a new strategic plan, broke ground on Trinity's first new building in forty years, and took on the identity of a university with several distinct academic schools (the College of Arts & Sciences, and the Schools of Professional Studies, Education, Nursing, and Health Professions). The Alumnae Association of Trinity College proclaimed its support for the emerging Trinity Washington

University, and alumnae contributed impressive gifts to two capital campaigns that raised nearly $50 million.

Despite years of success, the old alumnae culture still struggles with diversity. Trinity's student body in 2020 is 95 percent Black and Latina, and about 80 percent of full-time students are Pell Grant recipients. Many students have attended several different colleges before enrolling at Trinity, often taking more than four years to complete their degrees. More than one hundred students are Dreamers, undocumented young women who have enormous talent. A more racially diverse student body is also less Catholic and more Evangelical, Baptist, and Muslim. Nursing, not English, is the most popular major. While Trinity sustains its daytime undergraduate women's college, men are also part of the university in coed professional and graduate programs. These changes require considerable rethinking of the structure and format of programs and services for our alumnae and alumni. Historically, Trinity alumnae gathered in chapters in major cities and came together in class reunions every five years; a "class scribe" kept everyone informed via an annual written report printed in the "class notes" section of the magazine. Those structures no longer work for more recent graduates, many of whom graduate well outside of the traditional four-year timeline, so the very idea of the "class" is different for them; with many demands for work and family, they have little time for conventional alumnae social events; and social media has replaced the class scribe with more instantaneous updates on friends and classmates.

Beyond those superficial changes, the racial gap among alums across the years is painfully evident, with very few Black alumnae attending traditional events like reunions. Engaging Black and Hispanic alumnae remains one of Trinity's major challenges. An alumnae survey in 2019 indicated that these more recent alums prefer professional networking events, career services initiatives, and continuing education programming over the traditional cocktail parties and social events of past eras in alumnae relations.

In an unexpected way, the COVID-19 pandemic is also driving change in the Alumnae/i Relations office's structure, programs, and services at Trinity. With the traditional reunion events canceled, and even the older alums now Zooming, we are moving rapidly to new formats for gathering and staying in touch with our graduates. The single large reunion weekend with only the five-year reunion classes is unlikely to occur ever again; in its place we will have a range of smaller programs appealing to different alumnae and alumni interests and affinity groups, leveraging technology to be more inclusive and featuring a broader range of voices in planning and presenting programs than the previous volunteer structure allowed. New forms of programming and delivery systems will also make it possible for our graduates to engage more directly with today's Trinity students, providing a more robust mentoring system as students prepare to enter professional life.

Every new president comes with a change agenda, and the current climate for racial equity in higher education portends even greater institutional change. New presidents should engage alumni in strategic planning discussions with particular attention to these issues:

- Demographic change is already a reality for many colleges and universities, and this will accelerate as the United States heads into the time at midcentury when there will no longer be a White majority; planning for demographic change in the alumni body is an important part of institutional planning. The plan should encourage the formal organization of the alumni association to work with the university on specific initiatives to promote greater racial equity and inclusion among students and alumni.
- Students will be even more likely to migrate through several different institutions; take longer than four years to complete degrees; identify more with an affinity group than a class (such as a major program group, a significant cocurricular activity group, or a sports team); attend part time; and be working and even raising children while going to college. These changes will have a large impact on alumni programs and services in the future, from reducing reliance on class year cohorts to changing the narrative about who goes to college in the twenty-first century.
- Changes in the programs and delivery systems for all of higher education are urgent, hastened by the pandemic but likely made permanent by future market conditions. Making sure that alumni understand the big picture for what is happening in higher education, and engaging them in some of those changes such as online continuing education, will help them to remain engaged and supportive.

KELLYANNE, NANCY, AND THE PERILS OF PROVOCATIVE ALUMS

"You must strip her of her Trinity degree!"

"You must give her an honorary degree!"

Colleges and universities love to boast about their famous graduates, but sometimes those same graduates can cause significant controversy. The nomination of Brett Kavanaugh to the Supreme Court incurred significant protests among alumni of Yale Law School. Duke University alumni protested Trump Senior Advisor Stephen Miller's role in crafting harsh immigration policies. Critics wonder why the University of Pennsylvania is silent about its famous alumnus, Donald J. Trump.

Trinity has no shortage of noteworthy alumnae. Nancy Pelosi, Trinity Class of 1962, is the first and only woman elected to be Speaker of the House—twice. Kellyanne

Conway, Class of 1989, served as a White House Counselor to President Trump after successfully managing his 2016 election campaign. Each of these women has a record of accomplishment and also has incurred much controversy.

Speaker Pelosi is a Democrat who, among many other political issues on her agenda, is an advocate for women's rights including being pro-choice. Over time, I've grown accustomed to receiving letters from conservative Catholic alumnae demanding that I publicly denounce Speaker Pelosi and even revoke her degree. On the other hand, many Trinity alumnae also express a great deal of pride and support for Speaker Pelosi, and her classmates are always delighted when she hosts them for reunions.

Many alumnae did not know that Kellyanne Conway is a Trinity alumna until I conducted a straw poll prior to the 2017 presidential inauguration. In that survey, I asked alumnae what advice they would give to Conway as she undertook her responsibilities as White House Counselor. More than six hundred alumnae responded, and 85 percent of the responses were intensely negative about Conway and her boss. Many alums demanded that I denounce her publicly and revoke her degree. A small group of alumnae organized on the other side and petitioned me to award her an honorary degree.

I did not plan to make any public statement about Conway one way or the other. However, a few weeks after the inauguration, President Trump issued his travel ban targeting immigrants from seven nations with large Muslim populations. Because Trinity has a large population of immigrant students and a majority of Black and Latina women, I wrote a blog addressing the ways in which the Trump administration manipulated facts about immigrants to spread fear. In the seventh paragraph, I mentioned Conway's penchant for, in her words, "alternative facts." I did not consider the paragraph particularly harsh, but I did think it was important to mention her role.

A *Washington Post* reporter read my blog and wrote a story about my decision to criticize Kellyanne Conway publicly, including an interview with Conway, who complained about "disparate treatment" because I did not publicly criticize Nancy Pelosi. The story gained wide circulation, resulting in a deluge of comments—most positive but some quite vituperative. The most interesting part of the controversy was the fact that we received nearly $50,000 in donations from alumnae and others expressing support for the position I took.

Should a college president speak publicly about controversial issues involving alumni? Some critics claimed that I should have nothing to say, and instead, in the words of one correspondent, a graduate of Trinity, "stay out of the political circus and not judge other alumnae at all, sticking to celebration of their many and diverse accomplishments." I disagree. Teaching is one of the most important jobs of a president—we teach in every speech we give, every blog we write, every public statement we make, and every action others observe. Presidential teaching should advance the mission of the university and its values in freedom, truth, and equity. Certainly, prudence requires careful consideration of any public statement criticizing an alumna or alumnus. But real leadership also sometimes requires making that statement clearly and unequivocally.

New presidents should consider several strategies for dealing with controversial alumni:

- Focus on the critical issues that relate to institutional mission to discern whether a need arises to address something a graduate has said or done that impacts the university's students, faculty, or staff; all issues are not necessarily pertinent to the institution, and it's important to be very selective in choosing which battle to fight.
- Be a good role model for how to exercise freedom of speech appropriately, addressing the issues at stake for the institution and its constituencies, but avoiding personal characterizations (i.e., the difference between saying that the politician said something that is not true, and why that is harmful, versus calling the politician a liar.)
- Honor freedom of speech in response. If someone wants to reply to your statement, of course let that happen, and be as transparent as possible in letting all points of view be known publicly. You don't need to answer all of the people who will criticize you for speaking out; if you've done your job well, you will have made your point—and don't overdo it; know when to stop.

FUNDRAISING BUILDS ALUMNI ENGAGEMENT AND LOYALTY

Can a college change dramatically and still claim the loyalty and financial support of its alumni? Trinity has faced this question in the last three decades, and the answer is a resounding "Yes!" But sustaining alumni loyalty and support amid institutional change requires three critical elements: communication, testimonials, and success.

Communication

Communication—continuous, transparent, and rapid—is essential to sustain support in a dynamically changing institution. This is true for all constituencies, but especially for graduates whose connections are largely episodic and often informed by rumors passed along by classmates and friends.

As we were planning to launch a capital campaign to mark Trinity's centennial in the late-1990s, the husband of an alumna called me to say he wanted to honor her fiftieth reunion with a major gift. I was delighted when he invited me to meet in his New York office. Once there, to my dismay, he pulled out a fairly lengthy list of all of the rumors they had heard about Trinity from his wife's friends and classmates. He grilled me on the racial composition of the student body, their SAT scores, performance in class, and potential to succeed. At one point in my interview, and somewhat exasperated by his hostile tone, I said to him bluntly, "Look, I'm paid to give you these answers, of course. Why don't you come down to Trinity, spend a day on campus with our students and faculty, and then decide for yourself?"

He took me up on my dare; the couple spent an entire day on campus sitting in on classes and talking to students and faculty. I stayed in my office and let them roam at will. At the end of the day, they came into my office smiling, expressing great satisfaction with their experience. Then, with a flair, he pledged $1 million on the spot, making it a challenge to get other alums to join in the campaign. At that time, in 1999, it was the largest single gift Trinity had ever received. We raised the match quickly because they spread the good word about Trinity—in a sense, they gave permission to our donor's classmates and friends to show support.

Testimonials

Testimonials—affirming statements from alums and important institutional partners who became benefactors—soon became frequent enough that people took notice. When a prominent philanthropist, a business leader not otherwise related to Trinity, chose to make a major scholarship gift to support our students, alumnae noticed; his gift validated their alma mater in a way that was far more persuasive than another speech by the president.

Moved by that expression of generosity from someone who was not an alumnus, the Class of 1969—always conscious of their status at the apex of social change across generations—decided to devote their fiftieth reunion gift to funding micro-grants to help seniors graduate on time, a remarkable choice for a fiftieth anniversary class. "69 to the Finish Line" became one of the most successful reunion giving initiatives ever at Trinity, raising nearly $500,000 from a class with no singular major donors. The class leaders took the time to talk with students and to learn about their aspirations and challenges. The class even made a video about the needs of today's Trinity students, making the case far more effectively than any slick consulting piece might have done. Subsequently, and not to be outdone, the Class of 1970 launched a similar initiative with considerable success.

Success

As Trinity's transformation continued, we received more public attention for our success in serving historically marginalized students, and our wealthiest alumnae donors took notice. Multimillion-dollar gifts are not predicated on good stories alone, but on solid evidence of financial, reputational, academic, and strategic success.

One great benefactor, an alumna who owns her own company, spoke to her friends among a number of other college and university presidents and trustees, asking them about Trinity to investigate our reputation for quality; she came away impressed. She increased her giving substantially and launched a challenge campaign to urge other alumnae to do the same, sharing with a select group the insights she had gleaned from doing her own research on Trinity. Her insightful leadership has had a positive impact on the willingness of other alumnae to increase their contributions to Trinity.

New presidents face high expectations from trustees, alums, and faculty to get some big "wins" early on in fundraising. But sustained fundraising success requires durable relationships supported by research and planning.

- Establishing open, honest, and continuous communication with prospective donors gives them opportunities to explore the institution themselves, to talk with students and faculty or other constituents, and to understand the challenges and how their investment will help enlarge the life of the institution. Always make the case for that big gift from a posture of success, not need—while the university might need that $1 million right now, the donor will be more likely to write the check knowing that it will help one hundred students to graduate on time next year.
- Even while working on building relationships with major donors, take care to pay attention to the larger body of alumnae and alumni whose gifts are essential to support the college in the Annual Fund, and who will become larger donors over time if they feel welcome and included.

CONCLUSION: TRUST AND STEWARDSHIP

New college and university presidents have tremendous demands on their time and energy, and staying focused on priorities is challenging in the best of times. In the post–2020 landscape for higher education, presidents will have to deal with the consequences of the global pandemic in the many ways it has forced higher education to change, to innovate, to step back from cherished traditions, and to move forward with new modes of teaching and learning. At the same time, demographic, economic, and political factors are likely to drive even more dramatic change in campus populations. As new generations of graduates enter the alumni body, they will also carry expectations for greater inclusion and a more contemporary style in alumni relations.

In this new climate for higher education, effective and transparent communication with alumni will be more important than ever before as colleges and universities strive to regain their financial footing, rebuild enrollments, and recover revenues lost in the pandemic era. Fundraising, always an urgent priority, becomes even more complicated at a time when so much change may cause some alumni to wonder if they should invest in their alma mater.

Presidents need to design their communications with alumni to educate all graduates about the changes that are occurring not only at the university but also throughout higher education, and even invite alums into strategic planning discussions to build support for initiatives. Fostering leadership among alums who can also carry the institutional message forward is vitally important, especially when change is also likely to provoke controversy and resistance.

Finally, new presidents should always be mindful of the trust that alumni invest in them. The status of alumni in the community and their professional reputations are entwined with the status and reputation of the university—the better we do, the prouder they become. Conversely, when scandals rock universities and presidencies, alumni trust is shaken and possibly destroyed.

A president's most precious stewardship is the reputation of the institution, which is bound to the president's own reputation for integrity. The ultimate measure of a president's success is not the money raised or buildings constructed or championships achieved but rather how well the president enlarged the university's reputation for academic excellence: the value that endures across generations, uniting diverse groups of alumni in the common quest for intellectual growth and achievement. Presidents who are careful stewards of the university's reputation will have the trust, respect, and enthusiastic support of the alumni.

CHAPTER 18

The Power of Communication

SANTA J. ONO

In April 2009, when I was a faculty member and administrator at Emory University in Atlanta, I took my first baby steps into the world of social media by posting to Facebook a photo of myself at a university carnival. I took those first steps reluctantly, urged on by a student group.

Since that initial post, I have posted thousands of Facebook updates, tweets, and Instagram pictures and videos; first at Emory, then later at the University of Cincinnati, and now at the University of British Columbia (UBC). I have engaged in Ask Me Anything sessions on Reddit, hosted podcasts and Facebook Live conversations, sent video greetings to far-flung events, and, more traditionally, delivered countless speeches and penned op-eds and columns on a variety of subjects.

At first, I didn't find it easy to engage with people through social media. By nature, I tend to be rather shy and private. However, I pushed myself to do so because I believe that actively and personally engaging with the world on behalf of the university I lead makes that university more accessible and positively affects its public image. Social media, in particular, enables me to connect more authentically with a wider audience and has helped me achieve success as an academic leader. However, while I engage frequently on behalf of the institution, I still find it difficult to share much of my private life on social media.

My involvement in social media grew as I became more comfortable with using it. When I went to the University of Cincinnati as provost, the communications department there suggested I get a Twitter address and become more active on Facebook. After I became president, my Twitter following grew to about seventy-seven thousand—the largest number of any university administrator.

A question that many people ask me is why you personally? Why not delegate to a vice president of communications or other staff? Why should the president of the university be directly involved?

I would reply that a president has to be a communicator. Direct communication from the president is crucial to a university's reputation; to the building of its brand identity; and, above all, to its success in strengthening and facilitating relevant, meaningful community connections. A president is in a unique position: I strongly believe that, as president, if you're not using all possible means to send out messages to advance the institution, then the institution loses.

My evolution as a leader has centered on strengthening relationships and building community. It's important to me to be accessible and collaborative, and to listen to and learn from those I lead and serve. Communication—especially via social media—has been an important part of that. While I focus on social media here, the medium doesn't matter as much as a drive to connect authentically with the community to advance the institution, and to actively engage with both internal and external audiences in order to build a better university.

SOCIAL MEDIA: A WINDOW TO UBC

UBC has more than eighty-five thousand students, faculty, and staff spread out over two main campuses and several other locations throughout British Columbia. There is no way I can meet everybody, of course, but social media makes it possible for many individuals to have direct contact with me. I'm grateful to be made privy to our community's concerns—to know everything from a student worrying about a roommate who is coughing to a faculty member wondering where to get guidance on moving a course online. When appropriate, I'm able to respond rapidly (always mindful that I don't put the institution in a difficult spot), though often I refer the message to someone who can respond more effectively. I find that engaging with members of the community on a personal level builds trust, a trust that serves the institution well.

My tenure here at UBC has been built from the start on a solid foundation of trust and vulnerability, a foundation which has been strengthened for the past four years by bold social media engagement.

Certainly, communications can be a tricky game. While I've enormously enjoyed engaging with our campus and the wider world on social media, it can also be a difficult pursuit. Anyone can follow your social media posts—including people who don't like the institution or who do not like you. My style of informal communication has the potential to put the institution at risk, and there are times when social media is not the appropriate venue. I try very hard to think before I share because I represent the university, and I don't ever want to discredit it or hurt people. There are times when situations are very sensitive or there's a potential legal issue and I could get the institution into more trouble by posting something than by taking a step back. It's important to learn when not to communicate or when to switch gears to a more appropriate medium.

Over my years on social media, I've learned to develop a thick skin. My posts often attract negative comments—sometimes related to the post, and sometimes wildly off-topic. Though often sorely tempted, I never respond to these comments, though I do reply to genuine requests for information or clarification.

Besides a thick skin, you need an awareness of your own comfort level and your communications style when you assume the presidency. Are you more reserved and formal? Do you like the office of the president to maintain a certain distance and dignity? If so, then focus on speeches, op-eds, and blog posts. If your style is more informal, then add social media to the mix. I believe in projecting an informal, accessible image, so I am very active on Twitter, Facebook, LinkedIn, and Instagram—both for photos and for videos through IGTV. However, I leave the very casual and informal channels such as Snapchat and TikTok to UBC's student recruitment staff. Once I started a Snapchat account, but my daughter persuaded me to stop using it.

The medium you use also has to be appropriate to the message. For example, I find Instagram is best for informal communication—perfect for posting a photo of a snowball fight on campus, but not so good for announcing a major policy change or grieving the death of a student. Facebook, Twitter, and LinkedIn are good for celebrating the achievements of UBC and its people, but also for linking to more substantial messaging on other channels, such as the main university website. You also need to take into account the demographics of each medium. Instagram, TikTok, and Snapchat skew younger, while Facebook is used more by an older audience. Twitter is good for reaching out to the media and the broader community outside the university.

This is where your communications team comes in. They can help you learn your communication strengths and weaknesses, and the best communication vehicles for particular messages and particular audiences. They can also advise you when you're not sure whether a particular message or medium is appropriate.

This point brings me to perhaps my most important piece of advice for a new president: meet early with your communications team—not just those in your office, but the entire portfolio. There has to be a partnership and a solid understanding of what you're doing as president and how you want to communicate. If you're the kind of president who wants to have a visible presence, your team needs to know that, and you need to have regular, intentional conversations about what that looks like to you. Certainly, you won't get it right from day one—I've been doing this for more than a decade, and I definitely don't always hit home runs. It's always going to be a work in progress, but, over time, those communications experts will understand you and you will understand them. You will develop a natural alignment and trust through regular meetings and discussions.

In particular, to ensure that my communications and those of the institution are in sync, I meet with the vice president of external relations and her senior team every few weeks to go over our communications strategy. We map out themes and talk about what I want to communicate in general for the months ahead, as well as more specific topics for the immediate future. Once a year we strategize about how to build a story arc around strategic priorities for the upcoming year. We discuss how to weave in my social media messaging with other communications channels, including IGTV, YouTube, podcasts, print communications, and radio and television interviews.

Early on in my tenure at UBC, I let the communications staff know that I wanted to be hands-on with my communications. I would estimate that upwards of 95 percent of my daily posts on LinkedIn, Instagram, Twitter, and Facebook come directly from me, uncensored and unfettered by an approval process. This makes the communications people somewhat uneasy as, naturally, they're more comfortable when they control the messaging; but they also realize that it's to UBC's advantage to let me be me. My social media posts reflect my own personality, not just an institutional point of view, and are therefore more interesting, unexpected, and yes, sometimes challenging.

Since my @ubcprez account was created in 2016, I've sent out over eighteen thousand tweets, almost eight thousand Instagram posts, and thousands of Facebook updates. These posts have been on a wide variety of subjects. I'll post links to institutional news (e.g., how we're doing in the latest rankings, which professors are winning awards, which students are receiving prestigious scholarships, how our athletic teams are doing, and which alumni are being honored) and sector news (e.g., government funding announcements, changes to policies regarding foreign students, research agreements, etc.), as well as to local and regional news and to items that pique my own interest (science and music stories, especially).

Not surprisingly, a few of those thousands of posts have gone awry. For example, in a recent multichannel post, I used the word *lame* to lightheartedly describe my own musical performance. Since high school, I've used that word to mean "less than stellar." Today though, the word suggests a derogatory characterization of a physical condition. When a couple of faculty members saw my post and brought that to my attention through replies to the post, I was able to replace the word *lame* with *unpolished* on Instagram and Facebook; on Twitter you can't edit posts, you can only delete them, so I let the post stand along with the replies that pointed out my error.

Besides the risk of saying the wrong thing, there are other perils. For example, when you, as a university leader, post on social media, you leave yourself open to criticism, name-calling, and trolling. For example, when faculty, staff, or students disagree with a decision taken by the university (whether to cancel classes because of weather, for instance), they feel the need to vent to me on social media.

Once you're active on social media, you also need to prepare for a possible loss of privacy. Students have posted on Instagram when my dog went to the vet, when I've gone out to dinner with my family, when I've been walking around Vancouver, and on many other occasions, for example. As someone who's shy by nature, I sometimes find this lack of privacy a little discomforting, but I've had to get used to it and accept it as a way to further engage with students.

There are other challenges as well. Faked and hacked social media accounts are a fact of life. The former president of Harvard, Drew Faust, didn't have a Twitter account, so someone out there decided to "help" her out by creating a fake one. Barack Obama, Joe Biden, and others have had their Twitter accounts hacked. You have to be prepared for eventualities such as this. Once you set up a social media account, you not only need to use it, but you (or more probably your communications team) also need to monitor it and be prepared to respond to challenges.

Despite these risks, on balance, I believe that my being active on social media has been good for the university. It allows me to reach students, faculty, and staff in ways that would be impossible with more traditional media. And it allows me to have a conversation with them. People respond to my posts with comments and questions that allow me to get a feel for issues and concerns and that allow them to feel that someone at the institution is listening. Whether it's a student complaining about a vending machine that isn't being replenished or a parent announcing that their child has been accepted at the university, it's a way of establishing a connection.

A CHANGING SOCIAL MEDIA LANDSCAPE

More than a decade after first dipping my toes into the waters of social media, I obviously still have much to learn. When I posted that first photo on Facebook, MySpace was still the leading social media site (though Facebook surpassed it the very next month). The social media landscape continues to change, as do other forms of communication. I enjoy writing op-eds, for example, and believe they are a great way to reach key influencers, but many of the newspapers that publish them are facing an uncertain future. You and your communications team need to keep apprised of these trends, as you will need to adjust to circumstances that can affect how we communicate.

One obvious example of this is the COVID-19 pandemic. As we all know, the initial onset of COVID-19 created a rapidly changing and confusing situation. At the University of British Columbia, as elsewhere, the university community was demanding immediate information on how COVID-19 would affect them. Students wanted to know what would happen to their classes, faculty wanted to know how their teaching would be affected, and researchers worried about what would happen to their labs, to name just a few examples.

Because we weren't able to provide all the answers people were seeking as quickly as they wanted, rumors and falsehoods proliferated on Reddit, Facebook, and

Twitter. We clearly needed to communicate with our various audiences quickly, transparently, and candidly—but we were hampered by rapidly changing circumstances, government guidelines on what could be communicated, and the sheer size and complexity of the university.

One of the vehicles we chose for communicating during the crisis was a weekly video message from me to the university community. The video—which is always under ten minutes in length—blends reassurance, updates on how COVID-19 is affecting the university's operations, and a celebration of UBC's people and their actions during the crisis. It provides links to further information that students, faculty, and staff would find useful and always ends with a short musical performance by a UBC student or students (which are also posted separately to my Instagram account). Seen by over ten thousand people each week, the video (along with a transcript) is posted on my website, Facebook, Instagram, and YouTube channels, and publicized through all the university social media channels.

I record the video message at my home, using equipment and staff provided by the university's audiovisual facilities. At the same time, I record short messages and speeches for various online events, since COVID-19 has made in-person speeches impossible. These are then saved on the cloud, and links to the videos are sent to the event organizers.

I have found this weekly routine to be efficient while allowing me to stay in touch with the university community even when in-person communication is impossible. I can envision continuing to employ this way of communicating even after the pandemic ends. Although I used videos before COVID-19—mostly to send short greetings in lieu of an in-person speech to groups meeting at the university—videos have now become a much more important part of my communications toolkit; a toolkit that began with a single post to Facebook years ago and currently includes a wide range of tools, each suitable for a different purpose as I engage with the university community and the wider world.

To summarize, how much you embrace social media or depend on more traditional media such as speeches and op-eds will depend on your own comfort level and style. What's important is to be authentic and to coordinate closely with your communications team as you engage with both your internal and external audiences in order to build a better university.

CHAPTER 19

Navigating and Communicating About Controversial Situations

RONALD A. CRUTCHER
WITH ANDREW R. TILLMAN AND ASHLEIGH M. BROCK

This chapter draws on my experience as president of the University of Richmond to offer three critical lessons for navigating and communicating about controversial situations. I focus in particular on how to prepare for, manage, and communicate about some of the most pressing current controversies any new president might face, from a racist incident to an uncomfortable past to a free speech controversy.

LESSON ONE: NO ONE LEADER ALONE CAN CHANGE THE CULTURE

Over fifty years ago, I began my undergraduate studies on the bucolic campus of Miami University in Oxford, Ohio. Having studied cello at Miami since the age of fourteen with a professor named Elizabeth Potteiger, I had assumed that I would feel right at home on the campus where I had already spent so much time.[1]

Yet this familiarity did little to quell the profound alienation that I felt as a first-year student navigating the predominantly white spaces on campus. As I quickly learned, it is difficult to feel you belong when you are just one of two African Americans in your residence hall—and just one of about ninety African Americans within a student population of ten thousand. Making matters worse, my university—like most universities at the time—had no real programs to build inclusive communities for the few students of color on campus.

Thinking back to my graduation in 1969, I distinctly recall believing that the world would look far different by the year 2000; that institutions of higher education, in particular, would have learned how to use diversity as an educational benefit to change the campus culture—and ensure that all felt included and thrived, regardless of their race, ethnicity, religion, class, gender, or sexual orientation.

Recent events in our country—and across the globe—remind us that issues of equity and inclusion are as much of a challenge for colleges during the twenty-first century as they were during the twentieth century, from the "Great College-Yearbook Reckoning" to the barbaric death of George Floyd.[2] At Richmond we were reminded that our own work to build a thriving and inclusive intercultural community remains incomplete when we experienced a spate of racist and xenophobic incidents on campus in January 2020. In particular, several students of color and international students were targeted with hateful epithets written on their residence hall room doors.

Understandably, news of these deeply disturbing incidents ignited outrage across our campus and beyond. The university's Black Student Alliance, the Multicultural Student Solidarity Network, and our student governments issued a public statement saying the university had failed to ensure every student is treated as a "valued member of our community."[3] The Chinese Students and Scholars Association wrote me to express their shock and dismay. Parents started calling and emailing me with concern about their children's safety on campus. Local media were flooding us with inquiries. Our board of trustees wanted to know how we planned to respond.

Every college president will almost certainly face such a crisis, given that racism and other social inequities remain pervasive and pernicious forces in our country. While there is no one-size-fits-all solution to bias incidents, I offer the following three strategic steps as a foundation for navigating these difficult and painful moments.

First, put in place a bias response team *before* you find yourself on the hot seat. In this particular instance, I drew on the expertise of our Bias Resource Team to help coordinate the university's response. This team, which comprises everyone from our general counsel, chief of police, and head of university communications to our university chaplain, director of counseling services, and head of multicultural affairs, convened almost immediately and began considering our options for an effective response and community caretaking. The team helped ensure that affected students and groups received the care and support they needed; they worked with me to issue a prompt statement condemning the bias activity and reaffirming our university's shared values; and they recommended learning opportunities for the broader university community.

That brings me to my second point: in the immediate aftermath of a bias incident, serve as listener-in-chief, offering spaces where students can share their experiences, concerns, and suggestions. When I learned of the hateful incidents on our campus, I invited affected groups, including multicultural leaders and the Chinese Students and Scholars Association, to meet with me and other university leaders, so that they could inform our next steps. I also made a point of being present at student-led initiatives, from a speak-out on our university forum to a silent protest at a men's basketball game. Ultimately, I hosted a campuswide community meeting that brought together more than five hundred people to listen to students' experiences and expressions of hurt, anger, frustration, and concern.

Listening to students speak up about the burdens they had borne on Richmond's campus was one of the most painful moments I had ever experienced as a university president. I was especially pained when a young Black woman told me she had been singled out in class and asked to speak for all Black folks. Her story was at once surreal and familiar, mirroring one of my own experiences as a college student over fifty years ago—*fifty years ago*! Yet, as difficult as it was to learn that we were falling short in our effort to build a more welcoming, inclusive Richmond, this listening was, and is, essential work. From these important conversations, university leaders and I were able to develop a suite of actions that addressed students' most urgent concerns, including establishing a President's Student Cabinet to ensure student voices are heard consistently by university leadership and committing to the creation of a permanent multicultural space on campus.

A third and final point is to invest in the long-term work of building a skilled intercultural community. In the summer of 2019, the University of Richmond issued the report *Making Excellence Inclusive*, which defined a skilled intercultural community as one in which all members have the capacity to interact with each other in honest and direct ways across divides, from race and gender to politics and religion.[4] No single leader alone, however, can change the culture, promulgating from on high the creation of an inclusive community. Based on my forty-three years of experience in higher education, a leader must encourage the engagement and leverage the expertise of all community members to foster meaningful and sustainable change.[5]

To that end, we are using a distributed leadership team approach consisting of a Senior Administrative Officer for Equity and Community, who sits on the President's Cabinet and reports to the two executive vice presidents; an Institutional Coordinating Council representing faculty, staff, and students from across the university; and specific responsibilities assigned to each of the vice presidents. While this model is experimental and has been in place only since summer 2019, I have been pleased to see departments and divisions across campus establish new commitments to diversity, equity, and inclusion. Cultivating a campus culture in which empathy, kindness, and respect are part of the DNA is ultimately the best defense against the forces of hate and the recurrence of bias incidents.

LESSON TWO: UNCOMFORTABLE PASTS CAN LEAD TO CONVERSATIONS THAT POINT TO WAYS FORWARD

Over the past forty years, I have had the opportunity to live and travel extensively in Germany in pursuit of my musical career as a cellist. As an active observer of a different culture, I have been fascinated to watch the German people grapple with their history and confront their past transgressions. I have been especially struck by the ongoing project to install *Stolpersteine*, or stumbling stones, on the sidewalks of German towns and cities. These commemorative concrete cubes with brass plates, inscribed with the names and fates of thousands of Holocaust victims, are subtle yet consistent reminders that almost physically force those traversing the sidewalks to remember the past.[6]

As a university president, I have carried with me my memories of this important German practice and considered what we in higher education can do to ensure that we examine the full scope of our histories and keep memories alive for future generations. American colleges and universities are steeped in long and often inspirational histories, but if we are honest about our pasts, there are also aspects of our histories that we have ignored for too long and left out too often, from ties to slavery and segregation to the displacement of Indigenous communities.

Recent events remind us that college presidents can suddenly find themselves on the defensive when societies experience what cultural theorist Nelly Richard calls "eruptions of memory" after years of forgetting or only superficially engaging with uncomfortable pasts.[7] In the immediate aftermath of the controversy surrounding racist photos in Virginia Governor Ralph Northam's medical school yearbook in February 2019, universities across the country experienced eruptions of memory as they grappled with disturbing moments in their own histories, often documented in yearbook photos.[8] This process of remembering, bubbling under the surface for years, was then accelerated after George Floyd's death sparked the most widespread social upheaval since 1968, prompting universities such as Princeton to remove the name of Woodrow Wilson from its public policy school and other universities to commit to removing racist relics from their campuses.

This growing engagement with uncomfortable pasts is essential. As a nation, we have never fully examined and psychologically grappled with the aftermath of slavery, segregation, lynching, and ongoing systemic disparities. But college presidents must tread carefully, recognizing that any attempt to rewrite an institutional narrative or rename a building will likely be met with accusations of erasing or changing history. To be sure, such criticisms miss the point. To remove a statue or rename a building is not to deny that complex historical figures such as Woodrow Wilson made real contributions to American life. Rather, as the American Historical Association writes, such work is about determining who is "worthy of civic honor."[9] Responsibility falls on the president to demonstrate that the process of researching and shaping a more inclusive university story is a community effort, grounded in the complexities of the past.

At Richmond, I took two strategic steps to propel our own inclusive history work forward. First, recognizing that some members of our community would need a clear impetus or reason to engage with this work now, I launched our effort with an event our community was eager to celebrate: the fiftieth anniversary of the first African

American residential students to enroll in the university. Second, I established the Presidential Commission for University History and Identity, charged with reexamining our past to identify people and narratives previously excluded from our institutional history—and recommending ways to acknowledge and communicate our history inclusively. Recognizing the diversity of viewpoints in our community, and reflecting our commitment to inclusion, I ensured the Commission's membership included not only experts but also every constituency the university serves, from faculty, staff, and students to alumni, trustees, and administrators.

After seven months of work, the Commission made several recommendations, including enlisting a public historian to research and write a report about our landscape's historical ties to slavery, as well as to examine two towering figures in our university's history, Robert Ryland and Douglas Southall Freeman, whose names adorn campus buildings. After another six months of work, we had learned that before the university acquired the land on which it now sits, it had for more than a century been part of a series of plantations run on enslaved labor.[10] Research also suggested that there is an enslaved burial ground on our campus—and that the university had desecrated it while developing the campus in the early and mid-twentieth century. Finally, while research continues on Ryland and Freeman, it is increasingly clear that both men have complex, knotty legacies.

When confronted with unpleasant truths about institutional history, presidents are likely to both face great pressure to act quickly and have the power to do so. This reality presents several dangers for presidents. While a rushed process might appease one part of your community, it could very well alienate another part of your community. Many people are strongly attached to ingrained institutional narratives and myths, and I have been on the receiving end of my fair share of emails criticizing me for raking up the past. A rushed process could also flatten the complexity of the past, skimming only the surface of what is known about your institution and thus doing a disservice to all.

Uncomfortable pasts can lead to conversations that point to ways forward. To be successful, however, I believe there are at least two key steps presidents must take. First, slow down. At Richmond, students passed a resolution demanding that we remove the name of Robert Ryland, the university's first president—and a slave owner—from our oldest campus building. We engaged student leaders in dialogue as part of the work and research of the commission, both hearing from them directly regarding their motivations and concerns and taking it as an opportunity to educate them on the historical facts of our past. Some students were surprised to learn that, as my predecessor at Richmond, historian Edward L. Ayers writes, Ryland was not only a Baptist minister implicated in slavery but also a man who "worked alongside his black fellow Baptists, trying to sustain the marrow of his faith and of theirs even as he paid Caesar what Caesar demanded."[11] I should note that the Rylands are also valued members of our university community today, and it is important to us as an institution to give them time and space to share their perspectives too.

Second, recognize that you and your administration are not the sole custodians of the university's past and story. At Richmond, I established the Burial Ground Memorialization Committee to engage a range of stakeholders, including descendants of the enslaved, about memorializing the burial ground and the land's connections to enslavement. While forming another committee sounds both uninspiring and unimaginative, when done well and strategically, well-staffed committees can lay the groundwork for an iterative process of sharing research, listening to feedback, seeking input, and working with experts. In so doing, you have more opportunities to bring the community along with you as you seek to tell a fuller, more inclusive story of who you were, are, and aspire to be.

LESSON THREE: RESPOND TO CONTROVERSIAL SPEECH WITH MORE SPEECH

As I sat around a dinner table with a group of my peers in the summer of 2019, they turned to me when our discussion pivoted to the state of free expression on college campuses. My dinner companions were a diverse group of intellectuals, journalists, politicians, and business leaders, but they all shared a common concern that today's students lacked the resilience and resolve of previous generations. They had read stories of student protestors silencing controversial speech in the name of inclusion, from Yale University to Middlebury College. "Are college students really that fragile?" one person asked me. "How would they have ever persevered during the Civil Rights Movement when the First Amendment was at the heart of our efforts to build a more inclusive society?"

Many of my peers and I came of age in the 1960s, and we knew all too well that free speech challenges were not a new phenomenon for higher education. We had marched, participated in peaceful protests and sit-ins, and fought with our own institutions to recognize and protect our rights on campus during the Civil Rights Movement and the Vietnam War. From my own experiences of marching in the aftermath of Dr. Martin Luther King Jr.'s assassination to serving as a conscientious objector to the Vietnam War, I had come to believe that free speech is the single greatest tool we have to fight for a more just and equal society.

Of course, not everyone feels the same. One lesson I have learned from my tenure as a university president is that if a free speech issue has not yet erupted on your campus, it's not a matter of if, but when. And when it does happen, you are likely to find yourself walking on a political tightrope, navigating any number of obstacles that could knock you off balance. Given the US has entered a second era of widespread civil rights activism, one might expect a kinship to emerge between today's college students and those of us who were on the front lines of protest in the 1960s. Today's students, however, are more likely to believe that free speech conflicts with inclusion than my generation, and they might try to shut down debate when a controversial speaker comes to campus, as happened to Charles Murray at Middlebury in 2017.[12]

At a time when 61 percent of Americans say higher education is heading in the wrong direction, consider too that the general public—87 percent of whom believe that it is more important to protect free speech than to shield students from potentially offensive ideas—could lose even more faith in higher education if you handle a free speech incident poorly.[13] To top it all off, federal funding for education is often tied to the political whims of the moment. President Donald Trump, for example, directed federal agencies to withhold funding from higher education institutions that failed to comply with existing laws regulating free speech. College and university presidents who ignore these political and social trends do so at their own peril.

Experience has taught me that responding to controversial speech with more speech is the best way to navigate a free speech challenge on campus and maximize it as a learning opportunity. I was reminded of this in the fall semester of 2018 when a conservative and libertarian law school student organization invited Ryan T. Anderson of the Heritage Foundation to speak on our campus.[14] Many faculty, staff, and students called for me to disinvite Dr. Anderson, stating that his views were transphobic. Many LGBTQ+ students and employees said Dr. Anderson's presence made them feel unsafe. I empathized with these students and members of our community. As a Black man in America, I too have experienced the pain, discomfort, and at times fear that can come from the words of others.

Yet, even though Dr. Anderson's beliefs are not my beliefs and I strongly support transgender rights, my leadership team and I insisted that we allow him to speak. Dr. Anderson's thinking was influencing decision makers and had been cited in two Supreme Court cases. As several law professors pointed out, their students needed to be familiar with the case law Dr. Anderson would be referencing, whether or not they agreed with it. Moreover, as our law school dean wrote in a community message, one of our law professors would be providing a rebuttal to Dr. Anderson immediately following his remarks. In my mind, this was an important opportunity for discussion and debate, one in which we could model for our students how to hold speakers accountable for their words and actions and, if they so choose, how to protest peacefully. Indeed, as educators, I believe we have a responsibility to help students craft counter-arguments and develop both the internal and intellectual strength necessary to weather perspectives they find personally challenging. In my opinion, we do not help them develop those muscles by insulating them from speakers who offend.

Ultimately, Dr. Anderson came to campus, and members of our community protested his appearance vigorously but peacefully. Students dressed in white stood in silence, one by one, holding signs of protest. After Dr. Anderson delivered his remarks, Richmond Law Professor Jud Campbell joined him on stage for a spirited debate, modeling for our students how to marshal arguments against someone with whom you disagree. A group of law students lined up during the question-and-answer period to ask probing and pointed questions of Dr. Anderson. One of the protestors, who identified as transgender, later spoke about the experience of engaging Dr. Anderson one-on-one after the event. "Coming into this was really hard for me because it's really easy to vilify someone when you haven't met them," the student commented in our student newspaper. "It's hard to hate someone when you meet them."[15] I'll go out on a limb here and suggest that this meeting between a young adult and someone he perceived to be his enemy was among the most valuable educational experiences that student had all year. Indeed, this exchange—and the event overall—exemplified that our campuses can serve as laboratories for democracy, crucibles for learning how to live and participate actively in a democratic society.

Reflecting on the whole Ryan Anderson episode two years later, I do wish I had handled one thing differently, and that is how I communicated in response to requests from our LGBTQ+ community to cancel the event. In each case, I responded that Dr. Anderson's visit had no bearing on our commitment to ensure trans* students' full participation, inclusion, and thriving on campus. Perhaps I sounded overly legalistic, but I believed this moment provided an important learning opportunity in which our students would come out the other side better equipped to fight for a more inclusive society.

While free speech controversies on college campuses create an impetus for more speech and action, I would have done well to remember the words of Jeremy Waldron, who, in his book *The Harm in Hate Speech*, writes that the aim of hateful speech is to "compromise the dignity of those at whom [the speech] is targeted, both in their own eyes and in the eyes of other members of society."[16] Dr. Anderson's visit and his views evoked genuine anger, fear, and distress among our trans* community and allies. I wish that in addition to vigorously defending the right of Dr. Anderson to speak on our campus, I had also sent out an equally vigorous message to our entire community publicly reaffirming our commitment to our LGBTQ+ students, faculty, and staff and our values of diversity, equity, and inclusion.

"The University itself need not remain neutral in regard to ideas or beliefs expressed on campus," maintains our university's *Recommended Statement on Free Expression*. "The University enjoys its own freedom to respond or communicate the institution's values and principles."[17] My last piece of strategic advice is that every free speech controversy presents presidents with an opportunity to reaffirm their university's cherished values and institutional mission. It is critically important to lead by example in such instances, exercising your own right to counter-speech to uphold the dignity and worth of each community member.

CONCLUSION: KEY TAKEAWAYS

When COVID-19 swept across the country, shutting down universities and wreaking havoc in its wake, I initially felt fear and even terror; there was no playbook to address this global pandemic. But then as I paused to take stock of my feelings, I thought back to how I had led universities through major crises and challenges before, first as provost of Miami University during 9/11 and then as president of Wheaton College during the Great Recession. While I wish the United States had been spared these national traumas, I recognized that these terrible events had helped prepare me to lead Richmond through the crisis of COVID-19. Even if there was not a universal playbook on which to draw, I had accumulated over the years a variety of reliable plays that could be run to help the university community navigate the obstacles ahead and reach the goalposts.

Based on this chapter's case studies, I would like to conclude by offering five key takeaways that will help any new or future college president successfully navigate and communicate about controversial situations. First, put someone in charge of crisis communications starting on day one of your presidency and, with the assistance of that individual, develop a clear, inclusive process for generating universitywide communications about controversial situations. Proactive contingency planning will help ensure that you do not find yourself scrambling on the defensive—and will save you many headaches.

Second, and directly related, time is of the essence when communicating about potentially divisive events, but not at the cost of accuracy. Leaders will always face the dual pressures of speed and accuracy.[18] If you are too slow to communicate, you may lose control of the narrative. If you are too fast, you may make factual errors, undermining your credibility. To thread the needle, quickly send out a communication reassuring the community that the incident has your full attention, reaffirming the university's values, and committing to following up when more information becomes available. Such an approach shows empathy and concern for the community, generating both good will and time, while avoiding the pitfalls of getting ahead of the facts and stating a position you later have to walk back publicly.

Third, think carefully about if and when to respond to social media campaigns. While it is critically important for the university to monitor their community's social media activity, especially since it can serve as an early warning system for unfolding campus controversies, I have found it best to respond indirectly to social media advocacy campaigns—or, in some instances, not at all. College presidents must recognize that social media is an important way in which today's college students express themselves. To ignore an advocacy campaign simply because it is waged on a platform foreign to many presidents' college experiences is to risk being out of touch with the lived realities of today's students. At the same time, given the ways in which social media accounts can manipulate, obfuscate, or mask the identities or aims of its users (one only has to look to Russian troll farms' use of US-based platforms during the 2016 election campaign for chilling examples of this), I would advise caution about jumping into the fray. In general, having the president respond to messages on uncurated social media or to anonymous letters is not advantageous, and can sometimes have unintended consequences. A sharply worded tweet or ill-advised Facebook post could go viral, causing even greater public relations damage than the crisis du jour. Rather, as a first step, another senior university official—a vice president or dean, for example—should respond that they are aware of the social media campaign and, if necessary, outline any action that is being taken to get more information.

Fourth, do not be afraid of being vulnerable when communicating about controversial situations. Presidents do not have the same daily interactions with students as professors do, so it can seem at times as if they are detached bureaucrats rather than the committed educators they are. That's why it is especially important for presidents to be authentic and empathetic in their communications and give students a sense of who they are and what they believe. When I met with Richmond students after the racist and xenophobic incidents on our campus, for instance, I not only listened carefully to them to understand the depth and seriousness of the situation but also shared with them my own painful experiences with racism. This helped students better understand that I was not detached from their lived realities but had in fact had similar experiences. This vulnerable and empathetic approach, in turn, helped me gain students' trust and reassured them that I was committed to fostering a truly inclusive intercultural community.

Last but not least, always center the university's mission and values when deciding whether and how to communicate about and respond to controversial situations. As president, you will likely receive an endless stream of requests asking you to speak out on essentially every injustice on the planet. I remember when Donald Trump was elected president in November 2016, I received some pressure to condemn his rise to power, and I was tempted to do so. Then it occurred to me that I would have never released a statement if the candidate I supported, Hillary Clinton, had won. So, I decided to keep my views private. This is not to say that presidents should disengage from politics. When President Trump issued an executive order targeting immigrants and refugees from seven countries in Africa and the Middle East in January 2017, I did issue a statement condemning the administration's actions.

The difference this time was that the White House's actions directly threatened our values of diversity, equity, and inclusion—and could undermine our work to foster an inclusive intercultural community. University presidents, then, must walk a fine line when navigating controversial situations, defending institutional values while refraining from partisanship.

These five takeaways are not silver bullets for navigating and communicating about difficult situations. But I am confident that they will serve any new college president well as they develop their own style of leadership and address the challenges that will inevitably come their way.

CHAPTER 20

Leading Through Disaster with Courage, Purpose, and Resilience

GAYLE E. HUTCHINSON

The pessimist complains about the wind. The optimist
expects it to change. The leader adjusts the sails.

—JOHN C. MAXWELL

E nsuring the safety and welfare of students, faculty, and staff is a monumental responsibility of every college and university president. Accordingly, the president
must be confident and knowledgeable about emergency management, including continuity of operations for a variety of scenarios that may threaten life and/or the institution at any time, and be ready to lead through crisis at a moment's notice. Frankly,
it is not a question of if these events will occur, but when. It is incumbent upon you,
as a new president, to learn and know the steps to campus emergency preparedness
and management.

How prepared are you to lead your campus through an emergency, disaster, or crisis? As soon as you arrive on campus, I encourage you to work with university/college
emergency operations personnel to assess the strengths and weaknesses of the campus emergency management plan, and, if need be, revise it. Take it upon yourself to
know the plan well. Make sure you can easily access it at all times whether or not you
are on campus. Empower your emergency operations personnel to lead students, faculty, and staff in emergency preparedness and response exercises to a variety of threat
scenarios and participate with them. In fact, I encourage you to spend as much time
on emergency management planning and practice as you would on other university
matters like strategic planning, budget, personnel, and fundraising. The bottom line
is that you and your campus can never be too prepared when it comes to mitigating
and managing threats to campus and ensuring everyone's safety and well-being.

The first emergency I encountered as president occurred in the seventh month of
my inaugural year at California State University, Chico (Chico State). It was Sunday
afternoon, February 17, when local officials declared the Lake Oroville dam unsafe,

threatening all life below it. A state of emergency was declared and evacuation orders issued prompting 180,000 residents to leave the low-lying areas downstream from the dam. Thousands of displaced residents found shelter in the city of Chico.

Located thirty-five miles upstream from the dam failure, Chico State was not in imminent danger, but many of our students, staff, and faculty lived in the evacuation area. I activated our campus emergency operations center (EOC), which immediately began the continuous monitoring of the Oroville dam failure, and state and federal emergency response efforts that were taking place. The campus EOC also sustained contact with the California Office of Emergency Services (Cal OES), and the university remained on standby prepared to assist with emergency response if we were called upon to do so.

Our university simultaneously focused on the needs of our employees and students who were directly impacted by the evacuation. To assist them, we launched a series of campus communications that provided information about support services with a list of resources to call. Employees were also encouraged to call human resources for assistance with leave options and other matters. Faculty reached out personally to students whose studies were disrupted by the evacuation and granted them leniency. Food and housing referrals were provided by our Basic Needs Office to students within the evacuation area. Because the dam failure was not a threat to the campus itself, Chico State remained open; classes and daily campus operations remained on schedule.

Threats and hazards to campus will come in many forms and levels of complexity such as natural disasters (e.g., fire, flood, earthquake), system failures (e.g., boiler chiller, electrical), epidemics (e.g., measles and flu), pandemics, cyberattacks, civil unrest, acts of violence, accidents/injuries, chemical hazards, and more. Damage to the Oroville dam is a good example of a community system failure. Our campus response to the threat was timely and appropriate. At the time, I didn't realize that the Oroville dam failure would be the first of many threats and critical incidents that would require a campus emergency response and management. In the first four years of my presidency, Chico State experienced

- damage to Oroville dam and the evacuation of more than 180,000 people (February 2017);
- highly public suicide outside one of the tallest building on campus (March 14, 2018);
- the murder of a homeless person by another homeless individual on the steps of the administration building (October 31, 2018);
- the deadliest fire in California history, the Camp Fire, which caused 52,000 people to evacuate and left 85 dead (November 8, 2018);

- major flooding of Chico State residence halls and other facilities after a cloud-burst and torrential downpour (April 18, 2019);
- explosion of propane tanks and fire on a commercial property adjacent to campus (December 31, 2019); and
- the pivot to virtual instruction and services as the university responded to the COVID-19 global pandemic (March 25, 2020).

The Chico State emergency management plan (EMP) was implemented with each critical incident listed here. Upon the conclusion of each emergency response, the campus EOC conducted and filed an after-incident report and held a series of meetings with various constituent groups to debrief and learn from our actions. Lessons learned were used to continually update our campus EMP and were integrated into training exercises as we constantly prepared campus for the next risk and threat to come our way.

Generally, I think it is safe to say that new presidents don't receive a lot of training in emergency management, leaving emergency response skills to be acquired while on the job. I know that was true for me. Learning about emergency management and recovery in the throes of a crisis is like learning to fly a plane while you build it. Therefore, the purpose of this chapter is to provide you with an overview of emergency management and the steps to prepare yourself and your campus.

DEVELOPING AN EMERGENCY MANAGEMENT PLAN

A university president has three important responsibilities during an emergency: (1) protect life, (2) protect property, and (3) resume university operations (business continuity) as soon as possible. A comprehensive and detailed campus emergency management plan is essential. A campus EMP includes strategies designed to help campus prevent, prepare, respond, and recover from threats, hazards, and disasters. EMPs should provide guidance for a range of potential emergencies. Each response scenario defined within the plan aims to ensure the safety and well-being of students, staff, and faculty by minimizing exposure to danger. Emergency preparedness begins at the top, so it is up to you and members of your cabinet to lead efforts to train your campus in elements of emergency preparedness.

It's important to realize that emergency situations are often dynamic and unpredictable. Relevant and accurate information regarding the details and status of a crisis may be difficult to collect, or relevant information may change rapidly as the crisis unfolds—as we observed throughout the nation's response to the novel coronavirus and the resultant COVID-19 pandemic. As such, the EMP is an important guiding document. The president and senior leadership must set the expectation that the university's emergency response will be nimble and adaptable to meet the demands of a crisis under shifting circumstances. A university that is able to pivot on a dime in the midst of a critical incident is a university that will be able to save lives and sustain itself.

What Are NRF and NIMS?

Threats and hazards know no boundaries, thereby requiring a coordinated community emergency response and recovery effort. It makes sense then that local governments, support agencies, businesses, and the university use a common emergency protocol and nomenclature with the aim to make response more effective and efficient. Consequently, there are two Federal Emergency Management Agency (FEMA) documents among others that you will find helpful: the National Response Framework (NRF) and the National Incident Management System (NIMS). As defined, the NRF addresses the transboundary nature of threats and hazards, provides structure and mechanisms needed to manage disasters, and establishes a common approach to domestic incident management.[1] NIMS works to unite emergency response teams and facilitate effective collaboration across jurisdictions and agencies at a more localized level, which includes institutions of higher education.[2] Make sure the campus EMP incorporates the NRF framework and aligns with the terminology, principles, and procedures specified by NIMS.

FEMA also offers a number of resources along with a professional development series on the topic of NIMS that you and your emergency response team will find beneficial. Handily, NIMS provides a template for emergency management that is scalable to the size and complexity of the crisis.

Determining the Emergency Operations Center

The organizational structure of the university emergency operations center as defined in your campus EMP should align with the federal NIMS Incident Command System. I provide quite a few acronyms in this section, but they will come in handy later as you pursue greater knowledge about emergency preparedness.

The Incident Command System (ICS) is a standardized hierarchical structure that allows for a cooperative response by multiple agencies, both within and outside of government, to organize and coordinate response activities without compromising the decision-making authority of local command. ICS ensures that the most pressing needs are met, and that precious resources are used without duplication or waste.[3]

The ICS is designed to facilitate an institution's emergency response using five functional groups: command, operations, planning, logistics, and finance administration. I will admit that it took several emergencies before members of the EOC, cabinet, and I developed proficiency in working with and across these five functions. In hindsight, I believe we could have been more familiar with this command structure had we used case studies and hands-on simulations to practice it ahead of time.

As president, you should consider tailoring the campus EOC organizational structure to the demands of the crisis and the needs of the institution. But, remember that aligning the structure with the ICS enables the EOC to communicate more effectively with governmental and nongovernmental agencies engaged in emergency response and recovery.

Informing the campus community about the purpose of the EOC and the relevance of the five functional areas of emergency response will help clarify how and why decisions are made, who makes decisions, and why certain actions were taken during a crisis. Faculty, staff, and students outside of the EOC will want to be involved and helpful during an emergency. The president and cabinet should welcome this assistance when it makes sense and it is safe to do so. In fact, presidents should think seriously about how to coordinate emergency management actions with principles of shared governance as established on their campus. And, in keeping with the spirit of shared governance, the campus community must be kept informed about the status of a crisis through frequent and focused communications, and consulted at appropriate times. Engaging the expertise of faculty, staff, and students, when safe to do so, is essential to the quality and success of emergency response and to recovery initiatives. Acts of inclusiveness also strengthen a sense of community on campus and uplift morale.

Aligning the EOC structure with that of ICS streamlines interactions and communications between the university and outside agencies and community partners because all of you are implementing a common emergency management and communications structure designed to optimize collaboration and unify response efforts.

THE PHASES OF EMERGENCY MANAGEMENT

There are four phases to emergency management: prevention/mitigation, preparedness, campus emergency response and continuity of university operations, and continuity of university operations with long-term recovery. For the purpose of this chapter, the focus is on campus emergency response and continuity of university operations, and university operations with long-term recovery using Chico State's response to the deadliest wildfire in California history, the Camp Fire, as an example.

I. CAMPUS EMERGENCY RESPONSE AND CONTINUITY OF UNIVERSITY OPERATIONS

It is generally known that summer wildfires in California are a common occurrence. However, wildfires in California have increased in their frequency and severity in recent years. The Camp Fire began around 6:15 a.m. on November 8, 2018, in Pulga, California, a Ridge community roughly thirty-five miles east of Chico. When the fire started, the winds were blowing at fifty miles per hour. At one point, the fire was moving roughly eighty football fields per minute, consuming everything in its path. During the first six hours of the Camp Fire, the rural Ridge communities of Concow and Paradise were obliterated. Fifty-two thousand people were evacuated. Over nineteen thousand buildings were destroyed, most of which were people's homes. The Camp Fire was extinguished eighteen days later leaving eighty-five people dead, tens of thousands of people homeless, and thousands of pets and livestock displaced. Total acreage burned was 154,000.[4]

The fire burned close to the city line of Chico and within five miles of the Chico State campus. Chico residents observed the fire burning on the Ridge from their homes. The smoke from the fire resulted in severe air pollution not just in Chico and the county, but in most of northern California.

On the morning of November 8, 2018, I was sitting in the Portland, Oregon, airport with my wife, waiting for a flight to Reno, Nevada, where we were scheduled to meet with alumni and donors later that day. My chief of staff called me around 8:12 a.m., literally right before we boarded the plane. She explained that a fire was burning in the foothills east of town (known as the Ridge) and the town of Paradise was being evacuated. She reported that the cabinet activated the EOC in my stead. The cabinet and EOC command core began assessing the level of threat to campus and the region based on information that was flowing from the California Office of Emergency Services, county and city agencies, and news outlets. At the time, no one except those in the belly of the fire truly understood the gravity of the situation.

Our flight path from Portland to Reno took us over the Sierra Nevada Mountains and, in the distance, we could see the bellow of smoke rising from the inferno. Once I was safely in Reno, my staff informed me that the fire was raging out of control. All roads leading off the Ridge (and there were only four) were jammed with people escaping with their lives. With that news, I knew I needed to return to campus immediately. Normally, Chico is a three-hour drive from Reno. On this day, it took us longer than six hours. As the associate vice president of advancement drove us back to campus, I remained in constant contact with the EOC as they managed the situation and we began outlining emergency actions to be taken.

Initial Campus Emergency Response

As I mentioned earlier, as president you have three primary responsibilities during an emergency: (1) protect life, (2) protect property, and (3) resume university operations (business continuity) as soon as possible. As the Chico State EOC monitored the Camp Fire, our initial efforts were focused on the whereabouts, safety, and well-being of our students, faculty, and staff. All immediate actions during our initial emergency response were laser focused on life safety.

The EOC took these immediate actions related to protecting life and property and resuming university operations:

- Monitored constantly the status of the fire and community needs through NIMs communication strategy and other reliable sources.
- Activated and continuously operated the campus emergency notification system.
- Began identifying and reaching out to students, faculty, and staff evacuated from the fire.
- Canceled classes on the afternoon of Thursday, November 8, and all day on Friday, November 9. As the Camp Fire raged, students who could were encouraged to leave the area for the weekend. All other students who could not leave and who were not affected by the fire were asked to shelter in place.
- Accounted for and assisted all students living on campus including international students.
- Provided shelter to twenty-eight Red Cross volunteers in our gymnasia; provided housing to the California State University Critical Response Unit, which comprised twenty-six officers from other campuses, for nine days as they assisted local law enforcement.
- Provided showers in our locker rooms to firefighters and other first responders during their shift changes.
- Opened our largest auditorium, which has a capacity to hold 1,200 people, so that the town of Paradise and Cal Fire could conduct community meetings, and we supported this event with Chico State public events staff.
- Kept open the Hungry Wildcat food pantry for displaced students as well as students who regularly rely on assistance while campus was closed during the emergency.
- Launched an imperfect needs survey to identify the most urgent needs of students, faculty, and staff directly impacted by the Camp Fire.
- Established a comprehensive communications strategy that would provide continuous information to students, staff, faculty, alumni, parents, the system office, and the public using campuswide announcements, social media platforms, the Chico State website banner and links, internal memos, a calling center, and video messages directly from the president.
- Established a centralized office where employees could retrieve paychecks and receive a free N95 mask to help with extremely poor air quality.
- Placed a list of frequently asked questions and answers in both English and Spanish on the university website and updated it daily.

- Communicated frequently with other emergency agencies, both government and nongovernment, school districts, county and city officials, and in our case the California State University chancellor, and determined additional ways that the university could assist the community.

The EOC worked around the clock for the first thirty-six hours of the Camp Fire. Once it was clear that Chico State was no longer in imminent danger of the fire, the EOC convened each morning at 7:30 a.m. and worked straight through into the late evening each day, nearly fourteen hours a day for eighteen days. Each morning the EOC and cabinet met as a whole group to receive an incident status report. We would then review and assess our decisions and actions to date. Next, we determined daily objectives and identified tasks to be completed. After the morning briefing, the EOC would disperse with each cabinet member working with emergency leads and facilitating the work that needed to be done to accomplish objectives and tasks. Each evening before going home, EOC members would reconvene, hear a status report on the fire, assess progress made on campus objectives and tasks, and identify challenges rising. We continued this practice weeks past the eighteen days during which the Camp Fire roared in an effort to return campus to a long-term operational focus.

Lessons Learned During Initial Campus Emergency Response
The EOC recorded and archived all decisions, actions, and lessons learned in what's called the after-incident report. Lessons learned were used to improve and revise the EMP as we prepared for future crises. The following are selected lessons learned during our initial emergency response to the Camp Fire:

- *Define clearly "essential personnel."* When I closed campus to everyone but essential personnel, I thought that faculty and staff would know that essential personnel meant the university police department and skeletal work crews in the areas of facility management, health and wellness services, human resources, risk management, food service and housing, cabinet, and members of the EOC. What I didn't anticipate was how upset associate vice presidents, deans, department chairs, directors, academic senate officers, and student government officers became when they learned that they were not included in the definition. Many faculty members were disappointed by the news as well. All concerned informed me that their work was "essential." In many ways, they were right. Moving forward, I found it important to define essential personnel ahead of time and determine roles and responsibilities of all employees during emergencies. Additionally, I suggest that you make sure that your campus EMP is able to integrate consultation with the academic senate and principles of shared governance into the campus emergency response, when appropriate and safe to do so.

- *Appoint secondary and tertiary members of the EOC.* When an EOC member becomes ill or needs to stay home for some reason, a predetermined designee should take the member's place on the EOC. Much like an understudy takes over for the lead in a play, the transition should be seamless. In the event that the member and designee are unable to attend the EOC, then an appointed third person should be able to step in and continue the work. Unfortunately, I did not realize the importance of taking this step until one of our EOC members took ill and had to stay home.

- *Maintain the health and well-being of each EOC member.* This is a difficult task but one that is essential because emergency response requires all-hands-on-deck for the entirety of the event. Some emergencies are short in duration while others could go on for months. As president, you should insist that EOC members take a day or two off for their own health. Create a staff rotation system to ensure members can take time away and replenish their energy. Additionally, keep the EOC situation/meeting room clean and sanitized daily in order to significantly reduce the spread of disease.

- *Be prepared for secondary emergencies that may emerge as a result of the first.* The smoke from the Camp Fire was so thick that it blanketed Butte County where the fire originated, along with areas to the south and west. Chico was smothered in smoke. San Francisco, which is located roughly 150 miles southwest of the Camp Fire, reported its worst period of hazardous smoke since 1999.

Campus provided N95 masks to members of the EOC, essential staff working on campus, and any student or employee who wished to obtain one. For weeks, Butte County Public Health and Cal OES encouraged everyone who ventured outdoors to wear an N95 mask for their own safety. There were times when the air quality inside the EOC meeting room was so poor that we wore N95 masks indoors too. For those buildings that were open with limited service, facilities management changed the air filters frequently during the eighteen days of the fire.

Poor air quality was a contributing factor to canceling classes at Chico State. Our sister campuses located in northern California were also making decisions to close based on air quality. It became apparent that campus presidents were not using the same standard of air quality upon which to decide to close campus. This inconsistency created confusion around the California State University system and confusion for students, faculty, staff, and parents. A lesson learned here was to determine a reliable common standard for air quality against which decisions to close campus could be made.

Based on the severity of the Camp Fire and thickness of smoke that engulfed the region, I declared a campus state of emergency, thereby closing campus and continuing the cancellation of classes from November 12 through November 26. As it were, we only lost five and a half days of instruction (November 8–16). The reason more class time was not lost was that Chico State never schedules classes during the week of Thanksgiving, so there was no loss of instruction during the week of November 18. The provost and I worked with the chancellor's office to write a letter of justification to the Department of Education explaining why classes needed to be canceled.

Students were concerned about completing coursework during the time that classes were canceled. Faculty, department chairs, and deans worked hand-in-hand with advising and student support services to allay student fears and concerns. Aaron Draper, lecturer in the Department of Media Arts, Design, and Technology, shared a heartfelt letter with his students. The provost asked his permission to send a copy of his letter to her leadership team in hopes it would serve as a model for faculty communicating with students. I share it with you here:

Dear Students:

Our CSU Chico President, Gayle Hutchinson, has decided that it would be best to cancel classes next week. I support this decision 100%. The air quality is unhealthy to breathe and many students, faculty and staff members have been affected by what officials are calling the Camp Fire. It is the largest fire in the history of our state. During this week off I don't want you to think about your homework assignments. Don't think about what will be due when you return. In fact, I don't want you expending any energy or thought on your studies at all. This might sound counterintuitive coming from your professor. When we return to school I will bear the burden of figuring out how to account for our missed time and this burden will not be passed onto you.

But while our classroom learning has been paused, there is an opportunity for another type of learning. Learn what you can do to help our neighbor. For those of you who live locally, find a way to volunteer to help those affected by the fires. If you have the means, donate anything to help with the recovery effort. (I've listed a link at the bottom of this page.) Learning how to help your fellow humans is just as important as academic learning—in fact, I believe it's even more important. Let this week be a time when you can grow closer to others by serving them. Don't view this time as a vacation but view it as an opportunity to enrich your life by helping others. There is no greater way to enrich yourself than by helping someone else. But don't text, email or send snaps. People are feeling alone and vulnerable and many don't have service or have lost everything they own (including their phones). The only way to reach them is by being with them in person. Listen to their stories.

Understand what they could never convey in a text. Share their emotional burden. If you are not local and have gone home to avoid the polluted air and danger, please spend time with your families. Many have lost their loved ones and their homes. Enjoy both of yours. And even though you are far away from the tragedy, please reach out to those you left behind. These kinds of communications will bring us all closer together. I care about each and every one of you.

Sincerely, Aaron

A commitment to learn from each crisis will help you and campus emergency personnel deepen your knowledge about emergency response and recovery in ways that will help your campus be better prepared for managing the next one.

II. ONGOING EMERGENCY RESPONSE AND CONTINUITY OF UNIVERSITY OPERATIONS

When Cal Fire declared the Camp Fire extinguished on November 25, the fire had raged for eighteen days and had burned over 240 square miles. Over fifty-two thousand people had been displaced overnight. The town of Paradise and other "Ridge" communities were annihilated. Over five thousand firefighters were sent to the scene.

As you can imagine, emergency shelters were established immediately in neighboring communities. The city of Chico, just fifteen miles away, saw its population rise from 92,000 to 112,000 within hours of the evacuation. City parking lots and neighborhood streets were jammed with fire refugees camping and/or living in their cars and trailers. Many Chico State faculty, staff, and students were directly impacted, with roughly 310 losing their places of residence.

Within twenty-four hours of the fire starting, the Chico City Council passed an ordinance banning price gouging on housing. FEMA and other governmental agencies arrived in Chico and began providing evacuees with essential information and services almost instantly. Everyone knew that life for survivors as well as life for host communities would not be returning to normal anytime soon.

For months, local residents volunteered at human and animal shelters, medical facilities, and assisted with management of supply aid. Concerned citizens from out of the area made their way to Chico to volunteer as well. Local residents welcomed Camp Fire survivors, many of whom were friends and family members, into their homes and onto their land and vacant lots. The City of Chico along with the other neighboring host communities literally changed overnight, straining civic resources and infrastructure.

As time passed, Chico State continued to assist with Camp Fire response and recovery. We understood that recovery would take years to complete. At the same time, we had over sixteen thousand students who were not impacted by the fire anxious to return to campus and resume their studies on Monday, November 26. In short order, the campus needed to be readied for them with all campus daily operations (instruction and support services) up and running.

As president, you need to keep five steps associated with ongoing emergency response and continuity of university operations top of mind:

- Continually assess threats to the safety of students, faculty, staff, and the larger campus.
- Review campus business continuity plans and make adjustments needed for a return to university operations (e.g., student learning, support services, operations maintenance).
- Address any challenges that disrupt or continue to disrupt university operations.
- Communicate the status of the crisis and the university frequently to onstituent groups using all communication and social media platforms.
- Maintain campus engagement by continuing to provide support to impactedcommunities.[5]

Working with vice presidents and emergency leads for long hours day after day planning and implementing acute emergency response and support makes it easy to understand why the transition from an initial emergency response to one that is sustained is fluid and subtle. Another way to describe it would be your EOC's ability to maintain immediate emergency actions while incorporating slightly longer-range goals and strategies for emergency response and continuity of operations into its daily planning sessions. The following selected actions we took during Chico State's sustained response to the Camp Fire provide good examples:

- Continued all efforts identified during our initial emergency response.
- Established a temporary no harm policy for staff who could not work because of campus closure.
- Analyzed the results from the needs survey sent to faculty, staff, and students asking how the Camp Fire had impacted them and their families, and what type of help they needed.
- Established the Wildcats Rise Recovery Fund for students, staff, and faculty directly impacted by the Camp Fire. By early spring 2019, more than 5,100 people donated, raising over $700,000. A campus committee comprised of faculty, staff, and administrators determined criteria for eligibility and awarded funding to more than 500 students, staff, and faculty.

- Identified and called all staff and faculty living in the areas devastated by the fire. The director of human resources and the human resources team made these calls.
- Planned a Chico State resource fair for staff, faculty, and students to be held on the first day of our return to campus, November 26. The resource fair provided information about employee leaves, benefits, and the employee assistance program (EAP), along with information and lists of resources for housing, food, and medical assistance. Social service contact information (e.g., for obtaining a new driver's license and Social Security card) was provided too. Laptop computers were on hand for those needing to access one. Wellness counselors also were available for anyone who wished to talk to a professional, and therapy dogs were on hand for anyone who wished to pet one.
- Sustained the opening of the Hungry Wildcat food pantry whose numbers rose to roughly two hundred students per day while campus was closed.
- Identified classroom and meeting spaces for the Butte County Office of Education and Paradise Unified School District who were working to return over six thousand students to school.
- Established the "Teaching the Camp Fire" website.[6] This resource page was developed by concerned faculty who convened a faculty learning community sponsored by the Office of Civic Engagement. These efforts are discussed later in the chapter.
- Hosted humanitarian chef José Andrés and the World Central Kitchen along with celebrity chef Guy Fieri at the BMU auditorium on November 22 as they prepared and delivered a Thanksgiving meal to the town of Paradise and first responders with Cal Fire.

Lessons Learned

No one, on campus or in the community, expected the grand outpouring of help and support from individuals, institutions, and organizations that began flooding in from around the state, country, and world. So, one of our first lessons learned was the need to manage "good will" volunteers and agencies. We immediately realized that the university could serve as an important community liaison in this regard. As volunteer organizations and university researchers began making their way to the area, they were encouraged to contact the Chico State community liaison. When the liaison received questions and offers of community help, she would redirect inquirers to appropriate people and/or agencies in the region. The Chico State community liaison helped alleviate the high volume of calls made directly to town, city, and county officials who really needed to remain focused on Camp Fire emergency response and recovery efforts.

Additionally, a group of Chico State faculty came together forming a learning community called Teaching the Camp Fire. They quickly established a Teaching the Camp Fire webpage where resources and best practices for engaging students and conducting research were listed. Early on in their meetings, faculty recognized that well-meaning scholars and scientists descending upon the burn scar needed a reminder about ethical behavior, so they developed a list of guiding principles, which appear in the appendix to this chapter.

Another lesson learned was how challenging it was to balance resuming regular university operations while simultaneously addressing the severe needs of campus members whose lives had been devastated by the Camp Fire. Many students who returned to campus from out of the area did not understand the extent of devastation experienced by Camp Fire survivors. It demonstrated to me the importance of getting campus operating back to "normal" for those unaffected while at the same time demonstrating compassion and empathy as we sustained help and support to those in need. This bifurcation of understanding was a strong motivator for faculty to involve students in learning about and participating in Camp Fire recovery and rebuilding efforts through research, course work, and service learning.

Overseeing campus Camp Fire volunteerism was developed after the fact. Many groups and individuals from campus volunteered to assist with Camp Fire emergency response, and I'm proud to say that they made significant contributions to recovery efforts. For instance, Chico State nursing students were some of the first volunteers on the scene. Activated by Butte County Public Health, Chico State nursing students assisted with setting up one of the first shelters in Chico for Camp Fire evacuees. Marriage and Family Therapy (MFT) graduate students were also called upon to assist with emotional and mental health at area shelters. The Department of Anthropology Human Identification Lab was asked to assist with the collection and identification of human remains. This small team of scientists and graduate students was one of the first on the ghastly scene, and they worked tirelessly helping identify victims, thereby providing closure for their families. Learning about the good work of campus volunteers after they were engaged made clear that campus needed to develop a reporting mechanism so that campus volunteer groups could record their efforts and the EOC and cabinet could monitor it.

I addressed earlier in this chapter the importance of maintaining the health and well-being of each EOC member when you are in the midst of a crisis situation. It would be short-sighted not to also acknowledge that it became very clear to me in the Camp Fire crisis in particular that sustaining my own health had to be a priority. It has been my experience that it is often a struggle to maintain balance between the demands of the job and one's physical health in the best of times. While a president's health and well-being are always important to effective performance, in times of university emergencies they are paramount. Your observable presence and thoughtful guidance, actions, and decisions are essential to calm the inevitable uncertainty that quickly sets in and to provide leadership that sustains university operations. Hence, the president must practice self-care so as to maintain mental, physical, and emotional health and to model that behavior for the leadership team. Good health fuels the endurance you need to lead well.

III. CONTINUITY OF UNIVERSITY OPERATIONS WITH LONG-TERM RECOVERY

When first responders packed up and moved on to the next emergency, Camp Fire refugees and neighboring communities assisting them still had to manage the recovery and rebuilding of the areas left stranded in the burn scar. Debris removal from affected areas was the first item on a long list of things to accomplish. Hundreds of dump trucks carried debris off the Ridge daily, congesting area traffic and damaging roads for months on end. In what is now known as the largest clean-up project in California history, the debris that was cleared from the Ridge was twice that removed from the World Trade Center after 9/11.[7]

Continuity of university operations and long-range recovery goals for campus and community include five actions for the president's consideration:

- Continue care and support for students, faculty, and staff impacted by the crisis.
- Return campus back to its full range of university operations (e.g., instruction, service, scholarships, activities, sports, events, etc.).
- Keep the university engaged as a regional leader and partner in community redevelopment efforts.
- Improve the university's emergency management plan based on lessons learned from the critical incident.
- Improve upon university practice and processes through a lens of resilience and innovation.

When the EOC finished its Camp Fire–related functions on December 1, 2018, there was still much work to be done. Subsequently, I formed an ad hoc group to oversee university efforts, the Post Camp Fire Recovery Task Force, and charged them with monitoring progress on five key university objectives related to long-term Camp Fire recovery: (1) student support, retention, and recruitment; (2) faculty/staff support, retention, and recruitment; (3) employee and student housing; (4) community support; and (5) campus climate. Aside from me, membership included the cabinet, dean of students, director of environmental health services, chief of staff, members from the senate executive committee, chair of staff council, the university camp fire liaison, director of off-campus student services, university communications staff, director of human resources, chief of police, and the director of facilities management services. The task force met regularly from November 30, 2018, through March 2019. As outcomes, challenges, and tasks were identified, task force members would lead work groups comprised of faculty, staff, students, and administrators to problem solve and solution build.

Since the vast majority of our students, staff, and faculty were not affected by the devastation of the Camp Fire, it was understandable that campus life seemingly hummed along while recovery efforts took place on the Ridge. However, underlying a façade of business-on-campus-as-usual, 310 students, faculty, and staff who had lost everything in the Camp Fire remained severely traumatized. Many more who shouldered a burden of responsibility as hosts and caregivers for disaster-wedged friends and family also struggled to cope.

A number of faculty and staff impacted by the fire took leave for the remainder of fall and into the spring semester. Others retired or resigned from the university and moved out of the area in search of safer places to live. Human resource staff continued to reach out and assist faculty and staff coping with the aftermath and encouraged them to take advantage of the employee assistance program consisting of Camp Fire support group meetings and/or opportunities for individualized counseling. While it was important for staff and faculty to take care of their personal needs and well-being, leaves and departures did create employee shortages in some departments across campus.

The Campus Assessment Response and Education (CARE) team under the direction of the interim vice president for student affairs continued to reach out and assist students in need. Students were also directed to the Wildcat Wellness Center and other campus programs for assistance with their physical and mental health challenges. Additionally, the director of off-campus student services worked tirelessly to help student fire survivors who were homeless secure temporary living arrangements.

The Teaching the Camp Fire faculty learning community invited all instructors to join them as they learned more about and practiced trauma-informed pedagogy. They also continued to encourage all faculty and staff to reach out and support our students in need. When appropriate, faculty allowed students to utilize alternative pathways to course completion. The faculty learning group continued to meet and determine ways to integrate service learning projects into their classes that would assist with rebuilding the Ridge communities. Faculty research efforts focused on the effects of the disaster and the science of resilience were underway as well. Faculty collaborated with researchers from universities and governmental agencies near and far.

One shining example of interdisciplinary collaboration (and there were many) was the Camp Fire Water Resources Monitoring and Research Symposium sponsored by the Chico State Center for Regenerative Agriculture and Resilient Systems. Speakers (including Chico State faculty and students) discussed their investigations into the effects of the Camp Fire and other Northern California wildfires on communities.

Faculty expertise and scientific acumen demonstrated through research and projects of inquiry deepened our understanding of causation, effects, and resilience born from devastation. With the Camp Fire as impetus, studies spanned from effects on the natural environment to resilience rising from humanitarian crisis. For instance, Dr. Jack Webster, civil engineer who focuses on water quality, launched a multiyear study on the effects of wildland fires on the quality of water downstream. And, Dr. Marianne Paiva, a sociologist, conducted the Camp Fire Oral History Project, interviewing and documenting the lived experiences of Camp Fire victims, especially those residing in the rural parts of the Ridge.

The Chico State ecological reserves incorporated fire and forest health education into its outdoor education and outreach program, highlighting best practice for wildland management such as advocating for prescribed burns as a way to reduce fire danger and make resilient ecosystems. Schoolchildren traumatized by the Camp Fire were able to return to the wilderness and learn about the benefits of fire and the ways people can live safely at the intersection of wildlands and community.

Communities look to regional universities and colleges for guidance, so it was important for Chico State to remain engaged over the long haul as a regional leader and anchor institution. To do so, I moved the Chico State Camp Fire liaison from the Center for Civic Engagement into the president's office and increased her time base to full time. The liaison's primary responsibility was to coordinate on-campus volunteer efforts and service learning projects with off-campus recovery efforts and keep the president apprised of all of them.

The Chico State Camp Fire liaison worked closely with the president's office and the director of off-campus student services located in the division of student affairs. Together, they participated in community and governmental long-term Camp Fire recovery meetings and groups; and at the time of this writing in 2020, they were still working on behalf of the university and in support of Camp Fire survivors and community recovery efforts.

This list of heroic actions, volunteerism, and service by faculty, staff, and students is long. I selected only a few to share here:

- The Career Center identified funding that sponsored paid internships to students helping Ridge community organizations, agencies, and businesses recover from the Camp Fire.

- The Camp Fire Liaison partnered with area organizations on a "Bulletin Board Project" to bring relevant and official information published on paper to rural residents living without access to the internet and limited cell phone service, if any.
- The Chico State Hungry Wildcat Pantry organized food and clothing for rural residents dry camping and without state and federal aid.
- The construction management department assisted FEMA with the design and development of a FEMA trailer village for fire survivors.
- The School of Social Work provided opportunities for BSW and MSW students to assist regional disaster case managers address the needs of over three thousand fire refugees with access to basic needs and social services.
- The Computer Animation and Game Development students captured a 3D virtual animation of the 132-year-old Honey Run Covered Bridge just weeks before it was destroyed by the Camp Fire. The virtual animation was significant to the planning and rebuilding of this treasured bridge.
- Understanding the historical significance of the Camp Fire, one of the president's executive assistants teamed with the dean of the library and developed a database of research and service projects conducted by faculty, students, and staff from Chico State and other universities. Once completed, it will be hosted by the university library and available for review upon request.

In higher education, we aim to educate the citizenry of the future, and the world is our living, breathing, learning laboratory. When students embrace the challenges of the world, like those students who helped with Camp Fire response and recovery, they deepen their understanding of themselves and discover the reward of helping others. They gain insight into humanity's ability to be resilient.

LESSONS LEARNED

As stated previously, the EOC convened and worked nonstop for eighteen days. At that time we had no way of knowing how long and complex the Camp Fire response and recovery efforts would be. It was only as time passed that the campus and community understood the full magnitude of the disaster upon us. Not surprisingly, we did not have a long-term recovery group established to continue monitoring progress after the EOC Camp Fire activity concluded in December 2018. In the future, the need for the EOC incident command to remain operational will be reviewed by the cabinet regularly and kept operational as long as needed. This action will enable the university to continue monitoring community recovery efforts and campus long-term recovery initiatives in a cohesive manner and without disruption.

When we debriefed and prepared an after-incident report, we knew with clarity that we needed to enhance our campus emergency training programs by increasing the number and types of scenarios for which we prepared emergency personnel and members of campus.

Possible decline in student enrollment at the university lurked in the shadows of the Camp Fire. Many students who attended the nearby community college had lived within the burn scar and ended up dropping out of their studies. Chico State receives a large number of transfer students from this community college annually, so we became concerned that our enrollments would drop the following year, and possibly years after. Drops in enrollment decrease revenue generated from tuition and fees. To help mitigate potential loss of revenue, I made a request to the system chancellor that Chico State be held harmless for significant declines in enrollment for a period of three years. It was our hope that that would be enough time to adjust our practices and stave off any effects that might result from loss of enrollment.

Additionally, we had received reports that a number of prospective students and their parents across the state were thinking of attending college somewhere else out of fear that our region was not safe from fire and/or that the university had literally burned down. We did not anticipate a statewide spread of misinformation at all. Immediately, we launched a media campaign to address this and promote the fact that Chico State was open and welcoming students, new and returning. During crisis management, a university communication strategy must include addressing reputational threats to the institution, something that we did not consider right away.

After a few months of helping Camp Fire victims, residents of receiving communities began to express signs and symptoms of compassion fatigue, the emotional and physical exhaustion decreasing one's ability to feel empathy for others. Everyone yearned for life to "get back to normal." Local media outlets started defining compassion fatigue for the public, and elected officials asked people to remain kind and civil. At the university, we communicated about compassion fatigue to campus and encouraged everyone to be understanding. Unfortunate angry outbursts directed toward fire survivors only compounded their stress and made them feel unwanted with no place to go. I cannot overstate that, as president, you must be aware of compassion fatigue coupled with anxiousness for things to return to normal no matter what type of crisis you are dealing with. It is a good idea to implement a communication strategy that reminds people to be patient, calm, and kind, and to stay focused on relevant campus response and recovery tasks that align with the university mission and values.

Living through a regional disaster is deeply personal. Supporting students, employees, friends, families, and strangers who have lost everything is daunting. Sustaining that "can do" attitude personally and professionally is exhausting. Leading through crisis is a marathon and requires fortitude as well as endurance. What fuels collective and meaningful action through it all is the strength, vitality, and resilience of the human spirit. Together, we can emerge from devastating events triumphantly.

Lastly, I encourage you to find ways to recognize, celebrate, and thank faculty, staff, and students, especially members of the emergency operations center. Also deserving of thanks are those on the front lines working day and night for weeks on end, not only in response to the crisis at hand, but in keeping university instruction, services, and daily operations up and running. Chico State is a leader because of the extraordinary faculty, staff, and students who are committed to our educational mission, dedicated to the success of students, and focused on advancing the health and well-being of surrounding communities.

EPILOGUE

*The greatest danger in times of turbulence is not the
turbulence but to act with yesterday's logic.*

—PETER DRUCKER

Four months after the one-year anniversary of the Camp Fire, the COVID-19 global pandemic forced many communities in the United States into lock down out of concern for public health and welfare. Universities and colleges across the country scrambled to place all courses and services online, then struggled to ensure that students, faculty, and staff could adequately connect to the internet and stay engaged in their studies and work. The magnitude of disastrous effects associated with COVID-19 is unprecedented and no doubt will have a transformative effect on higher education in ways not yet seen.

In response to the threat of COVID-19, Chico State once again activated its EOC at the beginning of March 2020. We immediately identified challenges to instruction, support services, and university operations. Emergency planning committees were also established quickly. We worked across academic disciplines and campus divisions to solve problems. If we tried an action and it didn't work or needed revision, we adapted and tried again. All in all, we kept students engaged in their studies and guided them to the end of the spring 2020 semester. As soon as grades were in and virtual commencement over, campus began planning for a predominantly virtual fall semester with limited in-person classes.

As I wrote this epilogue, Chico State's academic plans for fall 2020 were in place. Faculty and staff spent summer months improving their virtual teaching skills and revising their class content to meet student needs via digital platforms. Staff continued to improve student access to virtual instruction and support services. And, the university stood ready to switch from limited in-person to all virtual classes should circumstances surrounding COVID-19 demand that we do so.

As I work with my colleagues on campus to navigate the COVID-19 public health crisis, one thing is for certain: the Chico State EOC, along with dozens of working committees and campus members, are well trained in emergency management. Through our experience with critical incidents, especially that of the Camp Fire, our campus community has learned to come together as one university to manage crises, solve attendant challenges, and emerge from it with an eye toward the future and the unforeseen opportunities that present themselves along the way.

The story of how Chico State responded to the Camp Fire disaster is a window through which to examine the operation of campus leadership in a time of disaster. Decisions made were both technical and tactical. Use of the NIMS Incident Command System enabled the university to engage in a coordinated emergency response with area communities and agencies. What is embedded in my account is the important act of sense making, especially by the president and senior leadership. "Sense-making in crisis refers to the challenging task of developing an adequate interpretation of what are often complex, dynamic, and ambiguous situations."[8] It is the ability to understand and navigate context even as it evolves. Karl Weick views sense making during a crisis as "navigating by means of compass rather than a map."[9] Although useful for charted territory or existing destinations, maps can be rendered useless amidst the unpredictable nature of crisis. A compass, on the other hand, enables a president to set direction and adjust course as circumstance shifts, similar to a sea captain adjusting sails in a changing wind. Making adjustments in direction requires constant motion, learning, and renewal, all of which are essential ingredients for successful leadership during a crisis.

In closing, it takes courage to lead an institution through a crisis. Keeping a sense-making compass in hand while navigating the changing terrain of exigency will help you shape a purposeful campus emergency response. Galvanizing your institution to action paves the way for community resilience and recovery.

Teaching and Researching the Camp Fire

Guiding Principles

ADAPTED BY SUSAN ROLL AND MEGAN KURTZ

W e recognize the fact that to serve the recovery efforts of those impacted by the Camp Fire, it is crucial that we acknowledge and honor the principles of community-based participatory research: that those who live in a community are experts in their experience and must be central in all decision-making related to their recovery. To this end, we will make every effort to adhere to the following principles as we are teaching, researching, and working on the Ridge:[10]

Prior to consent, prospective participants should be asked, to the extent feasible, about unmet needs and provided assistance including referrals and resources to reduce risk and maximize benefit.

In the immediate aftermath of a disaster, survivors are often left behind with acute physical and mental health needs. Additionally, disasters can cause chronic impacts that impair social and economic stability, including loss of employment and the dissolution of social networks. It is imperative that the essential needs of community members are met for them to have adequate capacity to make a voluntary decision about participation in projects with the university.

Close monitoring of the consent process is key to address any misconceptions about the research.

When applicable, research teams and the Institutional Review Board (IRB) should ensure close monitoring of the consenting process during recruitment of participants on the Ridge. In disaster studies, especially in the immediate aftermath of a disaster, research teams must establish a standard plan (e.g., which may include a capacity or competence assessment screening questionnaire) for determining the decision-making ability of disaster-affected research participants to provide informed consent. As a precaution to eliminate confusion concerning the exchange of disaster aid for participating in research, consent forms may include a section requiring the participants to initial for indication they understand that they are participating in research and that their participation in the study is independent of disaster aid administered by local, state, or federal agencies or other entities.

Post-fire research and teaching should be encouraged for members of vulnerable groups that are underrepresented in the disaster research literature such as women, racial/ethnic minorities, and elderly and disabled populations.

Researchers should develop new strategies to overcome the perceived barriers to the conduct of disaster research with groups that require special protections or who may have unique vulnerabilities. Valuable, informative research data may be lost if studies do not include these populations in their disaster studies. This is especially true when conducting research to assess behavioral and mental health outcomes. Indeed, there is mounting evidence that members of vulnerable groups may experience significant long-term mental and physical consequences following disaster events.

Justice demands that research be carried out for the benefit of the population as a whole; therefore, systematic exclusion of protected or vulnerable groups from disaster research studies should be avoided. Failure to include these groups leaves a knowledge gap in our understanding of the impact of disasters across the entire population.

Minimize participant burden associated with multiple duplicative studies in the field through coordination and communication of efforts.

Survivors of disasters are often approached by many investigators, all seeking the same or similar information. This can result in survey and specimen collection fatigue and an overall increase in participant burden. A coordinated effort among researchers and funders could reduce duplication.

All research should have a plan for the timely dissemination of actionable research results back to key stakeholders.

One of the principles of ethical research is to provide results and feedback to stakeholders, and disaster research is no different in that regard. IRBs should require researchers to develop a dissemination plan for the results that clearly describes how the data will be reported back to participants and the community throughout the life cycle of the study. The plan must ensure a timely report back and should consider specific entities such as community groups and health educators that can help translate scientific findings into lay language. Methods of dissemination should be carefully considered to optimize information exchange with the community and may include town hall forums, newsletters, and use of social media.

CHAPTER 21

Design-Build

··

Making Sense of Routine and Transformational Change in Higher Education

MICHAEL M. CROW AND DERRICK M. ANDERSON

The conditions in which America's colleges and universities operate are less stable today than they have been at any point in recent history. As a consequence, few, if any, of this volume's readers will be expected to change *nothing* about the universities they are appointed to lead. To be a college president in the first decades of the twenty-first century is to be a manager of change. This chapter is therefore rooted in describing aspects of university change management that we have found to be important for facilitating institutional transformation. We also describe a process that we have termed "design-build" that has been adopted as a key instrument of transformation at our institution, Arizona State University (ASU).

Much can be written about the dynamic settings in which modern universities operate. And, indeed, on this topic, much *has* been written. Similarly, one does not need to look far for thoughtful and specific accounts of how various innovative universities have responded to the economic, political, and social instabilities of our time. And we are especially cognizant that the literature on organizational change is so well developed that it stands as its own subfield of management studies. Given these conditions, we are careful to acknowledge what this chapter is not: a scholarly contribution to the literature on change management, a detailed survey of university innovation, or a meticulous characterization of higher education's shifting industrial landscape.[1] Instead, this chapter provides a practical summary of some of our own experiences with university transformational change. Since ASU's transformation is still underway, the account provided here should be appreciated as one that characterizes much, but not all, of what has happened and much, but not all, of what may come.

ROUTINE VERSUS TRANSFORMATIONAL CHANGE

In our experience, routine and transformational change in higher education are best understood first in their relationships to organic change and design change. Through organic change, a university's structure and practices adapt in response to external pressure or environmental stimulus. Organic change tends to be incremental in scale and scope and in the general direction of a university's existing operational momentum. For example, universities that are already faculty-centric tend to become more faculty-centric by way of organic change. In this sense, we can think of organic change as routine change. This is, by far, the most common form of change in higher education. It is tremendously powerful and merits intense examination by anyone interested in academic leadership.

Designed change is in some ways the opposite of organic change. In describing design more generally, Herbert Simon, whose ideas inform much of our thinking, observed that to design is to "devise courses of action aimed at changing existing situations into preferred ones."[2] Simon was careful to note that good design "insulates the inner system from the environment, so that an invariant relation is maintained between the inner system and goal, independent of variations over a wide range in most parameters that characterize the outer environment."[3] If organic change is *natural*, design change is *artificial*. In fact, *artificial* is the term Simon uses to describe the "science" of design.

With Simon's help we can see design in almost every aspect of human affairs. Collective action is often initiated in organic, natural ways since it offers great prospects for survival and evolution. When the aspirations of the collective transcend mere responsivity to environmental pressures to include the pursuit of aspirational, normative goals, the resulting outcomes (e.g., objects, arrangements, organizations, institutions, or systems) are what Simon would call "artificial." And the process of creating these outcomes Simon would call "design." In this sense, survival and incremental evolution are organic and natural while social progress by way of a specific chosen normative path is artificial. Design is therefore critical to social progress. And social progress institutions, especially universities, are design artifacts.

Through this (overly) concise conceptual reckoning, we can come to at least three conclusions as they relate to universities and design. First, design plays at least some role in the formation of all universities, as all universities represent forms of collective action created to facilitate social progress by way of specific normative pathways.

Second, design is not required for the routine management of all universities. Once a university, through design, arrives at a generally stable configuration, its routine management and change may be carried out in incremental ways. Such routine management is highly responsive to external stimulation and change is organic.

Third, in the course of a university's evolution, design is again required if aspirations for change transition from routine to transformational. Whereas routine change involves incremental evolution in response to external stimulation according to a university's existing institutional momentum, transformational change involves radical pursuit of design-specified aspirations that redefine the why, what, and how of a university's operations. The difference between routine change and transformational change is therefore not a difference of degrees, but a difference of kinds. ASU's evolution since 2002 represents a transformational change. Because design plays a key role in building a new ASU, we call the approach to carrying out this transformation a "design-build" process.

ROUTINE CHANGE IN HIGHER EDUCATION

Routine change in higher education is incremental in scale and scope, in the direction of existing institutional evolutionary momentum, and responsive to environmental pressure. Most of what we understand about routine change comes from the theory and practice of university strategic planning. Prior to the 1980s, universities used long-range planning primarily for budgetary and fiscal reasons, drawing on processes that originated from corporate and military operations. For example, George Keller's seminal book *Academic Strategy: The Management Revolution in American Higher Education* brought greater rigor and a wider, more comprehensive lens to university strategic planning. With the goal of maintaining financial stability in the context of external pressures, university strategic planning in the 1980s contended with such environmental factors as growing enrollments, rapidly shifting demographics, and an increasingly fluctuating resource base. All these factors remain key consideration for university strategy officers.

The increased use of technology-enabled data collection and the adoption of increasingly sophisticated analytical approaches have allowed university strategic plans to become more comprehensive and aggressive in responding to environmental pressure. Even as some criticized strategic plans as "shelf documents" that were resented by faculty and never meant to be fully implemented, by the 1990s they had become so common that most universities had created strategic planning offices.[4]

Adding to the cacophony of external environmental pressure on universities, the 1990s was the era of New Public Management, which came with innovations in accountability regimes that often required public universities to articulate their strategic plans to oversight bodies. Taken collectively with demands from a growing body of accreditation, magazine ranking regimes, and state report performance scorecards, the landscape of external pressures facing universities had grown to be incalculably complex by the end of the 1990s.

Both routine change and transformational change come with risks and challenges. A challenge for routine change management through strategic planning is that the focus on promoting institutional stability through incremental responses to external pressures runs the risk of divorcing universities from their core missions when external pressures are complex and intense.

By many accounts, this dynamic is unfolding today. As pressures from state investment and regulation, accreditation, and market competition for enrollment increase, colleges and universities have started to take cues from each other in developing organizational missions that look different on the surface but in practice result in widespread institutional replication. The condition of similarity in organization and design across institutions, referred to as *isomorphism,* can have subtle consequences for universities.[5] For example, because membership criteria for the prestigious Association of American Universities (AAU) and the *U.S. News & World Report* rankings system both incentivize smaller class sizes and selectivity in admissions, strategic planning in some public institutions has yielded to these pressures to achieve greater reputational standing.

Selectivity and prestige, however, are not intrinsically worthwhile goals for institutions of higher learning; institutions value them primarily because they are instrumental to external systems of evaluation. When public institutions adopt these values and priorities, they not only forsake their historical purpose of providing educational access but also limit their options for responding to external pressures. For example, if state legislatures opt to decrease investment in higher education, raising tuition (thereby further decreasing accessibility) is just one potential response among many, but it indeed is the option that makes the most sense according to the perverse logic of preserving institutional prestige. Likewise, although the pressure for reaccreditation does effect a kind of institutional conformity to external standards, it does not necessarily mandate that institutions become more and more like their peers in mission and kind.

The lesson here is that strategic planning, if informed by the wrong set of priorities, may function as a lever for imposing isomorphic pressure and hold institutions back from pursuing their original design aspirations. The solution here is often transformation change.

TRANSFORMATIONAL CHANGE AND OUTCOMES AT ASU

Before examining ASU's transformation through the design-build process, consider a few key outcomes. ASU was founded as a territorial teachers' college in 1885, attaining university status in 1958, and conducting no significant research until 1980. In 2002, when one of us, Crow, became its sixteenth president, ASU operated like a state government agency. ASU was dependent on high levels of appropriations from the state legislature, receiving $9,230 per full-time enrolled (FTE) student and maintaining an operating budget of about $750 million. ASU's four-year graduation rate was low, just 28.4 percent. Only 22 percent of undergraduates received Pell Grants, and 71.2 percent of the student population was white, with only 17.2 percent of students reported as underrepresented minorities. Research undertakings were small, accounting for just over $120 million in expenditures annually.

The effectiveness of ASU's design-build process is borne out by various metrics relative to the 2002 baseline. ASU has grown to become the largest university by enrollment in the nation, increasing enrollments by 116 percent to nearly 120,000 students across four campuses and online by 2019. By 2018 the university's operating budget had risen to $3.1 billion, even as state investment per FTE student decreased by 66 percent to $3,141. Degree production increased by 133 percent, and the four-year graduation rate nearly doubled, increasing to 51 percent. ASU students receiving Pell Grants increased by 36.8 percent to 37,000, and more than 22 percent of freshmen are from families meeting federal poverty guidelines. Minority enrollment increased by 310 percent, with underrepresented minorities now comprising 39.3 percent of ASU's enrolled population; and enrollments of first-generation students tripled to over 23,583. Across all groups, freshman persistence increased by 11.5 percent.

ASU's improvements in student access and success should be appreciated in the context of its unprecedented improvements in research excellence, generally seen as a concern for highly selective or elite institutions. Since 2002, research expenditures have quintupled to $618 million. Among 915 institutions participating in the National Science Foundation Higher Education Research and Development (HERD) survey, ASU ranks forty-first in research expenditures, ahead of the University of Chicago, Princeton, Brown, and Caltech. ASU is in the top ten in multiple HERD categories including anthropology (first), transdisciplinary research (second), social sciences (fourth), and humanities (fifth). Additionally, ASU ranks seventh in research expenditures among the 760 research institutions without a medical school in the HERD survey.

What makes these research outcomes more remarkable is that they were achieved while maintaining roughly the same number of faculty, with noninstructional staff per 100 FTE students at 12.9 compared to the national median of 25. Moreover, ASU has reduced the cost of the state to produce a degree by approximately 75 percent and lowered the needed resources per student from the state by more than 50 percent. ASU's instructional costs are 21 percent below the average of all four-year public universities nationwide.

ASU's approach represents a viable design for many public institutions to emulate, and although it is not vision- and mission-agnostic, it does accommodate a diversity of possible organizational aspirations. Critically, ASU's transformation was not achieved by the formation of a traditional, long-term strategic plan. Instead, we began with a powerful vision that was embraced by faculty, staff, and the community at large; defined a set of design aspirations as parameters to guide our transformation; and effected a cultural shift toward academic entrepreneurship that gave wide latitude to individual units and departments to implement ASU's new vision.

DESIGN-BUILD IN PRACTICE

We do not contend that all American colleges and universities, even those that are publicly supported, should strive to emulate ASU's design-build process, nor do we argue that ASU's model represents a singular, superior path for transformational change. The strength of American higher education is in its institutional diversity and the ability of colleges and universities to meet community needs and educate local students. The needs of learners are highly individualized, demanding a wide range of options to accommodate the aspirations and learning styles of every kind of student. However, ASU's vision-based, design-build approach does represent a lean, flexible way for universities to carry out transformational change.

The model we describe is especially relevant for public colleges and universities, which we believe have special missions that involve serving the public that supports them. A systematic, collaborative design-build process that aims to rethink an institution's *why, what,* and *how* can be an invaluable tool in proactively leading transformational change. Here we discuss how higher education leaders can engage with this process on their own terms. Importantly, there is significant overlap between identifying the why (institutional vision) and the what (design aspirations). Figure 21.1 provides a general overview of this model.

Identifying the Why: Rethinking Institutional Vision

Routine change generally aims to update an institution's vision or mission statement or promulgates a new set of goals and priorities to better serve the existing vision and mission. The design-build process, in contrast, involves rethinking the vision from the ground up and articulating a new rationale for its existence that can form ordering principles that govern its operations. We caution that the four steps described below must be carried out without consideration to the pressures of isomorphism or internal inertia, two forces which often complement each other. For example, many faculty and administrators may have come to put a high value on the institution's national reputation and prestige and hold strong beliefs that operational decisions should be guided by these concerns. The goal of rethinking an institution's why—and the overarching purpose of the design-build process itself—is to challenge assumptions and

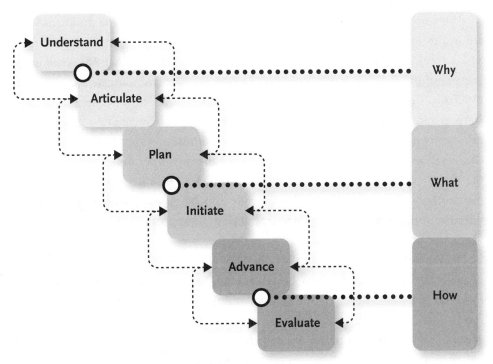

FIGURE 21.1 *A collaborative design-build process*

fundamentally reorient operations and culture. We believe that this is the starting place for any university transformation since it is, in our experience, the most meaningful and enduring remedy for resistance to change—a condition found at most, if not all, universities. This is true especially at universities that benefit from an array of real and perceived external and internal validation.

Although the prerogatives of internal stakeholders who are deeply invested in the operations and culture of the status quo must be considered as a matter of understanding organizational context, aiming to maintain extant organizational dynamics is mere "strategic planning" by any other name, not institutional design. We describe rethinking the institution's vision in terms of four steps divided into two phases; the first phase, *understanding the vision*, comprises three steps; and the second phase is *articulating the vision*.

The first step in developing a new institutional vision roughly aligns with the first phase of Simon's model of decision-making, the *intelligence phase*, which involves understanding and identifying problems and their social, competitive, and organizational contexts. Developing a vision suitable for your institution and the needs of its stakeholders requires consideration of the problems inherent to the institution's existing operating model and the assumptions that underpin it. Who are our stakeholders, and how does the existing model benefit or fail them?

It is important for a new college president to have a sense of the problems with an institution's existing operational model before beginning in their new role. ASU's transformation was initiated with a well-informed view that ASU embodied the prevailing logic of many public universities—academic bureaucracy, marked by change-resistance, rule formalization, over-specialization, bureaucratic routinization, and, perhaps most problematically, the conserver mentality—a dangerous mindset common among public and university administrators that prioritizes the conservation of resources above the mission of the organization. In our experience, the short-term improvements in operational efficiency sometimes associated with the tendency to view resources as intrinsically valuable, as opposed to instrumentally valuable to the mission of the university, almost always come at the expense of lost vision and purpose.

This first step requires a radically honest conversation about stakeholders, including accounting for who they have been, who they are, and who they should be in the future. If the stakeholders are the trustees and the governor, donors, or legacy families, it is critical to be honest about the fact that these are the parties the institution exists to serve—and the trade-offs that this entails for other groups, especially for low-income, disadvantaged, and minority students.

The second step to developing an institutional vision tracks to Simon's *design* phase, in which alternatives to solving problems are evaluated. What alternative institutional models, operational logics, or organizational configurations might an institution consider to deliver greater value to its stakeholders? Coming to an understanding of these options involves careful study of a variety of organizations, including universities, agencies, businesses, and more. Again, having a sense of a variety of models, logics, and configurations that could be implemented or drawn upon for inspiration prior to appointment as president of a college or university will allow the new leader to begin their period of service with a strong momentum and capitalize on a brief window of time, perhaps only a few months, to mobilize internal collaboration to support institutional transformation. The academic enterprise model adopted at ASU represents one possible option for public-serving institutions.[6]

Regardless of which existing models a new college president draws inspiration from, this step requires thoughtful consideration of how those models would need to be adapted to suit the needs of an institution and its particular stakeholders. Making a final determination on a suitable institutional model or operational logic to support the new vision coincides with Simon's *choice phase*, in which the most suitable option is selected based on criteria related to the vision.

A third step in the re-visioning process, which should be carried out simultaneously with the second, is to evaluate the institution's role in promoting broad-scale social progress. An underlying assumption of this step is that all colleges and universities exist to facilitate social progress, broadly defined, and each plays a distinct, differentiated role within the greater ecosystem of higher education. Many community colleges, for example, play roles such as preparing future workers through vocational training, helping adult learners to learn new skills, and offering more accessible, flexible options for students to advance along the pathway to matriculating at a four-year degree-granting institution. Some universities focus on research and training in numerous fields but aim to be the standard-bearer of excellence in particular disciplines, such as Johns Hopkins University in medicine. This third step therefore asks the new college president to understand what progress means for the institution's stakeholders and to reshape its priorities accordingly. It is possible that a new college president will identify new ways for an institution to achieve progress, and all but certain that they will find organizational structures and investments that do not align with a definition of progress as defined in terms of stakeholder needs.

Articulating the vision is the second phase of the re-visioning process. It is a single, fourth step that should be carried out continuously through the design-build process. Once a new vision has been established, it must be articulated *many times, in many versions, to many audiences*. Because the new vision does not represent the pro forma "mission" or "vision statement" common in conventional strategic plans, but instead reflects a transformational shift in the institution's values that must be adopted by students, faculty, and staff in order to facilitate operational and culture change, this new vision must be impressed deeply upon the university community.

Successful articulation of the vision requires communicating it to the specific needs and demands of different audiences through differentiated messaging in order to secure widespread commitment. The new vision and messaging to support it must be prominently displayed physically and digitally and should permeate public-facing and internal communications. The new college president should hire personnel based on their personal alignment with this vision and willingness to champion it.

Communicating the new vision to the community is also critical: the president should claim a prominent role as a public figure, conducting regular media interviews, writing op-eds, hosting community conversations and roundtables with local leaders, and facilitating prominent events that bring together the university community and the public. Over the course of several years, it may be necessary to work with members of the university community to refine aspects of the vision for greater impact. For example, the ASU charter, developed in 2014, is an expanded version of the original 2002 "New American University" vision statement. Our decision to refresh ASU's vision statement was not motivated by the need to secure greater internal or external support, but reflected that after twelve years, ASU truly had changed. Today, the ASU charter is the primary instrument through which ASU's core value proposition is expressed. It reads:

ASU is a comprehensive public research university, measured not by whom it excludes, but by whom it includes and how they succeed; advancing research and discovery of public value; and assuming fundamental responsibility for the economic, social, cultural and overall health of the communities it serves.

What: Developing and Implementing Design Aspirations

Simultaneously with developing and articulating a new institutional vision, an effective design-build process entails specification of design aspirations that serve as the criteria that define how it will achieve this vision. Design aspirations superficially bear some similarity to traditional university "mission statements," but they differ in that they play several specific functions in the design-build process. First, they directly inform the development of new organizational structures and the elimination and consolidation of others. Second, they shape priorities for faculty and staff. Third, they explicitly communicate cultural expectations and values. Finally, they act as the foundation for establishing the goals for strategic planning.

As the *what* to the *why* of the vision, design aspirations are *aspirational rather than descriptive*, especially in the first few years of institutional transformation. As mentioned earlier, the design aspirations should be developed simultaneously with the vision, as they will act as guidelines for implementation of the vision.

The design aspirations promote the fourth phase of Simon's decision-making model, *implementation*, in which the new vision and decisions to support it are put into practice and feedback mechanisms are established to track outcomes and determine corrective actions. ASU's design aspirations are shown in figure 21.2.

Implementation of a vision according to design aspirations should take place in two phases: *planning* and *initiating action*. In the *planning* phase, an effective design-build process mandates planning only in pursuit of a vision and only sufficiently to initiate action. This "lean planning" approach aims to avoid being overly long term, too specific, and time-consuming and demanding for participants. The design aspirations, if effectively developed in alignment with the vision, will already have done most of the work of determining what the institution is supposed to do to achieve its vision. Design aspirations, importantly, are not meant to fully replace strategic planning and goal setting, but they are intended to inform these activities. Because the institution has already developed a firm vision and established the design aspirations as parameters for achieving it, these issues do not need to be relitigated in subsequent formulation of goals and planning priorities.

Once goals are established, the *initiating action* phase can begin. A design-build logic informs new possibilities for initiating action that allows faculty and staff to be more agile, autonomous, and opportunistic. Because the design aspirations circumscribe what kinds of behaviors broadly contribute to the institutional vision, faculty

LEVERAGE OUR PLACE
ASU embraces its culture, socioeconomic and physical setting.

TRANSFORM SOCIETY
ASU catalyzes social change by being connected to social needs.

VALUE ENTREPRENEURSHIP
ASU uses its knowledge and encourages innovation.

CONDUCT USE-INSPIRED RESEARCH
ASU research has purpose and impact.

ENABLE STUDENT SUCCESS
ASU is committed to the success of each unique student.

FUSE INTELLECTUAL DISCIPLINES
ASU creates knowledge by transcending academic disciplines.

BE SOCIALLY EMBEDDED
ASU connects with communities through mutually beneficial partnerships.

ENGAGE GLOBALLY
ASU engages with people and issues locally, nationally, and globally.

FIGURE 21.2 *ASU Design Aspirations*

and staff should be encouraged to take action of their own accord. Although the planning process may have identified additional goals that they should work toward, the design aspirations themselves function as a self-sufficient set of guidelines. To maximize the utility of the design aspirations in motivating vision-aligned action, we also recommend that faculty and staff be encouraged to act under two specific conditions.

The first is to address urgent societal or managerial needs. Responding to societal needs demands that academic units be aware of their prerogative to mobilize internal resources to handle external challenges. For example, in the months preceding our writing of this chapter, we came to understand that as a consequence of COVID-19, Arizona's K–12 students and their parents would require greater access to new digital learning content. Within days, a web-based platform to aggregate learning experiences, tools, resources, courses, activities, and assessments from ASU and ASU partners was conceptualized and launched. Immediately branded "ASU for You!" the platform was used by tens of thousands of learners within just a couple weeks. This was made possible by, not in spite of, unit autonomy and a commitment to solving community problems.

A second condition for initiating action is to capitalize on emergent opportunities. By planning and taking action with agility, organizations can rapidly identify opportunities and mobilize to capture them, such as by hiring new personnel, developing proposals, creating partnerships, or negotiating new contracts with vendors. At many academic institutions, these kinds of actions require faculty and staff to navigate multiple layers of administrative approval, slowing down the opportunity capture process and compromising the opportunity itself. A critical part of breaking the "conserver mentality" that afflicts so many higher education institutions is empowering academic units with greater latitude to make decisions that are "pre-approved" by the logic of the institution's design. As we describe in greater detail in the next subsection, developing a culture of entrepreneurship is especially helpful to this end.

How: Driving Institutional Transformation

Before we describe the next two phases of the design-build process, it is important to revisit the importance of developing a culture of entrepreneurship that animates more effective operations. Higher education policy scholar Burton Clark gives a comprehensive overview of what an institution must do to establish truly entrepreneurial operations and culture:

> The entrepreneurial response offers a formula for institutional development that puts autonomy on a self-defined basis: diversify income to increase financial resources, provide discretionary money, *and* reduce governmental dependency; develop new units outside traditional departments to introduce new environmental relationships and new modes of thought and training; convince heartland departments that they too can look out for themselves, raise money, actively choose among sustainable specialties, and otherwise take an entrepreneurial outlook; evolve a set of overarching beliefs that guide and rationalize the structural changes that provide a stronger response capability; and build a central steering capacity to make large choices that help focus the institution. The entrepreneurial response in all its fullness gives universities better means for redefining the reach—to include more useful knowledge, to move more flexibly over time from one program emphasis to another, and finally to build an organizational identity and focus.[7]

ASU developed a culture of academic enterprise by adapting and implementing each of Burton's prescriptions to support its own transformation. For ASU, as we believe will be the case for many public colleges and universities, entrepreneurial culture is critical to motivating greater responsibility and accountability for outcomes at the unit and personal level. Although a clear vision and design aspirations that support it can motivate faculty and staff, the value of expressly setting the expectation for entrepreneurship and enforcing it through judicious investment in new initiatives and by freezing resources for academic units that refuse to take responsibility and ownership over their own outcomes cannot be overstated.

Moreover, for public colleges and universities that have grown dependent on external resources and have likely adopted the conserver mentality at all levels, becoming more entrepreneurial is not an option. The national trend toward state divestment in public higher education over the last several decades, and especially since the Great Recession, will likely only continue and even accelerate in the years ahead. Although academic units may initially show great resistance to increased expectations for achieving revenue sustainability, reaching conciliation with faculty and staff who are resistant to change at the expense of maintaining operational continuity, let alone driving growth, is self-defeating. At ASU, we found that although some faculty and staff pushed back in the early years of our efforts to foster a culture of entrepreneurship, over the long run a far greater number saw its benefits and embraced it. Success in this regard is linked directly to early and continued efforts to understand the problems and shortcomings of the prior model and to articulate the promise of the new model. The ASU experience shows that a well-reasoned and carefully, frequently articulated case for a new model can, over time, not only be accepted by the faculty, but embraced and promoted.

The next two phases in the design-build process can be carried out without an entrepreneurial culture, but both were developed in the context of ASU's transformation toward an academic enterprise model. The first phase of institutional transformation is advancing a new institutional design through structural change. Reorganizations are a contentious topic in any organization, be it public or private, and colleges and universities are no exception. Although a new college president may be fortunate enough to have a mandate to effect significant structural change, garnering support for reorganization through collaboration is still critical. Acquiring this support, especially from the academic units that are affected, will be considerably easier if faculty and staff have bought into the new vision and design aspirations and have been involved in the planning process.

Structural change can take many forms but generally will involve creating new units, combining or consolidating units, and eliminating others. Structural change can be conceived of in terms of the level at which they are promulgated (centralized or distributed) and the time scale at which they are implemented (comprehensive or incremental), as shown in table 21.1, which provides examples of this idea at ASU that are elaborated upon.

TABLE 21.1 *Structural change: An example from ASU*

	COMPREHENSIVE	INCREMENTAL
Distributed Design	ASU Downtown Phoenix Campus	School of Life Sciences
Centralized Design	Global Institute of Sustainability	Ira A. Fulton Schools of Engineering

Centralized approaches are most appropriate when trying to develop a new unit that leverages significant external investment, demands coordination between multiple units that may initially be resistant to working together, or is an experimental concept that no single academic unit has the ability to drive. Distributed design, in contrast, leverages a natural desire for collaboration between and within units, and draws upon extent momentum within the institution toward a new structural design. Reorganization can also take place through a single, focused effort (comprehensive) or as a longer-term evolution over time (incremental). To further illustrate what this means in practice, consider the rationale for ASU's design choices pertaining to the four academic units referenced in table 21.1:

- *ASU Downtown Phoenix Campus (Comprehensive/Distributed)*: ASU established a downtown campus in the heart of Phoenix that leveraged multiple sources of public, private, and philanthropic investments to relocate several units (law, journalism, nursing, and health) to be in closer proximity with local government and businesses with which they could collaborate. Although this effort took several years to fully complete, it was comprehensive because it was envisioned as a single, continuous design process; this effort was distributed because it drew together several units with a natural interest in reestablishing themselves in a new physical context that made more sense for their faculty and students.
- *School of Life Sciences (Distributed/Incremental)*: ASU established the School of Life Sciences in 2003 to create new opportunities for interdisciplinary collaboration, research, and teaching in the life sciences. This effort was incremental, reflecting several years of growth and optimization that ultimately resulted in tripling undergraduate enrollments and increasing graduate enrollments sevenfold over the course of eighteen years; it was also distributed, as it combined three traditional departments including biology, plant biology, and microbiology, which had strong incentives to work together to achieve greater financial synergy and facilitate transdisciplinary endeavors.

- *Global Institute of Sustainability (Centralized/Comprehensive)*: ASU's Global Institute of Sustainability was envisioned as a transdisciplinary unit that would draw upon dozens of different academic units, at all levels, to develop a first-of-its-kind research agenda around a broad range of real-world sustainability challenges. ASU secured a seed investment from a prominent philanthropist who had a strong interest in environmental conservation, but there was no single academic unit that was sufficiently comprehensive, transdisciplinary, and sustainability-focused to receive her gift. Therefore, establishing the institute was a centrally led effort, allowing ASU to motivate collaboration between many units and ensure that the donor's gift was invested appropriately; and it was comprehensive, as the institute was conceived and brought together as a single effort in the span of one year.
- *Ira A. Fulton Schools of Engineering (Centralized/Incremental)*: ASU's engineering program, in its current manifestation, was also established through a major philanthropic gift that supported the alignment of numerous departments under a new umbrella organization. Designing the Fulton Schools of Engineering centrally allowed us to bring together multiple engineering departments across two campuses under a new administration that reduced duplicated efforts by sharing resources; facilitated innovative, new transdisciplinary designs, such as by bringing the geosciences and astronomy together as the School of Earth and Space Exploration; and properly stewarded the donor's gift, which required a high level of central oversight. This effort was also incremental, as this evolution took place over the course of several years and two different reorganizations to iteratively redesign engineering programs.

The second phase of institutional transformation is evaluation of the institution's transformation. Extensive literature already exists on the practice of evaluating organizational strategic planning to determine a given plan's effectiveness in achieving its outcomes; although evaluating the outcomes of institutional transformation can draw from established methodologies, here we advocate a comparatively simpler approach that can be summarized in three questions. First, has the organization achieved its new vision? Second, is the organization acting in accordance with its design principles? Third, is the organization achieving the goals it developed as an extension of its vision and design aspirations? Because the first two questions lend themselves to more subjective answers, asking them in tandem with the third can provide a clearer picture of the institution's performance. Institutional goals, if they are developed in ways that accurately reflect the vision and design aspirations, are valuable for quantifying the effects of the design-build process. Over time, as the institution makes greater progress toward its vision and design aspirations in some dimensions and stalls in others, it will be necessary to revisit the first phase, advancement, to explore new possibilities for structural change to bring about the desired results. Progress, or lack thereof, toward the vision may also inform further efforts to articulate the vision in new ways and to new audiences to acquire greater internal and external support for further transformation.

CONCLUSION

While the process outlined here has broad applicability, we recognize that many factors stand in the way of transformational change. Many of these factors will be of special significance to the readers of this volume. We conclude by outlining three barriers.

The first is that colleges and universities are notoriously resistant to change. This is why routine change in higher education through incrementalism is so powerful. It often represents the smallest unit of change necessary for a university to survive. America's higher education system, for all of its originality and dynamism, still traces its lineage back to the monastic academies of fourteenth-century Europe. Insulated from the pressures of the market, the state, and society, they acted as guilds and used an apprenticeship model to facilitate discovery and learning for the sake of advancing knowledge itself, not for meeting social needs. In the twenty-first century, many universities carry on some form of this tradition, and consequently operate at a glacial pace and are late to adapt to learners' contemporary needs. Although faculty act as the engine for both knowledge production and teaching and learning, public-serving institutions will fail in serving the public if they reject change at the hands of faculty resistance.

Change resistance leads to a second problem that especially afflicts state-supported, public institutions: a "conserver mentality" that prioritizes organizational self-preservation. Faculty are often characterized as the primary barriers to university change, but bureaucratic and managerial functionaries may show equally strong resistance to change and similar proclivities toward rigidity, formalization, and specialization. This tendency is a function of organizational bureaucracy itself. As Anthony Downs writes, "No bureau can survive unless it is able to demonstrate that its services are worthwhile to some group with influence over sufficient resources to keep it alive. . . . If it is a government bureau, it must impress those politicians who control the budget that its functions generate political support or meet vital social needs."[8]

For universities, this means acting like public agencies that are risk-averse and preoccupied with survival. Downs further describes how, "Once the users of the bureau's services have become convinced of their gains from it, and have developed routinized relations with it, the bureau can rely upon a certain amount of inertia to keep on generating the external support it needs."[9] For both faculty and administrators, the conserver mentality gives rise to a lack of accountability: administrative offices and academic departments alike come to view themselves as entitled to receiving continued support and year-over-year budgetary growth. Resources become the focus at the expense of vision and, often, impact.

These dynamics lead to a third barrier: misplaced competition among internal stakeholders. Aiming to accommodate the needs of diverse internal stakeholders who view themselves as competitors for scarce resources rather than collaborators working toward a shared vision makes the effective implementation of strategic plans nearly impossible. In management theory, this is referred to as the "garbage can model" of organizational change, reflecting the way that problems, solutions, and decisions are haphazardly thrown into an anarchic choice arena. Final decisions and outcomes ultimately reflect an underlying lack of shared, internally coherent commitments to organizational goals, lack of common understanding of processes and solutions, and inconsistent application of time and effort to solving problems.[10]

Ostensibly, members of an organization are mutually committed to a similar mission and vision and play differentiated roles in achieving it, but in practice, poorly managed transformational change becomes a *bellum omnium contra omnes* (war of all against all). But this doesn't need to be the case. In thinking about transformational change as a design process, university leaders can invite otherwise competing stakeholders into a process that redefines the *why*, *what*, and *how* of a university's operations. The ASU experience demonstrates that resources will grow, outcomes will improve, and students will thrive.

CHAPTER 22

Work-Life Balance in the Presidency

Juggling Competing Priorities

PAMELA J. GUNTER-SMITH

Throughout my professional career, I have had the privilege of mentoring young people who ask about my career path and who aspire to follow it. As a professional woman in a nontraditional field (research science) with a family, I was often asked about work-life balance. Is it possible to excel professionally and still have a normal family life? How do you balance life and work equally well? I always gave my honest opinion based on my experience: it is impossible to achieve balance all the time, but if you are willing to choose strategically between competing priorities, you can have both. More simply put, you cannot have all of it all of the time.

When asked to contribute this chapter, I was surprised that I answered yes since I do not consider myself as having accomplished "balance." But then again, because I recognize that I continue to struggle with achieving balance in my life as a college president, I am in a position, if not to offer advice, to at least address the challenges that are particularly relevant to the presidency of a college or university.

When considering a presidency, I too asked colleagues who were currently in the position about how they find time to reflect, renew, and spend quality time with family. The advice given was to commit to one day a week, one weekend a month, and two weeks a year away from all things related to the presidency. I certainly have not been successful in following this advice. So what gets in the way? Here's my experience.

- *One day a week*: Failed, replaced by a few hours in the morning to work from home and contemplate the upcoming day. Some presidents work with their assistant to hold sacred this one day or its equivalent by disguising it on the calendar as a standing meeting off campus. Even with this, meetings or phone calls are scheduled because of a crisis or because it is the only time to meet with an important person.

- *One weekend a month*: Tried, but failed. So much happens on campus and elsewhere on the weekend—athletic competitions, concerts, open houses, and community events—making it almost impossible. My weekend more often than not becomes an occasional Sunday.
- *Two weeks a year*: Mostly successful, but not entirely. My husband and I normally take a two-week vacation in the summer to a destination that is several time zones away from campus and where communication must be intentional. I agree to check email twice daily but otherwise stay out of contact, knowing that people will reach me if necessary. This approach has worked for the most part, except for the summer in Ecuador on a trip to an eco-lodge in the Amazon rainforest when I had no phone and no internet and had to use a satellite phone to manage an emergency back on campus.

JUGGLING PRIORITIES

So what is it about the presidency that makes work-life balance so difficult? Why is it so hard? The job is more than "running" the institution. Unlike for other CEOs, many different constituents, both internal and external, require a president's attention. They include students, faculty, staff, community members, trustees, donors, parents, and alumni. Each has their own expectations of who the president should be and what the president should be doing for them. Each is important to the life and sustainability of a college or university, a president's primary concern.

Over my time as a college president (at this moment I'm in year eight), I have fashioned an understanding of my competing roles and have through some trial and error learned to juggle competing priorities. Below, I discuss several factors influencing allocation of my time across competing commitments.

First and foremost, the president is the framer and keeper of the institution's vision. The president sets the course for the future while working across units to develop the strategic plan. No one other than the president can do this, and while others in the administration are expected to carry the torch, the president has to be the one to continually communicate it to all stakeholders in various ways. This means seeking and taking opportunities to speak publicly about the institution, and not about one's self, at national and community meetings, as well as writing columns and meeting with small groups on campus.

The president is both the manager and coach of a team of talented individuals who operationalize the strategic plan and manage the day-to-day operations of the institution. Much like an athletic coach, the president understands the strengths, weaknesses, and ambitions of the players or, in this case, the members of the president's cabinet. To maximize their talents, a president must meet with team members collectively and individually to ensure the team is functioning at a high level. Without a constant check on the health of the team and the setting of institutional and individual goals, silos and competition for resources will erupt. Highly functioning team members can relieve the president of some of the day-to-day tasks of managing the institution. Delegating tasks requires trust, honest and open communication, and the setting of decision-making standards such that matters that must rise to the level of the president do.

The most valuable commodity a president has is time, and everyone (and I mean everyone) will expect the president to spend some of it with them. The campus community will feel that the president is absent and disinterested if the president is not visible on campus. Of course, it is not possible to attend every event, but you must be attentive to parsing out your time among various groups equitably. Otherwise, you may be accused of favoring one group over another. For example, students are a group that invite me to most of their events, and I attend as many as possible. My attendance has earned me a reputation for favoring students, which on the face of it may sound good, but not in the context of being disinterested in other campus groups. Since most of these activities occur during the evenings or weekends, this leaves Sunday as the only personal day left in the week. While not always successful, I try to leave Sundays unscheduled. It is equally important to set expectations as to which functions require the president's attendance and those events for which the president's attendance can be delegated to others. As president, I am ultimately responsible for setting the expectations regarding my event attendance, but my executive assistant (or a chief of staff) now makes that call for me.

Very early on in a new presidency, the community will come to call for institutional representation (you) on various boards and committees. Community involvement is key to developing positive town-gown relationships and opportunities for the institution. Carefully weigh the benefit of your involvement with respect to your goals for the institution. Likewise, avoid those that would indicate a particular political leaning. I currently serve on seven boards: one professional, three local community, two state or national associations, and our State Board of Education. Several of these affiliations preceded my appointment as president, but most came with my role as president. I have turned down or recommended colleagues for many more. Remember, not showing up is worse than not accepting an invitation.

Trustees, donors, and alumni are among the most important relationships to develop and manage. They can often be the same since trustees are among an institution's most generous donors and some may be alumni. These stakeholders particularly require the president's personal attention, including via lunches, dinners, conversations, and phone calls. The president must be the primary friend and fund-raiser for the institution. It is equally important to remember that after the courtship and honeymoon period are over in year one, trustees hire and fire the president. Developing good relationships and open communication with trustees, donors, and alumni is essential. Every presidency faces challenges, especially now; supportive trustees will back you if you have earned their confidence, and if they do not, you need to be aware of it. Invest time with your trustees beyond the official board meetings, and when appropriate, seek their advice. Most trustees want to give of their time and talent, not just their treasure.

Being a spouse/partner and raising children while serving as president can raise unique challenges. Some spouses enjoy being a presidential partner. Others do not. My retired husband serves on committees and boards both locally and nationally that support the interests of the college. He is seen regularly on campus and at events and serves as ambassador for both the college and me. Not every spouse/partner will relish the role, but it is important that spouses/partners show up at key times (e.g., board dinners). This means that it is essential that you place the same premium on negotiating the role of a spouse/partner and the time you must devote to your family as you would on your compensation. Consider an on-campus president's home as more of a benefit than just a place to entertain. Living on campus or nearby can facilitate family time because it is easier to go home for lunch or dinner prior to attending a function. Your spouse/partner might also accompany you to meetings where you can spend an extra day or two together, at your own expense, of course.

Also, incorporate children into campus activities and events as appropriate. Athletic events, concerts, and picnics are fine, but not professional meetings or board and donor dinners, for example. Each campus has its own culture, but remember that children will be children. They will need to forge friendships unrelated to the institution and have permission to be themselves.

I have yet to say much about how to achieve work-life balance during a presidency. What is most important is that you develop and maintain habits of wellness. My president colleagues with whom I have honest conversations have different ways of managing wellness. Many presidents maintain a residence away from campus or town, where they are not immediately identified as "the president." Doing so relieves you and your family of having to meet the community's expectations of the presidential persona or the brief college business meeting that often occurs while in the grocery store checkout line.

Many presidents follow some sort of wellness regimen—hiking, biking, running, strength training, yoga, meditation, etc. Find something you enjoy. Much of a president's life revolves around meals and receptions. I have followed the advice of one of my president mentors: eat enough to be sociable at events, but otherwise eat before going. Moreover, it is difficult to talk and mingle with a full plate. Hopefully, this eating approach will also help you avoid the freshman fifteen.

Remember that the presidency is just a moment of time, not a lifetime. It is important to maintain your relationships with friends and family. Understand that the many friends you cultivate during your presidency are in reality those of the institution and will appropriately transfer their loyalty to the new president once you leave. Don't be disappointed.

I have purposefully not given advice as to how I manage my own sense of well-being as president. Each must find their own path toward peace and tranquility during the times of stress that will come more frequently than you anticipate. I am up early at the gym for strength and cardio training daily. I find most of my needed reflection time before going to the office and in the evening after campus offices close for the day and the phones are silent. I avoid bringing problems home to dinner. I have cultivated a small group of president colleagues with whom I can share ideas and discuss challenges openly and honestly. I have maintained my core group of life-long friends. I also maintain an off-campus residence. While I manage to get there only every six weeks or so (prior to COVID-19), I can spend a long weekend working there away from the public eye. My president colleagues who have taken my recommendation of acquiring an off-campus hideaway have found it to be sage advice.

Fortunately for me, I also have a spouse of four decades who reads me and knows when I need time and space from my day-to-day president's life. He arranges mini-vacations and then has my assistant block out the time on my calendar. This said, after eight years in my role as president, I feel I am still working on work-life balance.

WHY BECOME PRESIDENT?

If the job of being the CEO of a college or university is so demanding and, frankly, so intrusive, why take on the role? It is important to find joy and fulfillment in the role even when dealing with the challenges. It cannot be a job, but rather a calling to serve. Certainly, ensuring the success of the institution and its future is my first priority. As a research scientist by training, I am energized by finding solutions to complex issues; setting a strategy to achieve an objective. I often say, "Every problem has a solution; the task is to find it."

My greatest joy comes with the opening of school in the fall and commencement exercises in the spring. I see the anxious faces of students and parents as they start their collegiate journey and share their pride as graduates walk across the stage to receive their diplomas. I know many of the graduates and welcome their hugs on the stage. Our educational experience is truly transformative, and I feel that I have played a role in their success and future.

When I am having a difficult day, I often leave my office, walk the campus and chat, or have lunch with students. This provides the "balance" in my day and a reminder of the importance of the work I do—serving students.

I started this chapter with the advice often given to new presidents about how to allocate time for self and work-life balance. I admitted that I failed the first two suggestions but have generally managed the third—two weeks a year without working for, and on, the college. Because of COVID-19, however, I failed to follow any of the rules—even the third. Nevertheless, I did manage to spend a long weekend at a very quiet lakeside B&B, relaxing by listening to the water, the rustling of the leaves, and the chirping of birds and finding the time to write this chapter. After spending the last six months here on campus working on COVID-19-related issues, I now feel sufficiently refreshed to return to the juggling act of balancing competing priorities at the college. I am ready to launch the next semester on campus and keep all of the balls in the air!

CHAPTER 23

Being "Contemplatives in Action"

....

Purposeful Planning for Life After the Presidency

DANIEL R. PORTERFIELD

A presidency is a worthy end in itself, but it is by no means the end.

—ELAINE TUTTLE HANSEN

College presidents often make time in their hectic schedules to help colleagues and mentees think about major life transitions: students looking for first jobs, alums changing professional sectors, faculty moving into administration, senior officers considering the presidency. It's one of the joys of the job.

Yet, many campus leaders don't make time to ponder or plan their own future directions. It's understandable. Many presidential initiatives imply an ongoing commitment to stay in office. Even being suspected of looking elsewhere can erode a leader's standing with stakeholders. And then there's the fact that the daily demands and pressures of the role can take over one's mind and shut down personal considerations.

None of these factors, however, changes the reality that every presidency will eventually come to an end. This is unalterable. It's inspiring to me that many of the presidents with whom I've served went on to take fulfilling roles in academia, government, nonprofit leadership, and the private sector. One reason why is that they were able to look forward to the next chapter in ways that also helped them thrive in their presidencies.

How to do this? To me, the key is purposeful introspection, a lesson I absorbed from three longtime Jesuit educators—former Georgetown presidents Timothy Healy, SJ; Leo O'Donovan, SJ; and Phil Boroughs, SJ, the current leader of Holy Cross College. Each modeled the Jesuit ideal of striving to be a "contemplative in action," one who reflects constantly as part of a calling to help and serve others.

It comes down to this: Reflection enhances action, and action enhances reflection—a beneficial cycle that brings together our inner lives and our social roles. As contemplatives in action, we can put our values to use in decision-making. We can better understand helpful and unhelpful forces working within and upon us. We can evaluate new work experiences—the good, the bad, the confusing—in light of core beliefs and commitments that transcend any job we happen to hold.

Even for people with chaotic calendars, there are many ways to contemplate purposefully—through meditation, prayer, conversations with friends, walks, therapy, mindfulness, imagination, writing, conversation, service, exercise, listening to music, and simply dwelling in silence. Some people like structure, while for others reflection is more freeform. What's key is to get started.

From my experience, there are three categories of reflection that, collectively, can help deeply engaged campus leaders prepare for future stages of their careers. In drafting this chapter, I solicited thoughts on this approach from expert sources—fellow former presidents who have made successful transitions to new endeavors. Perhaps the very best advice I could give any new president is to get to know your peers. There's no better source of perspective, understanding, inspiration, and friendship.

PERSONAL REFLECTION

In the quiet of the evening, or in moments of doubt or pain, we ask ourselves: Who am I, really, beyond the title I hold and the confidence with which I carry myself at work? What has shaped me? What do I value most? What do I fear? When am I fulfilled, and when am I not? Who relies upon me? What kind of a person am I trying to be?

This is a running conversation of the soul. Our interior monologues, and the actions we take in response, are central to our identities. They give us self-knowledge and feelings of authenticity. They help us regulate our emotional burners. These are the kinds of reflections that provide solace in draining times or help us fight through disillusionment—although they also can prompt honest reckonings of our own mistakes. The Jesuits call this discernment—the effort to know and heed our true heart's calling.

Recently, I asked Kim Benston, now back on the Haverford College faculty after having served as its president between 2015 and 2019, what questions helped him most during four highly successful years leading the institution: "Why do I love the job? Why does the work matter?" he offered. "What have I learned, what do I still need to understand and do better, and what are other ways to address the pressing issues in my job? Am I a president, or just playing a president?"

Returning to these themes allowed Benston to see the presidency "*as an extension of* rather than a departure from" his vocational identity as a scholar—helping him move more comfortably both into and, eventually, out of the position. When he resumed teaching and research, he did so not with regret but with feelings of coherence and freedom.

Jane Dammen McAuliffe, who led Bryn Mawr College from 2008 to 2013, drew strength from the values and commitments she developed over her lifetime. "Bring your existing concerns and passions with you," she advises new leaders, "and maintain those priorities beyond your role." Professionally, she says, "continue scholarly research and academic activities to keep anchored in the academic world and sustain your re-engagement after your presidency is over." And personally, she urges never to forget that family and relationships will "provide perspective and balance."

Such considerations help presidents work in ways consistent with who they are *and will be* when their service is over. In McAuliffe's case, this ethos fueled her determination to carve out time for scholarship, which positioned her in 2014 to join the Library of Congress as Director of the John W. Kluge Center and Office of Scholarly Programs. In that role she completed three research projects that she'd nurtured during her presidency—a new book on the Qur'an and two Norton anthologies, one on the Qur'an and one on Islam.

While I was working at Franklin & Marshall (F&M) College from 2011 to 2018, the discipline of personal reflection helped me hold firmly to values like family, service, respect for others, gratitude, fairness, and justice. I tried to start each day by challenging myself to align my actions with these values, to try to be the same person every day for my family, my students, and my colleagues. If I felt hurt by slights or criticisms, the reflection process helped me remember that a leader shouldn't take things personally. It also reminded me to be myself on the job and do things I valued, like advising students and sitting in on classes. This practice was good for my decision-making and for my relationships—and it kept before me the central fact that *I'm in the job but not the job.*

INSTITUTIONAL REFLECTION

At the same time, it's essential for leaders in every stage of a presidency to think beyond themselves with as much objectivity as possible about their institution's values, emerging needs, and trajectories—again, both to enhance the quality of our work and to prepare for its inevitable completion.

Some questions include: What do our stakeholders want and need from the institution at this time? What likely changes in the world will require changes in the institution? What is the most important work that I can do right now? How can I help others do their best work? How strong are my relationships with key stakeholders?

Contemplating these questions can help leaders do a better job setting priorities that will serve the institution. They help us remember that organizational needs can change even over the course of a few short years and that great institutions will shape lives and society far longer than the time-bound work of any individual working within them.

Such reflection also helps leaders guard against the tendency to romanticize their place within the institution, advises Elaine Tuttle Hansen, who left the presidency of Bates College to lead the Johns Hopkins University's eminent Center for Talented Youth. "The institution will not, cannot, should not, stay married to you, even if you are in love," she says. "So, if you do feel this kind of (irrational but not rare, I think) bond, prepare yourself for the inevitable divorce."

Janet Morgan Riggs, who led Gettysburg College with distinction from 2008 to 2019, encourages chief executives to think regularly about "fit" by asking themselves two questions: "Am I the right person to lead this institution at this particular time?" and "Is my work in this role facilitating my personal and professional goals?" If the answer to either is no, she cautions, "it's time to think about something new." And, with that, it's imperative for presidents to keep in mind the reality that sometimes the timing or drivers of change come not from within, but from external factors like board decisions or personal circumstances.

Riggs also advocates making a concerted effort to seed the ground for successors, which requires imagining the institution without oneself in it. A good way to do this is to develop a strategic framework that extends past one's term in office and thus gives the next president a roadmap and momentum for the early years. At the same time, she urges that presidents avoid constraining their successors to any single course of action.

In different ways, every former president I've spoken with makes the point that these roles are ephemeral, and it's in leaders' interests to try to view their institutions and their own roles in them dispassionately. Not easy, of course. I like the generous long view taken by Haverford's Kim Benston: "My overall goal," he told me, "was for the Haverford presidency to be the most attractive such position imaginable so that my successor would be someone prepared and positioned to lead the college to its greatest years yet." Benston's understanding was that it was his job to make sure the institution would thrive after his departure.

Informed by Jesuit values and the institution builders I worked for earlier in my career, this is how I saw the presidency as well. Extraordinary leaders like former University of Miami president Donna Shalala and Georgetown University president Jack DeGioia had shown me that the development of great institutions is a collective and communal act, guided or prompted by the executive, but not dictated.

Acting on this belief in the collective, I started my work year at F&M with an inclusive collegewide strategic planning initiative. Faculty, staff, students, trustees, donors, alums, and community members were all invited to contribute through meetings, working groups, surveys, and pilot projects. After a great deal of discussion and synthesizing, a working group I commissioned presented the strategic plan, *Claiming Our Future*, to the faculty and the board and received overwhelmingly positive endorsements.

The elements of the plan were exciting—a talent strategy to enroll students from the full American mosaic, innovations to bolster the holistic student experience, investments in faculty excellence, and ideas for new facilities. For the purposes of this chapter, however, more important than the actual details of the plan is the fact that the campus community made it and owned it.

That is to say, it was *our* plan, not my plan—and therefore I could give it to my successor knowing that *Claiming Our Future* was *our* work, not my work. Of course, the president must lead and take responsibility—but building a broad, shared partnership for the future is much healthier for organizational development and, ultimately, any chief executive, since we all serve for one time, not all time.

Because this was my approach, during my first few years as president, my institutional reflection tended to focus on building capacity. How could I help the college grow its applicant pool and donor base? How could I best support an effective culture of faculty governance? How could I best deploy the board in the service of the institution? How could I help keep equity and student success at the core of the college's development?

These considerations influenced my words, deeds, and decisions. It was always about building the institution and its culture and academic strength for the long term. The mindset I developed became, in effect, to work myself out of the institution, which ultimately helped strengthen the campus and made my eventual inevitable transition easier.

In late 2017, I was approached by the search committee charged with selecting the next president and CEO of the Aspen Institute, a global nonprofit whose mission is to drive change toward a free, just, and equitable society. I entered the process with curiosity and excitement because I knew the opportunity aligned with my values and because I felt confident that it would not harm F&M if I moved on at the end of the academic year. While the Aspen Institute does eminent work on higher education, it also covers many issues that I had not spent much time on, including health care, technology, climate change, and economic inequity. And, it utilizes myriad methods of change with which I was familiar but had no expertise, including adult leadership development, network building, education campaigns, policy advocacy, public convenings, public arts, closed-door dialogues, and the cocreation of solutions with the grassroots communities it hopes to assist.

This opportunity spoke to me for many reasons, and the timing was right. However, if not for a third way of being a contemplative in action that I had learned years before at Georgetown, I wouldn't have been ready to compete for the Institute's president and CEO position when the chance to do so came to me unexpectedly.

DIRECTIONAL REFLECTION

Directional reflection is the act of thinking forward to envision new pathways for giving and serving. It involves taking stock of one's strengths and weaknesses, values and motivations, developed skills and lessons learned—and then exploring how those qualities might be used in new roles and contexts. The process can be daunting because it requires us to embrace uncertainty, risk, and change—but it's personal work that leaders can assign themselves, and the payoffs can be deeply rewarding.

A good way to start is to take stock regularly of how one is growing and changing as a leader through the stages of a presidency. There's a lot to digest, for sure.

Some of this growth comes from developing invaluable leadership skills related to finances, risk, strategy, operations, crises, employees, communications, community building, conflict resolution, advocacy, fundraising, and cross-cultural engagement. Some comes from the expansion of one's professional network to include fellow college presidents, leaders of myriad diverse institutions, and change-makers in thought, innovation, and philanthropy. Some comes from one's exposure to new issues and concerns. And some comes from the new paradigms within which a chief executive needs to think and work—like, for example, the need to show demonstrable outcomes, or own a problem, or plan for multiple scenarios, or win over supporters from the general public.

Directional reflection also entails learning about the missions and mandates of other institutions, from foundations to companies to cultural organizations to government. The presidency offers many opportunities for those who take the initiative to join boards, form partnerships, or become friends with leaders in other sectors. It's well worth the time to observe how those organizations work and, as Jane Dammen McAuliffe told me, "keep an open mind about how your work might translate outside of the university."

Many college presidents underestimate what their role has prepared them to do or lead outside of the academy. Former Vassar College President Catharine "Cappy" Hill, now the managing partner of Ithaka S+R, a nonprofit education research organization, told me: "Being in a position where you are responsible for an array of constituencies, from eighteen-year-olds to eighty-year-old alums, from tenured faculty to unionized staff, gives you a deeper insight into how higher education works and fails in America. You can use those insights to contribute to society in a different way."

Similarly, for Elaine Tuttle Hansen, the regular practice of making persuasive speeches to a wide variety of audiences—"pitching, reassuring, and articulating our plans and actions"—is fabulous preparation for one's next goals and roles. She argues that the "performative part of the job" gives presidents the opportunity "to translate and expand their understanding of their own personal goals in their current role and how they will carry those philosophies to the next job." Be open, she advises, "to unlearning our sense of loyalty to one institution and one sector," and "focus instead on the larger concerns that motivated you to become a president in the first place."

For me, those motivating "larger concerns" were, in fact, the primary focus of the Aspen Institute, which made the opportunity resonate. The interview process required me to share my values, describe my management and organizational development philosophies, and explicate their potential relevance for the institute. I could do this because I had been thinking about these topics for years.

As I advanced in the process, it fell to me, of course, to share these explorations with my F&M board chair and then, when I accepted the position, with the full campus community. During those last seven months on campus, there was a lot to navigate, and having strong relationships made all the difference. How we exit our institutions truly matters, and I hope I did so well.

Now, more than two years into my service at the Aspen Institute, four insights stand out:

The first is that while I draw upon lessons learned in the academy every single day, twenty years of good work in higher education really isn't relevant to my standing or success in this context. It's a fresh start and future-focused, with all that entails—as it should be.

The second is that, while there is surely life after the presidency, and life after the academy, American higher education has many features that are beautiful beyond words. I'm thinking of the dignity of students in formation, the power of breakthrough discoveries, the electricity of a vibrant learning community, and the spirit of teamwork that holds it all together. Cherish all this while you're in it—and advocate for its support when you are gone.

The third is that, when we leave our roles, what endures are the relationships. Every week I get the chance to talk with or help out friends or former students who made my work at F&M so rich. Sometimes I can invite alums or colleagues to take part in the programs of the Aspen Institute, and sometimes I can use my new platform to draw attention to the quality of the college. It's all very rewarding.

Finally, as 2020 made all too clear, we inhabit a world in pain. The manifestations of inequity and mistrust are everywhere, which has made the work of campus leaders both harder and more urgent. Higher education can and must make real differences, right now. As contemplatives in action, we must constantly seek to discern what is needed from us and then apply ourselves accordingly. These are uncertain times, but one thing is for sure: The will and skill college presidents are using today to drive change from the academy will be a great resource in the future as well—from any role, in any sector.

CHAPTER 24

The Post–COVID-19 Era

What Future and New Presidents Might Consider

JAMES SOTO ANTONY, ANA MARI CAUCE,
LYNN M. GANGONE, AND TARA P. NICOLA

As of the submission of this book's manuscript, the world remains in the grip of the COVID-19 pandemic. The effect of the pandemic on human lives cannot be overstated. It has been a global tragedy. In the United States alone a tragic number of individuals have died as a result of COVID-19, with the loss and grieving made more difficult by social-distancing protocols. The effect on the global economy has been enormous, with record numbers of people losing jobs and their very livelihoods. The disproportionate impact of these health and economic impacts has also been evident. Lower-income as well as Black, Brown, Indigenous, and Latinx individuals and families have borne the brunt of the pandemic in ways that are both heartbreaking and unimaginable.

Against this backdrop, though not entirely divorced from its elements, the impact of the pandemic on higher education has been profound. Among its effects are an almost complete pivot in how instruction has been offered to students, with many institutions—for the first time ever—transitioning to entirely or primarily remote learning for students and remote meetings and work-at-home arrangements for most administrators, faculty, and staff. Most campuses have either restricted, or in many cases eliminated, on-campus housing options for students, placing our less advantaged and international students in particular peril. Research programs were disrupted, and in some cases completely stalled. Every campus has grappled with how to operate in an uncertain environment; how to implement public health protocols such as COVID-19 testing and contact tracing; how to support faculty and students who, up until this point, have not been familiar with remote-learning platforms and technologies; and how to address access to the software and hardware that make this all possible. And many of these adaptations have again differentially impacted our less economically advantaged students whose access to hardware, software, and broadband is more limited or nonexistent. What started quite suddenly as a patchwork of quick solutions has, over a period of months, become the "new normal"—people conducting business via videoconference, classes being offered in synchronous and asynchronous modes, and dramatic reductions in on-campus and in-person teaching even at those colleges or universities that welcomed students back to campus.

Campuses that provide training for health-care professionals—doctors, nurses, dentists, and pharmacists, as well as physical therapists and medical technicians—have had to revamp their training programs and accreditation processes. And academic hospitals and medical centers have often been on the front lines, fundamentally changing their operations to be able to accommodate COVID-19 patients from their local communities while working to develop new treatment approaches for the disease and/or serving as sites for clinical trials. They too have often moved key operations online, from routine medical visits to mental health treatment, while at the same time making major adaptations in order to deliver needed care to those suffering from COVID-19 or complications from it.

Campuses with intercollegiate athletic programs have had to make very difficult decisions about whether and how to carry out everything from recruiting and practices to travel and competition. Even fundraising and alumni relations have been upended, with large galas and get-togethers, often tied to sporting events or arts performances, canceled or moved online. No corner of the higher education enterprise has been left untouched.

The list of rapid and fundamental changes that higher education has experienced over the course of the pandemic could fill many pages. Most everybody understands that these changes have been difficult to manage. And most of us harbor deep anxiety about the effects on student engagement and learning during this time. Students have, simply put, not received the same experience they otherwise would have known. Faculty have never worked harder, and under such uncertain conditions. And our staff have been pushed to their limits as well—maybe even beyond their limits. Compromises have been made at every level. While some have thrived, too many students and faculty have experienced exhaustion and demoralization, with the need for mental health support burgeoning throughout our higher education and our entire country.

The human toll, the suffering, the illness and death, the declines in engagement, the exhausting demands, and the general uncertainty have affected us all. But, as we have already noted, all members of our community have not been equally affected. While some staff members have been able to work remotely, such as those in IT and finance, others have had to perform their jobs in person, such as those carrying out campus maintenance or housing and food services for those students who are in our dorms. Those with caretaking obligations, whether for children or elderly parents or relatives, have been especially stressed, and we will need to pay special attention to the widening of the gender gap in career progression as the crisis resolves. Members of our Black, Brown, Indigenous, Latinx, and communities of color have not only borne more of the COVID-19 burden but also have had to bear witness to members of their community murdered by those who we expect will protect us, not kill us. Add to these burdens the brazen display of racism and white supremacy in the US Capitol siege at the start of 2021, and one cannot help but feel the righteous anger of our communities of color, an anger we should all share even if we are not equally affected. We cannot successfully recover from the effects of the COVID-19 crisis without also focusing on how to deal with the longstanding issues of systemic inequity and racism that our institutions of higher education have perpetuated and bear a responsibility to address. How do we even begin to fully account for everything that has challenged higher education during this time?

Even with the above, incomplete attempt to characterize the impact of this moment on higher education, we have not yet begun to discuss the budgetary implications of this period. Simply, the impact on higher education budgets has been *devastating*. Every institution has had to make tough financial choices. Many have furloughed or laid off employees. Institutions that are more economically compromised have even had to thin the ranks of tenured professors, a status of faculty that is sacrosanct in higher education. Some have dramatically reduced services and course offerings. Others have closed programs in ways that were painful and carried a real human toll. Deficits abound, extensive borrowing is quite common, and Moody's ratings are plummeting, further exacerbating institutional financial viability. For public institutions, continued reductions in state budgets have had a compounding effect on institutional finances. For all institutions, lost auxiliary revenues have been impossible to replace, decreases in enrollments have stretched highly tuition-dependent colleges and universities, and unanticipated costs associated with addressing the pandemic's many demands have caused many institutions deep fiscal pain.

LOOKING TO THE FUTURE

Amid all the pain and very real devastation, there have been silver linings and lessons learned that will make for a stronger future. Unprecedented levels of creativity have been unleashed, and new ways of working and learning have emerged. And though while we write this, the pandemic is not yet over, higher education leaders are already asking themselves which practices, enacted under the most difficult circumstances imaginable, will they keep, at least in some form. Many are considering allowing some staff members to work remotely, for a day or two or in some areas perhaps indefinitely, cutting down on space needs, eliminating commute times, enhancing quality of life, and providing more personal flexibility. We are asking ourselves whether we should be incorporating more remote learning not as a necessity, but as another way of enhancing learning and flexibility for some students—whether in a "flipped classroom" or hybrid format, such as having both remote and in-person study sections. It is not unreasonable to assume that in the future all instructors will be expected to incorporate technology into their pedagogy and be able to adeptly move a class online during emergencies, making "snow days" a thing of the past. We are questioning whether we need to travel as often for business and professional meetings. Indeed, attendance at board or conference meetings has been higher than ever with the flexibility and reduced cost of virtual convenings. And we are questioning the ways in which our institutions have failed to more fully address issues of inequity and systemic racism with more energy and urgency than we have in decades.

For better and worse, COVID-19 has upended almost every aspect of what we do and how we do it. And, as we enter an era in our nation and world of increased uncertainty, unpredictability, and violence, where the threat of new pandemics, political, or environmental crises appear much more imminent, anyone interviewing for a presidency role will surely be asked why they are seeking such a position in this unprecedented time; what they've learned from their leadership and management experiences during the COVID-19 era; and how those lessons learned would guide their approach, strategies, and plans for the institution they wish to lead. What you can say will depend on the position you last held, how your institution functioned during this period (which varies tremendously), and how broad your knowledge of the entire enterprise of higher education is in reflecting on the past and preparing for the future. It is a question that you should fully understand in all its permutations and prepare for.

This is a time for incredible self-reflection as you consider a presidency during this period of change, that will no doubt reverberate for years to come as rapid demographic changes, new technologies, and modes of communication and connection affect the ways we teach, do research, and interact with our communities. The presidency will be much more difficult and, potentially, much more rewarding. Perhaps you have always been attracted to a presidency and have been thinking about it for a long time. But, that is not enough. Ask yourself, "What is it about a presidency *now* that propels me to seek this particular leadership role?" What are the characteristics you possess that will make you uniquely qualified to lead an institution? During this global pandemic, many leaders have stepped away from leadership roles, saying they were leaders for growth, not for retraction and turnarounds. Are you a leader who can lead in crisis? Lead a turnaround? Be confident as a change-management "guru"?

For this book we have chosen individuals whose lived experiences—and institutional types—vary greatly. Inside each of these chapters lie clues to being the type of president necessary for higher education now and in the future. Yes, we have focused on some of the practical aspects of the work—managing athletics, knowing and working with your board, understanding government relations, being adept at financial management—but we have also chosen true leaders who have faced adversity and thrived. If you are able to read between the lines, what you will read, beyond function, is about tenacity, courage, knowledge, resiliency, and a deep commitment to higher education and the students we serve. The president of the twenty-first century is a futurist, a compassionate leader, and a "tough cookie." The global pandemic has only magnified the challenges that were already there. You now have the opportunity and the privilege to serve higher education in what some say are its darkest moments. As American poet Amanda Gorman said in her inaugural poem, "There is always light, if only we're brave enough to see it, if only we're brave enough to be it." We invite you to be brave enough to be a college or university president *now*—to be the light.

Notes

INTRODUCTION

1. James Soto Antony, Ana Marie Cauce, and Donna E. Shalala, eds., *Challenges in Higher Education Leadership: Practical and Scholarly Solutions* (New York: Routledge, 2017).

2. Throughout this book, the term *president* is used most often. However, some of our authors use the term *chancellor*. For the purposes of simplicity, we view the terms as interchangeable.

CHAPTER 1

1. University of Washington, "Race & Equity Initiative," https://www.washington.edu/raceequity/.

2. Patti Payne, "Bill Gates Calls Fight Against Covid-19 'Defining Moment of Our Lifetimes,'" *Puget Sound Business Journal*, April 23, 2020, https://www.bizjournals.com/seattle/news/2020/04/23/bill-gates-covid-19-defining-moment-exclusive.html.

CHAPTER 2

1. Howard Gardner, *Leading Minds: An Anatomy of Leadership* (New York: Basic Books, 1995).

2. Richard P. Chait, William P. Ryan, and Barbara E. Taylor, *Governance as Leadership: Reframing the Work of Nonprofit Boards* (Hoboken, NJ: Wiley, 2005).

3. Gardner, *Leading Minds*.

4. Robert Kegan and Lisa Laskow Lahey, *Immunity to Change: How to Overcome It and Unlock the Potential in Yourself and Your Organization* (Boston: Harvard Business Review Press, 2009).

5. Judith B. McLaughlin, *Leadership Transitions: The New College President* (San Francisco, CA: Jossey-Bass, 1996).

6. Jerome Murphy, *Dancing in the Rain: Leading with Compassion, Vitality and Mindfulness in Education* (Cambridge, MA: Harvard Education Press, 2016).

7. Robert Greenleaf, *Servant Leadership: A Journey into the Nature of Legitimate Power and Greatness* (Mahwah, NJ: Paulist Press, 1977).

8. Ronald A. Heifetz and Marty Linsky, *Leadership on the Line: Staying Alive Through the Dangers of Leading* (Boston, MA: Harvard Business School Press, 2002).

9. Erik H. Erikson, *Childhood and Society* (New York: W. W. Norton & Company, 1950).

10. Michael D. Watkins, *The First 90 Days: Proven Strategies for Getting Up to Speed Faster and Smarter* (Cambridge, MA: Harvard Business School Press, 2013).

11. Nannerl O. Keohane, *Thinking About Leadership* (Princeton, NJ: Princeton University Press, 2012); Susan Resneck Pierce, *On Being Presidential: A Guide for College and University Leaders* (San Francisco, CA: Jossey-Bass, 2012).

12. Anita Roddick, *Business as Unusual: The Triumph of Anita Roddick* (London: Thorsons, 2001).

13. Gerardus Blokdyk, *RACI Matrix: A Complete Guide* (Plano, TX: 5STARCooks, 2018).

14. Bernie Roseke, "Project Management Plan—The 12 Core Components," Project Engineer, https://www.projectengineer.net/project-management-plan-the-12-core-components/.

15. Sharon Salzberg, *Real Happiness at Work: Meditations for Accomplishment, Achievement, and Peace* (New York: Workman Publishing, 2014).

CHAPTER 5

1. Emma Pettit, "Will Covid-19 Revive Faculty Power?," *Chronicle of Higher Education*, August 26, 2020, https://www.chronicle.com/article/will-covid-19-revive-faculty-power.

2. For example, in some states such as Michigan trustees are elected by voters throughout the state.

3. William G. Bowen and Eugene M. Tobin, *Locus of Authority: The Evolution of Faculty Roles in the Governance of Higher Education* (Princeton, NJ: Princeton University Press, 2015), 27–45.

4. American Association of University Professors, American Council on Education, and Association of Governing Bodies, *Statement on Government of Colleges and Universities*, (Washington, DC: American Association of University Professors, 1966), https://www.aaup.org/report/statement -government-colleges-and-universities.

5. AAUP, ACE, and AGB, *Statement on Government*.

6. Willis A. Jones, "Faculty Involvement in Institutional Governance: A Literature Review," *Journal of the Professoriate* 6, no. 1 (2011): 117–35; Willis A. Jones, Neal H. Hutchens, Azalea Hulbert, Wayne D. Lewis, and David M. Brown, "Shared Governance Among the New Majority: Non-Tenure Track Faculty Eligibility for Election to University Faculty Senates," *Innovations in Higher Education* 42 (2017): 513, doi:10.1007/s10755-017-9402-2.

7. James T. Minor, "Assessing the Senate: Critical Issues Considered," *American Behavioral Scientist* 46, no. 7 (2003): 967, doi:10.1177/0002764202250122.

8. William G. Tierney and James T. Minor, *Challenges for Governance: A National Report* (Los Angeles: Center for Higher Education Policy Analysis, 2003), 13, https://files.eric.ed.gov/fulltext /ED482060.pdf.

9. Tierney and Minor, *Challenges for Governance*, 14.

10. See William O. Brown, "Faculty Participation in University Governance and the Effects on University Performance," *Journal of Economic Behavior & Organization* 44 (2001): 129–43, doi: 10.1016/S0167-2681(00)00136-0; Gerald R. Kissler, "Who Decides Which Budgets to Cut?," *Journal of Higher Education* 68, no. 4 (1997): 427–59, doi:10.2307/2960011; Gabriel E. Kaplan, "How Academic Ships Actually Navigate," in *Governing Academia: Who Is in Charge at the Modern University?*, ed. Ronald G. Ehrenberg (Ithaca, NY: Cornell University Press, 2014), 165–208.

11. Robert E. McCormick and Roger E. Meiners, "University Governance: A Property Rights Perspective," *Journal of Law and Economics* 31, no. 2 (1988): 423–42.

12. Brown, "Faculty Participation in University Governance."

13. Brendan M. Cunningham, "Faculty: Thy Administrator's Keeper? Some Evidence," *Economics of Education Review* 28 (2009): 444–53, doi:10.1016/j.econedurev.2008.07.005.

14. For example, Brown utilizes SAT scores, the Gourman rating (a ranking of graduate programs), and faculty salaries. By contrast, Cunningham uses endowment per student.

15. William G. Bowen, *Lessons Learned: Reflections of a University President* (Princeton, NJ: Princeton University Press, 2011), 21.

16. For the importance of attracting high-quality faculty to governance roles, see Scott Cowen, *Winnebagos on Wednesdays: How Visionary Leadership Can Transform Higher Education* (Princeton, NJ: Princeton University Press, 2018).

17. Public goods are typically "non-excludable and non-rivalrous." Thus, once produced their benefits cannot be limited to the producer, and enjoyment by one person does not diminish their use by another. Sometimes because the producer of a public good does not enjoy their full benefit, they can be underproduced. Instead, free-riders can benefit from them without paying or contributing. With respect to shared governance, many faculty members can get all of the benefits without ever participating. See S. Rockart, "Free-Rider Problem," in *The Palgrave Encyclopedia of Strategic Management* (London: Palgrave Macmillan, 2016).

18. James W. Dean and Deborah Y. Clarke, *The Insider's Guide to Working with Universities* (Chapel Hill: University of North Carolina Press, 2019), 12–30.

19. Cowen, *Winnebagos on Wednesdays*, 127.

20. Robert Birnbaum, "The End of Shared Governance: Looking Ahead and Looking Back," *New Directions in Higher Education* 127 (2004): 5–22, doi:10.1002/he.152.

21. Pettit, "Will Covid-19 Revive Faculty Power?"

22. William A. Herbert and Jacob Apkarian, "Everything Passes, Everything Changes: Unionization and Collective Bargaining in Higher Education," *Perspectives on Work* (2017): 30–35.

23. From 1975 to 2015, the proportion of faculty in American universities who are off the tenure track has increased from 55 percent to 70 percent. See *Trends in the Academic Labor Force, 1975–2015* (Washington, DC: American Association of University Professors, 2017), https://www.aaup.org/sites /default/files/Academic_Labor_Force_Trends_1975-2015.pdf.

24. American Association of University Professors, "Timeline of the First 100 Years," https:// www.aaup.org/about/history/timeline-first-100-years. The AAUP was founded in 1915 to promote a strong faculty role in university governance. During much of its existence, the organization focused its efforts on protecting faculty academic freedom. In 1971, after significant internal debate, the AAUP voted to "pursue collective bargaining as a major additional way of realizing the Association's goals in higher education."

25. Peter Schmidt, "AAUP Leaders Face Backlash over Unionization Emphasis," *Chronicle of Higher Education*, February 26, 2014, https://www.chronicle.com/article/aaup-leaders-face-backlash -over-unionization-emphasis.

26. Nicholas C. Burbules, "How Unions Weaken Shared Governance," *Chronicle of Higher Education*, October 28, 2013, https://www.chronicle.com/article/how-unions-weaken-shared -governance/. Burbules also suggests that unions weaken shared governance by undermining relationships between administrators and faculty: "There is a self-fulfilling dynamic here: treating people as untrustworthy adversaries makes them regard you that way in return— and so the general climate between faculty and administrators gets worse. The kind of coerced 'shared governance' that union advocates have in mind is foreign to building and maintaining the kinds of relationships that professors and administrators should be striving to strengthen. Such relationships are slow to build—and easy to damage." For a point-by-point response to Burbules, see Ernst Benjamin, *How Unions Strengthen Shared Governance: A Response to a Chronicle Opinion Piece on Unions and Shared Governance* (Washington, DC: American Association of University Professors, 2013), https://www .aaup.org/sites/default/files/Unions-Shared-Gov.pdf.

27. Colleen Flaherty, "Federal Appellate Court Decision Could Make It Harder for Adjuncts to Form Unions," *Inside Higher Education*, March 14, 2019, https://www.insidehighered.com/news /2019/03/14/federal-appellate-court-decision-could-make-it-harder-adjuncts-form-unions#: ~:text=Uncertainty%20for%20Non%2DTenure%2DTrack,say%20in%20institutional%20decision %20making. This principle is set forth in *National Labor Relations Bd. v. Yeshiva University*, 444 U.S. 672 (1980), which holds that because the faculty of private universities held managerial power, they were not able to unionize under federal labor law. In 2015, the National Labor Relations Board (NLRB) narrowed its interpretation of the *Yeshiva* holding to provide greater leeway for faculties to unionize based upon the argument that, in practice, they had less authority in shared governance than contemplated by the Supreme Court. In 2019, the DC Circuit Court of Appeals created some doubt over whether non–tenure track faculty could unionize by remanding a case involving the University of Southern California Roski School of Art and Design back to the NLRB for further proceedings.

28. This idea is bolstered by provisions empowering the senate. See, for example, the Constitution of the University of Oregon, which provides: "[t]he Statutory Faculty of the University of Oregon delegates its governance authority to the University Senate." See The University of Oregon Senate, "Constitution," https://senate.uoregon.edu/governance-2/constitution/.

29. Typically, faculty who serve as managers are not in the bargaining unit. So, for example, many natural scientists are not part of the bargaining unit because they employ and manage research faculty in their laboratories. In addition, sometimes the bargaining unit is designed to exclude certain

schools or types of faculty. For instance, the bargaining unit of the University of Oregon does not include law school faculty.

30. Barbara A. Lee, "Governance at Unionized Four-Year Colleges: Effect on Decision-Making Structures," *Journal of Higher Education* 50, no. 1 (1979): 578, doi:10.1080/00221546.1979.11779995. In her study of six universities and colleges with unions, Lee finds that in those universities where faculty had considerable autonomy, the governance structures were only "minimally affected" by unionization. In one case, however, the union worked to abolish the senate. She also suggests that if unions developed more support or perceived a jurisdictional threat from the senate, "the senate could easily be weakened or abolished by the union."

31. Another reason to keep the roles of union separate from shared governance is that relationships between the union leadership and the administration naturally tend to become strained during contract negotiations. This antipathy could spill over into senate deliberations and harm the governance of the institution.

32. Clark Kerr, *The Uses of the University* (Cambridge, MA: Harvard University Press, 2001), 180.

33. See Adrianna Kezar, Tom DePaola, and Daniel T. Scott, *The Gig Academy: Mapping Labor in the Neoliberal University* (Baltimore, MD: Johns Hopkins Press, 2019).

34. American Association of University Professors, *The Role of Faculty in Conditions of Financial Exigency* (Washington, DC: American Association of University Professors, 2013), https://www.aaup.org/sites/default/files/FinancialExigency.pdf. Subsequent unilateral reports and communications by the AAUP have argued for a greater role of the faculty in budgetary matters, perhaps not coincidentally as the organization has become more active in union organizing. For example, in its 2013 report on program elimination as a result of financial exigencies, the AAUP recommends that "faculty members must be involved in consultation and deliberation at every stage of the process beginning with a determination that a state of financial exigency exists."

35. Bowen and Tobin, *Locus of Authority,* 151.

36. Bowen and Tobin.

37. Peter D. Eckel, "The Role of Shared Governance in Institutional Hard Decisions: Enabler or Antagonist," *Review of Higher Education* 24, no. 1 (2000): 15–39, doi:10.1353/rhe.2000.0022; George Keller, "A Growing Quaintness: Traditional Governance in the Markedly New Realm of US Higher Education," in *Competing Conceptions of Academic Governance: Navigating the Perfect Storm*, ed. William G. Tierney (Baltimore, MD: Johns Hopkins University Press, 2004), 158–76.

CHAPTER 7

1. Kim Parker, "The Growing Partisan Divide in Views of Higher Education," Pew Research Center, https://www.pewsocialtrends.org/essay/the-growing-partisan-divide-in-views-of-higher-education/.

CHAPTER 9

1. PwC Health Research Institute, *America's Future Academic Medical Centers: Forging New Identities in the New Health Economy* (New York: PwC Health Research Institute, 2019), https://www.pwc.com/us/en/industries/assets/pwc-psof-amc-report.pdf.

2. Joint Commission International, "Academic Medical Center," https://www.jointcommission international.org/en/accreditation/accreditation-programs/academic-medical-center/#537f0f3910414 f4f928992273026691d_281b7ac097024d10a26dc1d308684557.

3. Association of Academic Health Centers International, "Academic Health Centers," https://www.aahcdc.org/About/Academic-Health-Centers.

4. Elizabeth Brown and Jared Woollacott, *Economic Impact of AAMC Medical Schools and Teaching Hospitals: Executive Summary* (Washington, DC: Association of American Medical Colleges, 2018), https://www.aamc.org/system/files/2019-09/economic-impact-executive-summary-2018-March.pdf.

5. Atul Grover, Peter Slavin, and Peters Willson, "The Economics of Academic Medical Centers," *New England Journal of Medicine* 370, no. 25 (2014), doi:10.1056/NEJMp1403609.

6. David Irby, Molly Cooke, and Bridget C. O'Brien, "Calls for Reform of Medical Education by the Carnegie Foundation for the Advancement of Teaching: 1910 and 2010," *Academic Medicine*

85, no. 2 (2010): 220, doi: 10.1097/ACM.0b013e3181c88449; Kenneth M. Ludmerer, *Time to Heal: American Medical Education from the Turn of the Century to the Era of Managed Care* (New York: Oxford University Press, 1999).

7. Ludmerer, *Time to Heal.*

8. Ludmerer, *Time to Heal.*

9. Ludmerer, *Time to Heal.*

10. Johns Hopkins Medicine, "About Johns Hopkins Medicine," https://www.hopkinsmedicine.org/about/history.

11. Kenneth M. Ludmerer, "The Rise of the Teaching Hospital in America," *Journal of the History of Medicine and Allied Sciences* 38, no. 4 (1983): 389-414, doi:10.1093/jhmas/38.4.389; Ludmerer, *Time to Heal.*

12. Irby, Cooke, and O'Brien, "Calls for Reform of Medical Education"; see Abraham Flexner, "Medical Education in the United States and Canada: A Report to the Carnegie Foundation for the Advancement of Teaching," *Bulletin of the World Health Organization* 80, no. 7 (2002): 594-602.

13. Flexner, "Medical Education."

14. Ludmerer, *Time to Heal.*

15. Ludmerer, "The Rise of the Teaching Hospital in America."

16. Ludmerer, *Time to Heal.*

17. David M. Shahian, Paul Nordberg, Gregg S. Meyer, Bonnie B. Blanchfield, Elizabeth A. Mort, David Torchiana, and Sharon-Lise T. Normand, "Contemporary Performance of U.S. Teaching and Nonteaching Hospitals," *Academic Medicine* 87, no. 6 (2012): 701, doi:10.1097/ACM.0b013e318253676a; Laura Burke, Dhruv Khullar, E. John Orav, Jie Zheng, Austin Frakt, and Ashish K. Jha, "Do Academic Medical Centers Disproportionately Benefit the Sickest Patients?," *Health Affairs* 37, no. 6 (2018): 864, doi: 10.1377/hlthaff.2017.1250; Laura G. Burke, Austin B. Frakt, Dhruv Khullar, E. John Orav, and Ashish K. Jha, "Association Between Teaching Status and Mortality in US Hospitals," *JAMA*, 317, no. 20 (2017): 2105, doi:10.1001/jama.2017.5702.

18. Betty Anne Johnson, "The Accreditation Status of Student Health Services at Academic Medical Centers," *Joint Commission Journal on Quality Improvement* 23, no. 3 (2000): 160, doi: 10.1016/s1070-3241(00)26012-4.

19. Bernadette Mazurek Melnyk, Kate Gawlik, and Alice M. Teall, "Evidence-Based Assessment of Personal Health and Well-Being for Clinicians: Key Strategies to Achieve Optimal Wellness," in *Evidence-Based Physical Examination: Best Practices for Health and Well-Being Assessment*, ed. Kate Sustersic Gawlik, Bernadette Mazurek Melnyk, and Alice M. Teall (New York: Springer Publishing, 2021), 723-35.

20. Gary Claxton, Matthew Rae, Anthony Damico, Gregory Young, Daniel McDermott, and Heidi Whitmore, *Employer Health Benefits: 2019 Annual Survey* (San Francisco, CA: Henry J. Kaiser Family Foundation, 2019), http://files.kff.org/attachment/Report-Employer-Health-Benefits-Annual-Survey-2019.

21. National Center for Science and Engineering Statistics, "Academic Research and Development," https://ncses.nsf.gov/pubs/nsb20202/academic-r-d-in-the-united-states.

22. Ludmerer, *Time to Heal.*

23. Mark Wietecha, Steven H. Lipstein, and Mitchell T. Rabkin, "Governance of the Academic Health Center: Striking the Balance Between Service and Scholarship," *Academic Medicine* 84, no. 2 (2009): 170, doi: 10.1097/ACM.0b013e3181938d94.

24. PwC Health Research Institute, *America's Future Academic Medical Centers.*

CHAPTER 10

1. Carol Dweck, *Mindset: The New Psychology of Success* (New York: Ballantine Books, 2008), 57.

2. Carol Dweck, "Carol Dweck Revisits the 'Growth Mindset,'" *EducationWeek*, September 23, 2015, https://www.edweek.org/ew/articles/2015/09/23/carol-dweck-revisits-the-growth-mindset.html.

3. Pauline R. Clance and Suzanne A. Imes, "The Imposter Phenomenon in High Achieving Women: Dynamics and Therapeutic Intervention," *Psychotherapy: Theory, Research & Practice* 15, no. 3 (1978): 241–47, doi:10.1037/h0086006.

4. The University of Texas at Austin, "Mentorship Program," https://orientation.utexas.edu /content/mentorship-program.

5. Idrees Kahloon, "The Leveller," *New Yorker*, March 9, 2020, https://www.newyorker.com /magazine/2020/03/09/thomas-piketty-goes-global.

6. Andrew Howard Nichols, *Segregation Forever? The Continued Underrepresentation of Black and Latino Undergraduates at the Nation's 101 Most Selective Public Colleges and Universities* (Washington, DC: Education Trust, 2020), https://edtrust.org/wp-content/uploads/2014/09/Segregation-Forever -The-Continued-Underrepresentation-of-Black-and-Latino-Undergraduates-at-the-Nations-101 -Most-Selective-Public-Colleges-and-Universities-July-21-2020.pdf.

7. Jon Marcus, "Most Americans Don't Realize State Funding for Higher Ed Fell by Billions," *PBS News Hour*, https://www.pbs.org/newshour/education/most-americans-dont-realize-state-funding -for-higher-ed-fell-by-billions.

8. National Center for Education Statistics, *The Condition of Education*, US Department of Education, https://nces.ed.gov/programs/coe/indicator_cha.asp#:~:text=Total%20undergraduate %20enrollment%20increased%20by,students)%20between%202010%20and%202018.

9. Organisation for Economic Co-operation and Development, "Education," https://data.oecd .org/education.htm.

10. Kahloon, "The Leveller."

11. Michael Mitchell, Michael Leachman, and Kathleen Masterson, *A Lost Decade in Higher Education Funding* (Washington, DC: Center on Budget and Policy Priorities, 2017), https://www .cbpp.org/research/state-budget-and-tax/a-lost-decade-in-higher-education-funding.

12. State Higher Education Executive Officers Association, *State Higher Education Finance: FY 2018* (Boulder, CO: State Higher Education Executive Officers Association, 2019), https://sheeo.org/.

13. Marcus, "Most Americans Don't Realize."

14. Raj Chetty, John Friedman, Emmanuel Saez, Nicholas Turner, and Danny Yagan, "Mobility Report Cards: The Role of Colleges in Intergenerational Mobility," NBER Working Paper Series No. 23618, December 2017, doi:10.3386/w23618.

15. Miami Dade College, *Score Card 2019–20* (Miami, FL: Miami Dade College, 2019), https:// indd.adobe.com/view/70b3278d-e9a0-4b95-8de7-fb4037443c0c.

CHAPTER 13

1. Rick Staisloff, "Want Breakthroughs That Last? Consider Your Business Model," *Chronicle of Higher Education*, October 23, 2016, https://www.chronicle.com/article/want-breakthroughs-that -last-consider-your-business-model/.

2. Thomas R. Bailey, Shanna S. Jaggers, and Davis Jenkins, *Redesigning America's Community Colleges* (Cambridge: MA, Harvard University Press, 2015).

3. Community College Research Center, "Community College FAQS," Teachers College, Columbia University, https://ccrc.tc.columbia.edu/Community-College-FAQs.html#:~:text=A %20CCRC%20study%20of%20Virginia,%2Dto%2Dface%20completion%20rate.

4. RBK Group, "Evaluating and Promoting the Financial Viability and Success of Our Postsecondary Institutions" (presentation, SHEEO—State Agency Workshop, Boston, MA August 6, 2019).

5. Donna M. Desrochers and Richard L. Staisloff, "How Ohio Community Colleges Use ROI to Make the Most of Student Success," Jobs for the Future, Inc., https://www.jff.org/what-we-do /impact-stories/postsecondary-state-network/how-ohio-community-colleges-use-roi-make-most -student-success/.

6. RBK Group, "Evaluating and Promoting the Financial Viability and Success of Our Postsecondary Institutions."

7. RBK Group.

8. This example, along with the others, is presented to illustrate and illuminate strategic financial management principles and practices. It is not meant to be a detailed analysis or assessment. There will probably be many book chapters, journal articles, and full books on this subject.

9. Staisloff, "Want Breakthroughs That Last?"

10. Walter Brooks, Scott Carlson, Ellen Herbst, and Richard Staisloff, *Building the Streamlined College: Change Management and the Modern CEO* (Washington, DC: The Chronicle of Higher Education, 2019), http://rpkgroup.com/wp-content/uploads/2019/10/Chronicle-of-Higher -Education-Building-the-Streamlined-College.pdf.

11. "Strategic Finance Capacity," Postsecondary Capacity Assistance Research Convening, Harvard Graduate School of Education, Cambridge, MA, August 1, 2018.

12. "Strategic Finance Capacity."

13. "Strategic Finance Capacity."

CHAPTER 14

1. Larry W. Jones and Franz A. Nowotny, eds., *An Agenda for the New Decade: New Directions for Higher Education* (San Francisco: Jossey-Bass, 1990).

2. Caroline Sotello Viernes Turner and Samuel L. Myers, *Faculty of Color in Academe: Bittersweet Success* (Needham Heights, MA: Allyn and Bacon, 2000); JoAnn Moody, *Faculty Diversity: Problems and Solutions* (New York: RoutledgeFalmer, 2004).

3. Laura I. Rendón and Richard O. Hope, *Educating a New Majority: Transforming America's Educational System for Diversity* (San Francisco: Jossey-Bass, 1996).

CHAPTER 15

1. US Department of Education, National Center for Education Statistics, Integrated Postsecondary Education Data System, "Total Fall Enrollment in Degree-Granting Postsecondary Institutions, by Level of Enrollment, Control and Level of Institution, Attendance Status, and Age of Student: 2017," https://nces.ed.gov/programs/digest/d19/tables/dt19_303.50.asp.

2. US Department of Education, "Total Fall Enrollment."

3. US Department of Education, National Center for Education Statistics, *The Condition of Education*, https://nces.ed.gov/programs/coe.

4. Elizabeth J. Akers and Matthew M. Chingos, *Are College Students Borrowing Blindly?* (Washington, DC: Brookings Institution, 2014), 2.

CHAPTER 19

1. I previously recounted this story in Ronald A. Crutcher, "Toward a Thriving and Inclusive Intercultural Community," *Liberal Education* 104, no. 4 (Fall 2018), https://www.aacu.org/liberal education/2018/fall/crutcher.

2. Emma Pettit and Zipporah Osei, "The 'Great College-Yearbook Reckoning': Why Scholars Say Blackface Images Aren't Outliers," *Chronicle of Higher Education*, February 7, 2019, https:// www.chronicle.com/article/the-great-college-yearbook-reckoning-why-scholars-say-blackface -images-arent-outliers/.

3. Chris Suarez, "University of Richmond Officials, Students and Athletes Respond to Racist Vandalism in Dorms," *Richmond Times-Dispatch*, January 27, 2020, https://richmond.com/news /local/updated-university-of-richmond-officials-students-and-athletes-respond-to-racist-vandalism -in-dorms/article_20c32290-7810-56e9-8b68-3c1146e93491.html.

4. *Making Excellence Inclusive: University Report and Recommendations* (Richmond, VA: University of Richmond, 2019).

5. See also Freeman A. Hrabowski III, with Philip J. Rous and Peter H. Henderson, *The Empowered University: Shared Leadership, Culture Change, and Academic Success* (Baltimore, MD: Johns Hopkins University Press, 2019).

6. See Eliza Apperly, "'Stumbling Stones': A Different Vision of Holocaust Remembrance," *Guardian*, February 18, 2019, https://www.theguardian.com/cities/2019/feb/18/stumbling-stones -a-different-vision-of-holocaust-remembrance.

7. Nelly Richard, *Eruptions of Memory: The Critique of Memory in Chile, 1990–2015*, trans. Andrew Ascherl (Cambridge, UK: Polity Press, 2019).

8. Brett Murphy, "Blackface, KKK Hoods and Mock Lynchings: Review of 900 Yearbooks Finds Blatant Racism," *USA Today*, February 21, 2019, https://www.usatoday.com/in-depth/news

/investigations/2019/02/20/blackface-racist-photos-yearbooks-colleges-kkk-lynching-mockery
-fraternities-black-70-s-80-s/2858921002/.

9. American Historical Association, "Statement on Confederate Monuments," August 28, 2017, https://www.historians.org/news-and-advocacy/aha-advocacy/aha-statement-on-confederate
-monuments.

10. Lauranett L. Lee and Shelby M. Driskill, '*Knowledge of This Cannot Be Hidden': A Report on the Westham Burying Ground at the University of Richmond* (Richmond, VA: University of Richmond, 2019), https://president.richmond.edu/inclusive-excellence/report-pdfs/burying-ground-report.pdf.

11. Edward L. Ayers, "The Trials of Robert Ryland," *Baptist History & Heritage* 48, no. 2 (2013): 12–27.

12. *First Amendment on Campus 2020 Report: College Students' Views of Free Expression* (Washington, DC: Gallup-Knight Foundation, 2020), https://knightfoundation.org/wp-content
/uploads/2020/05/First-Amendment-on-Campus-2020.pdf.

13. Anna Brown, "Most Americans Say Higher Ed Is Heading in Wrong Direction, but Partisans Disagree on Why," Pew Research Center, July 26, 2018, https://www.pewresearch.org/fact-tank/2018
/07/26/most-americans-say-higher-ed-is-heading-in-wrong-direction-but-partisans-disagree
-on-why/.

14. See also Ronald A. Crutcher, *I Had No Idea You Were Black: Navigating Race on the Road to Leadership* (Seattle: Clyde Hill Publishing, 2021).

15. Logan Etheredge, "Law School Speaker Gives Controversial Talk on Transgender Issues, Incites Protests," *Collegian*, September 12, 2018, https://www.thecollegianur.com/article/2018/09
/ryan-anderson-delivers-controversial-talk-on-transgender-issues.

16. Jeremy Waldron, *The Harm in Hate Speech* (Cambridge, MA: Harvard University Press, 2012), 5.

17. University of Richmond, "Recommended Statement on Free Expression," December, 2019, https://president.richmond.edu/initiatives/free-expression/recommended-statement-free-expression
.pdf.

18. See, for example, Andrew Caesar-Gordon, "Speed Versus Accuracy in Crisis Comms," *PRWeek*, October 28, 2015, https://www.prweek.com/article/1357205/speed-versus-accuracy
-crisis-comms.

CHAPTER 20

1. Federal Emergency Management Agency, "National Response Framework," US Department of Homeland Security, https://www.fema.gov/media-library/assets/documents/117791.

2. US Department of Homeland Security, *NIMS: Frequently Asked Questions* (Washington, DC: US Department of Homeland Security), https://www.fema.gov/pdf/emergency/nims/nimsfaqs.pdf.

3. Corporation for National & Community Service, "The Incident Command System," https://
www.nationalservice.gov/sites/default/files/olc/moodle/ds_online_orientation/viewf265.html?id
=3139&chapterid=908.

4. "Camp Fire (2018)," *Wikipedia: The Free Encyclopedia,* https://en.wikipedia.org/w/index.php
?title=Camp_Fire_(2018)&oldid=993234096.

5. Adapted from US Department of Homeland Security, *National Disaster Recovery Framework*, 2nd ed. (Washington, DC: US Department of Homeland Security, 2016), https://www.fema.gov
/media-library-data/1466014998123-4bec8550930f774269e0c5968b120ba2/National_Disaster
_Recovery_Framework2nd.pdf.

6. California State University, Chico, "Teaching the Camp Fire," https://www.csuchico.edu/team
-teaching/campfire/index.shtml.

7. CalRecycle. "One Year After Deadliest Fire in State History, California Completes Camp Fire Debris Cleanup," https://www.calrecycle.ca.gov/blogs/in-the-loop/in-the-loop/2019/11/21/camp
-fire-debris-removal-complete.

8. Joseph A. Brennan and Eric K. Stern, "Leading a Campus Through Crisis: The Role of College and University Presidents," *Journal of Education, Advancement and Marketing* 2, no. 2 (Autumn/Fall, 2017): 120–34.

9. Karl E. Weick, "Leadership as the Legitimation of Doubt," in *The Future of Leadership: Today's Top Leadership Thinkers Speak to Tomorrow's Leaders*, ed. Warren G. Bennis, Gretchen M. Spreitzer, and Thomas G. Cummings (San Francisco: John Wiley & Sons, 2001).

10. Recommendations adapted from Joan P. Packenham, Richard T. Rosselli, Steve K. Ramsey, Holly A. Taylor, Alice Fothergill, Julia Slutsman, and Aubrey Miller, "Conducting Science in Disasters: Recommendations from the NIEHS Working Group for Special IRB Considerations in the Review of Disaster Related Research," *Environmental Health Perspectives* 125, no. 9 (2017): 094503. doi:10.1289 /EHP2378.

CHAPTER 21

1. These issues are more fully addressed in Michael M. Crow and William D. Dabars, *The Fifth Wave: The Evolution of American Higher Education* (Baltimore, MD: Johns Hopkins University Press, 2020).

2. Herbert A. Simon, *The Sciences of the Artificial*, 3rd ed. (Cambridge, MA: MIT Press, 1996), 111.

3. Simon, *The Sciences*, 8.

4. Karen E. Hinton, *A Practical Guide to Strategic Planning in Higher Education* (Ann Arbor, MI: Society for College and University Planning, 2012), 7, http://campusservices.gatech.edu/sites/default /files/documents/assessment/a_practical_guide_to_strategic_planning_in_higher_education.pdf.

5. Joseph Ben-David, *Scientific Growth: Essays on the Social Organization and Ethos of Science* (Berkeley: University of California Press, 1991); Pierre Bourdieu, *Homo Academicus* (Stanford, CA: Stanford University Press, 1988).

6. For more on the academic enterprise, see Michael Crow and Derrick Anderson, "Higher Logic," *Trusteeship* 26, no. 3 (Summer 2018), https://www.agb.org/trusteeship/2018/summer /higher-logic; Michael Crow, Kyle Whitman, and Derrick M. Anderson, "Rethinking Academic Entrepreneurship: University Governance and the Emergence of the Academic Enterprise," *Public Administration Review* 80, no. 3 (2020): 511–15, doi:10.1111/puar.13069.

7. Burton Clark, *Creating Entrepreneurial Universities: Organizational Pathways of Transformation* (Bingley, UK: Emerald Publishing Limited, 1998), 136.

8. Anthony Downs, *Inside Bureaucracy* (Boston: Little, Brown and Company, 1967), 7–8.

9. Downs, *Inside Bureaucracy*.

10. Michael D. Cohen, James G. March, and Johan P. Olsen, "A Garbage Can Model of Organizational Choice," *Administrative Science Quarterly* 17, no. 1 (1972): 1–25, doi:10.2307/2392088.

About the Editors

JAMES SOTO ANTONY is dean of the Graduate Division and Education Studies professor at the University of California San Diego (UC San Diego). Prior to his arrival at UC San Diego, Antony served on the faculty of Harvard University, where he was faculty director of the Graduate School of Education's Higher Education Program and codirector of the Management Development Program. He also held faculty and leadership roles at the University of Washington (1995–2012), including professor in Educational Leadership and Policy and adjunct professor in Sociology; associate vice-provost and associate dean for academic affairs in the Graduate School; and associate dean for academic programs in the College of Education. There, he served as director for two graduate degree programs (the Graduate Program in Higher Education and the Intercollegiate Athletic Leadership Program) and was the founding executive director of the Center for Leadership in Athletics. He was an associate provost for Yale University (2012–2015), where he worked on issues ranging from faculty development and diversity to undergraduate leadership development within Yale College. Antony earned his baccalaureate degree in psychology, his master's degree, and his PhD in higher education and organizational change, all from UCLA.

ANA MARI CAUCE is the president of the University of Washington (UW), where she leads the institution in advancing its mission in four key areas: providing a leading-edge student experience, conducting research and scholarship that has a global impact, upholding the UW's dedication to its public mission, and infusing the entire university with a commitment to equity and innovation. A member of the UW faculty since 1986, Cauce became president in 2015, having previously served as provost and executive vice president and dean of the College of Arts and Sciences. She has received numerous awards, including the Dalmas A. Taylor Distinguished Contributions Award from the American Psychological Association for her research on psychological well-being amongst ethnic and racial minority youth and the Distinguished Teaching

Award, the highest honor the University of Washington gives to faculty members for their work with students in and outside the classroom. She is a fellow of the American Academy of Arts and Sciences. Raised in Miami after emigrating with her family from Cuba, Cauce earned a BA in English and psychology from the University of Miami and a PhD in psychology, with a concentration in child clinical and community psychology, from Yale University.

LYNN M. GANGONE is president and CEO of the American Association of Colleges for Teacher Education (AACTE). Previously, she served as vice president at the American Council on Education (ACE), dean of Colorado Women's College, University of Denver, the executive director of the National Association for Women in Education, and as vice president of development, as well as vice president/dean of students, at Centenary University. She has held faculty appointments at two colleges of education, the George Washington University Graduate School of Education and Human Development as a visiting professor, and a full professor (clinical) at the University of Denver's Morgridge College of Education. She consults, writes, and speaks on education leadership, advancement of underrepresented men and women, strategic planning, and change management. Gangone received an EdD and MEd with a concentration in organizations and leadership from Teachers College, Columbia University; an MS and CAS in counseling psychology from the University at Albany, State University of New York; and a BA in political science from the College of New Rochelle.

TARA P. NICOLA is a doctoral candidate at Harvard University. Her research focuses on issues concerning access, choice, and equity in higher education. She is especially interested in evaluating policies related to the college admission process. Prior to studying at Harvard, Nicola was a research associate at the National Association for College Admission Counseling. Her work has been featured in *Education Week*, *Inside Higher Ed*, and *The Hechinger Report*. Nicola holds an EdM in education policy and management from the Harvard Graduate School of Education, an MSc with Distinction in higher education from the University of Oxford, and a BA in English from Johns Hopkins University.

About the Contributors

DERRICK M. ANDERSON is the managing director for University Design at Arizona State University, where he is also a senior advisor to the president and associate professor of science and technology policy. His research focuses on institutional design, especially as it relates to the economic, political, and managerial control of knowledge-intensive enterprises. He teaches courses in organization theory, public policy, and science and technology policy.

SUSAN E. BORREGO is the former chancellor of the University of Michigan–Flint. Throughout her extensive career, Borrego has been an advocate for students. Whether working alongside them in community service projects, supporting student athletes and artists, or shaking the hands of graduates and their families at graduation, Borrego understands students are the heartbeat of a campus. She has served on numerous national boards, task forces, and as a speaker at national meetings.

ASHLEIGH M. BROCK was the assistant to the president at the University of Richmond. She is currently chief of staff in the Office of the President at Wake Forest University.

CAROL T. CHRIST is the eleventh chancellor of the University of California, Berkeley. A celebrated scholar of Victorian literature, Christ is also well known as an advocate for quality, accessible public higher education; a proponent of the value of a broad education in the liberal arts and sciences; and a champion of women's issues and diversity on college campuses. Prior to being named chancellor in March 2017, Christ spent more than three decades as a professor and administrator at UC Berkeley and served as president of Smith College.

MARY SUE COLEMAN is president emerita of the Association of American Universities (AAU). She also is president emerita of the University of Michigan and former president of the University of Iowa. During her career, Coleman has been a national leader in higher education. *Time* magazine named her one of the nation's "10 best college presidents," and the American Council on Education honored her with its Lifetime Achievement Award in 2014.

MICHAEL M. CROW is an educator, knowledge enterprise architect, science and technology policy scholar, and higher education leader. He became the sixteenth president of Arizona State University in July 2002 and has spearheaded ASU's rapid and groundbreaking transformative evolution into one of the world's best public metropolitan research universities. The inaugural recipient of the ACE Award for Institutional Transformation, Crow is an elected fellow of the American Association for the Advancement of Science (AAAS) and the National Academy of Public Administration (NAPA).

RONALD A. CRUTCHER is president and professor of Music at the University of Richmond; he previously served as president of Wheaton College (MA). Throughout his career, Crutcher has actively promoted access, affordability, and inclusive excellence. He writes and speaks widely on the value of liberal education, the democratic purposes of higher education, diversity and inclusion, and free expression on college campuses. He also serves as chair of the board of directors at the American Council on Education.

MICHAEL V. DRAKE, MD, is president of the University of California. Drake previously served as president of The Ohio State University (OSU) from 2014 through June 2020. Prior to his six years at OSU, his entire academic career has been at UC, including as chancellor of UC Irvine for nine years and as systemwide vice president for health affairs for five years. Drake has published numerous articles and co-authored six books. He is a former chair of the board of directors of the Association of American Universities and the National Collegiate Athletic Association. He is also a former chair of the board of directors of the Association of Public and Land-grant Universities, and currently serves as a member of that board.

SHEILA EDWARDS LANGE is chancellor of University of Washington Tacoma. She previously served as president of Seattle Central College. Edwards Lange has a wide range of experience in higher education administration and has been a leading advocate for diversity and inclusion throughout her career. She has served on a number of national, state, and local committees and boards to advance equity and inclusion in education, including as a charter member of the National Association of Chief Diversity Officers and a past president of the Women in Engineering and Program Advocates Network (WEPAN).

MARK D. GEARAN is director of the Institute of Politics at the Harvard Kennedy School. From 1999 to 2017, Gearan served as the president of Hobart and William Smith Colleges (HWS), becoming the longest-serving president in HWS history. A leading voice at the intersection of education and public service, Gearan has held numerous leadership roles in American politics, government, and education.

ROSS GITTELL is president of Bryant University. Gittell previously served for nearly a decade as chancellor of the Community College System of New Hampshire, a seven-college system with twenty-six thousand students. He also served as the James R. Carter Professor and Department Chair for the Department of Management at the University of New Hampshire and as Adjunct Lecturer on Education at the Harvard Graduate School of Education. Gittell is active on many boards and commissions and is extensively published.

PAMELA J. GUNTER-SMITH is president of York College of Pennsylvania—the first woman and person of color to lead the college. She previously served as Drew University's provost and academic vice president and has held academic appointments at Spelman College, The George Washington University, and the Uniformed Services University of the Health Sciences. She is president of the William Townsend Porter Foundation, a member of the Association of Independent Colleges and Universities of Pennsylvania (AICUP) Board and the Pennsylvania State Board of Education, Central Board of Directors for WellSpan, and the National Association of Independent Colleges and Universities (NAICU) Board of Directors.

GAYLE E. HUTCHINSON is the twelfth president of California State University, Chico (Chico State) and the first female to hold the position in the university's history of over a century. Since taking office, Hutchinson has led the campus in developing a new university strategic plan and campus master plan. She also led the university's response and recovery efforts to the devastating Camp Fire of 2018 and the COVID-19 pandemic. Prior to her presidency, Hutchinson served as provost and vice president for academic affairs at California State University, Channel Islands.

BOB KUSTRA was president of Boise State University, Idaho's largest public university, for fifteen years. During his tenure, he oversaw unparalleled growth that redefined the university in academics, research, and athletics. He also was a member of the National Collegiate Athletic Association (NCAA) Division I board of directors and executive committee and served on the Presidential Task Force on the Future of Intercollegiate Athletics. Prior to his time at Boise State, Kustra was president of Eastern Kentucky

University and also had a long and distinguished career in public service in Illinois, serving two terms as lieutenant governor following ten years in the Illinois legislature.

KATHLEEN McCARTNEY is president of Smith College. Prior to Smith, McCartney was dean of the Harvard Graduate School of Education—only the fifth woman dean in Harvard's history. McCartney has conducted research on childcare and early childhood experience, education policy, and parenting. She is the author of nine volumes and more than 160 journal articles and book chapters.

PATRICIA McGUIRE has been president of Trinity Washington University since 1989. Previously, she was the assistant dean for development and external affairs at Georgetown University Law Center, where she was also an adjunct professor of law. McGuire writes and speaks on a wide variety of topics concerning higher education, women, and Catholic education, and her articles have appeared in a wide variety of publications. *Washingtonian* magazine named her among the "150 Most Powerful People in Washington" and the "100 Most Powerful Women of Washington."

BARRY MILLS served as the fourteenth president of Bowdoin College from 2001 to 2015. During his tenure, Mills underscored the primacy of Bowdoin's academic program and worked with the faculty to redefine a liberal arts education for the twenty-first century. Under his leadership, Bowdoin committed to create a diverse student body admitted to the college on a need-blind, no-loan basis—a policy that continues today. Most recently, Mills was interim chancellor at the University of Massachusetts Boston.

JANET NAPOLITANO is a professor of Public Policy and director of the Center for Security in Politics at the University of California, Berkeley. A distinguished public servant, Napolitano served as the president of the University of California from 2013 to 2020, as the US Secretary of Homeland Security from 2009 to 2013, as Governor of Arizona from 2003 to 2009, as Attorney General of Arizona from 1998 to 2003, and as US Attorney for the District of Arizona from 1993 to 1997. Napolitano is the recipient of nine honorary degrees as well as the Jefferson Medal from the University of Virginia, that university's highest honor.

SANTA J. ONO is the fifteenth president and vice chancellor of the University of British Columbia. Previously, Ono served as president of the University of Cincinnati and senior vice provost and deputy to the provost at Emory University. He is chair of the U15 Group of Canadian Research Universities and on the board of directors of Universities Canada and past chair of Research Universities of British Columbia.

DAVID W. OXTOBY is president of the American Academy of Arts and Sciences. He is president emeritus of Pomona College, and he was a visiting scholar at the Harvard Graduate School of Education prior to becoming president of the American Academy. He has been recognized as a leader in American higher education, at the forefront in advancing environmental sustainability, increasing college access, cultivating creativity, and pursuing academic excellence in the context of an interdisciplinary liberal arts environment.

EDUARDO J. PADRÓN is president emeritus of Miami Dade College (MDC). Padrón is widely recognized as one of the top educational leaders in the world, and he is often invited to participate in educational policy forums in the United States and abroad. In 2016, Padrón received the nation's highest civilian honor, the Presidential Medal of Freedom, for his decades of work in making higher education both accessible and inclusive.

DANIEL R. PORTERFIELD is president and CEO of the Aspen Institute, a global nonprofit organization committed to realizing a free, just, and equitable society. He has been recognized as a visionary strategist, transformational leader, devoted educator, and passionate advocate for justice and opportunity. Prior to leading the Aspen Institute, Porterfield served for seven years as the president of Franklin & Marshall College.

MICHAEL H. SCHILL is the eighteenth president of the University of Oregon (UO) and holds a tenured faculty appointment in the UO law school. As president, he has launched a series of initiatives to advance the university's priorities of enhancing academic and research excellence, supporting student access and success, and improving campus experience and diversity. Prior to coming to the UO, Schill was the dean of the University of Chicago Law School. He graduated from Princeton with a degree in public policy and earned his JD from the Yale Law School.

SUSAN D. STUEBNER is president and professor of social sciences and education at Colby-Sawyer College. Prior to Colby-Sawyer, Stuebner was the executive vice president and chief operating officer at Allegheny College and also spent a decade at Lycoming College in a variety of senior-level administrative positions. She currently serves as a member of the National Association of Independent Colleges and Universities (NAICU) Board of Directors, a Commissioner on the New Hampshire Department of Education Commission on Higher Education, and also recently completed a term on the Council of Independent Colleges (CIC) Board of Directors and the National Collegiate Athletic Association (NCAA) Division III Membership Committee.

CYNTHIA TENIENTE-MATSON is the president of Texas A&M University–San Antonio (A&M–SA). Among her many accomplishments at A&M–SA, Teniente-Matson led the university's successful transformation from upper-division to comprehensive master's university in addition to achieving the US Department of Education Hispanic Serving Institution (HSI) designation. Teniente-Matson has been recognized worldwide and nationally for her leadership and serves on numerous national educational-governing and local civic boards.

ANDREW R. TILLMAN is the president's senior writer and strategic communications advisor at the University of Richmond.

Index